Blenheim Preparation

The English Army on the march to the Danube

BLENHEIM PREPARATION

THE ENGLISH ARMY ON THE MARCH TO THE DANUBE
Collected Essays

by
Dr David G Chandler

in collaboration with
Christopher L Scott

edited by James Falkner

Foreword by His Grace The Duke of Marlborough

SPELLMOUNT
Staplehurst

British Library Cataloguing in Publication Data:
A catalogue record for this book is available
from the British Library

Copyright © David Chandler 2004
Maps © Spellmount Limited 2004

ISBN 1-873376-95-2

First published in the UK in 2004 by
Spellmount Limited
The Village Centre
Staplehurst
Kent TN12 0BJ

Tel: 01580 893730
Fax: 01580 893731
E-mail: enquiries@spellmount.com
Website: www.spellmount.com

1 3 5 7 9 8 6 4 2

The right of David Chandler to be identified
as the author of this work has been asserted by him
in accordance with the Copyright, Designs
and Patents Act 1988

Typeset in Palatino by MATS, Southend-on-Sea, Essex
Printed in Great Britain by
TJ International Ltd, Padstow, Cornwall

Contents

List of Maps

Foreword

by His Grace The Duke of Marlborough

Living near Blenheim Palace I am, somewhat inevitably, often reminded of my famous ancestor and his great victory of 1704. David Chandler believes Blenheim to be the most important battle in British military history, even ranking it above that of Waterloo in 1815. No doubt some people will contest this; nevertheless, Blenheim was a most significant conflict and was of immense consequence in the development of this country's national identity, foreign policy and the role it subsequently took for the next 210 years in European and world affairs right up until 1914.

It has been assumed by several historians, and many of the general public, that the victory of 1704 was – so to speak – 'self-created', or even 'magically established' by the genius of 'Corporal John', his general officers and his men. But this is only a half-truth. In this book the author correctly stresses the abilities of William III and his role in creating both the Grand Alliance and the professional English Army from his succession in 1688 onwards; especially during the almost-crisis years from 1697 to his death in 1702. Therefore, Dr Chandler has interestingly divided *Blenheim Preparation* into equal parts in order to fully describe the evolution of English military history from 1688 to 1704. In Part One he analyses the development of 'modern warfare', and then in Part Two he discusses the famous campaign and battle in more detail, incorporating the views of privates, sergeants, captains and generals who fought under or against 'Milord Duke' (including one Belgian general, defeated with the French at Blenheim, who went over to Queen Anne in 1705 and became a Field-Marshal in the service of Austria!). This is an important and fascinating book, drawn from David Chandler's forty years of work and writing. Over the last ten years David has unfortunately been ill, but he is now, thankfully, back to better health and writing once more, with some help from his friend Chris Scott, and I trust readers will enjoy this, his fourth book on what he has been instrumental in naming 'the Marlborough period'.

To complete this Foreword, I would like to append an extract of a letter from John Churchill to his wife, Sarah, written shortly after he had been in a hot and dangerous action at the Battle of Elixhem (18 July 1705), fighting himself among his English Horse:

'. . . this gave occasion to the troops with me to make me very kind expressions even in the heat of the action which I own to you gives me great pleasure and makes me resolve to endure anything for their sakes.'

John Churchill was a very special man.

Marlborough

2004

DEDICATION

to
The then Capt A de P Gauvaine, The Cheshire Regiment,
and the 16 RMA Sandhurst Officer Cadets and one Driver, with whom
I first visited Blenheim on 1 September 1972
(and where we all shared the fateful days at the Munich Olympics
on 5–7 September when the world changed for the worse)

And to
the now former Capt R J P Barker, RE,
and the 58 Officers, NCOs and OR Sappers of the 14th Independent
Topographical Squadron commanded by Maj R Dash RE
from Mönchengladbach who on 14 June 2000
(with slight assistance from me in England), enjoyed the same great
battle of Blindheim (13 August 1704).

I would like to include Maj Graeme Cooper, The Green Howards, who
launched *The Guild of Battlefield Guides* at the
National Army Museum, London, on 29 December 2003,
which will be invaluable in maintaining the standard of help given to
enthusiasts who enjoy visiting battlefields.

Acknowledgements

This book is a collection of articles which I have written over the last forty years as a military historian. Most were produced during my time at RMA Sandhurst from where I retired in 1994. Eight years ago, my friend, Lionel Leventhal of Greenhill Books, suggested to me that I should publish a series of my Napoleonic lectures and articles as a suitable 'farewell salute' to mark my retirement; a sort of *'apologia mea'* from the MoD. This work proved popular. It has been issued in both hardback and paperback versions, and the latter is still in print. As a result, therefore, I have been tempted to produce a series for a similar collection of my Marlburian material – rather like the Napoleonic series. Here then, is the result of my past and more recent Marlburian efforts: 'something old, something new' which I hope may interest my reading public.

For many years I have long felt that large numbers of excellent articles have been 'swallowed up', permanently locked away in specialist magazines which had an enthusiastic but minority audience. Similarly, lectures which were researched, written and delivered to student bodies or various conferences have become lodged in filing cabinets. Some of these may not be worth keeping, I grant you, but a number here and there may be 'gems' which should see the light of day once more before they get lost for ever. On that basis and through the offices of my good friend, Jamie Wilson of Spellmount Publishing, come these, the fruits of my considerable efforts – if I may so call them.

Unfortunately, since deciding to undertake this book, the project has been delayed for ten years due to my serious illnesses just six months after retiring, and some further problems two years ago. So I must firstly thank Jamie Wilson and his charming wife, Beverly, for being so patient and supportive of a 'wounded soldier' – or rather 'author', despite there having been times when lack of inspiration and fitness on my part has reduced me to a non-producer! However, I am a determined Yorkshire-man (and proud of it) and I have grown more and more resolute to win through and begin to write again. In these efforts I wish to thank a great friend, Chris Scott, who is also a fan of 'Milord Duke' and who has done some interesting work on both Sedgemoor and Ramillies. Chris has come to my rescue several times and used his period knowledge and wordsmith skills to help me with my 'strange' writing. In this book he has helped with this acknowledgement, the main introduction and the important modern chapter introductions; and also in many other different ways. I therefore thank him a great deal. I must also thank my Editor, James Falkner.

Before making my further acknowledgements I should perhaps say that although this book has seventeen chapters, it has been planned to fall into two halves. The first part, after an overall summary of 'The Art of War', considers the changes, good or bad, to the English Army between 1685 and 1702, drawing attention to the efforts of King William III and his servants. However, it is not intended to be an overall military history of this monarch's epoch, which today tends to be overlooked – except perhaps as part of Professor John Childs' notable trilogy on the English Army from 1660 to 1702. This section deals with the notion that an army develops from the results of earlier work put into it, good or bad, and also fits into the political and military context of its era. It argues that Marlborough's Army is partly the product of the excellent but unsung work of William III, a great military administrator if a rather unlucky commander, save for the great siege of Namur in 1695. Marlborough's great military achievements need to be seen in relation to the earlier background of the army he commanded and for work on this subject I am indebted to, and must bring the reader's special attention to R E Scouller's praiseworthy *The Armies of Queen Anne*, which, published thirty-eight years ago, produced vital information on the administration of the Marlburian period.

In the second part I become mainly involved in discussing Marlborough's abilities and especially those which brought about the dramatically significant campaign and Battle of Blenheim – events which turned Great Britain into a major European power and indeed gave her a position of importance in the affairs of the world. The later chapters give an overall comment and summary until, finally, the Epilogue covers Bolingbroke's famous panegyric on the Column of Victory at Blenheim Palace, and I thank the Eleventh Duke of Marlborough for his permission to quote this inscription 'in toto' in my Epilogue, and indeed for his Foreword.

I now wish to acknowledge the names and organisations who have kindly permitted me to re-use the results of my earlier research and written efforts.

Part One

I wish to thank Dr William Davies for permission to re-use my chapter on 'The Art of War on Land', first published as Chapter XXII of *The New Cambridge Modern History*, Vol. VI, (1970), and reproduced here by permission of the Press Syndicate of the University of Cambridge. Similarly, I thank Carl van Wodtke, Managing Editor of *Primedia Enthusiasm Publications History Group*, formerly of *Great Battles* magazine, and C Brian Kelly for allowing me to use my early work 'Royal Aspirations Crushed' – here Chapter II, 'Beginnings: The Battle of Sedgemoor'. The same notable magazine has also kindly allowed me to re-use as Chapter XVIII my article, 'England's Greatest Soldier' from *MHQ: The Quarterly Journal of Military History*, Vol. 3, No.1, Autumn 1990.

I thank even more Dr Peter Dennis for allowing me to use two of my articles originally published in the Australian *War & Society*, namely 'A Study of the Fluctuating in the Strength of English Pay in Flanders, 1688–1697' (Vol.1, No. 3, September 1982), here Chapter III, 'Fluctuations', and 'The Secretary-at-War 1683–1697, William Blathwayt In Flanders' (Vol. 5, No. 2, September 1987), now Chapter IV, 'The King's Servant'. Both are reproduced by permission of The University of New South Wales.

Next, I thank the still little-known military history publisher, Roxby Press, linked to the Bob Merrill Co., for whom I wrote the article 'Cavalry in the Age of the Sun King 1643–1715', originally published in the late Colonel John Lawford's book, *Cavalry*, and here Chapter V, 'The Horse'.

I am deeply indebted to Dr C W ('Kes') Schulten, President of the Commission Internationale d'Histoire Militaire, in the Acta of Washington, DC, August 1975, where I gave my paper 'Variations in Infantry Tactical Methods in the English and other armies, 1588–1713' and here as Chapter VI, 'The Foot'. Chapter VII, 'The Guns' has not been published before, but I am grateful to Professor Sir Michael Howard, who discussed this subject with me at KCL in 1974.

The first two-thirds of Chapter VIII, 'Fortification and Siegecraft' have not been published, but I included the final part in a lecture given at the Grolier Club, New York on 27 January 1989 and which was published as 'The Art of Science', part of *The Age of William III and Mary II – Power, Politics and Patronage, 1588–1702*. For its use I thank Professor Robert F Maccubbin, of the Department of English, College of William and Mary, Williamsburg, VA, USA, Editor of *Eighteenth Century Life*.

There are three personal friends I wish to thank: Dr Gary Sheffield and Wyn Rees, Editors, and Matthew Bennett, Review Editor, of *The Sandhurst Journal of Military Studies*. I especially thank them for their and the Editorial Board's permission to reproduce my article 'Some Aspects of Logistic Support of King William III' from Issue 2, 1991, pp.1–10, here Chapter IX, 'Supply'. Chapter X, 'Casualties' has not been published before, although again Professor Sir Michael Howard kindly discussed this paper at KCL in 1975.

Part Two

Turning to the study of the great Duke of Marlborough and the campaign and Battle of Blenheim, I am most grateful to the Editor of the *Journal of the Royal United Services Institute for Defence Studies* (*RUSI*) for the use of a piece I wrote in Vol. 118(3), September 1973, pp. 11–19, entitled 'Marlborough as a Military Commander'. For my own reasons, this is Chapter XI, called 'The Old Corporal'.

Over the years, I have enjoyed a long friendship with *History Today*, and I treasure a copy of the first Issue (January 1951) on my bookshelves. In my *On the Napoleonic Wars* (Greenhill Military Paperbacks, 1994 and 1999) I used no fewer than five articles previously published in that worthy journal. There are not so many pieces included in this book, but with three they still win the prize – whatever it might be! I am very grateful, therefore, to have been allowed by the current Editor, Peter Furtado, his predecessor, Gordon Marsden MP, and Jacqueline Guy and Marion Soldan for the following: 'The Campaign of 1704', which appeared in two Issues – Part One in Vol. 12, December 1962, pp. 854–62; and Part Two in Vol. 13, January 1963, pp. 33–43. These appear as Chapter XII, 'Donauwörth 1704' and Chapter XIII, 'Blindheim 1704'. I would like readers to know that I have added footnotes *passim* to the *History Today* chapters, and elsewhere *passim*.

I am grateful to Brian Robson, Dr B Holden Reid and Dr Peter Bowden of the *Journal of the Society for Army Historical Research* for permission to use part of my book, *The Journal of John Marshall Deane* (Special Publication No. 12, 1981), pp. vii–xviii and 1–26; and also for my much earlier article 'From the Other Side of the Hill: Blenheim' (Vol. 41, June 1963, pp. 79–93). These appear as Chapter XIV, 'Private John Marshall Deane' and Chapter XV, 'The Count of Mérode-Westerloo'.

It would be remiss of me not also to thank my long-time friend, Lionel Leventhal of Greenhill Books, London for his permission to use part of my recently republished book, *The Marlborough Wars* (1999) and parts of the earlier version of *Robert Parker and the Comte de Mérode-Westerloo* (pp. 159–86) – especially the latter that was originally published by Longman in 1968.

Chapter XVI, 'Allies', has never been published, although it was once read at the Staff College for a BCMH meeting on 21 November 1992. Finally, my 'Prologue' in Part One and 'Epilogue' in Part Two are new material. While acknowledging my debts to individuals, I cannot neglect an institution. For over forty years, the RMA Sandhurst Main Library has been a vital asset and I wish publicly to thank, among the present staff, Mr Andrew Orgill, the Librarian, Mrs D M Hillier and Mr M Franklin.

To conclude these acknowledgements, I wish to thank my many friends, both personal and professional, who have helped me over the years. I do so in this public manner, but I assure them of the personal nature of my thanks. I prefer to list them in alphabetical order, but if I were a millionaire, I would have presented each and every one of them with a signed copy of this volume – my twenty-eighth book since 1965!

As a very old man, the Duke of Wellington once rather sadly commented: 'I should have given more praise.' I do not intend to embarrass any of my friends by itemising what each has done for me, but most of them will know. Many have helped me during my illnesses since 1994, and I am most grateful to you all. The reader may recognise several names. Most are military historians, but not necessarily all are professionals, nor are Marlburian or Napoleonic themes a main interest among them, but after almost forty years of work and play, they make up a 'fair number' of kind associates and friends. Sadly, I shall inevitably leave out certain names unintentionally, and that will be by mistake and my loss, but I have done my best.

Very sadly, several more distinguished friends have died relatively recently over the last ten years before the completion of this volume – and I must mention the following who were good and esteemed friends, both young and old: Mr Stephen Beck; Mrs 'Maddie' Butler; Miss Cecilia Cardwell; Field Marshal Lord Carver; Brig-Gen Lawton (Jimmy) Collins (USA); Mr Barry Denton; Col John Elting (USA); Mr David Fortescue; Mr John Gaylor; Mr Bert Gisbey; Prof Stuart Kirby; Col Friedrich Nachazel (Austria); Prof Harold Parker (USA); Mr John Rushworth; Rev Gerald Solomon and Mr Arthur Starkie. They are all sadly missed by the author.

Finally, as always, I must thank my kind, caring and long-suffering wife, Gill (my 'minder'-secretary-ADC-driver-cook-'Pooh Bah' and general help) and also my three sons Paul, John and Mark, but especially the second named, who has over the last ten years, shown loving support through my various unfortunate illnesses.

As was the frequent method in the 1700s, authors published a list in alphabetical order of *The Names of the Subscribers* and also mentioned their Patrons and friends. I have now listed below (correct at press cut off date) the names of many of my personal friends and associates covering the period from 1960 to the present. I have listed them for reasons that are different from the 1700s, although some will have been interested purchasers. But whether they will have – or not – so done, I simply salute you one and all warmly!

Professor & Mrs John Adair
Dr Ernst Aichner (Bavaria)
Mr John Allen
General Juido Ammoretti (Italy)
Dr & Mrs Duncan Anderson
   (Australia & England

Mr Simon Anglin
Mr James Arnold (USA)
Brig & Mrs Maurice Atherton
Dr & Mrs Steven Badsey
Mr Malcolm Balen
Mr Aram Bakshian (USA)

Dr & Mrs Alastair Bantock
Ms Jeri Bapasda
Capt Richard Barker
Mr Bill Barlow
Mrs Jean Baveystock
Prof & Mrs Ian Beckett
Ms Alla Begonnova (Russia)
Mr Graham Bell
Mr Matthew Bennett
Mr Andrew Birkin
Mr Patrick Birks
Col & Mrs Donald Bittner (USA)
Mr & Mrs Douglas Blausten
Mr Ron Blaxter
Mr & Mrs Edward Boaden
Mr Martin Boycott-Brown
Mrs Sue Bradbury
Sr Claudio Braggio (Italy)
Mr & Mrs Paul Britten Austin
    (Sweden)
Mr Ken Brooks
Prof & Mrs Neville Brown
Mr & Mrs Richard Brown
Dr James Bruce
Mr Paul Brunyee
Mr Benjamin Buchan
Rev & Mrs Rupert Bursell
Dr June Burton (USA)
Mr Jerry Camp
Mr Neil Carey
Lt General Sir Robin Carnegie
Mrs Sarah Cartwright
Mr P Catley
Prof & Mrs Gherardo Casaglia
    (Italy)
Dr & Mrs Eugenio Castellotti
    (Italy)
Mr Keith Chaffer
Mr Paul Chamberlain
Mr John Chapman
Mr & Mrs Ken Chapman
Mr Nicholas Chapman
Maj & Mrs Roger Chapman
Field Marshal Sir John Chapple

Col & Mrs George Chernykh
    (Russia)
Mr Marcus Clapham
Mr Lloyd G Clark (RMAS)
Mrs Wendy Clark
Mrs Yolande Collins (USA)
Prof Owen (Mike) Connelly
    (USA)
Maj Graeme Cooper (Green
    Howards)
Mr Andrew Cormack
Prof & Mme André Corvisier
    (France)
Mr & Mrs Gerald Crane
Mr & Mrs Jonathan Crane
Prof Terence N Davis
Col & Mrs Thomas (Tom) Davis
    (USA)
Miss Pat E Deans
Mr & Mrs Allan Dickinson
Mrs Henrietta Dixon
Col & Mrs Donald
Brig Gen Rob Doughty (USA)
Dr Vittoria Scotti Douglas (Italy)
Mr & Mrs Stephen Drake-Jones
    (Spain)
Prof Christopher J Duffy
Mr Chris Durkin
Mr Rod Dymott
Mr David Eastwood
Mrs Margorie Ellery
Dr Philipp Elliot-Wright
Dr Charles Esdaile
Lt Cdr Robin Eyre-Tanner
Lt Col James Falkner
Gen Sir Anthony & Lady Farrar-
    Hockley
Mr & Mrs Donald Featherstone
Avv Andrea Ferrari (Italy)
Dr & Mrs Ted Fike (USA)
Mr Ian Fletcher
Mr Ken Ford
General Sir Robert Ford
Mr Peter Furtado

Dr Richard France
Professor Francesca Frasca (Italy)
General Sir David Fraser
Mrs Hilary Freeman
Mrs Christine Gadsby
Professor John G Gallagher
  (USA)
Mr Joseph C Gallagher (Eire)
Mrs Juliet Gardiner
Mr John Garratt
Mr & Mrs James (Jim) Getz (USA)
Col & Mrs Gregory (Greg)
  Gardner (USA)
Dr David Gates
Col (retd) Tony Gauvain
Mr David Gibbons
Professor & Mrs Mordechai
  Gichon (Israel)
Lt Col & Mrs Jack Gill (USA)
Mr Joe Gleeson
Mr David Goodland
Mr & Mrs Phil Grabsky
Mme Natalia Griffon de
  Pleinville (France)
Lt General Sir Peter & Lady
  Graham
Mr Igor Gracholski (Latvia)
Brigadier Charles Grant
Major James Gray
Mr & Mrs Randal Gray
Dr & Mrs Paddy Griffiths
Mr & Mrs Alan Grimes
Professor and Mrs M Guichon
  (Israel)
Dr Alan J Guy
Mr & Mrs Rex Hammond
Major & Mrs Mike Hannon
Brigadier & Mrs Brian Harding
Mr Thomas Harding
Mr Kelvin van Hasselt
Dr J Hattendorf (USA)
Mr Philip Haythornthwaite
Dr & Mrs Tony Heathcote
Dr & Mrs John Hebbert

Dr Oliver Hemmerle (Germany)
Mr Charles Hewitt
Mr D Hollins
Professor & Mrs Richard Holmes
Mrs Eryl Holt
Sir Alastair Horne
Mrs Felicia Horne
Mr Peter Hofschröer
Professor & Mrs Don Horward
  (USA)
Professor Sir Michael E Howard
Mr Gerald Howarth MP
Col John Hughes-Wilson
Mr John Hunt
Captain Wilfred Huntrods
Mr John Hussey
Major Valentin Iacoboaea
  (Romania)
Dr (Arch) Carlo Invernizzi (Italy)
Mrs Jocelyn Jackson
Mr Lee Johnson
Mr & Mrs Ewan Johnstone
Mr & Mrs David Jordan
Professor & Mrs John Kane
Dr Naotaka Kimizuka (Japan)
Lt Col & Mrs John Kimmins
Maj Curtis S King (USA)
Dr David Kirkpatrick
Lt Col & Mrs Alon Klebanoff
  (Israel)
Mr Tad M Klupczynski (Poland)
Maj-Gen & Mrs John Knapp
  (USA)
Lt Col Nick Leadbetter
Mr & Mrs Nigel de Lee
Mr & Mrs Lionel Leventhal
Mr & Mrs Mike Lindsay
Mr & Mrs Mark Lumsden
Ms Kathleen McDermott (USA)
Mr Denis McGowan (Belgium)
Mr & Mrs Sean McKnight
Mr & Mrs Tadashi Maeda
  (Japan)
Bishop Michael Mann

Their Graces, The Duke &
Duchess of Marlborough
Mrs Sandra Marshall
Colonel Mike Martin
Dr Giulio Massobrio (Italy)
Maj G Barry Matthews
Mr & Mrs Stephen Maughan
Mr Tony Merchant
Dr & Mrs John Metcalfe
Lady Janet Middleton
Major Gerry Miller
Dr Allan R Millett
Ms Judith Monk
Miss E P Moore
Mrs Judith Moore
Col Hans Moser (Germany)
Dr Rory Muir (Australia)
Mr Rob Mulligan (USA)
Dr George F Nafziger (USA)
Mr Robin Neillands
Mrs Linda Newman
Dr Mark Nicholls
Mr Rafael Bianco Nieves (Spain)
Mr Jonathan North
Ms Andrea Novin (USA)
Prof Jeanne Ojala (USA)
Prof Andrew J O'Shaughnessy
(USA)
Mr Andrew Orgill
Mrs Julia Page
Capt Richard Pantall
Dr Rick Parrish (USA)
Mr Alan Pearsall
Mrs Megan Perry
Mr & Mrs Tim Pickles (UK &
USA)
Mr Tom Pocock
Mr & Mrs Alfonso Torrents dels
Prats
Mr Mike Quick
Maj Mike Ransom
Lt Col Harold Raugh Jnr (USA)
Ms Christine Rawling
Dr Michael Rayner

Sir Robert Ricketts (Bt)
Brig & Mrs Jon P Riley
Maj Gen A S Ritchie CBE
Mr Hamish Robertson
Mr Mike Robinson
Mr Alan Rooney
Mr & Mrs David Rooney
Prof Gunther Rothenberg (USA &
Australia)
Sir Charles & Lady Rowley (Bt)
Dr Ian Roy
Mr Richard Rutherford-Moore
Mr & Mrs Michael Sackett
Mr John Salmon
Mr & Mrs Eric Sanctuary
Mrs Sarah Saunders-Davies
Snr Roberto A Scattolin (Italy)
Dr Alan Schom (France and USA)
Dr C M (Kes) Schulten (Holland)
Lt Col & Mrs Jim Schultz-
Carafano (USA)
Prof Don Schurman (Canada)
Mr & Mrs Chris Scott
Maj Robin E Scouller
Col (rtd) & Mrs Dick Sexton
(USA)
Lt Col John Sharples
Dr & Mrs Gary Sheffield
Mr Bob Siegel (USA)
Mr Keith Simpson MP
Mr Howard G Sledmere
Mr & Mrs Bob Snibbe
Mr Digby Smith
Dr Oleg Sokolov (Russia)
Mr & Mrs William Spray
Mr & Mrs Tony Stalley
Field Marshal Sir John Stanier
Mrs Irene Starkie
Commodore & Mrs Patrick E D
Stearns
Mr David Steele
Lt Col David R B Storrie
Mr & Mrs Hugh Street
Mrs Elisabeth de Stroumillo

Dr & Mrs Brian Swann
Dr & Mrs John Sweetman
Mr & Mrs Ron Taft (USA)
Mr & Mrs Tony Tallents
Maj Paul Thomas
Mr Arnold Thornton
Dr & Mrs Francis Toase
Dr Haruo Tohmatsu (Japan)
Dr Simon C Trew
Dr Peter Tsouras
Dr John Tucker
Mr Andrew Uffindell
Mr & Mrs José Uhagon
   (Spain)
Mr Mark Urban
Mr & Mrs Bob Verner-Jeffreys
Ms Helen Walch
Mr & Mrs Stephen Walker
Mr Charles Walther (USA)
Col Peter Walton
Mr George Ward
Mr David Watkins
Mr Charles Webb
Capt & Mrs Ken Webley
Dr Ben Weider (Canada)

Mr David Weidner (USA)
Their Graces, The Duke &
   Duchess of Wellington
Col & Mrs Mark Wells (USA)
Mr Charlie Wesencraft
Mr David Westwood
Brig & Mrs Michael Wharmby
Mr John White
Mrs Daphne Wilcox
Capt & Mrs Neil Wiley (USN)
Mr Ralph Willatt
Mr Alan Willey (Australia)
Mr & Mrs Guy M Wilson
Brig Henry Wilson
Col John Wilson
Mr Richard Wilson
Mr Paul Wisken
Mr Carl von Wodtke (USA)
Maj & Mrs Derek Woodroffe
Mr Geoffrey Wooten
Mr & Mrs Peter Wraight (USA)
Mr Michael Yardley
Dr Vladimir Zemtsov (Russia)
Dr Alex Zotov (Russia)
The Unmentioned Friend

ABSIT OMEN

'Everyman, I will go with thee, and be thy guide,
In thy most need to go by thy side.' Anon.

Introduction

Generalship is the highest form of military leadership. The correct exercise of command in war is one vital requirement for the achievement of success – and, in the event of defeat, for retrieving or at least minimising the effects of failure. Of the many senior soldiers and sailors entrusted with high command in the history of wars, only a very few aspired to the skill of the 'Great Captains'; even fewer received the accolade in their own lifetimes, as its conferment normally needs the confirmation of posterity when all the dust has settled and a reasonably objective assessment has emerged. Nevertheless, John Churchill, First Duke of Marlborough certainly belongs to this highest category and he owes much of the opportunity to win this reputation to the trust placed in him by King William III. William himself does not deserve to be listed very high as a military commander, but his stubborn opposition to French policy and force of arms, and his skill as a trainer of men – both Dutch and English – were significant.

It is common practice to speak of the 'art and science of war'. The scientific elements of warfare change constantly as new weaponry, methods of communication and transportation become available, but many aspects of the art of war, which includes generalship, remain much the same, generation after generation, or at least retain clearly discernible characteristics in common – as this study of the great fighting and training commanders will reveal. Field-Marshal Wavell (1883–1950) reminded us that this was so when he quoted the requirements of a good general as described by the Greek philosopher, Socrates (c. 400 BC):

The general must know how to get his men their rations and every other type of stores needed for war. He must have imagination to originate plans, practical sense and energy to carry them through. He must be observed untiring, shrewd, kindly and cruel, simple and crafty; a watchman and soldier; lavish and miserly; generous yet tight-fisted; both rash and conservative. All these, and other qualities, natural and acquired, he must have. He should also, as a matter of course, know his tactics, for a disordered mob is no more an army than a heap of building materials is a house.

This passage is almost as relevant today as when it was composed. The essentials of generalship and high command are unchanging. However, people tend to be very different and we must consider how men acquire these skills, how they achieve the rank of General, and become worthy to be remembered as a great one. It is thus interesting and important to consider the development of young officers.

I have been involved, for over thirty-three years with the wonderful Royal Military Academy Sandhurst, where young men and women begin this process, and perhaps I may therefore refer to a few memories, descriptions and comments relating to my times at that institution. As this is a book about military history, the army and its leaders, I believe it is fitting to include reference to my late department at Sandhurst where young officers studied history, armies and leaders.

Of course, neither King William III nor the great Duke of Marlborough conceived of the formal training of officer-cadets as such in their own periods, but the authorities began to consider and train some young men at The Armouries in the Tower of London and at certain other fortresses, to become professional gunners and engineers. The Great Duke, as an old man in 1715, saw the need to train the artillery and above all the need for commanders to understand and link together the horse, the foot and the guns – which today we call the combination of arms. After his death in 1722 there would be almost twenty years still to pass until, what eventually become the Royal Military Academy of Woolwich, opened in 1741; and it would still need another sixty years, until the Royal Military College, Sandhurst opened its gates in 1802. As Marlborough saw the need to reorganise the British Army in 1715, so in 1947 the two military colleges were finally merged into the new Royal Military Academy Sandhurst.

PROLOGUE
The King and his General

O! for a Muse of fire, that would ascend
The brightest heaven of invention;
A kingdom for a stage, princes to act
And monarchs to behold the swelling scene.
Shakespeare, *Henry V*

Two highly gifted men should be accorded the accolade of recognising and establishing the principle of the freedom of Europe from domination by one nation. Both men were caught up in the military and political events of their age. Both were inevitably embroiled in home and international affairs. Both had brilliant careers with great achievements, yet both were prone to making mistakes and had certain flaws in their characters. I write of William of Orange and John Churchill. Both men were highly capable but almost totally different types of people, although, to coin a popular adage, both had powerful women 'behind them'. King William III (1650–1702) was crowned King of England in 1689, and with his wife and co-sovereign, Mary II, ensured the Protestant succession and ended England's covert subservience to French policies. John Churchill, Earl of Marlborough, was raised by Queen Anne to the rank of Duke in 1703, and together with his wife, Sarah, née Jenyns, dominated court life and English foreign policy for a decade. Yet all was not cosy. All three royal Stuarts, James II (at one time Marlborough's patron) and his daughters, Mary and Anne, had wildly clashing opinions of William of Orange's abilities and personal qualities, while all four royals had different, often sharp and bitter views about John and Sarah Churchill, as we shall see.

King William III would die early in 1702, but not before the Second Grand Alliance had been successfully negotiated and circumstances set in motion for the achievement of his life's desire – the defeat of France and Spain. He had created an alliance of European powers: England and Holland were supported by Austria, Denmark, Prussia and other central German countries and later by Portugal and Piedmont. Set against this large power was the might of France, Spain, Liège, Cologne and isolated Bavaria.[1] John, Duke of Marlborough's star was not to rise until these powers fought, but at its height he had supreme political power over England and great influence in Holland. During the ensuing wars, Marlborough, appointed Captain-General by Queen Anne in 1702, was able to realise his military ambitions and abilities, displaying both in his daring and vital Danube Campaign and his brilliant victory at the Battle of Blenheim.

William was, of course, eager for England and Holland to become close European powers, especially in alliance against Louis XIV and his allies if war was to begin, which seemed likely. All of William's adult life had been involved with 'le Roi Soleil'. From 1672, when France invaded Holland, he had fought him, and he nursed a bitter memory that during that first clash, the Dutch only survived by the desperate gambit of opening the dykes and allowing the sea to flood their land. So, when his Catholic father-in-law, James II of England, became unpopular through his stubborn religious attitudes and folly of baiting Parliament, William seized the opportunity of uniting the two Protestant countries by 'invading' England on 5 November 1688[2] at Torbay. Churchill and the English Army changed sides in the field. The Whig Parliament decided that James, having fled, left the throne vacant and Mary and her husband were technically the heirs. The result was the Bloodless Revolution. William had denied Louis his English satellite and set England firmly in the Protestant camp, but he also brought England into his anti-French wars by convincing Parliament in 1701, when 'le Roi Soleil' recognised James II's son as James III, legal King of England, that this (along with economic clashes) was 'the last straw' in the breakdown of Anglo–French relations and paved the way for the open war of the Second Grand Alliance – the treaties of which both William III and John Churchill had negotiated with amazing diplomatic skill.[3]

We must now discuss the relationship between William III and the newly created Earl of Marlborough – his royal prize for changing sides at the critical moment. Churchill had abandoned long years of friendship with James II and although he wrote stating his reasons were centred on religious problems, citing his need to insist upon remaining a Protestant, he had in fact betrayed the king whose throne he had protected three years before from another Protestant claimant, Monmouth. William and Mary were understandably cautious of this ambitious man with highly developed political and military capabilities.[4] Having deserted one monarch, he could easily desert another, and he had a reputation for court intrigue.

Marlborough was, like everyone at court, a fully fledged schemer. His paramours were all 'advantageous beds', and his rise in society and his military career were due, in part, to his patronage by aristocratic and royal circles. However, he became increasingly fascinated by the art of war, and his broad experience was developed and honed over several years.[5] His first commission (or 'a pair of colours') was in the Foot Guards on 14 June 1667. The following year he was attached to the Tangier Garrison and served in the heat against the African Moors, probably fighting on the fleet in the action against Algiers in 1670. Next he moved into the Marines in the Duke of York's Admiral's Regiment, and fought at the naval battle of Solebay in 1672 against the Dutch where he won promotion to Captain of Marines. After that he was attached to an English contingent commanded by Charles II's bastard son, James, Duke of Monmouth in French service, and next against the Dutch of William of Orange. In 1673 he was awarded a composite regiment and was commended by Louis XIV in person for deeds at the Siege of Maastricht.

In 1674 he was appointed to command The English Regiment under 'le Roi Soleil' himself, and subsequently undertook two important and valuable years on the staff of the Great Turenne. Churchill prospered through his martial education and rose rapidly through his royal patronage. However, by learning his trade in their ranks he was also learning how to defeat the French – but this is still in the future. Then came his recall to England, to the rank of Lieutenant-Colonel in the Duke of York's Regiment of Foot. Stage by stage, John Churchill became a very good soldier and was as popular in the army as he was at court.

Around 1678 he married the beautiful and gifted, but domineering and argumentative, Sarah. She was his blessing and his bane. Sarah Jenyns (or Jennings) had come to court in 1672, where she made a very important friend in the young Princess Anne. The two became close confidantes and shared secrets and court conspiracies. John too gradually became included in the friendship, and when Anne married George, Prince of Denmark in 1683, the four people became a powerful and almost unbeatable lobby. Their friendship was remarkable, and in a time of intrigue and corruption, it remained free from scandal. But it did have its rewards for the Churchills. In 1682 John had been created Baron Aysmouth of Scotland and had sufficient revenues in 1683 to purchase the Royal Regiment of Dragoons. Thus began his training with the cavalry and knowing just what could be achieved by this arm. But he was interested in artillery too, despite being unable to secure the post of Master General of the Ordnance! One of the remaining passions he continued to share with his erstwhile long-term friend and patron the Duke of York, as their religious differences were exacerbated by the fiercely Whig Sarah, was a fascination with artillery and the art of defending and attacking fortresses.

After two more years of a balanced court life, came the upheaval caused by the death of Charles II. In 1685 the Duke of York became James II, and Monmouth landed and raised his standard in Lyme. Churchill was immediately promoted to Major-General and led the first response force into the West Country. He conducted a brilliant campaign of manoeuvre in containing rebellion, shadowing and harassing his quarry, and eventually playing a major role in its destruction at Sedgemoor. At the beginning of his reign James II was very popular, but within three years his unwillingness to compromise on religious and political matters, and his staunch Catholicism, lost him most of his support and many of his friends. He seemed unaware of the cost of losing the friendship of his most mighty subjects.

Churchill, now Lieutenant-General and virtually second-in-command of the Army, had to play a very complicated and clandestine alliance game, balancing between William of Orange and the Whig magnates on the one hand, and James II and his Tory supporters on the other. It all came to a head when William landed and marched through Wincanton, while James dithered at Salisbury. Deciding that James was about to lose, Churchill rode over to William's camp and joined the service of the Stadtholder. Many of his officers followed him, effectively taking their regiments with them. Although William and Mary declared that Parliament should decide who was to be king, it was said Churchill 'carried the crown in his saddlebag'.

We need not describe most of Churchill's career here, for that follows in Part Two, but we should note the effect had upon it by the relationship between the Churchills and William and Mary. From the start of 1688, Queen Mary was very suspicious of her younger sister, Princess Anne, believing that she was over-friendly with John, and more especially Sarah. Despite supporting her husband's taking of the crown, Mary disliked Churchill for having abandoned her father and, in her eyes, his great ingratitude for the many years of special friendship and patronage showered upon him, first as a royal page and later as a senior army officer. She also suspected that this over-powerful lord had not broken all ties with her father and acted at times as his spy in her husband's court; a suspicion enhanced by several of Churchill's mercantile interests having contacts at St Germain near Versailles. Indeed, there were secret dealings involving codes and combinations, including the famous – or infamous – '00' contact letters of 1708 and later. It is certain Marlborough was in touch with his nephew, the Catholic James FitzJames, Duke of Berwick and Marshal of France, who won the Battle of Almanza for Philip V's cause in Spain during 1707.

It soon became apparent that the King and Queen did not wholly trust or like John Churchill, despite creating him Earl of Marlborough in April 1689.[6] Both the new monarch and the new Earl were also 'rivals' in playing power politics, and such rivalry soon showed its teeth. Marlborough had already been made head of the English Army when war broke out with France, and he was despatched to Flanders to serve under Prince Waldeck at the brief Battle of Walcourt. Marlborough quickly impressed Waldeck. 'M. the Count Marlbaroy [sic] is certainly one of the most gallant men I know . . .' wrote the Prince, 'despite his relative youth.' William meantime was heavily engaged in Ireland fighting James II and the Franco–Irish Jacobites, so on returning home, Marlborough was soon preparing troops for the Irish campaign. Ruling England alone in his absence, Mary wrote to her husband: 'I can never either trust or esteem him.' The Battle of the Boyne, in July 1690, saw the beginning of the collapse of the threat and Marlborough was summoned to Ireland to finish the work. He fought two well executed engagements, Cork and Kinsale, which forced the French to return to the Continent and the Irish Army to disband.

Although very happy with the military achievements on his behalf, the relationship between King and General deteriorated. Queen Mary maintained her obvious dislike for the Marlboroughs, but Princess Anne resolutely backed her friends. Tension increased due to affairs in the Army. The English Army was 'put out' by the large number of Dutch troops stationed permanently in England, and the favours accorded to them, especially the Dutch 'Blue' Guards. Senior Dutch officers appeared to have preferential treatment in rewards, offices and titles[7] and their lesser brethren were even gaining posts in English regiments. Marlborough became the 'voice of the English Army', which caused a lot of 'bad blood' among the High Command. However, some European generals were full of admiration for his military ability and his international diplomatic skills. 'Kirke hath fire, Lanier thought, Mackay skill and Colchester bravery; but there is something inexpressible about the Earl of Marlborough,' wrote Prince de Vaudemont in 1691. He continued: 'I have lost my wonted skill in physiognomy, if any subject of your Majesty can ever attain such a height of military glory as that to which this combination of supreme perfection must raise him.'

So far, so good, but William III was tempted several times to crush this seemingly overpowerful Earl, but he patiently bided his time. In 1692 William thought he had discovered a sign of Marlborough's treachery when a good general was left to be killed during a raid against the French.[8] He said, 'Were I and my Lord Marlborough private persons, the sword would have to settle between.' Marlborough lost all his positions and tenured possessions, and indeed was confined in the Tower for several months – hardly a way of laying future foundations for useful co-operation between two such men! Events in the Royal Family were now to influence Marlborough's fortunes. Princess Anne gave birth to a son, the Duke of Gloucester, and Mary died suddenly soon afterwards in 1694. Without her constant pressure on him, William relented and realised that a man of Marlborough's talents was better gainfully employed than left to nurse a grievance. The Grand Alliance, which William had worked so hard to achieve, looked unsteady, and Marlborough was the man to whom he could look to repair it. Marlborough too was to become Gloucester's tutor, but that was cut short by the unexpected death of the Prince.

William suffered from a trio of sorrows: his Queen, his sister-in-law's son, and his painfully assembled political plans all seemed to have collapsed. England, Austria and Holland were in confusion. Had all his work since 1672 come to nothing? France's power was gradually ascending and Louis was growing triumphant when the long-awaited death of Charles II of Spain occurred in 1700. King Louis won the golden prize he had schemed for as the Spanish crown was willed to his great-grandson, to be known as Philip V. Although France and Spain were not completely linked by treaty, William and much of the rest of Europe feared such a formidable combination and all had made treaties with France to protect their own interests. Louis now broke all agreements, grasped and wielded the powerful alliance, invading the Southern Netherlands (Belgium) to reassert Spanish claims there. The ageing William had to begin his negotiations all over again. Almost despairing, he decided to trust Marlborough and his talents with much of the work and despatched him into the world of international political wheeling and dealing.[9]

It was now apparent that Anne would inherit the English throne, and accordingly John and Sarah Churchill would become very powerful indeed. The Earl would be handed considerable power in military circles again, and those would include influencing the affairs of the Dutch Army. William had never intended this to be the case, although it had been foreseen by Mary. He was a brave man and a realist, and accepted the inevitable – that Marlborough would take over the military and international political aspects of his realm. So he shared his plans with him and set him on the road to rebuilding his dream.

However, despite the likelihood of full war also looking inevitable, Parliament was not in agreement and refused to fund it. Still the tiring monarch, his general and his loyal servants managed to prepare the Army, with controlling measures and training programmes. There was hardly time to re-organise or to undertake massive reforms, but there was just time to set things in motion and to prepare for war utilising the small army of the hiatus of 1697.[10] Here, then, was the final achievement of William III. He overcame personal enmity for the realisation of his dream and the protection of his faith and his two countries.

From his early life, William, Prince of Orange, had learned, during an unhappy childhood, to hide his feelings. His health was never strong and he suffered from both asthma and chronic dyspepsia. He loved his wife, and her death in 1694 shook his heart. Perhaps it was this that caused him to swing away from generous instincts, for he abandoned affection and instead ruled by policy. But his determination, courage and patience enabled him to triumph over all opposition. Above all he refused to accept defeat or recognise failure. If necessary, he was prepared to die in a last ditch attempt to succeed. He loved Holland first, and England next, but only just! William had been a foreigner. His Dutch friends were disliked and his Dutch officers were envied and distrusted. His frequent, and vital, visits to Holland were criticised in Parliament and he was seen as not being enough of an Englishman to sit upon the English throne. William was a shy man all through his life, and hated pomp and show, preferring to remain silent; he was also reputedly incapable of geniality. Nevertheless, William saved England from the planned absolute monarchy of James II. He had emancipated her from the French bondage into which Charles II had sold her, and he had transformed her into one of the greatest powers in Europe safe from any threat France could pose. Furthermore, he improved the finances of the nation, especially with the creation of the national Bank. He insisted upon and protected the liberty of the Press; rendered military force controllable by legal process and law; and while he guaranteed the Protestant succession, he improved and supported religious tolerance – although Catholics were still suspected and controlled by debarment from office until the 1820s.

As an army general William III was never able skilfully to plan and execute great campaigns, and several of Louis' marshals, such as Condé, Turenne and even Luxembourg were superior to the Anglo–Dutch monarch. Perhaps he was most able in avoiding the disastrous results of a defeat, but we must remember his important victory at the Battle of the Boyne in 1690 and his greatest achievement in the capture of the mighty fortress city of Namur in 1695. Being more dogged than brilliant and having more perseverance than skill, he could still inspire his soldiers and sailors, and this inspiration meant they carried out his well thought-through plans. This, in turn, meant that the grand strategy of his foreign policy could be achieved and thus in many ways led to the future victories of the great Marlborough from 1704 to 1711, and indeed to those of a century later – those of Admiral Nelson, whose achievements built upon William's great naval victory of La Hogue on 23 May 1692, by Admirals Edward Russell (1653–1727) and George Rooke (1650–1708), which wrested control of the Channel from the French.

Such then was William III. He was a great English monarch and there stands a suitable statue of him with his Queen, side by side, in London. He also stands alone, a golden monarch upon a golden steed in Kingston-upon-Hull. Amazingly, there is no major public statue of Marlborough. Perhaps there are reasons for this, but surely 'Corporal John' should be immortalised in bronze or stone? Perhaps such a statue should be set outside Waterloo Station, from where the trains run so often to Brussels, the city he liberated after Ramillies; and perhaps it ought to face towards France, the nation whose political expansion he and his King set out to curb and control.

Two great men, therefore, planned and constructed this challenge to France. They were the architects and champions of the Grand Alliance and the victors of the great War of Spanish Succession. The Battle of Blenheim (1704) set a precedent of victories which saw the freedom of Europe wrested from the hands of 'le Roi Soleil'. William had no ambition to dominate or rule the whole of Europe himself, but he was determined no other nation would do so – a policy continued by successive British governments over the intervening centuries to this day, in opposing a series of would-be tyrants and doggedly, by political or military means, driving them off the world's stage.

NOTES

1   D G Chandler, *Marlborough*, Batsford, 1973; Spellmount, 1984; Penguin, 2001, especially pp. 45–60 and xiv–xv for the map of Europe.
2   John Childs, *The Army, James II and the Glorious Revolution*, Manchester, 1980, *passim*. (Childs avoids reference to Sedgemoor.)
3   Chandler, *op. cit.*, pp. 23–9. See also Childs, *op. cit.*, pp. 15–50.
4   W S Churchill, *Marlborough: His Life and Times*, 4 vols, London, 1933–8, especially Vol. I, pp. 356–74.
5   See Chandler, *op. cit.*, pp. 12–25, and Childs, especially *The Nine Years War and the British Army 1688–97*, Manchester, 1991.
6   S D Baxter, *William III*, London, 1966, pp. 299, 370 & 390.
7   Examples include A van Keppel, 1st Earl of Albemarle (1669–1718); G van Ginkel, 1st Earl of Athlone (1630–1703), and H van Schomberg, First Duke (1615–90), killed at the Boyne. Other important Dutch senior commanders (but not listed for titles by William III) include Graf G van Weldeck (1620–92); Graf H Solms (d. 1693); Heer H van Overkirk (1640–1708), and C H de L, Prince Vaudemont (1649–1723). The English troops loathed Solms.
8   See Churchill, *op. cit.*, Vol. I. Churchill is over-loyal to his ancestor. See also John Childs, *The British Army of William III*, pp. 209–39.
9   E & M S Grey, *The Court of William III*, London, 1910, pp. 351–83.
10 See Grey, *op. cit.*, pp. 368–83 for a good summary of William III.

PART ONE

A Military

DICTIONARY.

EXPLAINING

All difficult Terms in Mar-
tial DISCIPLINE, FOR-
TIFICATION, and GUN-
NERY.

Useful [for all Perfons that Read
the Publick News, or ferve in the
Armies, or Militia] for the true
underftanding the Accounts of
SIEGES, BATTELS, and other
warlike EXPEDITIONS , which
daily occur in this Time of Action.

By an Officer, who ferved feveral
Years Abroad.

LONDON:
Printed for *J.Nutt*, near *Stationers-*
Hall, MDCCII.
Price One Shilling.

CHAPTER I

The Art of War on Land

'The Devil's Teeth'

Compared with most areas of the world, Europe in the 17th and 18th centuries was both wealthy and important. Nevertheless, it suffered from numerous devastating wars as rival emperors, kings and princes tried to gain and keep power – prompted by egotistical, religious and financial motives they pitted armies against armies in a sort of 'great game' to become the supreme power. For example, the attempt by successive emperors of Austria to control the regions of central Germany succeeded in drawing various kings of Sweden, first Gustavus Adolphus and then Charles XII, into the conflict, while the kings of France, Louis XIII and especially Louis XIV, controlled by their cardinals, Richelieu and Mazarin, worked industriously to use the agonies of the Thirty Years War to establish their nation as the greatest power of Europe. To serve the political ends of rulers, international rivalry was linked to the cruel struggle between Catholics and Protestants and several large areas of Germany were ruined in the so-called name of God.

In the main, England was not involved in these terrible European struggles, although a few regiments, especially the Scottish Foot, entered the service of France as Le Régiment de Hebron, and campaigned during parts of the Thirty Years War. These intrepid soldiers were named 'His Majesty's Royal Regiment of Foot' in 1684, and later became the 1st of Foot and their 'long history' earned them the nicknames 'Pontius Pilate's Bodyguard' or 'The First and Worst'. A number of the officers, having seen action in Europe during the early 17th century, became sought-after men of experience who could train the quickly formed armies in England during the crisis between Charles and Parliament. The bitter struggle of the civil wars (1642–53) led not only to the execution of the King but to the Army having a political role of its own and the rule of the Commonwealth. However, when the guiding light of this experiment in democracy, Oliver Cromwell, died in 1658, it appeared that nobody could keep Army, politicians and country in harmony, and in 1660 Charles II was restored.

By the last decade of the seventeenth century the attitude of influential European opinion towards warfare was undergoing radical change. The

3

intolerance that embittered the wars of religion had largely ebbed away, except in regions exposed to the Ottoman; and although the increasing scope of hostilities led to the ever deeper commitment of available national resources, only the desperate French war effort after 1709, and the Homeric sacrifices borne by the Swedes in their protracted struggle with Russia, looked forward in any way to that patriotic inspiration destined, from 1793, to produce the *levée en masse* and 'total' warfare. Between the eras of religious and national wars the conduct of military operations tended to become 'limited', less perhaps in the sense that objectives were restricted to dynastic or commercial ambitions as that the fighting itself was increasingly regarded as a relatively gentlemanly affair governed by firm conventions. In any case, the impact of war on the civilian populations of Europe was still restrained by poor communications, which tended to channel campaigns to certain well-fought-over areas. Although the economic consequences were widely felt, wars varied considerably in the amount of direct misery they inflicted. The Great Northern War earned a reputation for ferocity, whilst in the south-east Turkish atrocities were occasionally avenged by Austrian reprisals. In the west, the two sackings of the Palatinate by the French forces, in 1674 and 1688, and the Allies' ravaging of Bavaria in 1704 are often cited as examples of the horrors of war; but the widespread contemporary outcry about these excesses suggests that they shocked the conscience of the age.

Nevertheless, the most striking feature of war during this period was the gradual growth in the size of certain armies, even though most armed forces remained small. At Rocroi, widely regarded in 1643 as a large battle, 23,000 French troops defeated approximately 27,000 Spaniards; sixty-six years later 80,000 Frenchmen fought 110,000 Allied troops on the gory field of Malplaquet. This reflected a general growth of military manpower as governments improved their financial and administrative systems. Between 1691 and 1693 it is estimated that France controlled some 440,000 soldiers; in war-time, however, the total fluctuated considerably according to national fortunes and in 1705 this number had shrunk to 250,000, although it subsequently recovered. Even in peace-time the French establishment rarely fell below 150,000 effectives. The Swedish empire, with a population of two and a half million, supported an army of 110,000 at its peak. Peter the Great built up a regular army (excluding Cossacks) of twice this size. The Austrian and Imperial forces varied between 100,000 and 140,000. These figures were matched, if not exceeded, by the Ottomans. England continued to pursue her incalculable way and her army differed in size at different periods: the lowest ebb was reached in 1698, when parliament restricted the strength to 7,000 on English soil and 17,000 in Ireland and overseas, but at the height of the Succession War a total of 75,000 native-born troops was attained. The forces of the United Provinces were of that order.

4

These larger armies must not be regarded necessarily as 'national' forces of home extraction. Large elements were made up of hired mercenaries. Thus the French employed Swiss, Scots, Irish and other foreign regiments to form no less than an eighth of their army in 1677; the Dutch used Danes and Brandenburgers, the English Hanoverians and Hessians, and the Austrians relied on large numbers of troops provided on contract by the States of the Empire, besides contingents of irregular infantry and cavalry supplied by the Croats and other inhabitants of the military frontiers (Militärgrenze). This 'international' appearance of many armies was made possible in part by the professional attitude of the adventurer element in all of them. The Irishman Peter Drake served in both Allied and French armies during the same war without embarrassment; the Flemish cavalry general, the Count of Mérode-Westerloo, switched from the Franco–Spanish to the Habsburg army and rose to high rank in both. Scorned by the rest of society as a wastrel, the professional soldier felt little compunction about changing sides if it suited his advantage. Yet this did not prevent individual units from acquiring a very high esprit de corps – the Maison du Roi, the English Foot Guards, the Swedish Drabants being outstanding examples – and the great commanders often inspired a high degree of personal loyalty in their men. Deeds of great gallantry were never lacking on the field of battle.

Transfers of service by soldiers of fortune were facilitated by the large similarity existing between armies. This was often more than superficial, for a series of strong influences, long-term and immediate, ensured that they developed along the same broad lines as regards tactics, equipment and theories of warfare. Throughout the second half of the seventeenth century, the influence of France predominated. Her forces were the largest, the best organised and (until Blenheim) patently the most successful in Europe. French military terms (or their derivatives), such as battalion and platoon, were incorporated in many languages. Charles II sent young officers to study their profession under Turenne: one was John Churchill, destined as the first Duke of Marlborough to become the scourge of his old French colleagues. Goaded by William of Orange, the United Provinces slowly reformed their forces on the French model. Peter the Great always relied heavily on German officers, especially in the higher ranks. The Austrians and Swedes developed their military systems more independently under Montecuccoli and Charles XI, but in most ways they reproduced the standard French pattern. Gallic influence was more marked in Germany, although Sweden was copied in Brandenburg–Prussia.

One major protagonist in the wars of this period continued to employ the organisation and methods of a much earlier age. While the Ottoman navy was already adopting certain western techniques, modernisation of the army was not seriously undertaken before the time of Bombardier

5

Ahmed Pasha, alias Claude Alexandre de Bonneval (1675–1747), who entered the sultan's service in 1729.[1] The Turks still relied on weight of numbers, their field-armies being the largest in Europe. The well-informed Count Marsigli, who was in Turkey in 1678–9 and 1690–1, placed the number of second-line infantry, sappers and pioneers (müsellems), raised by the provincial pashas and known generically as 'Seratculi' (serhadd kullari, slaves of the frontier), at 100,000, in addition to a maximum of about 54,000 janissaries, organised in three corps. With the other regular arms – janissary novices, cannoneers, armourers, water-carriers – the janissaries were described as 'Capiculi' (kapi kullari, slaves of the Porte). The standing ('Capiculi') cavalry of over 15,000 sipahis, senior and junior, was supplemented by something like 50,000 horsemen from the provinces, raised as tribute or under various forms of service related to the holding of public offices, tax-farms and land. Tributary contingents were provided by Transylvania (until its conquest), the Rumanian principalities, and the Crimea, whose Tartar horsemen played a notable part in Ottoman campaigning. The old 'feudal' host, based on zeamet and timar tenures was yielding in importance to the several types of 'Seratculi' cavalry – gönülüs (heavy), beshlis (light) and delis (scouts) – originally concerned with frontier defence but now recruited increasingly by all provincial governors out of the proceeds of tax-farms and by forced levies.[2]

Many features of the new-style French military machine were not of native origin, but it was the development of borrowed ideas by a series of great French generals and administrators that ensured their eventual incorporation into practically every European army. Most notable, after the tactical innovations of Maurice of Nassau (d. 1625) was the influence of Gustavus Adolphus, whose reforms amounted to a new type of warfare based on exploiting the higher fire-power achieved by an improved 'wheel-lock' musket, by increasing the ratio of musketeers to pikemen, and by careful standardisation of artillery calibres into the three main groups – siege, field and regimental. Gustavus was the first to realise the full implications of the improved artillery arm and he evolved his battle tactics round a complex fire-plan. Further, his new and compact tactical units, 400–500 men strong, increased mobility. Many countries imitated his innovations. Thus Cromwell and Prince Rupert adopted the 'cold-steel' cavalry charge; Montecuccoli replaced the unwieldy Habsburg *tercio* with the six-rank battalion. Most significantly, Richelieu absorbed the entire army of Bernard of Saxe-Weimar into the French forces and sent promising officers to serve under others among Gustavus's old comrades. As applied by Turenne, Condé and Luxembourg, the Swedish system provided one basis for French martial predominance. Unfortunately for France, her generals later misapplied Swedish principles, and it was left to Marlborough, Eugene of Savoy and Charles XII to redevelop Gustavus's doctrines. Hence Sweden had introduced a 'military revolution' that left a lasting imprint on the armies of the century after Gustavus.[3]

It was in the reshaping of military administration that France made her greatest original contribution. Richelieu, again, began the process, by creating a war secretariat to coordinate supply and organisation. His work was continued by Michel Le Tellier (1603–85) and his son Louvois (1641–91), who between them transformed an ill-trained rabble into the finest standing army in Europe, and whose reforms were imitated far and wide. They imposed close government supervision at all levels, although there was often a world of difference between practice and precept. A revised court-martial system dealt ruthlessly with cases of indiscipline and overt corruption. Irregular formations were suppressed and attempts made to end financial speculation in recruitment. Many abuses were eliminated by the careful allocation and supervision of funds, although the troops were still paid months in arrears.[4] Colonels of regiments received regular visitations by inspectors-general; drill, training and equipment were standardised as far as possible; distinctive uniforms were gradually introduced between 1672 and 1700. Precise regulations settled the numbers of battalions in the various regiments, the strength of cavalry squadrons, and many other points. The reorganisation of the supply services particularly engaged the attention of Louvois. A body of war commissaries was set up to supervise the different branches of the Quartermaster's department, which included the artillery, munitions, commissariat, remount, transport and ambulance services. The civilian intendants were to relieve the field commanders of as many supply problems as possible and report independently to Versailles on the conduct of operations. A comprehensive series of depôts (étapes) was established behind the frontiers to replenish supply-trains. All this greatly lessened the need to live off the countryside – a practice condemned by contemporary opinion and in any case inefficient, owing to the high desertion rates encouraged by sending men out to forage. Similar reforms improved the logistics of other European forces. The Austrian *General-kriegskommissariat* existed as early as 1650, but the General Supply Department *(Generalproviantamt)* became responsible for details of supply in the field. In England, the ancient Board of Ordnance provided many war materials besides artillery, but was supplemented in 1703 by the office of Comptroller of Army and Accounts to ensure that soldiers were issued with good equipment and regular subsistence money; the historic Royal Warrant of 1707 prescribed a scale of the correct clothing and equipment to be issued to each soldier. Such improvements were near to Marlborough's heart and it was his influence that procured them.

The French command structure was thoroughly revised. The celebrated *Ordre du Tableau*, first issued in 1675, minutely regulated the military hierarchy, clearly defining the privileges of each grade and the requirements for promotion. The ancient custom whereby generals of equal rank commanded in the field on alternate days was finally replaced by the principles that seniority was firmly based on date of commission to the rank, and that the highest commands were solely in the royal gift and subject to continuous review.[5] Thenceforward the social status of the French officer became theoretically less important than the rank he held. Old posts of dubious value, including that of *colonel-général*, were discontinued and new ones substituted, the most important being that of brigadier-general. Similar rank structures appeared throughout Europe, mostly owing something to the French, despite local variations and the strength of Austrian influence in Germany and Russia. Commissions in the intermediate and lower ranks were still bought and sold. In France they remained largely a noble perquisite, especially after 1715, although Louvois had attempted to make qualifying tests compulsory and set up training cadres for aspiring noblemen. Several European countries followed his lead.

By these means Le Tellier, Louvois and their imitators founded efficient standing armies. At the same time, a tendency towards over-regulation encouraged a deadening stress on correct procedures that afflicted the French and other armies at the turn of the century. Many field-forces, moreover, continued to suffer great hardships from corrupt contractors and war profiteers.

Certain developments in types of infantry weapons also transformed the art of war. The flintlock musket and socket-bayonet were fast replacing the old combination of matchlock and pike. The new musket incorporated many improvements. It was still a heavy weapon[6] but considerably lighter than the matchlock, so that the musketeer no longer required a rest to support the barrel. A second improvement was a reduction in the calibre, increasing the number of musket balls from 12 to 16 to the pound, and in the case of one French model to 24; as a general rule, each soldier carried 25 rounds. The firing mechanism was easier to operate, the powder being ignited by a spark produced through the action of flint on steel. Although misfires were still experienced, this mechanism was more convenient than the use of the burning slow-match, which had to be manually applied to the touch-hole and was frequently put out of action by dampness. The effective range of the flintlock did not noticeably increase beyond seventy-five to 100 yards, but the rate of fire, assisted by the growing use of paper cartridges, was almost doubled; a good marksman could loose off several rounds a minute. One weakness persisted: the ramrod continued to be made of wood and tended to snap in the excitement of battle. Yet the flintlock represented a considerable advance in weapon technology: 'Firearms and not cold steel,' Puységur (1655–1743) was to write, 'now decide battles.'[7] The flintlock was soon adopted as the standard infantry weapon. Part of Feversham's army had it at Sedgemoor in 1685; by 1700 the English, Dutch and French forces were almost completely rearmed with it, although matchlocks were still issued to French second-line troops as late as 1703. The Swedish government approved the pattern for a flintlock musket in 1692 and began distribution in 1696, but many Swedish units long retained the peculiar 'combination-lock' musket of older design, embodying features of both match- and flintlock. This weapon was also widely used by the Austrians, but they gradually replaced it with the *flinte* during the early years of the new century. Only in the Russian and Ottoman forces did the matchlock remain for a further period the standard firearm for most musketeers. Ottoman troops were very unevenly armed; the janissaries carried good muskets, but many of the territorial formations still fought with javelins, bows and arrows, and *coupies* (lances).

The transition from pike to bayonet, as the weapon of personal protection, came more slowly, for the 'queen of weapons' had many champions: for instance, d'Artagnan strongly resisted Vauban's attempt to arm the French infantry exclusively with the musket. The proportion of one pikeman to five or six musketeers was retained by all armies to the end of the seventeenth century. Gradually, however, the disadvantages of the pike came to be widely recognised. Its weight and unwieldy length (fourteen to eighteen feet) severely restricted the mobility of the battalions, whilst the musketry experts coveted the unit manpower the pike employed. Even before an effective alternative had been discovered, the emperor in 1689 ordered the substitution of the *Schweinsfeder* (boar spear)[8] against the Turk. The pike's value as a defensive weapon was also in doubt after the Battle of Fleurus (1690), where it was widely remarked that certain German battalions armed only with the musket had repulsed French cavalry attacks more effectively than other units conventionally armed with a proportion of pikes; in 1690 also, Catinat abandoned his pikes before undertaking his Alpine campaign against Savoy. Yet the development of a satisfactory replacement was very gradual. The *Schweinsfeder* was still an awkward weapon to convey, needing special carts. Attempts to fix a knife-blade or bayonet to the musket itself were not at first very successful. The 'plug' bayonet was in service in England as early as 1663 and on issue to certain French and Imperial units within the next twenty years, but this weapon's drawback, when fitted into the muzzle of the musket, was that it obstructed firing. As General Hugh Mackay, defeated at Killiecrankie (1689), pointed out: 'The Highlanders are of such quick motion that if a Battalion keep up his fire until they be near to make sure of [hitting] them, they are upon it before our men can come to the second defence, which is the bayonet in the musle of the musket.'[9] The difficulty was eventually overcome by the ring and socket bayonets, fitted round the muzzle. Different authorities credit both

Mackay and Vauban with this invention, the effect of which was to ban the pike from the field of battle. The Swedish Guards received the bayonet in 1700, and the changeover was completed in most armies three years later, although the French regulations of 1703 still refer to 'le combat à la pique et au mousquet'. Different armies produced their own versions – thus the Austrian model was shorter and squatter than the French bayonet which it originally copied – but the tactical implications were the same. The ancient and puissant pike disappeared from European armies, although its small brothers, the half-pike, the *spontone* and halberd, were retained for more than another century as the personal weapons of sergeants and junior officers, proving invaluable for correcting the alignment of the rank and file.

The effects of the improved weapons were far-reaching. The importance of the infantry soldier on the battlefield was greatly enhanced, the role of the cavalry became correspondingly less vital. New formations were gradually created to make the most of the increased fire-power; infantry lines were extended to provide a wider unit frontage, but battalions were reduced in size. At the Battle of the Dunes (1658), the French battalions consisted of 1,200 men apiece drawn up eight ranks deep: forty years later it was 700, in four or five ranks. The English battalion averaged approximately 500 men in 1702, drawn up in three ranks only, to achieve the maximum fire frontage. The Swedish units commonly contained 600 men in four ranks, covering an area in open order 185 metres long and six metres deep. In the Austrian army the regiment remained the basic major unit, but was grouped into battalions for tactical convenience; its size varied at different periods, consisting in 1695 of 2,300 men grouped in four battalions, but reduced by Eugene's reforms in 1711 to three battalions of five companies, each with a nominal strength of 140 men.

These changes encouraged a more aggressive employment of the infantry arm by commanders able to understand the true implications. At the same time tactics remained rigid. To secure maximum efficiency in firing and reloading, elaborate drill-movements were evolved. This inevitably meant the retention of strict linear formations and shoulder-to-shoulder drill. Both William III and Marlborough insisted on frequent exercises to develop disciplined fire-power. Many of the English were trained to fire by platoons in three firings, instead of by line, company, or even battalion volleys – the continued practice of the French and their allies. The English innovation had grown almost unnoticed over the years, but Marlborough recognised its tactical importance. Platoon fire conferred several marked advantages: greater continuity and accuracy was achieved by entrusting fire control to the subordinate officers; the opposing line received no respite from the rippling fire of the English platoons, for one third of the battalion was always in the act of firing; and equally important from a defensive standpoint, a further third of a battalion's strength was always loaded and available to repulse an unexpected attack. To beat off enemy cavalry, a battalion formed a hollow square, each division or quarter-battalion wheeling into position to form one face. The English infantry were trained to move as well as to stand and fight, and gradually the modern principle of fire and movement was evolved. After wearing down the enemy with platoon fire at seventy yards' range, the English battalions poured in a single, delayed volley, followed by a bayonet charge into the reeling enemy line. The French were less imaginative in their employment of infantry fire-power. Their battalions were expected to provide chiefly a static base behind which the cavalry could re-form after the charge. The retention of four- and five-men-deep formations from the days of the pike wasted fire-potential and hindered fast re-deployment; but Louvois had unimaginatively encouraged these concepts and it was not until Villars took command that the superior Allied techniques were partially adopted. The Swedes employed their infantry more effectively than the Russians. Charles XI introduced many improvements of drill in 1680; his son made few original contributions in this respect, but produced revised manuals in 1701 and 1708. The importance of the attack was constantly stressed. The Swedish infantry were ordered to counter-attack as soon as the enemy were reported advancing: at forty paces the two rear ranks fired a volley; advancing through the protective smoke, the two front ranks reserved their fire 'until one could reach the enemy with the bayonet'.[10] The Russian levies could rarely withstand such pressure.

One consequence of the association of linear formations and higher fire-power was a general increase in casualty rates. Steenkirk (1692), an action in which both armies were still largely armed with pike and matchlock, was widely regarded at the time as the severest infantry battle ever fought, each side losing some 4,000 killed and as many wounded out of 150,000 present; the brunt of the Allied casualties was borne by the advance guard of infantry. At Blenheim, after the change of weapons, there were over 30,000 casualties (besides prisoners) out of a joint total of 108,000 men; at Malplaquet the Allies lost one man in four; and at Poltava the Swedes suffered almost 4,000 casualties out of some 13,000 sent into battle. Exceptional losses on this scale evoked widespread outcry, and it is small wonder that many commanders preferred wars of manoeuvre. At the same time, sieges could be extremely costly: the capture of Lille, for example, cost the Allies at least 12,000 casualties.

By the last quarter of the seventeenth century, the science of defensive engineering had far outstripped the power of the cumbrous and short-ranged artillery. Rather ironically, Vauban never intended his fortifications to become the central focus of military operations: they were to conserve troops for offensives on other fronts. Nevertheless, an obsession

11

with fortification and its associated operations gripped both France and the United Provinces, inevitably inducing defensive thinking and a preference for limited wars. Vauban's 'regulation of the frontier towns' (1678–98) resulted in the building of thirty-three new fortresses and the renovation of several hundred more near the French frontiers. His Dutch counterpart, Coehoorn, also developed a formidable fortress barrier. The emperor somewhat ineffectively attempted to renovate the defences of the upper Danube (Villingen, Ulm) and north Italy (Milan, Mantua) against French incursions, besides setting in order the fortresses of the Iron Gate (Old and New Orsova, Mehadia) against the Turk. After the French, the Turks were originally the most renowned for siege warfare; but their failure before Vienna in 1683 reduced their prestige as besiegers,[11] whilst Eugene's capture of Belgrade in 1717 irreparably damaged their reputation for invincibility in defence. Vauban's influence really dominated both aspects of such operations.

The measure of impregnability that his 'three orders' of defence-works conferred on fortresses compelled generals to concentrate on sieges and on operations in support or relief of them. His system, in the simplest terms, was to make the widest possible use of enfilading fire, defence in depth, and sally-ports for sudden sorties by the defenders. Vauban perfected the system of Pagan (1604–65), which hinged on the bastion; he reinforced vulnerable salients with outworks and ravelins, and based all his fortifications on the natural configuration of the ground. Thus, employing night-raids and mining to delay the progress of a siege, the defence often possessed the upper hand until supplies and morale ran low. But Vauban also perfected the techniques of siegecraft, regularising the sciences of 'contravallation' and 'circumvallation'.[12] As a contemporary saying ran, 'a town defended by Vauban is a town held; a town invested by Vauban is a town taken'. He regarded each of the fifty-three sieges he personally conducted as an entirely separate problem, but his general principles were copied throughout Europe. After carefully siting their camp and making a full reconnaissance of a town's defences to determine the weakest sector, the attackers sapped forward by digging three 'parallels' – elaborate earthworks linked by indirect approach trenches and designed to hold troops for local defence and ultimately for the assault – until the edge of the enemy's glacis was reached. These pioneers were supported by small batteries employing direct or ricochet fire to make a breach through the selected sector of the parapet, whilst mortars swept the hostile defences. Once undertaken, the progress of sieges of this type could be almost mathematically calculated; one stage followed another until the defending commander, caught in the toils of Euclid, faced the alternatives of honourable surrender or a direct assault through the breach – with the potential consequences of fire and sword for both garrison and townsfolk. Such stormings were indeed rare, for they could entail enormous loss of life, while convention permitted defenders to capitulate on terms after a forty-eight-day period or in face of an imminent assault; but all sieges involved much preparation of material, consumed a great deal of manpower and time, and so constituted a drag on active warfare.

Regular fortresses were sometimes supplemented by permanent lines where conditions of terrain made these advisable. The Lines of Stollhofen, constructed in 1703 to command the ten-mile interval between the Rhine and the Black Forest, exemplified the more elaborate variety. Simpler specimens consisted of inundations, natural obstacles and fortified posts, designed to delay rather than forbid the advance of hostile forces. The difficulty of manoeuvring eighteenth-century armies made it hard to turn such positions, whilst a frontal attack was at a decided disadvantage owing to the inadequacy of the preliminary bombardment by the artillery of the day. Although, by consummate artistry, Marlborough forced the seventy-mile-long Lines of Brabant in 1705 and the Lines of 'Ne Plus Ultra' six years later, and Villars surprised Stollhofen in 1707, the use of fortified lines encouraged defensive warfare and justified Defoe's complaint that 'now it is frequent to have armies of 50,000 men of a side standing at bay within view of one another, and spend a whole campaign in dodging, or, as it is genteelly called, observing one another, and then march off into winter quarters'.[13]

Under these general conditions, victory or defeat or stalemate rested on the quality of individual generalship and on the size of the armies – otherwise so similar as a rule in equipment, weapons and tactical ideas. A few leaders were bold, but most were cautious, allowing the developments that favoured defensive war to dictate their style. Often, however, it was their governments who imposed this on them. From 1676 defensive warfare had appealed strongly to Louis XIV, influenced after the death of Turenne by Louvois and his assistant Chamlay, who waged war as administrators and moved armies like pawns on a chessboard. 'Journals' of detailed instructions were issued for every campaign; frequent reminders to avoid risks were sent to the front. 'Conduct yourself in such a way as not to compromise the reputation of my army,' wrote the king. 'I know there is no need to tell you what pain an unfortunate defeat would cause His Majesty,' reiterated the minister,[14] whose successors Barbezieux and Chamillart, constantly sounded similar notes of caution. Even the great Luxembourg fought brilliant campaigns of evasion during the Nine Years War, continually thwarting the efforts of the ailing William III to force a decisive action. Small wonder that lesser generals of the next generation such as Tallard and Vendôme hesitated to fight battles. Even when action was authorised by Versailles, royal directives restricted the initiative of the commander; in 1706 Louis ordered Villeroi 'to pay special attention to that part of the line which will endure the first shock of the English troops'[15] – advice which substantially contributed to the defeat at

Ramillies. Cautious Allied governments might hamper their generals with similar trammels. Through their field-deputies, the States-General frequently obstructed Marlborough's designs for battle: so did the Tory outcry at the 'butcher's bill' of Malplaquet.[16] The Habsburg Council of War (Hofkriegsrat),[17] to its credit, never attempted to dictate courses of action to commanders in the field, but some Imperial generals – Styrum and later Bayreuth – tended to favour siege operations. The Swedish army, of course, led in person by its soldier-monarch, enjoyed a comparatively free hand for the war of movement in which Charles XII delighted.

The preference for limited war was not shared by the truly great generals. Like Charles XII, probably the most daring soldier of his time, Marlborough, Eugene and Villars were often able to escape the deadening military customs of the day and to revive the spirit of movement and decision known to Gustavus Adolphus and Turenne before them. 'Make few sieges and fight plenty of battles,' Turenne had advised Condé; 'when you are master of the countryside the villages will give us the towns.'[18] As a general rule, the Turks shared this eagerness to give battle. Marlborough's four great victories proclaim his belief in the importance of the major action, even when undertaken at considerable risk. After Oudenarde, where the Allied army ran the peril of being divided and annihilated in detail as it crossed the Scheldt in close proximity to the French, Marlborough wrote: 'I was positively resolved to endeavour by all means a battle, thinking nothing else would make the Queen's business go on well. This reason only made me venture the battle yesterday, otherwise I did give them too much advantage.'[19] Eugene was similarly dedicated to action. In spite of his failure before Toulon (1707) and his inability to master Villars in the years following Marlborough's dismissal, he merits fame for his many victories against the Turk, the defeat of Marsin at Turin (1706), and his masterly cooperation with his English colleague. On the French side, Villars had the unique distinction of confining Marlborough and Eugene to a technical victory at Malplaquet: rallying the demoralised French forces, Villars enabled France to continue the struggle and win a not unfavourable peace after his culminating triumph at Denain.

As in every age, conditions of terrain and climate had much to do with determining the type of operations conducted in the various theatres of war. Shortage of green fodder and the bad state of the winter roads normally confined the campaigning season to the summer months, and even then the generally low agricultural yield of Europe tied the larger armies to the distances they could carry their bread. Hot weather brought dysentery to ravage the ranks; winter's cold produced frostbite, starvation or sickness in billets.

In western Europe wars were fought over four main theatres. First in importance was the 'cockpit of Europe', contained within the quadrilateral formed by Antwerp, Dunkirk, Namur and Maastricht, and largely dominated by the river basins of the Meuse and Scheldt. The comparatively high fertility, the facilities for attack and defence offered by the numerous intersecting waterways, and the wealth of its many towns made the southern Netherlands a good area for soldiering, besides its strategic situation for protecting the respective approaches to Paris and the Rhine. The many fortresses there made it a general's first preoccupation to protect his lines of communication. Beyond Luxemburg and the Moselle forts was a second front, the upper Rhine, which saw much fighting in the Spanish Succession War as it had done in the days of Gustavus and Turenne. The rich agricultural lands of Alsace and Lorraine were now protected by the fortresses of Strasbourg and Landau on the left bank, while the Stollhofen Lines shielded the approaches to the upper Danube and lower Rhine; the Black Forest area was mountainous and barren, armies having to convoy supplies through narrow passes before emerging into the plains of Franconia. North Italy, thirdly, figured prominently in both of Louis XIV's later wars. Here the Po valley, with its fertile acres, many cities and tributary watercourses, bore certain resemblances to the Netherlands. Operations frequently turned on control of the four fortresses of 'the Quadrilateral' north of the valley: Mantua, Verona, Peschiera, Legnano. From the north and west, enclosed by the Alps, the only means of easy access from France lay along the narrow Ligurian coast, which was exposed to seaborne operations; also vital to the French were certain passes: the Bochette, running north from Genoa, the valleys of the Bormida and Stura rivers, and the Colle di Tenda. The Brenner and Semmering passes similarly linked Italy and south Austria. Except in the mountains, summers were hot and winters mild. Very different was the Spanish theatre. The arid mountains dividing Portugal from Spain severely limited operations in the west of the Peninsula after 1704; most of the fighting took place in the east, in Catalonia (as in the Nine Years War) and Valencia, but even there the inhospitality of much of the countryside and the great heat of the summer months rendered effective operations difficult.

The Great Northern War ranged from the Baltic lands through Poland to the Ukrainian steppe beyond the Dnieper. In 1701–7 the focal area was Poland, where the Swedes fought hard campaigns along the Niemen and Vistula against the elector of Saxony. The swampy nature of much of this region (particularly the Pripet marshes), which presented a major obstacle in spring and summer, induced Charles XII to undertake several unconventional winter campaigns. His invasion of Russia meant traversing vast distances of forest and rolling plains besides a series of great river obstacles, and then the Russian 'scorched earth' plan forced him to strike south to the friendlier areas of the Ukraine, there to meet disaster after surviving the bitter frosts of early 1709. The tides of the Turkish wars flowed over half a dozen different regions of the Balkans. Three zones along the Danube are worth distinguishing in particular. The area of the middle Danube and the Hungarian plain saw Vienna besieged by the Turks in 1683 and the Magyar revolt two decades later; here the north bank of the river opened on to fertile regions, but to the south lay more barren areas. Farther down, the confluence of the Danube and Sava formed a second theatre, the scene of the Battle of Zalánkemén (1691) and successive contests for the key citadel of Belgrade, below which the dry hills of Serbia and Wallachia closed to the fortresses of the Iron Gate; away to the south-east, through the open country round Nish, stretched the high road to Adrianople. A great deal of fighting, including the Battle of Zenta (1697), took place north of Belgrade, in the Banat of Temesvár,[20] which linked the Danube with Transylvania and with the key Wallachian passes, the Vulcan and Red Tower.

Details of drill and minor tactics varied considerably from army to army, and even from regiment to regiment.

The troops normally assembled for a campaign in the vicinity of a fortress, carefully stocked with munitions and supplies during the previous winter. Such preparations were difficult to conceal from the enemy's spies; an army's broad intentions could often be deduced from the areas reconnoitred and the fortresses supplied. To achieve surprise, therefore, generals had to resort to deception. In the winter of 1703–4 the Allies made elaborate preparations at Coblenz and Philippsburg in order to deceive Versailles into believing that their main attack would be launched up the Moselle or against Alsace, not towards the Danube; in 1707 Villars lulled the Margrave of Bayreuth into a false sense of security by attending a ball in Strasbourg at the very time the French forces were secretly converging on Stollhofen. The area chosen for the assembly-camp was surveyed by a senior officer accompanied by representatives of all arms; outposts were established and the site carefully subdivided. The camp plan invariably reproduced the order of battle. The flanks were normally allocated to the cavalry, each squadron receiving a frontage of fifty paces with a similar distance dividing it from the next lines. The infantry were placed in a double line of cantonments, each battalion usually receiving a sector 100 yards broad with similar intervals. The artillery was generally parked in front or at the rear of the main position under the protection of a special guard; and the commissariat waggons were drawn up in an easily accessible area ready to issue supplies every four days. Junior officers laid out the lines of the regimental camps within the allotted areas before the main body of the army arrived. On reaching the appointed bivouac, the colours or standards were planted in the front centre of the unit area to provide a rallying-point and the men dismissed to prepare their meal. For protection from the weather, the rank and file often had to build rude shelters from whatever materials they could procure, but after 1700 tents were increasingly provided. Main guards and picquets were mounted, grand guards of infantry and cavalry were sent to the outposts a mile or more from the camp. These were under the command of the *maréchal de camp* or *General-Feldwachtmeister*, appointed each day from a roster and responsible to the commander-in-chief for security and discipline. If the camp was to be permanent, palisades and earthworks were constructed around the perimeter. Fortified camps could play decisive roles: in July 1704 Marlborough and Baden were not strong enough to attack the elector of Bavaria's entrenchments outside Ulm; in 1709 Peter fought the Swedes at Poltava close to a large encampment supported by a line of fortified outposts.[21]

This elaborate procedure was followed every time an army halted on the completion of the day's march. The camp survey party rode at least half a day ahead of the army, searching for a site with fresh water and protected flanks, and it was not unknown for it to run unexpectedly into the enemy; in 1706 Cadogan discovered Villeroi's army already camped on the very site round Ramillies that the Allies had intended to select. The plan for the following day's march was prepared jointly by the lieutenant-general of the day and the camp-commandant, for the commander's approval. Within range of the enemy, armies always marched in battle-order. The formation adopted would depend on the direction of the foe: if he was reported ahead, the army marched by 'wings'; if on the flank, by 'lines'.[22] The reserve, artillery and supply-trains were commonly placed in the centre along the best available road, under the orders of the waggon-master and his detachments of provosts or *archers*. The other columns used parallel tracks or struck off across country, headed by detachments of dragoons carrying fascines or straw-trusses for bridging streams or marshy ground, whilst groups of engineers laboured to improve the way. The battalions normally marched by column of platoons, temporarily narrowing the front by dropping files to the rear when necessary, but resuming formation as soon as possible so that the battle-line could be formed by a simple wheel of platoons.

An army rarely progressed more than ten miles in one day. On the march to the Danube, Marlborough's forces took more than five weeks to cover the 250 miles to the rendezvous with Baden at Launsheim. The main limitation was the weight of the cumbersome field-guns; the current practice of harnessing the horses in tandem, and of hiring civilian con-tractors to supply transport and drivers, did little to improve their general performance over the mud roads of Europe. The successful performance of long marches depended on the quality of the field administration. In many cases this left much to be desired, and nothing is more revealing than the contrast between the French and British forces in this respect during the campaign of 1704. On his first march to reinforce Bavaria,

Tallard lost a third of his effective strength through desertion and straggling in the Black Forest; before the second operation in July, half his cavalry horses contracted a murrain and had to be kept in quarantine. By comparison, the Allied army's longer march from the Netherlands to the Danube was conducted far more efficiently; advance preparations ranged from the provision of a new pair of shoes for the infantry at Heidelberg to an alternative set of communications. Measures of this type enabled Marlborough to execute a daring march down the flank of superior enemy forces, and to bring his men to the Danube fit enough to win the bitter struggle for the Schellenberg Heights; the English cavalry, in particularly fine fettle after the long march, earned Eugene's unstinted admiration. Painstaking administration and care for the men and horses were indeed two secrets of the high morale prevalent in the British forces, who dubbed Marlborough 'Corporal John', a reputation that enabled him to make calls on his men's endurance that few other generals would contemplate. Although Charles XII was equally popular with his men, his administrative talent was not so great; the loss of Lewenhaupt's single convoy at Lesnaja in October 1708 compromised the entire invasion of Russia. But it would be erroneous to believe that the British forces were invariably well equipped. The army that served in Spain under Peterborough, and later Galway, suffered terrible privations through mismanagement, seriously affecting its battle-power and contributing to the defeat at Almanza.

Most generals marched at sunrise and camped at dusk, but another secret of Marlborough's success was his use of night-marches to conceal his movements and save his army from the heat of the day. Captain Parker wrote of the Danube march: 'We generally began our march about three in the morning, proceeded four leagues or four and a half by day, and reached our ground about nine.'[23] This stratagem of advancing under cover of darkness was also used in tactical operations. Baden marched by night to attack the rear of the Turkish position at Nish, and Marlborough forced action upon unwilling adversaries at both Blenheim and Oudenarde by adopting similar measures. 'If they are there, the devil must have carried them. Such marching is impossible!': such was Vendôme's reaction to reports of the Allied army deploying over the Scheldt on the latter occasion.[24] An advance into battle was made in several columns to facilitate tactical deployment. Five was the number most frequently used; but Marlborough marched on Blenheim in nine columns, and at Poltava Charles XII let Rehnskiöld and Lewenhaupt advance with six of cavalry and four of infantry respectively. By deploying his men on as broad a front as possible, a general attempted to envelop his adversary's flanks; but over-extension had to be avoided to prevent units being cut off and crushed in detail. At Ramillies, Marlborough made the fullest use of interior lines against Villeroi's over-extended position, and employed the cover of a reverse slope to conceal

18

the transfer of the British troops from the right flank to the centre at the crisis of the battle. An eye for country was, of course, an essential attribute in a commander; the key to many actions lay in the proper exploitation of the natural advantages a position offered, or of the weather. At Narva (1700) the Swedes attacked the more numerous Russians under cover of a snow blizzard.

The development of formalised tactics materially restricted the possibilities of the battlefield. The elaborate battle-arrays needed much time to prepare: unless taken by surprise, either side had time to refuse action by withdrawing to some inaccessible position. Once battle was joined, a general's first preoccupation was to preserve his battle-order intact, for an unbroken line of battle was considered as important on land as at sea. This was no easy matter when the slightest irregularity of terrain could throw the carefully aligned battalions and even whole armies into confusion. The largest formation then in existence was the brigade, and this factor further complicated the deployment and handling of armies in action. Charles XII formed part of his army into self-contained corps in 1718, but this was a unique experiment. No army possessed even a divisional organisation at the end of this period.

Before battle, each army formed up in two or more parallel lines, 300 to 600 yards apart, thus permitting mutual support without unduly exposing the rear to the enemy's fire. General officers took post in a predetermined order according to rank, the station of greatest honour being the front line's right flank; the junior general present commanded the left of the second line. Brigadiers served with their own groups of battalions or squadrons, but all higher command posts were decided by seniority. In other respects, the principles governing battle-formations varied between nations. The standard seventeenth-century practice of drawing up infantry and cavalry units in alternate succession was continued by the Imperial armies, whose rectangular battle-formations, drawn up behind barricades of *chevaux de frise*, proved effective in checking the loosely controlled attacks of the Turkish masses. The French, on the other hand, stationed their cavalry on the flanks, employing them throughout the battle. By contrast, Marlborough and Charles XII placed much of their cavalry in reserve for use at the moment of crisis or decision, and left the preliminary fighting to the lines of infantry battalions supported by smaller detachments of horsemen. Similarly, the Turk kept his regular sipahis in reserve for the *coup de grâce*. Eighteenth-century authorities were to consider a well-planned battle-formation a major secret of victory. Turpin de Crissé, for example, wrote that 'Battles are won not by numbers but by the manner of forming your troops together and their order and discipline.'[25]

Once formed, the battle-line advanced directly to the front, halting frequently to rectify the alignments. Over-haste was considered fatal; 'slow but sure' was the rule. The theory was commonly held that the side that fired first was often defeated before it had time to reload; consequently the infantry was trained to hold its fire until the last practicable moment. At Blenheim, Rowe reserved his brigade's first fire until he was within sword's reach of the enemy palisades. Restraint of this order required a highly developed discipline. The tactical deployment of the British, French and Swedish infantry in battle has already been considered in connection with the changes in weapons. The other European armies conformed to the general pattern with a few individual idiosyncrasies. The Imperial regiments were notorious for their lack of uniform training, but most of their tactics were conventional and the 'firings' generally performed on a battalion basis. In one unique respect, however, the Habsburg infantry were ahead of the times – in using the Croats as a light infantry screen ahead of the main battle-formation. Turenne had experimented with the use of individual skirmishers, but the practice had been temporarily abandoned on the grounds that it obstructed the battalion fields of fire. The stolid discipline of the Imperial infantry indeed contrasted strikingly with the fighting methods of their Turkish opponents. Ottoman commanders relied on massed rushes to win infantry battles. The large numbers of irregular troops they commonly employed made more sophisticated tactics impossible. At this period the Turk rarely triumphed in open battle, provided the Imperialists preserved their battle-order and were not lured into premature pursuits in their eagerness to loot the viziers' rich encampments.

Despite the increased importance of European infantry as a battle-winning arm, the cavalry retained much of its ancient prestige and size, normally a fifth to a third of an army's strength. A total of 60,000 horse were in action at Malplaquet – by far the largest cavalry engagement of the age. The regiment remained the standard administrative unit, but for action the cavalry served in two or more squadrons of three troops apiece, fifty soldiers forming a troop. There were two main types of cavalry. The heavy cuirassier was armed with sword and pistols; wore breast- and back-plates, sometimes a steel cap – the last vestiges of functional armour. The dragoon was expected to fight on foot or on horseback as occasion demanded, and was additionally armed with a carbine. The Austrian army contained a third type in the hussar. Light cavalry of Magyar origin had been employed for centuries, but the first regular regiments were raised in 1688. These hussars had no place in the line of battle, but were used for raids, foraging and reconnaissance, in much the same way as the Turks employed the *beshlis* of the territorial cavalry.[26] The hussars were not universally admired: Colonel de la Colonie described them as 'properly speaking, nothing but bandits on horseback who carry on an irregular warfare'.[27] Similarly, the Swedish forces adopted a type of light cavalry from the Poles, and the Russians made great use of the mounted Cossack bands.

The tactical employment of the *arme blanche* (sword or sabre) varied considerably from army to army. The French tended to exaggerate the use of cavalry as an instrument of sophisticated fire-power, although both Turenne and Condé had believed in '*la charge sauvage*'. The parade-ground manoeuvres of the French cavalry, firing their pistols or carbines at the halt, troop after troop, made them extremely vulnerable to the 'knee by knee' twin-squadron charges of the English horse. Marlborough was insistent on the use of cavalry as a shock force: cold steel was the specified weapon and on campaign the English were issued with only three rounds of pistol ammunition – for personal protection while foraging. Similarly, Charles XII permitted attack only with the sword. A Swedish tactical innovation was the use of a wedge or arrow-shaped formation, three ranks deep, the troopers riding 'knee behind knee'. The Turk often employed his territorial horse in loosely coordinated attacks ahead of his foot soldiers, the Crimean Tartar being renowned for his superb individual horsemanship and ability to fire accurately from the saddle at full gallop, although he more than met his match in the well-handled Austrian cavalry, which under Baden and Eugene formed the finest arm of the Imperial forces.

The artillery included a variety of calibres, but there was little to choose between the different armies so far as the types and ranges of guns were concerned. The field and regimental artillery which regularly accompanied an army included small three-pounders, 'sakers' (six-pounders), 'demi-culverins' (eight-pounders), and larger pieces firing sixteen-pound and twenty-four-pound cannon-balls. Effective ranges varied between 450 and 600 yards according to type, and armies were provided with guns on a scale of one or two for each thousand men. Heavier metal was required for siege work: these pieces ranged from thirty-six- to sixty-pounders, supported by an array of mortars and brass petards; the Ottomans boasted a cannon that fired stone balls of 120 pounds, but it was unique. The 'train' was a vast, complex organisation embracing engineers, pioneers and supply services as well as gunners, though it varied in size from one campaign to another. The heavy guns were organised into separate 'siege trains': these did not accompany the armies but moved independently from fort to fort as the campaign progressed, the protection of the guns being entrusted to companies of infantry specially detached from the line battalions. Guns most influenced the conduct of wars, indeed, by their bulk and weight. The slow rate of march which they imposed was fatal to schemes of rapid or daring movement, although the increasing use of two-wheeled trails slightly improved their speed.

All things considered, the artillery arm made little progress. Certain armies ignored the professional gunner as belonging to an inferior social class, but the most important reason for this eclipse of the artillery was that the organisations responsible for providing and serving the guns were not usually integral parts of the regular army authorities. The English Board of Ordnance was a completely autonomous body; the Austrian *Büchsenmeister* (trained artillerists) regarded themselves as guildsmen rather than soldiers. Louvois slightly improved the organisation of the French artillery, reducing the number of calibres to six in 1679, but no real corps existed, despite the exertions of Claude du Metz. Once again, it was differences, not in the kind or quality of equipment, but of its correct employment, that distinguished the hostile batteries. During the Succession War the English guns were the best served in Europe, partly because Marlborough combined the post of Captain-General with that of Master-General of the Ordnance and paid the closest attention to the component parts of the artillery. In action he frequently sited the guns in person, as at Blenheim and Malplaquet; he insisted on the use of prepared powder-charges; he introduced a well-sprung cart for easier and faster movement of supplies and munitions. Above all, he nursed the professional interests of his gunners and engineers, assuring them their fair share of promotions and honours. Of much tactical significance was the English practice, originally Swedish, of attaching two light guns to each infantry battalion to provide close fire support. The Dutch and Austrians soon followed suit, and Eugene issued 'galloper guns' to the Imperial cavalry. The Turks experimented with firing small cannons from the backs of camels, but the results were not very satisfactory to man or beast. The French made rather less effective use of their guns on the battlefield, brigading them into rough groups of four, eight or ten pieces; but the terrible carnage inflicted on the Dutch Guards at Malplaquet was caused by a cunningly concealed French battery. On the whole, however, the artillery created more limitations than advantages. By reducing mobility to a minimum, it generally reinforced the unimaginative handling of armies.

Effective control of the various arms during operations was made more difficult by the virtual absence of any staff organisation. Louvois attempted to form the first rudiments of a staff system after Nymegen, but it failed to develop. Most commanders packed their staffs with relatives or sycophants. Marlborough planned and executed his great designs with the assistance of a mere handful of confidants – his secretary Cardonnel, Quartermaster-General Cadogan, and Henry Davenant, the financial agent. These men gave the Duke skilled assistance based on experience. Marlborough was also exceptional in his careful training of the aides-de-camp, who were expected to assess and report on local military situations as well as carry messages through the smoke of battle. Charles XII relied on advisers of the calibre of Stuart, Rehnskiöld and the wily Gyllenkrook, who was responsible for all aspects of supply and the production of maps and routes. With no intermediary divisional or corps headquarters, and only a few subordinate generals in charge of the various sectors of the battlefield, the commander-in-chief bore a very personal responsibility for every decision. Orders were often issued to colonels by word of mouth, but it was exceptionally difficult for a commander to keep a balanced view of the over-all progress of a battle, owing to the clouds of coarse-powder smoke that soon obliterated the scene. Success, then, was won by a general's ability to overcome the many limitations of the time, especially in coordinating the efforts of his men to make the fullest use of the advantages of improved fire-power.

The endeavours of the great captains attracted considerable attention from contemporary essayists and diarists. A few, like Defoe or Goslinga, the Dutch Deputy, were openly critical, but most of the chroniclers – themselves serving soldiers – appreciated the problems their leaders faced. The Count of Mérode-Westerloo has left an interesting description of service in the French armies, complementing Captain Parker's reminiscences of campaigning under William III and Marlborough.[28] Colonel Blackadder of the Cameronians betrays in his journal the conflict between his Presbyterian conscience, which condemned the loose talk and behaviour of many of his fellows, and pride in their martial achievements;[29] Captain Drake, Private Marshall Deane, Corporal Bishop and Serjeants Millner and Wilson speak for Marlborough's rank and file.[30] Count Marsigli made a comprehensive survey of the Ottoman army. The 'Old Campaigner', de la Colonie, painted a graphic picture of life in the Bavarian and Imperial forces. At a critical stage, Captain James Jeffereys reported at length Charles XII's operations.[31] Brigadier-General Richard Kane was to lay the foundations for deeper studies of the military art in *The Campaigns of King William and Queen Anne* (1745). Vauban's works on military engineering and Puységur's *L'Art de la Guerre* remain classics of military writing. These sources reveal that the last decades of the seventeenth century and the early years of the eighteenth were a period of military transition and general mediocrity, enlivened by only a few men of genius. Yet the period clearly foreshadowed major developments in equipment and tactics, and it proved that the profession of arms could be relatively humane as well as honourable.

NOTES

1   Exception might be made of the sappers, who gained from English and Dutch instruction during the Cretan war of 1664–9. See Gibb and Bowen, *Islamic Society and the West*, Vol. 1, Part 1, p. 171.
2   See L F Marsigli, *L'Etat militaire de l'empire Ottoman*, Amsterdam, 1732, Part I, pp. 61–143; also Gibb and Bowen, *op. cit.*, pp. 192–3 and 314–28.
3   See M Roberts, *The Military Revolution, 1560–1660*, Belfast, 1956; also R M Hatton, *Charles XII of Sweden*, London, 1968, pp. 525–6.
4   An English soldier was paid 8d. a day; a cavalry trooper reached 2s. 6d.
5   The post of Chief of Staff had not yet been created.

6 The English version weighed ten pounds; the matchlock fifteen pounds.
7 See J F Puységur, *L'Art de la guerre par principes et par règles*, Paris, 1748.
8 The Swedish invention used a shorter pike employed for metal barricades (or *chevaux de frise*) driven into the ground in front of the men.
9 H Mackay, *Memoirs, Letters and Short Relations*, Edinburgh, Bannatyne Club, 1833, p. 52.
10 General Magnus Stenbock's *Instructions*, Waxjö, 24 January 1710.
11 See J W Stoye, *The Siege of Vienna*, 1964, pp. 235–64.
12 Placed against the besieged town or to protect the besiegers.
13 Quoted in H Morley, *The Earlier Life and Works of Daniel Defoe*, London, 1889, p. 135.
14 Quoted in H Weygand, *Histoire de l'armée française*, 1938, p. 155.
15 Quoted in F E de Vault and J G Pelet, *Mémoires militaires relatifs à la Succession d'Espagne*, 1835–64, Vol. VI, p. 19.
16 See G M Trevelyan, *England Under Queen Anne*, Vol. III, 1934, p. 19.
17 The Instructions of 1675 and after the single *Hofkriegsrat*.
18 Quoted in Weygand, *op. cit.*, p. 155.
19 To Godolphin, 12 July 1708, from W Coxe, *Memoirs of the Duke of Marlborough*, Vol. II, 1847, p. 265.
20 See *The New Cambridge Modern History*, Vol. VI, 1970, pp. 580 and 610.
21 Ottoman camps were notoriously disordered and included many slaves.
22 Marching by one column or by complete battle-lines, foot in centre.
23 R Parker, *Memoirs…1683–1718, in Ireland and Flanders*, Dublin, 1746, p. 80.
24 See W S Churchill, *Marlborough*, Vol. II, 1947, p. 360.
25 *Essai sur l'art de la guerre* (1754), p. 124, quoted in G B Turner, *A History of Military Affairs in Western Society*, 1953, p. 23.
26 Marsigli, *op. cit.*, p. 99.
27 De la Colonie, *The Chronicles of an Old Campaigner*, London, 1904, p. 159.
28 See D G Chandler (ed.), *The Marlborough Wars*, 1968 (new edn 1998). The Introduction examines the authenticity of Parker's work.
29 *The Life and Diary of Lt-Colonel J Blackader* (ed. A Crichton), London, 1824.
30 *Amiable Renegade: the Memoirs of Captain Peter Drake* (ed. S Burrell), 1960; J M Deane, *A Journal of the Campaign in Flanders*, Edinburgh, 1846 (new edn, D G Chandler (ed.), 1981); C T Atkinson, 'One of Marlborough's men: Matthew Bishop', *JSAHR*, Vol. XXIII, 1945, p. 157; J Millner, *A Compendious Journal of all the marches, famous battles, sieges, etc.*, 1733.
31 *Letters from the Swedish Army, 1707–1709* (ed. R Hatton), Stockholm, 1954.

CHAPTER II

Beginnings

The Battle of Sedgemoor

Upon his restoration King Charles II ordered his father's nemesis, the New Model Army, to be disbanded. The country resented the military not only for attempting to run the country but for costing too much in the process, and today we still have a *Royal* Navy, and a *Royal* Air Force, but *the* Army because its ancestors were in fact very far from being 'royally disposed'. Four regiments (two infantry and two cavalry) were retained by the King to meet local crises, such as protecting his Coronation Decorations from being torn down by the London mob, but Charles astutely bound all early new regiments to him by allowing them to be called 'Royal' in their titles

As a result, the English army was, at first, only called 'Guards' and 'Garrisons', but very slowly the Army was created of 'subject troops' – and by the time of the death of Charles II in 1685 there were eight regiments of Foot and four regiments of Horse. As a result of economic policy and a fear of an armed force which might be manipulated for political ends, the Army was small, poorly trained, and 'slightly admired'. Despite this, Charles II, copying an idea of Louis XIV and traditionally abetted by his mistress Nell Gwyn, had created The Royal Hospital, dedicated to helping wounded and aged soldiers, and providing certain of them with somewhere to live.

Meanwhile, the King's brother – James, Duke of York – reorganised the artillery in the Tower of London, and some young officers were sent abroad to learn their trade; especially in France under Louis XIV. John Churchill was one such important example, having been trained by the great Marshal Turenne. Young Churchill had already been recognised as a brave and able soldier, having served as a marine officer with the Royal Navy and taken part in operations at Tangier in north Africa. These small improvements were slowly developing when Charles died and the Catholic James II succeeded. Almost at once an important crisis arose. In June 1685 James Scott, Duke of Monmouth, Charles II's Protestant illegitimate son, gambled his life and fortune and invaded the south-west of England. Churchill offered his services and his patron, now his monarch, promoted him Major-General and gave him his first independent command – albeit only temporarily.

Old battlefields are often fertile grounds for legend and myth – especially when they represent a special milestone in a nation's story, or, as Winston Churchill once described it, 'when they form punctuation-marks on the pages of secular history'.

The Battle of Sedgemoor, fought out on the misty early morning of 6 July 1685, outside the Somerset village of Westonzoyland, has contributed greatly to the national story, fact and fiction, truth and myth – sometimes they are hard to distinguish – and the story of Sedgemoor has certainly had its fair share of both.[1]

Its significance lies at several levels. First, it proved to be the last pitched battle to be fought on English soil. Although there was a skirmish or two associated with the early days of the Glorious Revolution in November 1688, and two small actions – one near Derby, the other near Shap Fell in Cumbria – associated with Bonnie Prince Charlie's rash invasion of 1745, none of these led to more than a dozen casualties a side and consequently don't earn the title of a true battle-royal. Of course the same is not true of Scotland (Culloden in 1746 was a battle by any standards). Wales had a brief action with a French Revolutionary force at Fishguard in 1797,[2] and as for feud-torn Ireland – well, enough said. But where England has been concerned, the Battle of Sedgemoor proved its last engagement of any size.

Secondly, had James Scott, Duke of Monmouth, triumphed in his daring attempt at a night attack on Lord Feversham's encamped royal army that summer night 319-odd years ago, it is distinctly unlikely that the House of Windsor would today be upon the British throne. The 'ifs' and 'buts' of history are notoriously uncertain, but a rebel success outside Westonzoyland might have triggered a chain reaction of support for the handsome, illegitimate 'Protestant Prince' at the expense of his Roman Catholic uncle, King James II, in the nation at large. In such a case, the present monarch would in all likelihood have been the Duke of Buccleuch – the direct descendant of 'King Monmouth'.[3]

Sedgemoor indisputably was the first major engagement fought by the reconstituted standing army as recreated by Charles II after his restoration to the throne in 1660. Certain regiments had fought in Tangier, on loan to Louis XIV or the Dutch, or indeed in Scotland, but 6 July 1685 was the first time that a substantial force of regular horse and foot, together with the train of artillery, had fought together in a concerted action. The tragic fact that they were called to use their energies against their fellow countrymen on such a significant occasion is illustrated by the refusal to grant a battlehonour for 'Sedgemoor' – to be proudly borne on regimental colours, guidons, mess silver or the like – to any of the ten formations engaged, the direct ancestors of the most senior regiments of the modern

British Army. Indeed, until very recently the Queen's Regiment (descendants of 'Kirke's Lambs' – later the 2nd Regiment of Foot – who earned a particularly bad reputation by their conduct after the battle) were forbidden to recruit in the West Country, where memories die hard.

To this day there is talk of ghostly happenings on the battlefield outside Westonzoyland on the night of the anniversary each year, although confusion over the Old Calendar (as in use in 1685) and the New Style – involving a ten-day difference (thus 6 July 1685 O.S. becomes 16 July 1685 N.S.) – causes one to regard some claims of 'sighting' in the mist with more than usual scepticism. One belief is that 'King Monmouth' never died but (like King Arthur) is only sleeping, awaiting his nation's call to return and lead his people in time of crisis.

Another is that since the Battle of Sedgemoor no monarch or member of the Royal family has ever visited the disaffected area of 1685. Queen Victoria, by one legend, would order the blinds of her railway coach to be drawn when passing through the countryside around Taunton. For this claim there is absolutely no evidence; for the former, the evidence is definitely on the other side. Just one year after the battle, who should visit Sedgemoor in person but King James II (who had also written a personal account of the Revolt in the West which is still to be seen in the archives of the British Library in London),[4] who came down from Windsor to see the field for himself. And – to slay the legend once and for all – Prince Michael of Kent attended the commemorative service in Westonzoyland Church on the 300th anniversary in July 1985.

What was the crisis that led to Norton St Philip and Sedgemoor all about? The death of King Charles II, 'the Merry Monarch', on 6 February 1685, without a legitimate male heir meant that the succession passed to his brother, the Roman Catholic James, Duke of York. To a substantial number of his Protestant subjects, here was a flagrant breach of the principle of a Protestant succession to the throne established in the reign of Queen Elizabeth I.[5]

This offended the consciences of many people living in Lowland Scotland, Cheshire and the West Country. There was also a widespread fear in Parliament and elsewhere that the new King would be unduly influenced by his powerful co-religionary, Louis XIV of France, who was openly persecuting his Protestant (or Huguenot) minority. The coronation period had seen much fraudulent adjustment of borough charters to ensure support for the new King – another cause of resentment in much of the country at large. To compound it all, there were widespread rumours of a mysterious 'Black Box'[6] said to contain incontrovertible proof that Charles II as a young man had in fact married Lucy Walters, the Duke of Monmouth's mother, and that consequently her son was perhaps the rightful and Protestant King.

Indeed, the question of the succession had dominated domestic politics since 1679, and the handsome young Monmouth had received much popular adulation during two passages through the West and Cheshire which encouraged certain exiled plotters – foremost among them the Presbyterian Earl of Argyle, Lord Grey of Warke, the Rev. Robert Fergusson (already known as 'the Plotter') and a number of republican and Cromwellian malcontents congregated in the Low Countries – to spin their webs of intrigue around the 'Protestant Prince' who was himself periodically in exile in their midst. These unscrupulous men played upon Monmouth's easy-going nature and credulity to persuade him to challenge by force of arms his half-uncle's accession to the English throne.

When news of Charles II's death reached the Continent, the plotters swung into action. After a period of preparation, Argyle set sail with some followers on 2 May to raise the Lowlands of Scotland, while Lord Delamere undertook to promote rebellion among the Cheshire Protestants. Monmouth was to raise an army in the West – where, he was assured, a great welcome awaited him – while disaffected London awaited the word to revolt in its turn. His power base threatened, and three separate but connected rebellions in distant parts of his kingdoms to contend with, James would be tumbled from the throne and the Commonwealth reproclaimed – or so the senior plotters intended.[7]

In fact, this plan was from the start overambitious and based on several false assumptions. Monmouth's finances were very slight – he was forced to pawn some of his regalia and his mistress, Lady Henrietta Wentworth, her jewels, to hire three vessels and purchase powder and arms for his part of the venture.

It was too late in that it came several months after James' coronation which permitted Monmouth's half-uncle to consolidate his position among his people; and yet it was too early in that Monmouth had not afforded James II sufficient time to show his true nature as a tyrant and thus disabuse his subjects of any feelings of loyalty towards him, as would most certainly have become the case by late 1688, the time of 'the Glorious Revolution'.[8] Even worse, Monmouth was slow – owing to amorous dalliance with Henrietta and adverse winds in the Channel – in setting out down the Channel, and it was only on 11 June that he arrived off Lyme in Dorset and landed with eighty-two supporters, four small guns, and weaponry for 1,500 men to raise his green standard emblazoned in gold, 'Fear Nothing but God'.

While local supporters flocked in to welcome the duke, news of the invasion rapidly reached the Court of St James's. In fact, James II had been alerted by his secret agents to what was in the wind for some time – before Monmouth even landed, steps had been taken to crush the Scottish rising (Argyle would be executed in Edinburgh on 30 June) and to recall regiments from service in the Low Countries to swell the small but tough and experienced Royal Army.[9] The shire militias were mobilised to meet the invaders, and an apprehensive Parliament hastened to place a price on the invader's head, while Lord John Churchill[10] – son of the MP for Lyme – was sent west with a cavalry force of the Blues and several companies of Colonel Kirke's Regiment to observe and harass the newcomers.

By 19 June the newly appointed commander-in-chief, Louis Duras, Earl of Feversham[11] (and a nephew of the great French Marshal Turenne), was marching down the Great Bath Road at the head of three battalions of Foot Guards and more horsemen, while behind him the 'Great Trayne' of guns from the Tower of London set out westward, escorted by Dumbarton's Regiment of Foot (the Royal Scots) and the remainder of Kirke's. Meanwhile a by-train of guns had left Portsmouth, accompanied by Trelawney's Regiment (today the King's Own Royal Border Regiment) under Lord Churchill's brother, Charles. The government also ordered the raising of eleven new regiments (all still existing today).

Monmouth, largely unaware of the forces of nemesis beginning to move against him, was enjoying a period of heartening support from the local population. A raid on Bridgport scattered some militia, followed by an advance from Lyme northward through Axminster (where the Devon militia recoiled before the burgeoning rebel host, now over 3,000 strong) and thence through Chard to Taunton, county-town of Somerset, where the warmest welcome yet was encountered and more recruits poured in to form a new regiment – the 'Blue', to add to the Red, White, Yellow and Green already formed. But Monmouth was a worried man – and so were his key advisers – for there were few signs of the gentry or estate owners who had rapturously greeted him in the region a very few years before. In an attempt to bring them in, it was decided to proclaim the duke King. 'Royal Proclamations' were read to an ecstatic crowd on 19 June, while twenty-six maids of Taunton presented colours reputedly made from their petticoats to the handsome 'King Monmouth'.[12]

The army marched on – now approaching 7,000 strong – to Bridgwater and another rapturous welcome on the 21st. But there was still no sign of the gentry joining the column, and from the distant rear news was coming in of a first brush for the Blues near Chard (on the 18th) and a more serious cavalry skirmish at Ashill the next day, neither of which had ended to the Rebels' advantage. Kirke's hard-marching companies of Foot joined Churchill's cavalry on the 21st. Meanwhile, in faraway Scotland, the 18th had also seen the final defeat of Argyle and the scattering of his Presbyterian Lowland supporters, and there were still no signs of the anticipated risings in either London or Cheshire.

What to do? Monmouth decided to press on for Bristol. The city was the second port of the realm, had great riches and arsenals of weapons to be tapped – and reputedly many more eager and well-to-do supporters waiting only the word to rise. But Lord Feversham, after burning the roads to the west, narrowly won the race and, while loyal militia occupied

Bristol, other parties broke down the bridges over the Avon. On 25 June Monmouth and his men came to Keynsham, managed to repair the bridge there, and briefly paraded on the east bank before a violent storm drove them back into the town. It afforded scant respite, for suddenly the sodden rebels found themselves under attack by royal cavalry from two directions, to their great alarm.

Through appalling rain, the rebels set out southward, planning to break east through Warminster towards 500 'mounted gentry' waiting in Wiltshire, or so it was said. After being repulsed from Bath, the demoralised host moved on to Philip's Norton (as the town was then known), arriving there on the 26th, the same day that Churchill at last joined up – none too willingly – with Feversham's main army south of Bath. The Royal commanders conferred, and it was decided to increase the pressure[13] on Monmouth. A Royal pardon was being proclaimed for all rebels who surrendered their arms with no more ado and Feversham's advance guard set out for Norton town. Early on the 27th they approached the outskirts.

The red-coated veterans were in for an unpleasant surprise. Not only did their foremost party blunder into an ambush in 'Bloody Lane', but the rabble stood their ground manfully, and by the time more heavy rain brought the engagement to an end that afternoon, some forty soldiers had become casualties, and even the arrival of several Royal guns had achieved little. As the royal army pulled back to Bradford-on-Avon, Monmouth decided to continue his move towards Warminster by way of Frome. There, news awaited him that soon dampened the short mood of exaltation that the success at Norton had inspired. The collapse of the Scottish revolt was now revealed.[14]

A despondent council of war was held, amid news of desertions from the rebel army. Monmouth himself was only narrowly dissuaded from deserting his followers and fleeing for France. Instead, he agreed to abandon the Warminster venture and issued orders for a retreat through Shepton Mallet and Wells towards Sedgemoor outside Bridgwater where, rumour had it, an army of 10,000 reinforcements waited.

Through yet more rain the march proceeded. Reaching Wells on 1 July, the demoralised rebels vented their bitter wrath on the cathedral – shooting at statues, ripping lead from the roof to make musketballs and attempting to desecrate the high altar. On the 2nd the despondent host reached the moor – to find just 150 'clubmen' waiting for them.[15] Marching into a silent and shuttered Bridgwater, Monmouth's men fell down exhausted in Castle Field, while their leader moved into nearby Sydenham Manor.[16] Incredibly, on Saturday 4 July, permission was given for rebels with homes in the vicinity to visit them. Many did not return. His army now numbered under 4,000 men.

The somewhat chastened royal army was meanwhile marching south and west so as to cut the rebels off from the south coast and the main areas of their support. Moving by way of Frome and Glastonbury to Somerton, Lord Feversham cautiously reconnoitered the approaches to Bridgwater, believing that he might need to undertake a siege of the place. On Sunday the 5th his troops moved forward to make camp on the outskirts of Westonzoyland, pitching their tents behind a large drainage ditch called the Bussex Rhyne. Less than three miles divided them from Bridgwater.

This fact did not go unobserved by a Monmouth supporter atop neighbouring Chedzoy church tower through his spyglass. Summoning his servant, Godfrey,[17] he sent him into Bridgwater to report what he had seen. Thus were set in motion a series of fateful decisions that were to lead, within twenty-four hours, to a gory night battle.

On receipt of his sympathiser's report, Monmouth had spied out the lie of the land from the turret on St Mary's church spire, and after sending Godfrey to ascertain whether the royal army had dug any fortifications to protect his rough camp (he reported that there were none), the duke called a council of war and declared his intention of carrying out a surprise night attack. Godfrey was pressed into service as local guide, and after a busy evening of preparations, at 11 pm the rebel regiments, well fortified with drink but under draconian orders to preserve total silence, set out eastward from Bridgwater, some 600 horsemen, 3,000 foot soldiers, four cannon and forty-two waggons strong. Monmouth's plan was to avoid the direct route to Westonzoyland down the Taunton highway (he knew that Feversham's far superior artillery was drawn up to command the road), and to make a five-mile, cross-country advance to attack the camp from the farther (or eastern) side.

It was a desperate gamble, given the ill-training and low morale of his remaining men. Feversham's and Churchill's 750 cavalry and 1,900 regular infantrymen were supported by all of twenty-six cannon, while three regiments of Wiltshire Militia (perhaps another 3,000 untried men) were stationed in nearby Othery and Middlezoy. Furthermore, the Royal commanders were professionals – as Monmouth should have known well, since he had served alongside several (including Churchill) in happier, younger days. As a result, sensible security precautions had been taken at last light, and when Feversham retired to bed at about 1 am on 6 July, there were cavalry patrols to the fore of the camp and a comprehensive system of pickets and sentries near the Bussex Rhyne,[18] while the cavalry horses had been left ready, saddled in the village in case of need.

There was a dense mist over the moor, however, and with the benefit of Godfrey's local knowledge of the watercourses, Monmouth just might have achieved the surprise on which everything depended. The baggage train and one gun with a squeaking wheel were left at the main road;[19] ammunition waggons and handlers dropped off at Peasey Farm; Chedzoy was bypassed; two ditches successfully and silently were passed.

31

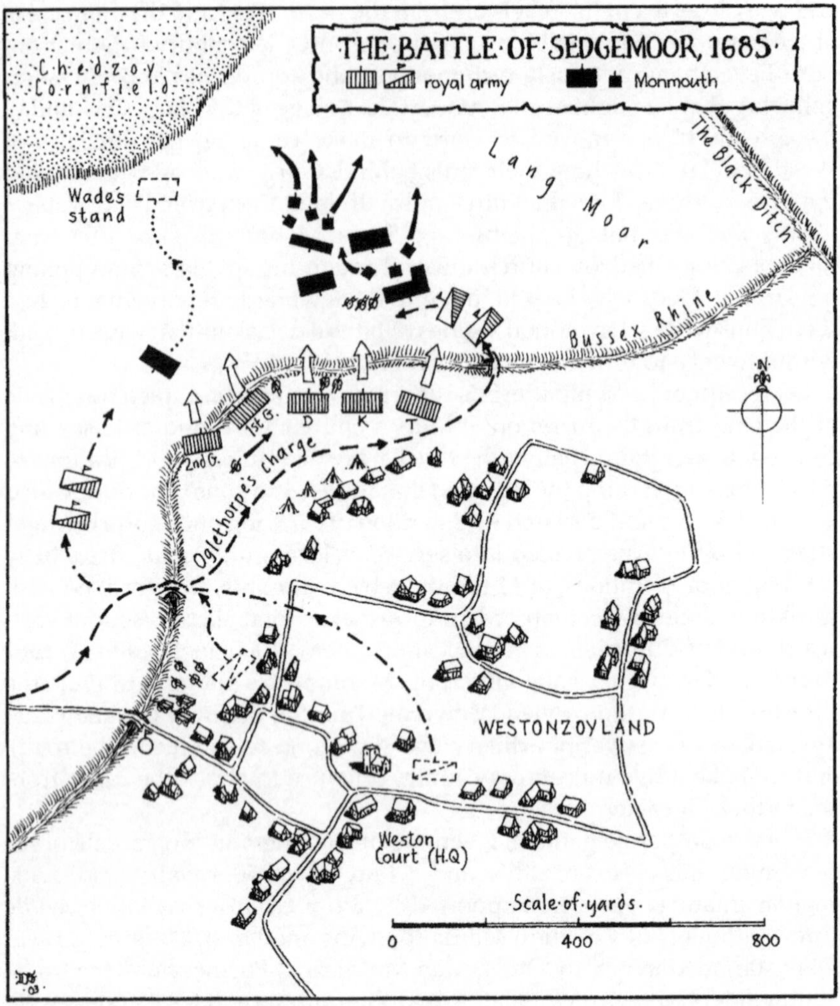
THE·BATTLE·OF·SEDGEMOOR, 1685·
royal army
Monmouth
Chedzoy Cornfield
Wade's stand
Lang Moor
The Black Ditch
Bussex Rhine
1st G.
D
K
T
2nd G.
Oglethorpe's charge
N
WESTONZOYLAND
Weston Court (H.Q)
·Scale·of·yards·
0
400
800

But then Monmouth's luck suddenly ran out. Godfrey missed the crossing point over the Langmoor Rhyne, the last obstacle between the rebels and their target.[20] In the fog-enshrouded darkness at about 2 am, the rebel column crowded up; discipline slipped, someone swore, a few clumsy pikes clashed and were dropped – and it was over for Monmouth.

Suddenly a shot rang out and all hell broke loose.[21] Monmouth decided to press on regardless.

The drums rolled out the alarm, and the disciplined royal redcoats seized their weaponry and ran in orderly fashion to take up their alarm posts in the line of battle, under Lord Churchill's command. Only two things were missing – their guns[22] some 500 yards to the left, whose civilian drivers had apparently fled at the first alert, and the commander-in-chief, who was so fast asleep in Weston Court that for some time his servants could not awaken him despite the din without. Both discrepancies would shortly be made good, however.

It was by now 2.30 am. Followed by Monmouth's perspiring foot regiments over the moor, Lord Grey of Warke lost the race to seize the upper crossing point over the Bussex Rhyne and his rough horsemen swung south and rode along its course across the front of the forming royal army. Dumbarton's men,[23] busy lighting their pieces of slow-match, let them pass, but the Guards battalion[24] next in line made no such error, and soon volleys of musketry were tearing into Monmouth's cavalrymen. Their ill-trained horses swerved away in terror, and in their flight plunged willy-nilly through their own approaching foot soldiers.

Monmouth's infantry regiments staggered on forward until they came up to the Bussex Rhyne, which, although deep, did not have much water in it. Instead of pressing over to get to grips with the outnumbered royal infantry before their dispositions could be completed, first the Yellow Regiment, then the Red (despite the entreaties of its commander, Major Nathaniel Wade[25]) came to a halt, and began – such as had firearms – to engage their foes with fire. The three guns of the rebel army – commanded by an anonymous Dutch gunner – made good practice against Dumbarton's (whose glowing matches they could dimly see through the dark), causing more than forty casualties. Monmouth was prominent among his men, half-pike in hand, trying to encourage them.

Dawn was now breaking, and the mist began to disperse, allowing the royal army to see what it faced. Lord Churchill extended his line to the right by transferring Kirke's[26] and Trelawny's regiments[27] from the left. Thanks to Bishop Peter Mews,[28] a visitor in the camp (and an old soldier from Civil War days), several Royal guns were drawn up by his servants and coach horses dragged them to the centre of the line. Their fire quickly silenced the rebel cannon. Next, an anxious Colonel Oglethorpe[29] arrived from the Taunton Road to swell the ranks of the Royal cavalry.

Last to appear was Lord Feversham, at last restored to consciousness,[30] who calmly assumed command of a battle which by then was already three-quarters won.

Indeed, all was nearly lost for Monmouth, his guns out of action, his musketry fire dying away as his men ran out of ammunition. And the disciplined royal volley firing was now having maximum effect in the gathering light. Judging his moment with nicety, Lord Feversham launched the *coup de grâce*. First, he unleashed two forces of cavalry[31] over the two plungeons, or cattle crossings, to take the hesitating rebel infantry in flank and rear. Then, judging the time to be right, he ordered the infantry battalions forward over the Bussex Rhyne.

At that point, Monmouth remounted his horse and with a few colleagues fled the field. Although Wade fought a model withdrawal with the Red Regiment's survivors, the other regiments broke and fled. Some 300 rebels already lay dead on the field. Another 1,000 would be slaughtered as they fled, beneath the swords of the pursuing dragoons or at the hands of the Wiltshire Militia. A further 500 or so would be dragged to St Mary's, Westonzoyland, turned into a temporary prison.[32] Summary justice was meted out – particularly by Colonel Kirke and his 'Lambs', as the full horrors of the hue and cry began.

The Revolt of the West was crushed with telling severity. As a grateful King James lavished rewards on Feversham and other officers, a strict inquiry was made through the disaffected counties, and many arrests made. Then, the jails bulging at the seams, Judge Jeffreys[33] and his 'Commission of Oyer et Terminer' were sent into the West to wreak their master's vengeance. By the time the 'Bloody Assizes' were over, some 333 had suffered the supreme penalty and a further 814 were sentenced to serve as virtual slaves in Barbados and Jamaica.[34]

As for 'King Monmouth', he was found by the Sussex Militia in disguise cowering in a ditch near Woodlands in Dorset, forty-eight hours after the battle. Conveyed to London, he abjectly pleaded for his life before his implacable half-uncle, offering to reveal the names of his supporters that he could remember. On 15 July he recovered his manhood sufficiently to die bravely under the axe on Tower Hill, before a vast and silent crowd.[35]

Apologists for Monmouth claim that he failed in his revolt because he never received the support of the gentry, and that he lost Sedgemoor because he had no prior knowledge of the existence of the Bussex Rhyne defending the approaches to the royal camp. The first claim is essentially correct. The second is – or should be – bogus since Monmouth and his army had passed through, or close by, Westonzoyland twice in the weeks before the battle.

NOTES

1. See D G Chandler, *Sedgemoor 1685*, Spellmount, 1995, *passim*.
2. P Chamberlain, *Waterloo Journal*, No.3, December 1997, pp.17–18.
3. See J N P Watson, *Captain-General and Rebel Chief*, London, 1979.
4. Account by James II (Harl. Mss), BM, No. 6845, *passim*.
5. G N Clarke, *The Later Stuarts*, Oxford, 1949.
6. Chandler, *op. cit.*, Appendix D.
7. R Clifton, *The Last Popular Rebellion*, London, 1984, *passim*.
8. K Merle Chacksfield, *1688: Glorious Revolution*, Wincampton, 1988, pp. 7–24.
9. J Childs, *The Army, James II and the Glorious Revolution*, Manchester, 1980, *passim*; also *JSAHR*, No.13, 1987, on 'Restoration Britain 1660–1688'.
10. W S Churchill, *Marlborough: His Life and Times*, London, 1967, Vol. I, pp. 130–207.

11   *Proceedings of the Huguenot Society*, Vol. XVV(3), 1991.
12.   B Bevan, *James, Duke of Monmouth*, London, 1947, pp. 220–7.
13.   Chandler, *op. cit*, pp. 31–7.
14.   *Ibid.*, pp. 38, 80 & 122 (on the 9th Earl of Argyle).
15.   *Ibid.*, p. 41 (on the 'Clubmen' of whom only 150 arrived).
16.   Monmouth had moved to Sydenham House at Bridgwater.
17.   Richard (or Benjamin) Godfrey (or Newton). He was illegitimate.
18.   Proposed for planning to march to Bristol after the battle.
19.   Chandler, *op. cit.*, Appendix B and page 180.
20.   Soothsayer, *c.* 1672. See Chandler *op. cit.,* first page.
21.   This pistol was fired by a Royal Army cavalryman near a picket.
22.   Some twenty-six guns, from the Tower Train and the Portsmouth Bye-Train.
23.   Dumbarton's Regiment of Foot (later 1st Royal Scots).
24.   The Royal Regiment of Guards (later the Grenadier Guards).
25.   Nathaniel Wade, a lawyer who was also Major of the Rebels; and see Chandler, *op. cit.*, pp. 78–9.
26.   Kirke's (or Queen Dowager of Foot – later The Queen's Regiment, now Princess of Wales's Royal Regiment).
27.   Trelawney's Regiment (today The King's Own Royal Border Regiment).
28.   Peter Mews, Bishop of Wells (and later of Winchester), who had been a soldier during the Civil Wars. He was visiting with Feversham.
29.   Oglethorpe's Blues (today The Blues and Royals).
30.   See Note 11 for details.
31   The Horse Guards (today The Life Guards) and the King's Own Royal Dragoons (subsequently 1st Royal Dragoons, now the Blues and Royals).
32   See Drummer Adam Wheeler, *Iter Bellicosum*, Camden Misc., Vol. 12; and Chandler, *op. cit.*, pp. 85–7.
33   Baron George Jeffreys of Wem; and see Chandler, *op. cit.*, pp. 84–7.
34   W M Wigfield, *The Monmouth Rebels*, Sutton, 1985.
35   W M Wigfield, *The Monmouth Rebellion*, Bradford-on-Avon, 1980, is an excellent work. Jack Ketch, the executioner, took four axe blows and a knife to sever Monmouth's head.

CHAPTER III
Fluctuations
English Troops in Flanders 1688–97

As we have seen, the size of the English Army grew considerably in the 1680s. Before Sedgemoor, James II and Parliament ordered sixteen new regiments to be raised. However, the early popularity of the king rapidly declined over the next three years, and James himself became more hostile to Parliament. Protestant versus Catholic issues became very serious and even posed threats to the chartered rights of the universities and large towns; in addition to these concerns, James began to appoint Catholics as officers in the army and raised some to high rank. In 1685 he massed the army at Hounslow Heath near London, ostensibly as a rendezvous, but really to bully Parliament, and to add insult to injury, he insisted certain important local citizens had dragoons billeted freely upon them in their homes.

Therefore, the army was now larger, but a national crisis was impending. James II would not give way on religious issues and pushed his ministers even further until certain politically powerful Parliamentarians opened secret negotiations with the Protestant Dutch Stadtholder, William of Orange and his wife, Mary, James's eldest daughter. They plotted a revolution. As a result, on 4 November 1688 William invaded England with a Dutch army and several well known 'disaffected Englishmen' near Torbay in Devon. Briefly resisted at Wincanton, it became a bloodless 'Glorious Revolution' – as more gentry, officers and English troops went over to William. John Churchill, recently promoted Lieutenant-General by his erstwhile close friend and patron, James II, slipped away from Salisbury and joined William too. Traditionally James realised he must escape when he overheard a royal sentry outside his own quarters whistling 'Lilli Bullero', a tune popular with William's troops! Friendless, James decided to flee to France and William III and Queen Mary II were crowned.

Parliament insisted on legal restraints on the new Williamite Army, and the artillery remained embodied. However, William vastly enlarged his forces to almost 100,000 men for his war against France, but on the signing of peace in 1697, Parliament immediately reduced the Army to 7,000 – it was the old issues of fear and expense again! In the meantime, Lord

37

Marlborough fell from favour; the king did not trust a General who changed sides and one who was openly critical of the numbers of Dutchmen getting lucrative army appointments. However, he did not move far from royal circles as he and his wife Sarah became great friends of Princess Anne, the Queen's younger sister.

King William III, constitutional monarch of the United Kingdom and Stadtholder of the United Provinces, was in a very real sense in personal control of the overall administration of the English war effort between the years 1688 and 1697. He was equally responsible for the operational employment of the English armies in the field and the maintenance of the unity of the international alliance that he and the Emperor Leopold of Austria had brought into existence to check the grandiose ambitions and flagrant territorial appetites of Louis XIV. In order to appreciate the complex reasons that caused considerable annual fluctuations in the number of troops England was prepared to employ for the war on the Continent, it is first necessary to review the main problems that William faced in his largely self-appointed crusade against 'le Roi Soleil'.

In the day-to-day running of the struggle, William relied to a greater or lesser extent on two men – namely William Blathwayt, who served as Secretary at War when in England and as Secretary of State when accompanying his master abroad, and Lord Ranelagh, Paymaster General of the Forces. These two men, together with William himself, formed an informal committee of three who between them directed all aspects of the war on land – apart from the crucial allocation of supply to finance the campaigns which remained the inalienable right of a jealous Parliament.

Blathwayt (who succeeded the less competent George Clark in 1690 and held his post until 1704) was indubitably William's 'eminence grise' in affairs relating to military administration. An administrator of great ability and loyalty, he more than made up for his relative inexperience of the realities of warfare by his tireless attention to matters of detail. Ranelagh, on the other hand, was a corrupt crony of Lord Carmarthen, Lord President of the Council, who was formally ministerial head of the English government until 1693 during William's long absences abroad, although in fact his real power was very slight. Indeed, William was the only irreplaceable figure in the whole administration.

Here it will only be feasible to mention the major and more obvious problems faced by King William and his key servants. Firstly, there were the constitutional and political complications involved in being the ruler of England and of the United Provinces at one and the same time. On many occasions, English and Dutch interests did not exactly coincide, and William consequently faced many tricky calculations of balance and priority. The fact that he never enjoyed absolute power in either nation meant that he could never ignore the various trends of influential opinion, for both the States-General and the Houses of Parliament controlled the power of the purse and without their grudging support there could be no prosecution of the struggle whatsoever. This financial difficulty was to underlie many of the disappointment of the years that lay ahead.

Secondly, there were problems posed by the armed forces themselves. During the war under consideration the Dutch army rarely put into the field more than 11,000 cavalry, 2,000 dragoons and 60,000 infantry, and these figures included a contingent of three English and as many more Scottish regiments 'in the Dutch pay', besides a considerable body of mercenaries. In terms of quality, however, since the debacle of 1672, the Dutch infantry and cavalry had attained a very creditable standard of discipline and battle-worthiness under William's personal supervision, whilst in the persons of Prince Waldeck Vaudemont, and Generals Ginkel and Schomberg, William possessed a cadre of sound senior commanders. The English army, on the other hand, was barely more than an ad hoc collection of regiments of varying standard. If we discount the militia, which stood at a strength of 80,000 men throughout the period and was never embodied for overseas service, we can say that William inherited a force of 31,000 regular soldiers, although in the course of the war this number was to be vastly expanded to as many as 93,635 (1694), including a total of thirty-two foreign regiments 'in English pay'. Initially the army's standards were deplorable, whilst despite their own opinion of their martial qualities the native-born leaders – these 'brave and haughty society officers' as Churchill calls them[1] – the Earl of Marlborough, Lords Cutts and Ormonde – lacked experience of command on the continental scale for several years. The friction and jealousies that bedevilled Anglo–Dutch military relations – typified by the irrational hatred many Englishmen felt for the unfortunate Count Solms – was not the least of the crosses that William was called upon to bear.

As Allied Captain-General and the inspiration of an international alliance, William faced a number of interrelated strategical problems. In the first place, his main purpose was to ensure the continuation of a military and diplomatic war of attrition against the forces of Louis XIV in the Netherlands region in the hope of bleeding the French white in terms of manpower and allies; in association with this war aim was a policy of economic strangulation of French trade, and it was to be this factor more than any other that brought France to accept the Peace of Ryswick; in practical terms, however, this often led to clashes between land and sea priorities, especially when the supply of funds was short – which was in effect every year. William's second preoccupation as a soldier-statesman was with the preservation of the unity of the Alliance, ceaselessly attempting to forestall French-inspired defections or the formation of a 'third force' of neutral powers. Thirdly, William had always to regard with great care the national security of both the British Isles and the

United Provinces from the danger of enemy attack – Ireland was to present the greatest problem here in the early years of the war – and associated with both this and the foregoing considerations was the question of his personal safety; rarely has an international figure been made the target of so many assassination plots by a vindictive foe that realised that William was compelled to pay attention to the private problems faced by his other allies – most particularly the Empire (engaged until 1699 in a large war with the Turk in addition to its commitments against France) and, from 1690, by Savoy in north Italy. Such problems imposed a heavy drain on England and Holland in the form of monetary subsidies. All these factors, therefore, played an important part in determining the scale of English forces serving in Flanders at any given time.[2]

As is only to be expected, the sources from which detailed information on military strengths can be drawn tend to be contradictory, but it is possible to draw broad conclusions from the comparison of available evidence. The most valuable sources are the eighteen large volumes of documents in the Public Record Office comprising what is known as 'King William's Chest'. An investigation of these volumes[3] has revealed a considerable amount of directly relevant information for most years of the war. A series of annual military balance-sheets and reports to Parliament have survived, and as several of these bear the signature and annotations of William Blathwayt, there is no reason to question their validity, especially as almost without exception they are drawn up in an identical form in the same hand.[4] A certain amount of corroboratory documentation is forthcoming from the Additional Manuscripts at the British Museum,[5] and wherever possible these have been used to check the 'official' lists drawn up by the Secretary at War and his clerks. It is also of interest to compare this primary material with the statistics provided by contemporary chroniclers of the wars and other published sources. In this respect two authors have proved particularly useful – namely Edward d'Auvergne, who served as Chaplain to the 3rd Regiment of Guards throughout much of this war, and who published an annual account of the events that transpired between 1691 and 1697;[6] and the French historian, the Marquis de Beaurain, who chronicled the career of the Duke of Luxembourg in considerable detail.[7] In addition I have consulted 'A True Relation' for the year 1689.[8] Passing on to secondary sources, the great work of Colonel Walton, *The Regular Army, 1660–99* and the even more useful volumes of Dalton relating to the Commission Registers, proved of great value between them in their complementary ways.[9]

Certain problems were, however, encountered from the outset with regard to the documentary sources. For one thing, many of the relevant papers bore no exact date; for another, it soon became evident that 'King William's Chest' was to some extent haphazardly assembled, and the odd undated record which close investigation subsequently proved to be relevant to, for example, 1689, was placed in Volume 13 considerably out of sequence, as most of the papers for this year are included in Volume 5. In consequence, a certain amount of academic detective work had to be undertaken to establish the periods to which such undated and out-of-sequence documents belonged, but fortunately the following-up of such clues as the changes in regimental commanders or comparison of totals with other dated papers bore considerable fruit, and it can be claimed with fair certainty that the documents have now been accurately dated and placed in their correct sequences. In the process, several assumed dates (added in pencil with question marks by past researchers) have been proved to be erroneous.[10]

Secondly, it has also proved very difficult to reconcile the figures given by the various sources for the same years. No small part of this problem is due to the fact that few sources calculated their unit strengths in the same way – and it is clear that all figures, from whatever sources, are at best only approximate. Thus Mr Secretary Blathwayt calculates the average establishment of an infantry battalion at 780 'private men', excluding officers, NCOs and staff from his main calculations; similarly, he calculates the average cavalry regiment at 300 troopers, and that of dragoons at 480 – though there are plenty of variations for larger-than-usual regiments (e.g. the Guards, or the Royal Regiment). D'Auvergne, on the other hand, calculates an English battalion at 600 men, and cavalry and dragoons at 130 and 150 per squadron respectively. Walton in general terms follows d'Auvergne's conventions, but at times adjusts his figures to allow for the wastage or special problems of particular campaigns or periods (for example his calculations of battalion strengths fluctuate between 600 and 500, and his cavalry squadron strengths between 100 and 150). But once allowance for this type of difference of basic calculation is made, a broadly accurate reconciliation can be achieved from the number of formations sent into the field in terms of regiments of infantry and cavalry, or, where the data is available, in terms of companies of foot and squadrons of horse.[11]

It is proposed to examine each year of the war from the following angles: first, we shall estimate the current strength of the English contingent in Flanders (including foreign troops in London's pay) and note any detected fluctuations during the twelve-month period. Secondly, wherever possible we shall estimate the proportion of the English army that these figures represent, and also calculate as percentages what they mean in terms of the Allies committed to the war in the Netherlands region. Thirdly, we shall conclude each annual survey with a brief resumé of the main trends of the year, suggesting reasons for any considerable fluctuations in the numbers of English troops present in terms of military or political preoccupations elsewhere. Lastly, as a general conclusion to

41

the completed series of annual surveys, an attempt will be made to draw the threads together, comparing the general picture of the scale of English involvement in Flanders during the years 1688–97 with that of the years 1700–13.

The story of the involvement of English troops in Flanders really begins in the second year of the Nine Years War, that is to say in 1689. The previous year saw little activity in the Flanders region, the main centres of attention being parts of Germany and of course England itself, where the 'Glorious Revolution' was effected towards the end of the year – a triumph of incalculable importance for William's cause, as at one stroke it provided him with hitherto undreamt of resources of manpower and specie (always providing of course that Parliament would support his plans and vote supply), and at the same time this coup represented a notable setback for French prestige by removing one of Louis XIV's most valued satellites to the opposite camp. It would seem that the new regime immediately made available for service in Flanders a force of 10,000 men, being the number promised in Charles II's treaty of 1678, the terms of which were now reinvoked.

By April 1689 there appear to have been 10,972 'private men' in the English pay on the continent, namely 706 cavalry and 10,266 foot.[12] This number (and the date) is confirmed by a document in the British Museum,[13] which is identical in most respects to that in 'King William's Chest', but in addition mentions the intention of raising '9 new regiments for Ireland'. A third document, clearly dated '20 September 1689'[14] reveals an overall drop of 1,002 men in the English 'Holland' contingent – which is explained by the withdrawal of 'Prince George's Regiment' (possibly incorporated in the Danish forces, 7,000 strong, 'expected' in Ireland) and a drop of 240 men in the Second Regiment of Guards; on the other hand, the 2nd Troop of (Life) Guards and the Scots Guards had received slight reinforcements. Nevertheless, the overall strength of the English army had risen dramatically over the period of six months from 30,866 in April to 76,846 on 20 September[15] – presumably the seventeen 'new' regiments had been mustered besides the hiring of considerable forces of Danes and three 'French' regiments (probably Huguenots), and the transfer of a considerable number of Dutch troops (including the Blue Guards, William's personal escort) into English pay. Thus the proportionate commitment of English troops to the Netherlands drops from about 32% of the army to a mere 14% and, as we shall see in the following year, this is not the end of the decrease.

It is of some value to compare these figures with those given in *A True Relation* by 'an English Officer' (whom we may presume to have been serving with the 2nd Troop of Guards from various clues he lets fall in the course of his narrative). This source provides a full list of the Allied forces present at Tillroy Camp immediately prior to the Battle of Walcourt (15

August 1689, N.S.), and includes 660 English cavalry and 7,160 foot, listing nine English battalions.[16] We possess a full list of the English units over the Channel in the previous documents cited, and the battalions either absent or only partly present at Walcourt – namely Collier's, the Royal Regiment, and a proportion of the 'Talmash' Guards (the 1st) and of the Scots, would total some 2,100 men – thus bringing the total of foot into line with the State Paper Figure of 9,260 foot in all.

A *True Relation* also reveals that Hodges', Churchill's, Hale's and Offarrel's were reduced by sickness to a mere '900 men' by 2 September, and were accordingly sent to garrison duty at Breda.[17] It would seem that this is a considerable exaggeration, for another document in the State Papers[18] gives the detailed 'absentee' returns for the period May to December, and this reveals that the 'official' figures for these three regiments only amount to a joint 330 absent from duty up to October! However, it was clearly in the Colonels' interests to minimise their losses so as to continue to draw full pay for their regiments, and a revealing *cri de coeur* from the Secretary at War's office shows that these unscrupulous officers were trying to burn the candle at both ends. Not only were they minimising their actual losses, but they were also trying to claim levy money 'for 929 men to complete the said Regiments, so that by this demand 599 men are dead, or runne away, since October last'.[19]

It would also appear from *A True Relation* that the total Allied forces in the Netherlands that year amounted to some 60,000 men in the field and perhaps we can place a further 20,000 in garrisons (although our informant does not mention any figure). In which case, the English were providing approximately one eighth part of the troops in the area.

Before leaving 1689, we must briefly consider the main events of the year which may explain the slight drop in the number of English troops in Flanders. William III was preoccupied with the consolidation of his position in England, and was busily preparing the conquest of Ireland, where the Jacobites were still in control. His main task was to expand the slight English forces to ensure the success of this scheme and at the same time guarantee the security of England, and several papers reveal the different expedients suggested for raising more men. Four regiments were to be sent out of Scotland (which at this period had a separate military establishment paid for out of Scottish funds), and companies were to be withdrawn from several battalions to form nuclei for the seventeen new regiments.[20] Other proposals were put forward advocating the reduction of the companies of Foot Guards to sixty men apiece, it being calculated that this would save the Crown some £12,773 p.a.,[21] and William's financial difficulties must never be overlooked.

Secondly, the English forces in Flanders had suffered some relatively slight losses at Walcourt perhaps '50 or 60 on our side, including a major',[22] and the usual wear and tear of sickness and desertion doubtless accounts for more absentees by the year's end. The English forces had earned a mixed reputation during this campaign. On the one hand Prince Waldeck 'would never have believed that so many of the English would show such a *joie de combattre* [at Walcourt]. M. the Count Marlboroy is certainly one of the most gallant men I know',[23] but the commander-in-chief had earlier reported 'I wish that these troops [the English] who are believed to be very brave, were as disciplined as they seem to be brave, M. de Marborough has much trouble with them.'[24]

The year 1690 was to prove the most critical twelve months of the whole war. A document entitled 'the Intended Disposition . . .' and dated 'for 1690' on the rear reveals that William intended to reduce the Flanders contingent to 5,360 private men – or a drop of 4,610 since the previous September. The total strength of the English army (all areas) is put at 75,764, so that barely 7% of the forces were to be left in Flanders.[25] In the event even fewer troops were left there. 'The Present Disposition' dated October 1690 (placing the overall strength of the army at 75,134, including two large Marine Regiments 5,000 strong) shows that only four and a half Regiments, or a mere 4,800 private men, were still in Flanders.[26] The details of these units are confirmed in 'A list of their Majesties Forces now in Flanders and of those ordered thither'[27] – an undated source which, however, certainly belongs to late 1690 (and not to '1693' as marked in pencil), as it lists in a Memorandum the name of the regiments 'now in Flanders' which tally in every respect with the names included in the other documents mentioned above.

As to estimates of total Allied strengths in Flanders for that campaign, we can only turn to de Beaurain, who places them at 37,000 in all, as opposed to a French strength of seventy battalions and 203 squadrons (or some 65,000 men).[28] If these figures are accurate (unfortunately d'Auvergne's lists only begin in 1691), the English contingent in Flanders would seem to have been only one eighth of the reduced Allied forces – but implicit faith cannot be placed in de Beaurain's estimates and he may have excluded all garrisons.

However dubious and incomplete some of these estimates may unfortunately be, there is no doubt that the English contingent dropped dramatically during the year. Why was this the case? Certainly the requirements of the conquest of Ireland were the main reason. A glance at Source 'E' reveals that five of the withdrawn infantry regiments were to be redeployed in England, doubtless to secure the country from any invasion threats, and the Royal Regiment of Horse is to be found in the Irish lists given in both this document and in Source 'G' (which relates to January 1691).[29] As for the war situation as a whole, 1690 saw the addition of Savoy to the Alliance, a considerable victory as it removed a fourth country out of the French sphere of influence (Cologne, Liège and England being the earlier three), and at the same time offered the Allies a good area for launching a 'second front' against France – 'the ancestor of the concept of the soft underbelly of Europe' in S B Baxter's considered opinion.[30] However, the task of keeping Savoy 'in the fold' was to involve a considerable sum in English gold each year, and there can be no doubt that William was finding himself very short of funds, as the documents considering ways and means of reducing army costs would seem to demonstrate. It has also been claimed that France had virtually lost the war by the end of 1690, as the economic effects of the trade denial policy were beginning to have an adverse effect on Louis' hard money economy. William's task from now on was to hang grimly on to his gains until France was exhausted and try to avert the possibility of the 'third party' – most particularly Denmark, Sweden, Hanover and Münster – intervening with offers of mediation.

Two setbacks during 1690 highlighted this danger. First, the death of the Duke of Lorraine deprived William of a good general and an invaluable smoother-over of doubts and dissensions within Germany itself. Secondly, the loss of the Battle of Fleurus (1 July 1690) by the ageing Waldeck spoiled the prestige earned at the Boyne ten days later, and this setback on the continent led directly to a Swedish offer of mediation in October – the eventuality William wished to avoid. Other disappointments suffered during the year, which also affected this matter, were Austria's failure at Belgrade (8 October), Piedmont's at Staffarda (18 August), and the defeat of the Anglo–Dutch fleet off Beachy Head (10 July) which caused a considerable – though abortive – invasion scare. A further blow to the cohesion of the alliance – indeed, the first real crack – came when the Spanish Governor of the Netherlands (the Marquis Gastañaga) refused to employ Hanoverian troops on contract. Parliament also proved difficult, and it took much persuasion and pressure on the King's part to gain a vote of £4 million for the next year's campaign prior to his departure for the United Provinces in January 1691. All in all, therefore, 1690 proved a mixed year.

The military deployment in Flanders in the early part of 1691 is shown in Source 'G'.[31] It will be noted that following the successes attending his arms in Ireland, William was already in a position to redeploy considerably larger forces on the continent than during the previous year. The English contingent rises to 11,144 private men (comprising one squadron of Dutch Guard Cavalry and sixteen battalions or eleven regiments of Foot). Clearly, therefore, the greater part of the reinforcement programme listed in Source 'F' above had been put into effect, and more troops besides, some from Ireland, more from Scotland, and the balance from the English establishment.

D'Auvergne largely corroborates this impression. He states[32] that the British contingent at the Camp of Gemblours amounted to fourteen battalions in all, and the list of formations he gives tallies exactly with those listed in Source 'G'. It would appear from our militant chaplain's account that the Allies placed 56,270 troops in the field that year, to match the fifty-four battalions and 168 squadrons of the French forces listed by de Beaurain.[33] Walton agrees with these estimates.[34] Thus the English contribution would seem to have risen to almost 20% of the Allied troops in Flanders.

We know that King William had asked Parliament during the previous 'difficult' session to vote supply for a total of 69,636 private men; he was not prepared to allow Lord Ranelagh, who presented the estimates on 9 October 1690,[35] to reveal the proposed disposition of this army (which represented a decrease of over 6,000 men on his previous request – see Source 'E'), 'but he will keepe noe more of them in his own Dominions than what he shall judge absolutely necessary for their security'; the rest would be employed in 'reducing of Ireland and the carrying on of the Warr against France with Vigour'. This same document suggests one reason for this decrease, revealing that there was already a deficit of £800,000 owing for the previous years. So we find the King trying once again to economise, now that the worst crisis in Ireland is over and the prospect of imminent invasion of England has receded. Such financial considerations were clearly given great priority, for we find, for example, Count Solms suggesting the merging of three regiments into one formation of three battalions of eight companies apiece throughout the English army, claiming that this reorganisation would effect a saving of £19–2–4 per diem or £344–2–0 if the system were applied to all '54 battalions in the service at present'[36] – and making 4,266 men available for service in new units. His advice fell on stony ground, however (no doubt vested interests were too deeply involved in the lucrative English regimental system), and his idea was never implemented.

As for the fortunes of the Alliance as a whole, 1691 was again a year of mixed fortunes. Although the Allies had jointly agreed to field 220,000 men (all fronts), the French reached the field first and captured Mons (8 April) after three weeks of siege. This was no small setback so early in the campaign (Sweden at once offered her mediation once again!), and the cohesion of the Alliance was in danger. First to profit from this was Max Emmanuel of Bavaria, who blackmailed William into supporting his candidature for the vacant Governorship of the Spanish Netherlands, tacitly threatening to withdraw his country's support from the Alliance if his ambition was not satisfied. William could only give way (December). Another disappointment was the refusal of Leopold to make peace with Turkey when occasion offered after the victory of Szlankamen (19 August), and indeed that distracting struggle was to continue to drain the Empire's resources until 1699. On the credit side, however, the year saw Ginkel's brilliant victory at Aughrim (12 July), which effectively ended the Irish war, while by adroit manoeuvring William managed to preserve

Halle and the very important arsenal and barrier fortress of Liège from falling into enemy hands. Leopold also made one positive contribution to the fortunes of the year by bribing the wavering Ernst Augustus of Brunswick into remaining within the Alliance and providing a contingent of 6,000 men a year by creating him an Elector of the Empire.

When William returned to England in the autumn to place his proposals for the coming year before Parliament, he once again found himself in difficulties. His request of 22 October for an army of 65,000 men met with a cool reception,[37] and it was only after much debate that the requisite vote was carried.

Two 'Dispositions of Their Majesty's Land Forces' for 1692 have survived the years. The first, dated simply '1692', reveals that the English contingent in Flanders had risen dramatically to include four troops of Horseguards, nineteen regiments of horse, four of dragoons and no fewer than forty-four battalions – or a total of 40,254 private men.[38] The second document, dated '1 December 1692', indicates that this strength was not maintained after Steenkirk, for the total is down to 34,127 (or eighty-seven troops, the guards and sixteen regiments of horse, sixteen of dragoons, two regiments and thirty-seven battalions). Nevertheless, even this figure represents an English contribution of almost 47% of the troops in Flanders if we are to believe d'Auvergne's figure of 'fourscore thousand' for the total Allied strength that year.[39] It would seem that the British Army (all establishments) stood at a strength of some 66,997 men by the end of the year.

The reasons for the alterations in the English forces in Flanders are not far to seek. The initial rise doubtless reflects the ending of the Irish war, which made large forces available for redeployment over the Channel. The subsequent decrease was partly due to the losses sustained at Steenkirk (3 August), which caused several regiments to be disbanded and others sent home or into garrison, fears of which were not allayed until after the naval battle of La Hogue (1 June). Most of the units that disappear from the Flanders section of Source 'I' re-emerge in England in Source 'J', where the home garrison rises from 12,020 to 16,044. The units disbanded or sent home include the Saxe-Gotha contingent, and we find in a memorandum to the list of troops William 'thinks necessary' for 1693 (as delivered to the House of Commons on 25 November 1692) a claim for a cash sum 'in lieu of the three Regiments of Saxe-Gotha which were under his Majesty's Pay this last Campagne; and which are now sent home, being in a very ill condition'.[40]

By the time the troops had been returned into Winter Quarters, the fortunes of the Alliance had taken several hard knocks. The French had fielded no fewer than 111,440 troops (106 battalions and 299 squadrons),[41] and with this great armament had succeeded in capturing the fortress of Namur (1 July), a prestige victory of great significance. Beaurain goes further and puts their strength at 125 battalions, 385 squadrons and 263 cannon and mortars.[42] Against such a formidable array, William was virtually at a loss, but with great courage he forced action on an unwilling opponent at Steenkirk, and although the outcome of this bitter struggle is normally represented as a defeat (for William withdrew from the field), it really amounts to a strategic victory, for he gave the French such a mauling (their officers losing no fewer than 619 casualties) that they gave up all further thought of attacking the critical fortress of Liège that year and entered winter quarters much earlier than usual.

This fabian half-victory and La Hogue apart, however, 1692 was a 'bad' year for William III. An assassination plot only narrowly failed, and the Earl of Marlborough's overweening pride and selfish ambitions for high command made his dismissal inevitable. This event caused a sensation in the army – and in English political circles. Nevertheless, all fear of a French invasion of England was now removed, and the economic war was going very much in the Alliance's favour. The French navy was soon to be laid up in the French ports through lack of funds, whilst Louis XIV had to suspend his proposed improvements at Versailles. When William increased his building programme at his favourite Dutch palace of Het Loo that same year, the lesson was clear for all of Europe to see – and the Alliance survived the crises on the field. It would also seem that the Anglo–Dutch forces in the Netherlands were in good heart and reasonable condition when they entered winter quarters. 'A survey of the Regiments in Flanders and Germany' lists eighty-three regiments, and reports that 47,182 men were present therein, only 1,659 (or 3½%) being sick and 2,034 (5%) absent.[43] These figures do not reveal a defeated or demoralised army.

As might be expected, however, Parliament was in an ambiguous mood when William presented his next requirements before it in late November. Three months earlier, Nottingham had written to warn William that he doubted whether Parliament would willingly vote the amount of supply necessary for the next year. Even if they eventually did so, the Secretary of State continued: 'It is not likely that Parliament would be of opinion that so great a share of the expenses should, or could, be spent in Flanders.' He assured the King that this rather pessimistic report he was making was only proffered 'to the end that His Majesty may judge whether some other measure may be taken both abroad and at home for the carrying on of the war at such a charge as probably may be had, rather than to think of doing it still at such Expense as perhaps cannot be furnished'.[44] William declared himself 'not a little surpriz'd' at this presumption, which was, for him, the equivalent of a furious outburst.

Nevertheless, the King chose to handle the Commons with great cunning. His estimate of requirements for the next year involved an overall increase of 2,598 men, but this 'pill' was cleverly disguised by an apparent *decrease* in the cost involved, by dint of reducing most of the

Dutch and Danish forces presently in the English service to the scale of pay provided by the United Provinces, i.e. the cost of paying 54,562 troops in 1693 would require over £41,000 less than had been needed to finance an army of 51,964 in 1692![45] This brought the House round, and, in Baxter's words, 'although the funds granted in 1692 were far too small, England remained a partner in the war on land.'[46] But it would seem that William was being more than usually devious with Parliament, deliberately understating his requirements for 1693, for another document entitled 'An Estimate of the Charge of 74,562 men for the Land Forces for the Year 1693', whilst it mentions the 119 troops of Horse, thirty-six of Dragoons and 656 Companies of Foot listed in Source 'K', goes on to quote an 'addition of foot' to the number of 10,610 foot and a further 9,390 troopers for the mounted arms of the service.[47] The charge arising from this increase, together with the cost of providing shipping for a proposed 'Descent into France' by some 48,000–70,000 men[48] – probably the prototype for the abortive expedition against Brest in 1694, reflecting an attempt to adopt a more maritime approach to the strategy of the war – is placed at £1 million *above* 'what is allowed' (presumably by Parliament). It would seem, however, that Parliament eventually approved the proposed increase in the forces, for Source 'M' mentions the twenty-five new Regiments as 'voted by the House', and puts the strength of the army, *probably* including officers and NCOs, at '83,121'.[49]

Throughout the Campaign of 1693, the Allies were labouring at a numerical disadvantage; for most of the year Louis' generals enjoyed a superiority of about 8:5. D'Auvergne paints an even blacker picture, claiming that the Allies proved capable of fielding only 60,850 men (sixty-four battalions and 151 squadrons) to the French 119,700 (130 battalions and 278 squadrons).[50] De Beaurain is in broad agreement, placing the French strength at 134 battalions, 292 squadrons and four regiments of dragoons at the outset, reducing it to ninety-six battalions and 201 squadrons following the detachment of the Dauphin's army for operations in Germany later in the year; Allied strength, the same source claims, started at sixty-one battalions and 142 squadrons, but rose eventually, when outlying contingents materialised, to eighty-three battalions and 142 squadrons of horse.[51] Walton declares that the English contingent at the camp of Parck totalled twenty-two squadrons and twenty-three battalions, or 87,100 men.

William, therefore, throughout the campaign, was on the defensive. His main aim was to save Liège, and by placing his army with great skill at Parck (whence it could cover both Liège and the Duchy of Brabant), he denied Louis XIV the chance of achieving anything really constructive. In the end 'le Roi Soleil' left the camp in disgust and returned to Versailles. Nevertheless, William's situation was soon critical enough; news of the loss of part of the Smyrna convoy caused a financial crisis in the City; the government found itself unable to raise loans, and by 24 July we find Godolphin, the Lord Treasurer, ruefully admitting that the Treasury was dry. William, therefore, had no recourse but to subsist his army by raising contributions locally, and this measure proved barely adequate. Meantime, Marshal Luxembourg was marching towards Huy, the outwork of Liège, and after its fall, William was forced to interpose his army between the French and the city. The result was the Battle of Landen (or Neerwinden) on 29 July, another defeat for William. The enemy's superior forces (80,000 French against 50,000 Allies) prevailed after a long struggle, but received such a pounding in the process that Luxembourg was in no position to follow up his success. William's army, however, quickly recovered from the setback, and were soon stronger than before. Mr Secretary Blathwayt, on the other hand, disgraced himself by fleeing for fifty miles without resting after the battle! The key civil servant had little taste for the realities of war, it would seem.

By thus imposing what proved to be a six-week delay on the French advance, 'William had again saved Europe'. The campaign was so far advanced that the French had to content themselves with the irrelevant prize of Charleroi (taken on 11 October) before entering winter quarters.

Once again William had successfully maintained his avowed strategy of holding on against the might of Louis XIV in the hope of eventually inducing the giant to accept a reasonable peace treaty. His return to London in October sparked off a governmental crisis which ended in the dismissal of the unpopular Nottingham, and this sop induced Parliament to vote £5 million for the continuation of the war. William asked Parliament, through the medium of his servant, William Blathwayt, for a total of 93,635 officers and men (or £2,220,421: 11:10 in terms of their pay),[52] sensing that the next campaign might hold the prospect of a great success if sufficient troops were procured. Parliament, as we have seen, agreed to this increase of eight regiments of horse, four of dragoons and twenty-five of foot – or 26,108 men in all. In the events, 1694 saw little decisive activity, either for better or for worse. Although the campaign opened later than usual, owing to protracted though ultimately unsuccessful peace negotiations with a tiring but still defiant France, the Allied forces were stronger than ever before and this led to a situation of stalemate. The British contingent in Flanders numbered 56,969 private men.[53] At first Source 'O' proved exceptionally hard to date, but in the end a clue was found in the inclusion of Lord Rada's name amongst the list of Foot Regiments; this nobleman only received command of his unit on 1 February 1694[54] and had relinquished it again by 1695, so the inference was clear. It was confirmed by turning the paper in question over and the discovery of the date '13 November 1694' clearly written on the rear. This document also places the total strength of the English forces at 88,210 private men (officers are not included here) – or 93,635 if we include officers[55] – and this would suggest that almost ⅝ths of the army was now serving in Flanders. Walton places the figure of English troops as low as 30,000,[56] but he is presumably leaving out the record thirty-two foreign regiments in English pay. Our informant d'Auvergne estimates the total Allied strength in the region at 91,320, or ninety-five battalions and 230 squadrons, besides the 7,000-strong garrison of Ghent, and places the French strength at 91,320 men (divided between three armies of 107 battalions and 226 squadrons) – 'which is a very great army though inferior to what they had the last year';[57] de Beaurain agrees about the French figures (citing 106 battalions and 219 squadrons), but estimates the Allied strength considerably higher.[58]

Apart from the capture of Dixmude and the regaining of Huy, the year saw little of startling note in the military field in Flanders, but elsewhere General Tollemache's attempted attack with a combined force on Brest proved a fiasco. For the rest, neither side dared risk a major battle – the odds were too nicely even – but by the end of the year it would be fair to claim that the initiative had passed from the French to the Allies.

William had scented victory, and he obtained money for 87,702 officers and men for 1695.[59] The strain of war finance was still very considerable, no less than £212,571–8–0 being paid out to Allies such as Savoy, Brandenburg, Hesse-Cassell and Saxony in the form of subsidies to keep them in the war, and Source 'P' shows that for 1695 alone there was an estimated deficit of £401,401–15–9, whilst a vast burden of debt had already been inherited from previous years.[60] William was determined to continue the war, however, although the sudden death of Queen Mary on 27 December 1694 almost robbed him of the will to live.

Following his bereavement, William's one wish was to finish the war, and although the French at one time seemed prepared to heed Mr Mollo's mission, the emissary in the end had to return to England with nothing accomplished. If negotiation alone could not secure peace, perhaps a great success in the field would be more productive. For 1695 William set his sights on Namur, and the death of Luxembourg had already removed one of the greatest obstacles between the King and his goal. The omens were propitious. For the first time since 1678, the Allies enjoyed a considerable superiority of manpower over France in Flanders. Our chaplain puts the Allied strength at 124,700 as compared to the French 98,850 in the field (besides another 20,000 in garrisons, most particularly in Namur itself).[61] It would appear that the English share in this force was a little under half, namely 56,309 private men (Dalton places the native English contingent at 29,100)[62] out of a total army strength, in December 1695, of 86,890).[63]

The climax of the campaign was, of course, the great siege of Namur. Marshal Boufflers fought a staunch defence, and it was not until 1 September that the garrison capitulated. The preceding months had seen the French bombardment of defenceless Brussels and their capture of

Dixmude in attempts to create diversions. The successful conclusion of the siege raised William's prestige to unknown heights. The church bells rang in England, and there would be little doubt that Parliament would vote the King what he desired for the rest of the war.

So it turned out to be. He requested, and obtained, supply to pay for 87,440 officers and men[64] – a slight decrease in the numbers requested the previous year – although the army's debt now stood at over £613,500. But Allied superiority in Flanders was now unquestioned. Their armies in 1696 totalled 130,250 troops in all, 68,550 'effective men' in Brabant besides 15,650 under the Prince of Hesse and 46,050 under Prince Vaudemont to the French 127,540 (and the foe was clearly demoralised and on the defensive).[65] The contingent paid for by England amounted to 56,449 rank and file (or more than half the Allied army) out of a total English army of 90,172 'private men'.[66] Never before had England produced a larger or more impressive army. William was proud of its quality as well as its size. Apart from a thwarted French invasion scheme (which diverted sixteen battalions from Flanders to England) and yet another attempted assassination, the year proved successful enough on a small scale, but the defection of Savoy (which signed a separate peace with France in July) was an unexpected complication. By this time the whole of Europe was clearly utterly war-weary, and the signature of a general peace was desired by all.

The details of the negotiations that dragged on well into 1697 do not concern us here. Military events were not particularly dramatic. D'Auvergne claims that the French produced some 150,000 troops to dispute the last campaign which centred on Ath and Brussels, whilst the Allies only proved able to field 104,756.[67] At last, in September 1697, the long war came to an unmourned conclusion. It only remained to disband the army. A paper from 'King William's Chest' (undated but clearly referring to the post-Ryswick 'run-down' of forces) shows that at one time there had been some seventy-seven battalions and some eighty-one squadrons of horse and dragoons in the King's pay, but by the time the undated document referred to, there remained but forty-three battalions and forty-six squadrons undisbanded.[68] Then Parliament took over. By 1698 the once imposing English forces had been reduced to a mere 10,000 in England and a further 12,000 in Ireland.[69] The wheel had turned full circle.

In conclusion, it is interesting to compare the scale of English military involvement in Flanders during the Nine Years War with that during the War of the Spanish Succession. Fortunately, an invaluable document exists in the Stowe papers in the British Museum[70] which gives a full comparative breakdown of the various forces in the English and United Provinces' pay between 1701 and 1711. From this it would seem that Queen Anne's involvement rose from 40,000 in 1701–2 by steady stages to a grand total of 70,188 by 1711. The Dutch, on the other hand, fielded a force of 44,992 at the outbreak of the war, but had raised it to 111,334 by the end of 1702, and ultimately attained the number of 137,600 by 1711. Thus the English contingent accounted for a bare third of the Allied troops in the Flanders region. However, it must be remembered that the English had a considerable army in Spain for much of the period, whilst the Dutch were practically free of commitments outside the immediate Netherlands area. Nevertheless, it still remains true that William never got more than 58,000 English troops (including those in 'pay') into the Netherlands – although this number represented up to 54% of the Allied army serving in the theatre – and that consequently the British military administration of Queen Anne's day proved capable of producing a larger army for service overseas. But this is not to decry William III's achievement. There was only one threat of an invasion of the British Isles in Anne's reign (early 1708), and an alien monarch of strong continental persuasions, 'Dutch William', had performed miracles of organisation and persuasion to field the forces on the continent that he did; and there can be little doubt that he and his invaluable assistant, William Blathwayt, did as much to reform and improve English military administration as in the previous generation the Duke of York and Samuel Pepys had achieved in their reorganisation of the Royal Navy.

NOTES

1. W S Churchill, *Marlborough: His Life and Times*, Vol. I, London, 1947, p. 288.
2. This summary was partly prepared from S B Baxter's *William III*, London, 1966, Chapters 19–25, probably the best biography yet published in English.
3. State Papers 8/1 to 18 (parts).
4. SP/8/15 folio 73.
5. Add. Mss 15897 ff. 88–90, 94, 106, etc.
6. E d'Auvergne, *The History of the Campagne in Flanders . . . 1691*, London, 1695, et. seq.
7. Marquis de Beaurain, *Histoire Militaire de Flandre, 1691–94*, two vols, Paris, 1755.
8. *A True Relation . . . in 1689* by 'an English Officer', London, 1690 (MoD Library).
9. C Dalton, *English Army Lists and Commission Registers, 1661–1714*, six vols, London, 1898–1904; C Walton, *History of the British Standing Army, 1660–1700*, London, 1894.
10. Sources 'A' to 'T' listed below.
11. G N Clarke, 'The Nine Years War', Chapter VII in Vol. VI of *The New Cambridge Modern History*, 1970.
12. SP/8/5, folio 12 (PRO). Source A.
13. Add. Mss 15897, folios 88–90 (British Museum). Source B.
14. SP/8/5, folio 304 (PRO). Source C.
15. Another undated document, misplaced in 'King William's Chest', mentions a total of 72,666 troops.

16   *A True Relation*, pp. 25–32.
17   *Ibid.*, p. 30.
18   SP/8/6, folio 84 (PRO).
19   SP/8/6, folio 25 (PRO). Source D.
20   SP/8/6 (6 December 1689) and SP/63/353 (PRO).
21   SP/8/6, folio 83a (PRO).
22   *A True Relation*, p. 14.
23   SP/8/5, folio 95, Waldeck to William III (PRO).
24   SP/8/5, folio 44, Waldeck to William III (PRO).
25   SP/8/8, folio 71. See also folio 36, which lists 75,764 ORs, including 5,360 in 'Holland' and presumably, therefore, lists the position in mid-year. Source E.
26   SP/8/8, folio 5 (PRO).
27   SP/8/14, folio 117 (PRO). Source F.
28   de Beaurain, *op. cit.*, pp. 62–3.
29   SP/8/8, folio 80 (PRO). Source G.
30   Baxter, *op. cit.*, p. 289.
31   SP/8/8, folio 80 (PRO).
32   d'Auvergne, *op. cit.*, pp. 63–6.
33   de Beaurain, *op. cit.*, p. 184.
34   Walton, *op. cit.*, p. 184.
35   SP/8/8, folio 6 (PRO). Source H.
36   SP/8/13, folio 12 (PRO).
37   Baxter, *op. cit.*, p. 298.
38   SP/8/13, folio 12 (PRO). Source I.
39   SP/8/12, folio 147 (PRO). Source J.
40   SP/8/14, folio 122 (PRO). Source K.
41   SP/8/13, folio 98 (PRO).
42   de Beaurain, *op. cit.*, p. 151.
43   KWC, SP/8/13, folio 90 (PRO).
44   Add. Mss 37991, folio 152 (27 August 1692).
45   SP/8/14, folio 122 (PRO). Source K.
46   Baxter, *op. cit.*, p. 309.
47   SP/8/14, folio 101 (PRO). Source L.
48   *Ibid.*
49   SP/8/14, folio 2 (PRO). Source M.
50   d'Auvergne, *op. cit.*, pp. 8 & 18.
51   de Beaurain, *op. cit.*, pp. 243–4; 253.
52   SP/8/15, folio 73. This document is of particular interest as it includes details of numbers of officers and NCOs – 4,803 and 9,801, or about one to five other ranks. Source N.
53   SP/8/15, folio 67 (PRO). Source O.
54   C Dalton, *English Army Commission Lists and Registers* (London, 1904).
55   See C Dalton, p. 7.
56   Walton, *op. cit.*, p. 276.
57   d'Auvergne, *op. cit.*, p. 21.
58   de Beaurain, *op. cit.*, pp. 332 & 354.
59   SP/8/15, folio 110 (PRO). Source P.
60   SP/8/15, folio 111 (PRO). Source Q.
61   d'Auvergne, *op. cit.*, pp. 18 & 23.
62   Walton, *op. cit.*, pp. 287–8.
63   SP/8/16, folio 95 (PRO). Source R.
64   SP/8/16, folio 53 (PRO). Source Ri.

65 d'Auvergne, *op. cit.*, pp. 36; 45; 56; 64–5.
66 SP/8/17, folio 13 (PRO). Source S.
67 d'Auvergne, *op. cit.*, pp. 42 & 59.
68 SP/8/17, folio 16 (PRO). Source T.
69 Baxter, *op. cit.*, p. 362.
70 Add. Mss Stowe 246 folios 21–4 (BM).

CHAPTER IV

The King's Servant

Secretary-at-War 1688–97

Throughout the major campaigns fought by the English Army in Flanders during the Nine Years War, overall control was, for the most part, vested in William III himself; the monarch was *de facto* as well as *de jure* commander-in-chief, and it was noted by many important contemporaries that he retained very close personal control over all aspects of the campaigns. Nevertheless, so many were his constitutional duties and other commitments, including being C-in-C of the Dutch forces as well as the English, that he found himself compelled to rely on certain key ministers and royal servants to an ever-increasing extent, particularly after the death of Queen Mary in 1694. In this chapter we shall examine the functions of one of the most important of these officials, namely the Secretary-at-War, William Blathwayt, in an attempt to demonstrate the extent to which William found himself compelled to delegate the reality as well as the appearance of power.

After a brief summary of Blathwayt's career and of the history of the post of Secretary-at-War, we shall examine the function carried out by this particularly astute man, both in time of peace and of war and for both the campaign and Winter Quarters season. Thereafter it is proposed to consider Blathwayt's relations with his monarch and his ministers, before concluding with an evaluation of his character and of his contribution to the war effort in Flanders.

In some ways he fulfilled the senior civil servant role under William III, undertaking many of the same tasks for the navy that Samuel Pepys did for Charles II and above all for James II. Pepys was retired in 1688 at the Revolution, while Blathwayt continued to hold office until 1704 – hence his importance to the reign of Queen Anne and the stories of Marlborough and Blenheim.

William Blathwayt (1649?–1717) had a varied career as a public servant between 1668 and his retirement in 1710. His first known employment was at the Hague as a member of Sir William Temple's staff in 1668; four years later he was conducting official business of an unspecified kind in Rome, and thereafter held further diplomatic appointments at Stockholm and Copenhagen. The real turning-point in his career came in 1683, when he purchased the post of Secretary-at-War from Matthew Lock. According to Luttrell[1] he added the post of Clerk of the Council in Ordinary to his appointments in 1686, and in February 1689 he was made Clerk to the Privy Council. He was called as a key witness in the Trial of the Seven Bishops, and on the outbreak of The Glorious Revolution accompanied James II to Salisbury in November 1688. He was still at least outwardly loyal to James as late as 8 December[2] but it is not known exactly when he deserted the King. However, he was fortunate to be assimilated by the new regime with so little trouble. He was in fact out of office between 4 February and mid-May 1689, but his replacement, John Temple, killed himself, and after a brief period when the Duke of Schomberg and John Churchill issued orders from the war office, Blathwayt was reinstated. The exact date is not known as there is a gap in the Entry Book from 6 April to 11 May,[3] but he was certainly back in office by 13 May.

Until 1692 Blathwayt was able to exercise his functions as Secretary-at-War from the London office, avoiding service in either Ireland or Flanders, but in 1692 William III decided to summon his Secretary-at-War to be in attendance upon him in Flanders. The next nine years of Blathwayt's life saw extensive service overseas, much of it in Flanders during the main campaigning seasons of 1692–7, and thereafter at the Hague negotiating the abortive Partition Treaties; each winter, however, found him back in London resuming the normal duties of his office (which were deputed during his absences to George Clark). After William's death, his life became less peripatetic and Marlborough took Adam Cardonnel (Blathwayt's clerk) into the field.

Blathwayt did all in his power to oppose the drastic reduction of the English Army after the peace of Ryswick, but to no avail.[4] He had been Member of Parliament for Newton in the Isle of Wight from 1685–7, but although re-elected in 1688 he never sat in the Convention Parliament, but used his successor to Newton, the Paymaster-General, as his mouthpiece. On 20 November 1693, however, he was returned as MP for Bath, a seat that he held without a break until 1710. He was latterly noted for his opposition to Robert Harley.

Besides his duties as Secretary-at-War, Blathwayt held two other offices of great significance – namely those of Surveyor and Auditor-General of Plantation Revenue (1689–1717), and Member or Commissioner of the Board of Trade (1696–1707). Although it is with his work as Secretary-at-War that we are particularly concerned here, the breadth of his competence should be appreciated in any attempt to judge his ability and contribution.

His marriage to an heiress (Mary Wynter) took place in 1686, but she died in 1691 and he never remarried. The last years of his public life were somewhat overshadowed by his disappointment at not being created Earl of Bristol (as was mooted in 1700), and by the investigations of the Commission for Public Accounts (1701–2) – particularly over food contracts – although he ultimately emerged with an unsullied reputation from their detailed investigations into alleged corruption and mal-practices associated with his office, a piece of good fortune neither Robert Walpole nor Marlborough was destined to share in the fullness of time. He was also disappointed at never being appointed a full member of the Privy Council. In the end he resigned the post of Secretary-at-War in 1704 (being succeeded by his *bête-noire*, Robert Harley) and finally retired from public life in 1707. Most of his remaining years were spent at his beloved house at Dyrham Park.[5]

Before analysing his functions as Secretary-at-War, a brief description of this office's antecedents is necessary. The status of the post was to grow markedly during Blathwayt's tenure, but in its origins it was a humble affair. It would seem that it sprang from the post of 'Scrivener of the Army' – or salaried secretary to the Commander-in-Chief – and it was not until the Civil War that the position began to emerge from obscurity. In 1657 the office received its first patent, and thenceforward the remuner-ation was placed on a public fiscal basis, being paid directly by the Exchequer instead of through the commander-in-chief as hitherto. From the first the post seems to have been an exclusively civilian appointment, but its relative lack of importance is reflected in the fluctuations of the salary. Originally this stood at 10/- per diem, but in 1670 this was raised to £1, and thence (1673) to £2, but by the end of the decade it had reverted to 20/-, and so it stood on Blathwayt's appointment. The status of the office had followed these fluctuations. In 1670, for example, the post had almost been re-absorbed into the establishment of the commander-in-chief, but from the early 1680s it had become very closely associated with the Secretary-of-State for the Southern Department. As a result, Blathwayt always owned two masters, namely the Commander-in-Chief *and* the Secretary-of-State, and despite the great advances made by his office during his tenure, it never achieved an independent status, although it nearly became a Secretaryship on one or two occasions.[6]

The reasons behind the increasing growth in the office's importance were not wholly associated with the occupant's talents as an adminis-trator. The circumstances of the time were equally important. First there was the fact that military affairs had come to occupy a preponderantly important place under William III – much more so than under either of his royal predecessors. Secondly, the concomitant expansion of the army to fulfil the increased military obligations[7] involved an equal increase in the importance and status of Blathwayt's office. This, thirdly, was particularly reflected in financial responsibilities associated with the post (these will be described below). Fourthly, the active distrust felt by Parliament for large-scale armed forces increased the scope of their interest in military affairs, and this in turn enhanced the position of the Secretary-at-War, who was one of the key links between King and Parliament, as will also be discussed below; this somewhat baleful Parliamentary interest was concentrated on the financial and disciplinary angles rather than on the operational side, and this again inevitably brought Blathwayt's office (and that of the Paymaster-General) into the limelight.

If in some ways Blathwayt's tenure marked an apogee in the history of his office, in others it marked the beginning of a transformation and even foreshadowed a decline in its real importance (immediately after his day). Blathwayt was the last of what we may term the 'civil service' occupants of the post. After 1704 it became a political appointment to an increasingly marked degree. Moreover, as the office never became independent of the Secretary-of-State's department, its tenure became increasingly regarded as a stepping-stone towards higher preferment by ambitious occupants. Thus, although James II once referred to the position as carrying cabinet rank,[8] it was never to attain that status in fact. Blathwayt was an ambitious man (despite Miss Jacobsen's assertions to the contrary), but he was no intriguer, and this straightforward aspect of his character caused him to miss several opportunities of really establishing his position. Those who followed him – Henry St John, Walpole, George Grenville, Sir William Wyndham and William Pulteney – were men of a different stamp. None attained cabinet rank, however, although Grenville did become a Privy Councillor in 1710 during his period of tenure.

All the same, this is not to belittle the work of William Blathwayt, even if to some extent it was a case of his having importance thrust upon him. Much of the day-to-day administration of the army's affairs fell to his lot, as will be seen and the fact that the inadequate machinery of the period could be induced to produce even a modicum of efficiency is no small tribute to his abilities as an organiser, delegator and controller. His overall value is reflected by the salary he eventually came to draw as Secretary-at-War. By 1689 this had risen from 20/- to £3 a day[9] and for several years he received the full emoluments of a Secretary-of-State (from February 1694) for the periods he spent in Flanders each year. This was something of a sop to console him for the repeated disappointments he suffered in respect of his hopes to be appointed Secretary-of-State on several occasions when a vacancy occurred, but it is also some evidence of the value of the man in the eyes of both the King and the Treasury.[10] His perquisites of office were considerable. He was entitled to two-thirds of the one shilling deducted from every pound of pay issued to the army, and this must have grossed him at least £1,000 a year. Additionally, of course, he received remuneration for his posts in the Plantations Office and the Board of Trade.

The peace-time tasks of the Secretary-at-War do not require detailed analysis here, but it is desirable to list the major responsibilities that fell to the lot of the Secretary-at-War in normal times in order to compare them with the vastly increased load of duty in times of hostilities. A study of the earlier – and later – parts of the manuscript sources listed reveal a fairly clear pattern of routine work. One of his major responsibilities was liaison with other Departments of State with overlapping interests in the military field. These included the Treasury, the Secretaries-of-State (to the senior of whom Blathwayt was directly responsible), the Commissaries of Musters, and, inevitably, the Board of Ordnance. Most of his functions in this respect were of a consultative rather than a decision-taking variety. Blathwayt had a say, for example, in drawing up proposed establishments for regiments of marines;[11] where the Victualling Board, Transport Commissioners, and the Commissioners of sick and wounded were concerned, his function was usually the transmission of royal orders, little more, and the receipt of reports on their implementation or otherwise.[12] There are signs that at times Blathwayt attempted to authorise Ordnance issues, but from the Board's reaction he seems to have had little success – his orders being abruptly rejected.[13] Probably his most important duty constitutionally and financially was his Secretary-at-War's attendance on Parliament for the presentation of the annual 'State of the Land Forces' and estimates for the following year. As this remained a war-time responsibility of enhanced importance, we shall return to it later. Thirdly, the War Office was charged with the preparation of military commissions, although their signature was the duty of the Secretary-of-State (except under certain special war-time conditions which will be mentioned later).[14] Fourthly, Blathwayt was required to sign the pay warrants prepared by the Paymaster-General, Lord Ranelagh, before cash could be issued to the regimental agents. The administrative procedures seem to have been somewhat imprecise, and determined by custom rather than precept, for in 1702 we find even the conscientious and rule-abiding Blathwayt citing *lex non scripta* as justification for some of his activities.[15] Another important duty was the preparation in triplicate of establishments for signature by the Treasury and a Secretary-of-State, together with the maintenance of the Muster books. In this respect Blathwayt was very careful to keep within the procedures first laid down in 1667 as emerges from his evidence to the Commission in 1702.[16]

Further tasks included the issue of 'Authority to beat up for recruits'[17] and conversely the supervision of disbandments (particularly in the 1698–9 period).[18] The Secretary also had to maintain a list of taverns suitable for the quartering of troops,[19] and often became involved in disciplinary squabbles over their misuse. Further disciplinary duties included the formal issue of the Articles of War to regimental commanders (and the receipt of due acknowledgements),[20] but his right to order General Courts-martial was convincingly challenged by George Clark, Judge-Advocate-General (although the particular case at issue was largely a misunderstanding on the latter's part)[21] – and it seems that the

Secretary's jurisdiction only extended to the level of Regimental Courts-martial.[22] A final selection of duties of the office included the removal of troops from the vicinity of the hustings on election days (really part of the Secretary-of-State's police duties but often delegated),[23] and the resolution of disputes over regimental precedence (although this power never extended to include the militia except in time of war, and on no occasion whatever covered the Royal Guards and Garrisons).[24]

The general impression, therefore, of the peacetime responsibilities of the Secretary-at-War is one of concern with the detail of military administration in a wide number of fields without much say in the formulation of policy except insofar as the office-holder was the royal mouthpiece in the Commons in the debates on the Mutiny Act and military supply, and held important financial counter-signature responsibilities.

In time of war, however, William Blathwayt's authority was vastly extended and in certain instances became practically indistinguishable from that of a Secretary-of-State. Two main factors accounted for this unique situation. First was the constitutional requirement made by the Convention Parliament requiring the King to be accompanied abroad on campaign by a Secretary-of-State (whose counter-signature of many orders and documents was deemed indispensable). This duty was not popular with either party concerned. Lord Nottingham (Secretary-of-State for the Southern Department) had avoided this irksome duty in 1690 by placing it squarely on the shoulders of the Secretary-of-State for Ireland, but a similar move in 1691 ended in failure when the junior Secretary-of-State, Lord Sydney, proved incapable of fulfilling the duties to the King's liking in Flanders. Second, for the campaign of 1692, therefore, Nottingham suggested that his subordinate, the Secretary-at-War, should accompany the King with enlarged powers to enable him to perform a double function. This suggestion also pleased the King. He had no wish to be saddled with an over-powerful political figure like Nottingham who might challenge the position of such Dutch favourites as William Bentinck. He therefore welcomed the appointment of a comparative nonentity of no great political interest, above all as Blathwayt's mastery of several languages, including Dutch and French, made him a potentially useful accessory, as did his reputation as a hard, reliable and inconspicuous worker. Accordingly, William virtually rolled the offices of Secretary-of-State and Secretary-at-War into one for the period of the campaigning seasons only, by conferring the Signet upon William Blathwayt.[25]

William Blathwayt does not at first seem to have welcomed this sudden promotion, but he had no option but to comply or resign, and as his wife had died the previous year he was relatively free of family commitments. Moreover, it seems likely that Nottingham baited his hook with some sort of undertaking that Blathwayt might well succeed to the post of junior Secretary-of-State on a permanent basis (vacant in spring 1692) if he acceded with a good grace. Blathwayt was sufficiently ambitious to be very attracted by this possibility (pace Miss Jacobsen), although it was never destined to become reality. Accordingly, he arranged for George Temple to be appointed Deputy-Secretary-at-War during his absences abroad, in the optimistic belief that the war would be of short duration.[26]

From 1692–7, therefore, Blathwayt was living a complicated double existence. During the campaigning season and the weeks immediately prior to its opening and following its close, he was serving abroad in the capacity of a de facto Secretary-of-State; during the winter months, however, he invariably returned to England to resume his more lowly status as *de jure* Secretary-at-War.

The functions performed by Blathwayt whilst in Flanders can be distinguished under seven main headings – transportation; food contracts; clothing and horse contracts; the distribution of subsidies to Allies; further diplomatic duties as the King's representative, and finally his influence on matters of patronage and discipline through his proximity to the monarch. Before discussing each aspect in turn, however, it is important to realise that there are virtually no signs of Blathwayt having a determinant role so far as policy or strategy were concerned. Nor did he exercise any immediate charge over the forces present in the war zone, although we occasionally find him signing movement orders – and commissions – on the King's behalf. Similarly, his direct authority over troops in England itself lapsed almost completely during his absences abroad. From first to last, then, William Blathwayt was a royal servant, obeying directives and carrying out the day-to-day tasks of military administration, rather than a formulator of policy.

Blathwayt's relations with the Commissioners of Transport were frequently strained and contentious, the basic irritant being, as it was in all other aspects of his work, the inadequacy of financial arrangements. From the correspondence preserved in Add. Mss 9729, we find him ceaselessly trying to extemporise means of procuring adequate shipping for various expeditions and 'descents'. On the one hand he was calculating the tonnage required to lift '40 battalions of 800 men' (arriving at a figure of 47,100 tons on the calculational basis of one ton per man and four per horse), which would cost £28,260. 8. 0. at £12 per ton per month, whilst 'Sea Provisions' and 'Transport Provisions' would cost at least another £30,000 over the same period.[27] So poor was the government's reputation as regards payment of debts that it is clear that the requisite shipping was very hard to find. An agent, Jonathan Ellis, reported on 28 April 1693:

We are just as we were, without money, and without orders going on still because we are not bid to stop, but going slowly for want of money to grease the wheels. We have the whole quantity of 35,000 tons of shipping yet we were ordered to take up . . .[28]

This, however, was still some 9,000 tons short of the total required, and when a desperate Blathwayt suggested an embargo on shipping presently in English ports as a means of securing the balance, the idea was rejected by the Committee of the Lords of the Treasury. Over the weeks that followed Blathwayt was bombarded with a flow of complaints, all requiring money. 'We are well assured they [the ships' masters] whatever orders are sent them, will not sail unless they have their month's pay beforehand, and wee have not yet received a penny of ye account, nor do the Lords of the Treasury seem to be in humour to give any for ye service . . .' (12 May);[29] 'wee have not yet one farthing on money towards the expense of the Descent' (16 May);[30] 'wee have not yet a penny of money towards the charge of the thing called "the Descent" [the amphibious landing at Camaret Bay] . . . I believe it is time to think of dismissing our shippes.' (30 May)[31] In the end this was also the decision reached by the King, and by late August all the laboriously gathered shipping had been discharged after a season of complete inactivity in the Bristol Channel and the Solent. The final blow had been the destruction of a large part of 'the Turkey fleet' which had made loans unobtainable in the City.

Another aspect of troop transportation that came within Blathwayt's competence was the evacuation of wounded back to England. A typical letter, dated 15/25 July 1692, from Ostend runs:

This instant there came here about 60 disabled soldiers of several regiments under the conduct of Ensign Scott, who expects soon as many more, which we hope next post may bring your order to Captain Price to receive them on board Their Majesty's Ship *Assurance* to transport them to England, for they have very little (if any) money to subsist on . . .[32]

A further letter, dated the 18th, reveals that the necessary authority had arrived. Judging from the amount of correspondence devoted to the subject, much of Blathwayt's time in Flanders was occupied in wheedling further supplies out of disgruntled contractors, and in trying to procure a minimum of specie from the Treasury to reduce some of the long-standing debts incurred. Even more time was spent dealing with pleas from regimental colonels desirous of securing their subsistence money. As Sir Charles O'Hara complained on 24 March 1692; 'I desire to know what wee are to do, wee are paid but to the 5th March . . . the officers are so poor they are not able to lend the soldiers anything . . .'[33] A week later he was repeating the complaint. Colonel Foxton was somewhat luckier.

Blathwayt wrote back to his appeal for his due (contained in a letter from Breda dated 21 March 1692) six days later: 'You complain with reason of ye want of money for the supplying, whereof I have made enquiry . . .', and went on to say that £180 was being forwarded by hand of a Captain Brown.[34] It appears that he had no personal power of the purse, but was in a position to bring pressure to bear on the Paymaster-General's representatives at headquarters, presumably by signing authorisations for the issue of funds.

His relations with the most powerful contractors were often terse. On 26 March 1695, for instance, M. Favisseau informed Blathwayt that if he was to fill the Reserve Magazine with the stipulated 900,000 forage rations, he would require immediately the 45,000 florins promised him on 1 February, 'and it is already necessary for me to disburse immense sums for the maintenance of the Flanders magazines.'[35] A further letter from the same source reported that General Overkirk 'requires me to issue daily 3,000 rations of forage from the Reserve Magazine into the local waggons, which is very hard on me as I have not received my 45,000 florins.'[36] It is not recorded whether the sum was ever forthcoming.

Many letters from and to the three most important contractors – namely Pereira, Medina and Machado (all Flemish or Dutch Jews of Spanish or Portuguese extraction) – take up a great deal of space in the Blathwayt papers. Almost all reveal the weakness of English war finance at this period. 'We are engaged in a manner which will make it very difficult for us to furnish the bread for the present campaign', complains Pereira on 16 July 1696, unless funds promised by 'Milord Ranelagh appear soon.'[37] According to Blathwayt's accounting, some £74,830 – 0 – 6½ 'rests to pay by Mr. Hill' to settle an account rendered by 'Messr's. Machado and Pereyral' [sic] for 1696, but a further letter from these gentlemen, dated 27 July, reveals that they considered full debt outstanding at 1,074,835 guilders.

Similar matters were sent to plague him regarding the issue of contracts and authorisations for the supply of clothing, new weapons and horses. Even gunpowder required Blathwayt's authority before an issue could be made. 'I have burnt all the powder I brought from England, and am in great want of more to Exercise the men,' wrote Colonel O'Hara to Blathwayt on 29 April 1692. 'The Governor can't furnish me without an order which I desire you will be pleased to procure . . . Count Solms promised us a new stand of pikes but methinks him something long in performing.'[38] The Secretary also found himself deeply involved in organising the issue of chests of medicines and the means to transport them to each battalion:

His Majesty commands me to mind you of providing your regiment with a good surgeon and surgeon's mate . . . His Majesty has directed that a small tumbrell or ammunition waggon be provided for every battalion which will be done by the office of artillery, and ten pounds will be given to each (regiment) for providing a good draft [sic] horse.[39]

This communication called forth a dozen letters from colonels, some like Edward Lloyd complaining that the earlier part implied that their medical arrangements were deficient whilst in fact they were 'as good as any in the Army',[40] but most enquiring exactly how they were to receive their £10 for the horse!

The diplomatic duties carried out by Blathwayt fall into two main sections. The first was concerned with the negotiation and payment of various subsidies to the smaller Allies such as Savoy, Denmark and Hesse-Cassel – matters of no small importance if their troops were to be expected on time for the opening of the following campaigning season.[41] The second group of duties related to the day-to-day running of the diplomatic service – receiving or requiring reports, making appointments to the various courts and recalling envoys, or issuing passports for people desirous of visiting England. But it is quite clear that he was not entrusted with matters of great moment. As the King wrote to Shrewsbury concerning the defection of Savoy in 1796: 'It is sometime since I wrote to you having nothing agreeable to communicate, nor answer to give your letters, but what I could trust to Blathwayt.'[42]

Nevertheless, many men believed that Blathwayt had the King's ear, and many were the petitions and pleas addressed to him on every matter conceivable. Officers desirous of promotion besought him to intervene with the King on their behalf, or on behalf of some friend.[43] Others, believing themselves the victims of injustice at the hands of Courts-martial, implored his intercession. For example one Mons Moreau (possibly an *émigré* French officer) who had been 'denounced in publick' and was afraid that he would be 'exposed . . . to the fury of the people',[44] was advised by Blathwayt that 'the best time to obtain His Majesty's ear is when he is hunting'[45] and a passport was enclosed to enable the suppliant to reach Loo. On other occasions he found it necessary to inform parents of the ill-doing of their progeny. He wrote to Sir George Fletcher on 8/18 June 1696:

I am very sorry to acquaint you with the misfortune that has happened to your son upon the late review of the English troops in Flanders, where His Majesty did not only notice of the many stores that were wanting to his troops but more particularly of his being absent from his command without any word or notice given . . . Whereupon His Majesty could nor forebear the giving orders for the breaking of him which is actually done to serve for an example and prevent the like misdemeanours in others . . .[46]

This letter resulted in a lengthy correspondence, the father being at pains to demonstrate that his son had been delayed at Harwich by the recurrence of an old complaint, namely a *'fistula in ano'*[47] The ultimate outcome is again not recorded. More seriously, Blathwayt was several times informed of newly discovered plots against the King's person. He was told, for instance, in a letter dated 10 June 1692 from one Faucheur, that 'the King's life is in danger through the conspiracy which I have discovered . . . A Swiss courier in the confidence of the King of England [James II] is to be sent to the English army in the hope of finding a chance to deliver his blow during the battle' (presumably Steinkirk).[48] Another concomitant task was the denial of rumours of serious decline in the King's health as he grew older.

Such, then, were the typical tasks undertaken by William Blathwayt whilst in attendance upon the King in Flanders – although those described here are far from exhaustive. There is no evidence that he was directly consulted or concerned in the higher direction of the war – indeed the evidence points to the contrary. Many men expected him to become a Secretary-of-State *de jure*, but the post never materialised, although the emoluments were awarded as a consolation prize, payable whilst Blathwayt was serving in Flanders (from 1694):

> But Mr Blathwayt not yet being declared secretary-of-state puts all our business much out of order, and it will be worse if necessity of state should put him by.[49]

So wrote Mr Stepney, Resident at Celle, in November 1692. The following October he returned to this theme:

> Methinks Mr Blathwayt is not in the humour he ought to be, and I apprehend his resentment of not being made secretary-of-state (as he expected and ought to have been) may make him lay down his other employment or at least no more to follow the King in Flanders which is as bad for those who are abroad. For certainly no other man can be found out who can acquaint himself with such capacity, honesty and diligence as he has done, which I apprehend His Majesty may perceive when it is too late.[50]

It must indeed have been frustrating in the extreme for Blathwayt to see such nonentities appointed to successive vacancies as Sir John Trenchard and Lord Jersey. Perhaps by 1695, however, he had come to terms with his disappointment, for, as a contemporary wrote, following the death of Trenchard in April 1695, 'Mr Blathwayt might have it, but seems to decline it, because, without envy, he is warmer as he is.'[51] It was also widely known that William held the Secretaryships as a whole in low esteem, a fact he made abundantly clear by leaving offices vacant for months at a time without designating successors. In sum, therefore, it can be said of Blathwayt that he was an ideal 'civil servant', who came to know his place – 'a good-natured, indispensable drudge' is how Miss Jacobsen depicts him.[52] He relieved William III of many a routine and irksome task, but his duties did not on any occasion raise him to the level of a statesman although at times he was expected to entertain foreign envoys in William's absences.[53]

A brief explanatory word must be interpolated here concerning Blathwayt's duties during the winter seasons, when he returned to London to resume his normal duties as Secretary-at-War. Basically, the additional tasks were twofold – looking after the well-being of the troops in their quarters, so far as that lay in his power,[54] and frequent attendance in Parliament, where he was the foremost spokesman of the Crown for military affairs in the Commons, besides of course the resumption of the normal duties of his office already listed. The most important task of his Parliamentary responsibility was the preparation and presentation of the annual 'State of His Majesty's Forces on Land' for the general approval of Parliament, and of course to obtain the vital voting of supply for the next year's campaign.[55] These tasks he performed with verve and skill, and William owed no small debt to the ability shown by his Secretary-at-War in answering the critics of his strategy and in wheedling from an often contentious and unforthcoming House the minimum of necessary supply for the continuance of the war. He became a past-master at the tactics and combinations required to circumvent Parliamentary obstruction.

To conclude, William Blathwayt must be regarded as first and last a royal servant of uncommon loyalty, tact and efficiency. He was indubitably hard-worked, but there was never a breath of scandal against him – no small achievement at that period of history. His skill and common sense relieved his master of much drudgery. On the other hand he was never a major figure in the administration nor a favourite at court. He was not entrusted with the greater secrets, nor was he a determining influence in making strategy or employing troops. He hated most of the time he spent abroad, and was no soldier himself. Indeed, after the defeat of Landen (1693) he fled as far as Breda without a pause when in fact there was no enemy in pursuit at all![56] For all his continuous proximity to the King, he enjoyed few of his confidences although he did receive a measure of the royal friendship. Matthew Prior's description of 'the Elephant', whilst rather cruel, perhaps holds something of the truth:

[He] is always the same, jocular and ignorant, disguising his want of knowing what is going on by affecting to keep it secret.[57]

Thus it cannot in all honesty be claimed that Blathwayt played the part of Berthier to William's Napoleon. He was first and last a functionary, an underling, little more. Full ultimate responsibility for both the triumphs and disasters of the war must therefore remain at the King's door; but without the able assistance of Mr Blathwayt, William III would have been at a sad loss in the discharge of his routine military responsibilities.

The main sources for this study are the following: the Additional Manuscripts at the British Museum include the Blathwayt Papers (Add. Mss 9723, 9724, 9725) from which a great deal can be gleaned; the same collection also holds many further letters from Blathwayt to Lord Nottingham (Add. Mss 37991–2) on diplomatic matters, whilst the Secretary-at-War's correspondence with the Commissioners of Transport (Add. Mss 9729) is also valuable. Of particular interest are the papers included in Add. Mss 36859–61 which relate to the minutes of the Commission for Public Accounts in 1702 which closely questioned Blathwayt on the functions and prerogatives of his office. The Flanders Letter-Books (Add. Mss 37991–2), the official correspondence of the Secretary-at-War (28694–28714), and the Egerton Mss 1626 and 2618, also contain a wealth of information, whilst at the Public Record Office, the War Office and State Papers series contain much relevant material, including WO:4:1, – 5:7 and – 30:17 and SP:77:56–8. The Calendars of State Papers and Treasury Books are also of considerable use.

Secondary authorities consulted include Clode, *The Military Forces of the Crown, their administration and government*; C Walton's *History of the English Standing Army, 1660–1700*; R E Scouller, *The Armies of Queen Anne*; H Gordon, *The War Office*, and Miss G A Jacobsen's valuable study, *William Blathwayt: a late seventeenth-century English Administrator* published in 1932. Although the last-named work is indubitably the most important biographical study yet to appear, its treatment of Blathwayt's military responsibilities is in some respects rather sketchy, the author clearly being more interested in her subject's work at the Plantations Office and Board of Trade. Finally, I found S Baxter's study, *William III*, of the greatest 'background' use.

NOTES

1 N Luttrell, *A Brief Historical Relation…*, Vol. I, London, 1857, p. 326.
2 Letter of that date, signed by him, ordering the artillery train from Brentford to Hounslow Heath. WO:4:1, folio 118.
3 WO:4:1, folios 126–7; 129; 132–3.
4 'I cannot and will not write our General [Prince Vaudemont] word that our House of Commons has finally pinned the basket…upon the number of 10,000 men for our whole army…' Porlock Mss, 11 January 1697/8, BL Add. Mss.
5 Biographical information based on the *Dictionary of National Biography* and on Jacobsen *passim*.

6   Clode, Vol. II, Appendix CXXIX, pp. 335–65. See also Lytton Bulwer, *Life of Palmerston*, 1871, pp. 272–4 for Palmerston's views on the growth of the office during his quarrel with Dundas in 1811.

7   See *War and Society*, no. 2.

8   G N Clarke, *Life of James II*, p. 642.

9   C Walton, *History of the British Standing Army, 1660–1700*, London, 1894, pp. 641 & 769.

10   Treasury Reference Book, Index 6431, folios 320–8, entry dated 7 February 1694.

11   Add. Mss 9755.

12   Add. Mss 9729, folios 2, 3, 4, 25, 31, 33, 35, 51, 55.

13   WO:55:333; Add. Mss 17771.

14   On the latter point, see WO:25:6 and Add. Mss 38861, folio 123 (reverse).

15   Add. Mss 36861, 30 November 1712 and 36859, folio 141.

16   Add. Mss 9732, folio 27.

17   WO:4:2, folio 100, dated 20 January 1704, for example.

18   Add. Mss 38704, folio 79; 9759, folio 13.

19   See WO:30:48.

20   WO:4:1, folio 10 (4 July 1685) and Add. Mss 38695, folio 179 (an acknowledgement).

21   See HMC Popham Mss, p. 262 and WO:30:17, folios 4–6.

22   WO:30:17, folios 49–53 (1686) and folio 174 (signed Bolingbroke) for 8 August 1704.

23   WO:5:7, dated 13 October 1695 & HMC F Russell Mss, p. 85, dated 26 March 1695.

24   Egerton Mss 2618, folio 175, WO:4:1, folios 37–8, 56, 85.

25   This subject is fully covered by Miss Jacobsen, *op. cit.*, Chapter XI.

26   HMC, Popham Mss, p. 276.

27   Add. Mss 9729, folio 2.

28   *Ibid.*, folio 25.

29   *Ibid.*, folio 12.

30   *Ibid.*, folios 33 & 35.

31   *Ibid.*

32   *Ibid.*, folios 51 & 55.

33   Add. Mss 9723, folio, folio 29.

34   *Ibid.*, folio 36.

35   Add. Mss 9725, folio 13.

36   *Ibid.*, folio 21.

37   *Ibid.*, folio 82.

38   Add. Mss 9723, folio 94.

39   *Ibid.*, folio 85.

40   *Ibid.*, folios 100–1.

41   Add. Mss 17771, folio 7 and Somers Tracts, Vol. III, No. 6 for a summary of subsidies paid out from 1701 to 1704 (*inter alia*). Also Add. Mss 9723, folio 66.

42   Dated 23 July 1686 from Gemblours, W C Coxe, *The Shrewsbury Correspondence*, p. 127.

43   Add. Mss 9723, folios 55, 72, and 9724, folio 35.

44   Add. Mss 9724, folios 58–9.

45   *Ibid.*, folio 81.

46   Add. Mss 9725, folio 13.

47   *Ibid.*, folios 75–7.

48   Add. Mss 9724, folio 15.

49 SP Foreign, Vol. 84, entry for 16 November 1692.
50 *Ibid.*, Vol. 60, entry for 4 October 1693.
51 Cited in Jacobsen, *op. cit.*, p. 254.
52 *Ibid.*, p. 257.
53 Baxter, *op. cit.*, p. 326.
54 WO:5:4, folios 27, 42, etc. for muster returns from WO sources.
55 See KWC SP/8/14, folio 122 and numerous other documents.
56 Baxter, op. cit., p. 314.
57 L G Wicklen-Legge, *Matthew Prior: A Study of His Public Career and Correspondence*, Cambridge, 1921, p. 315.

CHAPTER V

The Horse

The Cavalry of Louis XIV

The Revolution of 1688 was popular. Rumours that James II's Queen had been delivered of a baby son thus securing a Catholic succession had caused anxiety, but now James II was safely in exile at St Germain near Paris. No doubt this would provide Louis XIV with the opportunity to make trouble for England, especially in Ireland, but the vast majority of English people were relieved by the changes. King William III was a quiet, silent, reserved and serious man. His wife, Queen Mary II, showed signs of the family stubbornness and from the start she did not like the Churchills, man or wife, and was further angered by their close friendship with her sister Princess Anne, and her husband, George, Prince of Denmark. There would be trouble.

Despite having been created Earl of Marlborough in 1689, as we have seen earlier John Churchill disliked many of the Dutch generals and colonels who were now in high positions at court and reaped its sinecures, titles and financial benefits. William, however, needed to be careful dealing with this important figure, the Earl of Marlborough, who might return his loyalty to James II. Could recent events really eradicate the many years of friendship between them? Queen Mary advised her husband not to advance or trust Marlborough, but fortunately for John Churchill the opposition subsided when the Queen died in 1694. However, two years later there was a crisis when Marlborough was sent to the Tower in 1696 on suspicion of treachery. This was quashed, and the same year Marlborough was made tutor to Princess Anne's son.

The King now recognised Marlborough's abilities and without his wife's whispering gradually became friendly with him and made great use of him in international diplomatic matters. They worked together over four years and allegedly the two men saw eye-to-eye on many things. This was especially good for military matters as the Army was improved and Marlborough would soon be in a position to exploit his talents. He had trained in the Guards, as a marine, and also as a cavalryman. Meanwhile in France James II died in 1701 and Louis XIV recognised his son as James III, and openly pledged to support his attempt to recover the English crown and return

73

England to the French satellite status it had 'enjoyed' under Charles II. Louis' expansionist ambitions meant a major European war was likely against France by Holland and Austria, and the French Army was being readied for it. A series of reforms and reorganisations had brought about major improvements and, as an example, we shall now study 'Le Roi Soleil's' cavalry, who were known to be the best in Europe – but the English Horse would be ready for 1704.

A visitor to the great Palace of Versailles is left under no illusions about the proclivities of Louis XIV for the pursuit of *la gloire*, nor about the association of the horse with concepts of military triumph. In the Grand Court stands the huge bronze equestrian statue of the famous monarch – his steed's nostrils flared, its eyes glaring, its powerful hooves pawing the ground. Within the Palace, the same theme meets the eye time and again – the mounted conqueror riding in Roman triumph over the prostrate bodies of the vanquished – a theme repeated in paintings, tapestries and, perhaps most strikingly of all, in the fine bas-relief by Antoine Coysevox in the Salon de la Guerre, which depicts 'le Roi Soleil' in the role of Mars.

The mounted arm still played a vital role in the campaigns and battles of the second half of the seventeenth century, but this should not obscure the fact that in more ways than one *l'arme blanche*, sword or sabre, had passed its zenith and was slowly slipping into the first stages of a long decline. During Louis XIV's long and eventful reign[1] the realities[2] of the situation were often easy to disguise or overlook, but, as Professor Bodart's researches have illustrated, whereas between 1618 and 1648 mounted warriors had provided all of 35% of the armed power of France, over the next seventy years the proportion would drop to 30%, before plunging to little more than a fifth by 1780. This was a trend experienced by all European armies, only the forces of England, Russia and Turkey maintaining a reasonably steady and consistent level of cavalry representation.

The reasons for this general decline in numerical representation are not far to seek. Armies were, at least in times of war, larger than had been experienced since the days of Rome and Byzantium. To train, equip and mount a cavalryman was far more expensive than to provide an infantryman.[3] Although in some countries a would-be cavalry recruit was still expected to provide his own mount in the first instance, the cost of a suitable cavalry charger in England fluctuated between £12 and £15 during the quarter-century following the Glorious Revolution of 1688; in Ireland a dragoon's mount cost £5, a Spanish jade £9. Similarly, the cheapest remount available to the Dutch and Imperial services in 1693 cost all of 90 *patagons*, or approximately £10. At the same time the cavalry trooper's pay and subsistence was higher than that of the *fantassin* or humble foot-soldier, as he had to feed and care for his mount as well as himself. Thus, in the reign of Queen Anne a cavalry trooper received half a crown a day and 14/- (or 70p) a week subsistence-money to the dragoon's 1/6 (17p) a day and 8/2 (41p) a week respectively, but both fared far better than the infantry rank and file who received only 8d (about 3½p) a day to include 6d subsistence money before stoppages and routine deductions. It also took considerably longer to train a raw recruit into an acceptable cavalryman than it did to teach a country bumpkin the rudiments of foot-drill and musketry. Taking all these factors into consideration, the Marquis de Santa Cruz,[4] the Spanish military expert of the 1730s, estimated that '. . . the maintenance of 1,000 cavalry costs as much as the maintenance of 2,500 infantry'. In the French Army the situation was further aggravated where pay was concerned by the widespread practice of including a double-allocation of officers in each cavalry troop – half holding actual commands, the rest serving as *reformés* or ordinary troopers. Whatever the desirable social effects of such a system, it was indubitably an expensive one, for *reformés* drew pay as officers.

If expense was one factor leading to a decline in cavalry numbers, another was the rapid advance in the effectiveness of infantry weaponry and tactics during our period. The new combination (from about 1700) of flintlock musket and socket bayonet made the foot-soldier less vulnerable to mounted attack, and at the same time increased the vulnerability of the mounted soldier, At least until the mid-seventeenth century the cavalry had as a general rule been the battle-winning arm, but as the technological revolution in firearms took increasing effect the cavalry's superiority began slowly but surely to wane, although its social prestige remained as high as ever. 'Firearms and not cold steel now decide battles', Maréchal de Puységur[5] noted with typical realism. But this is not to claim that the day of the cavalry was wholly past. Such commanders as Marlborough, Eugene and Charles XII, as we shall see, still relied on their mounted arm to achieve the coup de grâce in their greatest battles; and if Napoleon[6] could still claim a century later that '. . . the cavalry represent the legs and eyes of an army; the infantry and artillery are its body and arms', this was equally the case in the earlier generation, if not even more so.

The roles of cavalry were indeed multifarious. When an army was on the march, they reconnoitred ahead or served to guard the flanks and rear against the possibility of a surprise attack. When an army entered camp, they provided vedettes and patrols, conducted foraging forays, protected convoys and escorted senior officers – or undertook raids into enemy territory to place hostile districts under contribution, contract or barefaced pillage. Other detachments hovered hawk-eyed close to the enemy's main positions, watching for signs of reinforcements or impending movement. Still others would lie quietly concealed in wood or lane, placed in ambush ready to surprise enemy convoys or small parties. On the day of battle, the mounted soldier, whether cuirassier, dragoon or light horseman, really came into his own. The squadrons[7] wheeled and manoeuvred over the field, supporting their infantry and guns with their carbines, pistols or swords, clashing with the hostile horse, charging and re-forming, until the cohesion and morale of one or other army cracked under the combined impact of cannonade, musketry and cold steel. Thereupon, in the event of victory, it was often the particular duty of the cavalrymen and dragoons[8] to head the pursuit, harrying the enemy's rearguard, affording the foe no time to rally or prepare his defended places. In the process of these duties the wheeling and huzzaing squadrons would sabre fugitives or round up prisoners. Sometimes they would be called upon to mount large-scale, deep-penetration raids into the enemy's countryside, bringing fire and the sword, rapine and destruction to areas singled out for military execution. If, on the other hand, the fortunes of war proved contrary on the day of battle, the cavalry's prime duty was not to escape the stricken field, but rather to cover the retreat of their discomfited comrades, delaying the enemy's pursuit and distracting his attention from the vulnerable and disordered hordes of weary and disheartened infantrymen. On occasion the cavalry would aid the wounded or exhausted by taking them up on to their mounts. Such were the routine tasks of cavalry in time of war.[9]

In the days of peace, they were less actively employed, but their days did not pass in complete idleness. For Guards units there was the routine of ceremonial duties and escorts for members of royal families, visiting dignitaries and other notables. In the days before the existence of any regular police forces, it also often fell to the lot of the horse to reinforce the magistrates and tax-collectors in the performance of their often unpopular duties. Dragoons might also be required by unscrupulous monarchs and governments to oppress discordant or simply unwelcome minorities by means of 'dragoonades' – the forcible billeting of rough soldiers on hapless civilian families upon whom they were free to wreak every indignity and havoc short of actual murder, whilst authority turned a blind and conniving eye on these activities. Louis XIV used such methods against the Huguenots and later the Camisards;[10] James II of England applied the same treatment to political opponents of his pro-Catholic policies; George I and II both employed the method in attempts to quell the Jacobite aspirations of the Highlands after both the '15 and the '45 Scottish rebellions. This type of activity did not endear the reputation of the cavalry soldier to the population at large, and later in the eighteenth century the great lexicographer, Dr Samuel Johnson, would feelingly bracket felons, bad stinks and Life-Guardsmen as equally unwelcome presences in lodging houses.[11]

But these were not the normal peace-time roles for those cavalrymen retained in service at the end of hostilities. Dragoons would be expected to assist with road building and bridge improvement. Regiments of Horse would form parts of fortress garrisons, or in large encampments near capital cities ready to overawe the 'vulgar' or keep Parliaments and Assemblies of Notables in a proper frame of loving and respectful subservience to their God-appointed sovereigns. And year in, year out, there were the perennial tasks of training to fulfil, of horses to be taken for grass, water and exercise, with the occasional visit to the smith or farrier to fix a loose shoe or to the leather-workers to repair some defective piece of tack. Such was the lot of the cavalryman retained in pay by his government. His was a routine and often boring existence no doubt, centring on ale-house sheds and meagre stabling for barracks, except for certain elite formations, were still things of the future; but such a life was infinitely preferable to that of the disbanded trooper or common soldier, dismissed the service and his regiment at the end of hostilities by economy-minded governments with never a word of thanks for his services and never a penny of pension to repay him for his expenditure of blood, tears and service in his country's cause. Only officers might hope for half-pay. For the rest, it was a question of finding whatever work was available; a few of the deserving might be fortunate enough to secure a coveted position as an in-pensioner or out-pensioner at Chelsea Hospital – founded for the comfort of old soldiers in their declining years by Charles II and his mistress, Nell Gwynn, or at the similar establishment at Kilmainham in Ireland. French old soldiers might hope for a similar place at the Invalides, founded for the same purpose as Chelsea by Louis XIV. But only a fortunate few could hope for such a sanctuary. For those without work – and there was precious little of it available in the seventeenth century – the outlook was bleak. Reduced to become beggars and public nuisances, they would have only recourse to the grim provisions of the Poor Law in the British Isles, or to the charitable propensities of religious orders in Catholic countries on the Continent. Small wonder that a proportion of old soldiers turned to crime in the hope of eking out a miserable existence. Where ex-cavalrymen were concerned, the dark calling of highwayman or common footpad was sometimes the final recourse – with the distinct likelihood of swinging at a noose's end at Tyburn always in their minds.

The purpose here is not to dwell on these aspects of a cavalryman's life, but rather to examine his military role – though the social context should never be neglected. The social prestige of the mounted soldier – like his pay – was superior to that of the common soldier in the rank and file of an infantry regiment,[12] but not markedly so. Although many cavalry troopers would be drawn from the servants of country estates, following their master's younger son to the wars perhaps, and would be expected to have means enough to bring a horse with them on first enlistment, others were failed tradesmen or small farmers, and all who donned the scarlet coat of Great Britain, the silver-grey of Austria, the black of Prussia (in the days before Frederick William II and his gifted son), the Bourbon white of France, or the dark blue of Sweden, were doomed to be regarded to a greater or lesser extent as social outcasts, for the military profession was not highly regarded by society at large. According to Daniel Defoe, in times of hardship '. . . the poor starve, thieve or turn soldier.'[13] The early seventeenth century poet Francis Quarles[14] put his quill right on the point when he wrote during the reign of James I:

> God and the soldier men, adore
> When at the face of danger, not before;
> The danger past, the same is each requited –
> God is forgot, and the soldier slighted.

This parlous reputation attached to those following a 'military life' was partly due to the social scorn and fear felt for the 'sturdy beggar' or vagrant[15] – the class from which many an unwilling soldier was recruited and to which he returned willy-nilly after discharge, and also to the reputation the profession earned, part deservedly and part unfairly, during the grim days of the Wars of Religion in France, during the even worse times associated with the Thirty Years War in central and southern Europe, and also from the days of the English Commonwealth and Protectorate of Oliver Cromwell, when the New Model Army proved itself not only a ready instrument of repression but also a potent political force – feared and distrusted by ex-Cavalier and Parliamentarian alike. In England's case the result would be a long-standing distrust of the military, reflected by the strict control of the estimates 'for Guards and Garrisons'[16] by Parliament after the Restoration of 1660 – for a time even the mention of the word 'Army' was taboo – and by the later annual Mutiny Act dating from 1669 in the aftermath of the Glorious Revolution. On the Continent, armies remained the instruments of their monarchs or (in the case of the United Provinces and the Serene Republic of Venice) of their oligarchic governments, much as they had always been, but this did nothing to enhance the popularity of the profession with society at large. All armies and all soldiers were regarded as public blights and private rogues and wastrels, to be avoided whenever possible.

During the seventy years under review, an army's cavalry was made up of four district types. First there were what may be termed Household Cavalry – forming part of the monarch's escort, or corps d'élite. In England this comprised the Life Guards, in Sweden the Drabants, and in Austria the Trabans. In France the Maison du Roi comprised Horse Grenadiers, the Gardes du Corps, the Gendarmes de la Garde, the Compagnie des Chevaux-Légers, and the two companies (or squadrons) of Musketeers – the Black and the Grey (named after the colours of their mounts). All these formations were privileged, and their officer-posts

78

highly prized; many indeed were reserved almost exclusively for Princes of the Blood or the most senior marshals and generals.

When serving in the field these crack formations were often brigaded with the most prestigous regiments of 'the Horse' – the generic term that covered many types of regular cavalry. Thus the English Life Guards early developed close ties with the Royal Regiment of Horse Guards ('the Blues'), and in France the Maison often fought alongside the Gendarmerie. For the rest, the Horse included cuirassiers (still wearing three-quarter armour in some cases at the beginning of our period but gradually reducing this until it comprised only helmet, back and breast, and, sometimes, tassets);[17] carabineers (armed, as the title suggests, with carbines or short muskets as well as the habitual sword and pistols), and finally the numerous Regiments of Horse, the backbone of the Line cavalry, many of which only existed in time of war whilst others were reduced to the merest cadres at the cessation of hostilities.

This was also often the fate of the third category of mounted troops – the Dragoons. These troops were less well paid than the regular Horse, and were generally treated as maids-of-all-work within the mounted arm. Dragoons were expected to fight on foot as well as on horseback, and to this end carried carbines, bayonets and hatchets as part of their standard equipment. They were also often ordered to serve in pioneering roles, and as storm-troops or 'forlorn hopes'.[18] Many commanders of note, including the Austrian Montecuccoli, regarded their dragoons as little more than mounted infantry, but there is no denying they performed many vital roles. They never wore armour, and were frequently equipped with distinguishing cross-belts which supported an ammunition pouch on one side and sword and bayonet on the other. Their high knee-boots made them somewhat clumsy in the dismounted role, and this earned the 'Jackbootmen' (as Brigadier-General Kane disrespectfully dubbed them) some telling criticisms.

Nevertheless, their numerical representation steadily developed over the years. By 1668 Louis XIV boasted fourteen regiments of dragoons to sixty-six of Horse, but by 1690 the former had been increased to number all of forty-three regiments. Peter the Great inherited only a single dragoon formation in 1700, but by 1711 he had all of twenty-four. William III commanded only seven regiments of English dragoons (to thirty-one Horse), but between 1707 and 1711 the Army Lists of his successor contain the names of eighteen units of dragoons and only eleven of native Horse. This steady development was largely due to economic factors: dragoons were paid less and their mounts were less costly than their counterparts in the regular cavalry as has already been noted. In social terms, therefore, the dragoon figured less prominently than the trooper of horse, but in the French service many famous families were proud to command dragoon formations – including the Boufflers, the Brissacs and the noble house of La Ferté.

Fourthly, there were the beginnings of what would in the fullness of time became the Light Cavalry, a type of horsemen originating in eastern Europe. The Russian prototype was the Cossack (See Appendix B), famed for both their horsemanship and their general indiscipline. Peter the Great attempted to integrate eight regiments of hussars within the regular Russian forces by 1710, but subsequently reduced the number. In southern Europe the rulers of Austria were not slow to copy their Turkish opponents, who employed large numbers of Beshlis and Delis in fast-moving but loosely organised clouds of light horsemen to protect their main forces. They were further induced to introduce similar troops within their armies when in 1683 the King of Poland, John Sobieski, marched to the relief of Vienna, tightly besieged by the Turks. The Polish army included numbers of the famous 'winged lancers', so-named on account of their lances gaily bedecked with feathers attached to their saddles. Of course Austria had employed Hungarian Magyar irregular horsemen since the fifteenth century, but only in 1688 did they formally raise their first regiments of Hungarian hussars on a semi-permanent basis. These cavalry were more heavily equipped than the light horse of the day, but did not rate as heavy cavalry in the light of the day. The term hussar derives from the Hungarian word *Husz*, meaning twenty reflecting the fifteenth-century feudal practice of conscripting one Magyar in every twenty for military service. France was relatively late in adopting light cavalry. The Chevaux-Légers of the Maison were not really light cavalry at all – but patterned themselves on the Musketeers, and it was only in 1692 that the French raised their first real hussar regiment, recruited from Imperialist deserters. However, it is also true that Cardinal Richelieu had raised a small unit of 'Hungarian Cavalry' in 1635, but this did not survive for long. As for Great Britain, her armies included no truly light cavalry formations until the mid-eighteenth century.

Light cavalrymen were not universally admired. If the regular cavalryman tended to scorn the dragoon, both affected to despise the hussar. The French soldier, Brigadier-General de la Colonie, described hussars as '. . . properly speaking, little more than bandits on horseback', and in 1706 William Cadogan, Marlborough's famous Quartermaster-General, congratulated himself on being captured by 'the French carabines [sic]' rather than '. . . falling into the hussars' hands, who first came up with me.' From Louis XIV's Carabineers he met '. . . with quarter and civility, saving their taking my watch and money.' His likely fate at the hands of hussars is not described, but they would seem to have enjoyed a somewhat barbarous reputation. Nevertheless, these rough, wild, indisciplined light horsemen proved very valuable for scouting, ravaging and raiding, even though no army at this time deemed them worthy of a place in the formal line of battle.[19]

The organisation of mounted formations at this period contained a myriad variations, but a reasonably standard impression can be presented. In all cases the regiment was the basic major formation. Sometimes cavalry or dragoons were organised into ad hoc brigades, but these were only temporary affairs adopted during active campaigning; there were certainly no cavalry divisions or corps, although it may be argued that the wings of cavalry placed on the flanks of the standard double battle-line of the day under Generals and Lieutenant-Generals of Horse approximated to the higher formations of later generations.

The cavalry regiment was, however, the basic administrative unit. It was sub-divided into two main parts: a regimental headquarters (which included the colonel, a lieutenant-colonel and a major, besides an adjutant, chaplain, surgeon and a kettle-drummer – or, in the case of dragoon regiments, a gunsmith and his servant), and a varying number of cavalry troops called 'companies' in the French service (comprising a captain, a lieutenant and a cornet, a quartermaster, two or three corporals of horse – or sergeants in the dragoons – and a varying number of troopers or dragoons making up the rank and file, not to mention two trumpeters, or, in dragoon formation, a pair of kettle-drummers or hautbois[20] players).

Guards and Household formations had more elaborate rank structures with additional posts. Precise strengths of cavalry and dragoon troops are impossible to suggest, but French establishments in the 1670s officially comprised twelve companies, each holding four officers and fifty troopers, Fluctuations were enormous, however, so a regiment's strength might vary between 300 and 450 men. Guards units were frequently larger – a Troop in the English Life Guards, for instance, holding all of 156 'gentlemen' – and Dragoon regiments tended to have rather more troops or companies than formations of line cavalry per se.

It will be noticed that no mention has been made of the squadron. This formation was never institutionalised in our period, but was created for use in battle by grouping two or more troops together under command of the senior troop commander. Such organisations were never permanent or administrative bodies. Thus a regiment of twelve troops might provide two or three ad hoc squadrons on days of action. Regiments of Dragoons, being generally larger, might form four or more companies. Some countries differed from the norm. Austrian cuirassier regiments, for example, commonly contained as many as 1,000 horsemen, who fought in some six squadrons. Swedish cavalry, by way of contrast, rarely comprised more than two squadrons in a regiment, which might, however, number up to 1,060 officers and troopers apiece at full establishment. Similarly, English regiments varied in size between 300 troopers (six troops or two squadrons) and 480 men in the case of dragoons (up to eight troops). But at every peace many formations were disbanded and most of the survivors reduced to the merest cadres. It is therefore impossible to give more than a broad approximation.[21]

The training of cavalrymen was often a long and laborious process. Brigadier-General Kane,[22] in his *Discipline for a Regiment of Foot upon action, also the most essential discipline of the Cavalry* (1745), summarised the requirements as follows:

> It is sufficient for them to ride well, to have their horses well managed, and train'd up to stand fire; that they take particular notice what part of the squadron they are in, their right and left-hand men, and file-leaders, that they may, when they happen to break, readily know how to form. Breaking their squadrons ought to be practised in their common discipline. That they march and wheel with a grace, and handle their swords well, which is the only weapon our British Horse make use of when they charge the enemy; more than this is superfluous ... Dragoons should be well instructed in the use of fire-arms, having upon occasion to make use of them on foot; but when on horseback, they are to fight as the horse do.

Kane, however, was basically an infantryman, and the production of a good troop of Horse called for much hard effort. The troops had to master four basic movements – the facings, doublings, countermarches and wheelings – and then become proficient in the 'postures' or exercise of arms, with sword, pistol and (when carried) carbine. Troops equipped with sabres were enjoined to use the sweeping cut to left or right; those armed with the broadsword were encouraged to use the point as well as the edge. Most cavalrymen were taught to slash first at their opponent's bridle headstall in the hope of causing the bit to fall from the mouth, rendering the horse uncontrollable. Dragoons, of course, also had to master infantry drills.

The employment of cavalry in battle varied considerably from country to country. In the second half of the seventeenth century, there was considerable doubt as to whether the mounted arm should be regarded as primarily an instrument of shock or as one of sophisticated fire-power. In France, the advocates of the latter long held the advantage. In many instances, French cavalry moved to the attack on the frontage of a single company, the remaining troops advancing one by one behind the leader, at a slow trot.[23] Each formation would discharge its pistols in turn, before wheeling to the rear, reloading as they went. Use of the sword was largely restricted to the general mêlée which would be engaged once the fire action was complete. Such formalised proceedings did not recommend themselves to such bright spirits as the Great Condé,[24] latterly it was mainly France's foes that espoused the cause of shock-action. Marlborough, for one, demanded that twin-squadron charges, delivered it should be noted at the fast trot, using cold steel, should be the norm. He went so far as to ban the use of firearms by cavalry except when at grass or on outpost duty. Prince Eugene of Savoy, the celebrated Austrian commander, was of much the same mind, and so was the firebrand Charles XII, King of Sweden. His cavalry were trained to charge at the gallop in vast arrowhead formations, the troopers riding 'knee behind knee' with the ensign at the apex rather than 'knee by knee' as was the practice in much of the rest of Europe.

Swedish horsemen were trained to baulk at no obstacle, and eventually became proficient at manoeuvring with a decisiveness and speed that no other country could match. Only the horsemen of the Ottoman armies could rival the dash of the Swedes, but they lacked the Swedish discipline, which, like Marlborough's, enjoined the immediate rally after the charge. The Turks tended to fight in a loose cloud or swarm of individual warriors rather than in a cohesive body, and provided their opponents maintained their formations or remained within the barricades of chevaux-de-frise set up on the battlefield, they would generally withstand the fury of the 'Turkish storm'.

Until the 1690s, however, the French cavalry remained the best in Europe in overall terms. Under Condé they brought off spectacular battle successes, as at Rocroi in 1645. Turenne used his cavalry equally adeptly in many an engagement both great and small, whilst the elder Luxembourg's horsemen swept all before them through the Flanders campaigns of the War of the League of Augsburg[25] – as at Leuze on 19 September 1691, when he surprised the rearguard of Waldeck's army, all seventy-five squadrons and five battalions, and proceeded to inflict 1,500 casualties upon them at the head of just twenty-eight squadrons; or at Landen[26] two years later, when French cavalry stormed the earthworks defending Neerwinden village at the fourth attempt, and thus signalled William III's defeat. These were great days for the French cavalry.

The next war, however, witnessed a reversal of fortune. Marlborough's well trained and disciplined squadrons – in close association at all times with their foot and guns – wreaked havoc time and again upon the proud cavaliers of France who, under the less inspired leadership of the latter-day Marshals of France, lost some of their old fire and dash. Nowhere was this better demonstrated than at Blenheim, where, in one celebrated engagement near the outset of the battle, eight squadrons of the vaunted Gendarmerie were routed by a bare five squadrons of English horse under Colonel Palmes. This event was witnessed by Marshal Tallard,[27] and when, after his cataclysmic defeat, he listed his reasons for the loss of the day, he wrote: 'First, because the Gendarmerie were not able to break the five English squadrons.' The previous year had witnessed an equally notable feat of arms when, at Eckeren, the Dutch General Hompesch had routed 1,500 French and Spanish horsemen in a desperate dyke-top engagement at the head of a mere forty Dutch cavaliers, and 'pursued them closely for almost a mile'.

In their various generations, Condé, Marlborough and Charles XII were the most skilled handlers of masses of cavalry at the level of grand tactics. At Blenheim, Ramillies, Oudenarde and Malplaquet, Marlborough clinched each successive engagement by the judicious husbanding and dynamic handling of his mounted squadrons at the climax of the battle. At Blenheim, he massed eighty fresh squadrons over the Nebel river in the centre to engage, and at the second attempt overwhelm, the sixty squadrons and nine battalions of Tallard's exposed centre. It should also be noted, however, that a tricky situation during the forward movement of the Allied centre was safely remedied by Prince Eugene's selfless sending of Fugger's brigade of cuirassiers – his sole reserve – to fall on the flank of Marshal Marsin's counter-attack which at one moment threatened Marlborough's whole deployment in the centre. The Duke's handling of his horsemen at Ramillies will be described later; at Oudenarde he extemporised a double envelopment by the Prince of Orange's squadrons on the one flank and by Natzmer's and Eugene's cavalry on the other of Vendôme's exposed wing of the French army; and at Malplaquet,[28] close-fought and dearly bought victory though it proved, it was the massive advance by the Allied squadrons, closely supported by Orkney's battalions (Marlborough invariably ensured that horse, foot and guns served as an integrated combat team in all his battles) swept through the abandoned redoubts in the French centre to engage, and defeat, Marshal Villars' horsemen on the plain beyond – an action involving all of 30,000 horsemen, 'one of the greatest cavalry actions in history' in Winston Churchill's just opinion. Indeed, Marlborough's relationship with his cavalry was always rather special. After Elixhem in 1705, for example, where he had led cavalry charges in person, and almost been killed, 'This gave occasion to the troops with me to make me very kind expressions, even in the height of the action, which I own to you gives me much pleasure . . .', as the Duke wrote to his wife, Sarah. He was clearly not the son of the first Sir Winston Churchill, sometime Captain of Royalist Horse in the Great Civil War, for nothing.

For the bold handling of cavalry in action, Charles XII of Sweden held no peer. At Klizow (1702), twenty-one Swedish squadrons routed thirty-four Saxon squadrons (who were employing pistols) with cold steel. At Narva the previous year, great wedges of Swedish horsemen had charged through a dense snow blizzard to crash through and over the Russian earthworks. Charles was also ahead of his time in his doctrine of pursuit *à l'outrance* after a victory. Thus, following his pursuit of General Schulenburg's Saxons in 1704, the Swedish cavalry hounded the survivors for nine days without respite, eventually catching up with them at Sanitz. Without hesitation, two regiments of unsupported Swedish cavalry proceeded to charge a mixed force of several thousand Saxons and scattered them all. Denison[29] justly remarks that the Swedish cavalry

'. . . was the natural outcome of his [Charles'] daring and chivalrous spirit'. Later that same year, when his army faced disaster at Poltava, the Swedish squadrons again distinguished themselves against overwhelming odds.

All in all, the cavalry of the late seventeenth and early eighteenth centuries saw some great days and brought off some notable achievements. And if the future lay more with the hurrying hordes of flintlock-bearing infantrymen and the ponderous smoke-shrouded cannon – at least insofar as primacy on the field of battle was concerned – the future also held some great days for the mounted arm handled by such accomplished leaders as Seydlitz, Murat and J E B Stuart. In the words of *The Hitopadesa*: 'The horse is the strength of the army. The horse is a moving bulwark.'

APPENDIX A

An Example in the Future:
English Cavalry at its Best – 1706

The Battle of Ramillies – 23 May 1706[30]

On Whitsunday 1706 there took place a mighty trial of strength some twenty miles south-east of Brussels in what was then known as the Spanish Netherlands, the heartland of 'the Cockpit of Europe'. Ranged against the Duke of Marlborough's Allied army – 123 squadrons, seventy-four battalions and 120 guns, or approximately 62,000 men in all – were the forces of Marshal Villeroi – 132 squadrons, seventy battalions and seventy guns, making a total strength of perhaps 60,000 French, Spanish and Bavarian troops. This battle is a good representative engagement for a number of reasons: it took place early in the campaign of that year, and both armies were therefore fresh; the sides were evenly matched; neither had planned to fight on that exact date or in that precise area – it was an 'encounter battle' that escalated from a minor early morning brush; and its history saw great and imaginative use of cavalry, both during and after the battle, particularly on the part of John Churchill, First Duke of Marlborough. As for the French, they were smarting to avenge their great defeat at Blenheim two years earlier, and Villeroi was under specific orders from Louis XIV to force or accept a major battle as soon as possible.

Although both armies knew of the other's general proximity, neither anticipated a major battle on 23 May. Cadogan and a camp-survey party, escorted by 600 horse, was seeking a site for the Allied army's next stopping-place on the well-watered plain of Ramillies, when, in the early-morning fog, he blundered upon the enemy already occupying the provisionally selected ground. The news was rushed back to the Duke, who rode forward with his staff to confirm his Quartermaster-General's impressions. Until the mist cleared, he could not decide whether he faced all or only a part of Villeroi's army, and the Duke's first order was for all his cavalry to come up in case he was opposed by only a covering force. But suddenly, at about 10.30 am, the sun broke through and the curtains of fog rapidly rolled back, revealing the full splendour of the French army occupying the ridge running from near the village of Taviers to the south, past Ramillies and Offus to Autre-Eglise behind the Little Gheete and its marshes to the north – the whole position forming a concave arc some four miles long. Marlborough realised the possibilities of the situation for the Allies: the enemy were over-extended; the Little Gheete's marshes would obstruct their left wing and protect his own right if he adopted a shorter front; similarly, the Mehaigne river beyond Taviers and the French-held outpost of Franquenay precluded all danger of the left of his position being turned; and, most important of all, his trained eye for ground picked out a useful re-entrant running from behind Foix-les-Caves to the north to opposite Ramillies in the centre – a feature that he might well make good use of to transfer troops unseen by the foe and thus make the most of a position based upon 'interior lines'. Soon aides were spurring eastwards to bring up the army, which fanned out into eight columns.

The French were equally taken by surprise: their intelligence had placed Marlborough a full day's march distant, and all their tents were still pitched behind Ramillies. But now the trumpets blared and the signal-guns recalled the foragers, and the French hastened to form their lines of battle. To make the most of the open plain some one and a half miles wide to the south of Ramillies, Villeroi massed eighty-two squadrons, including the Maison du Roi, with several interlaced infantry brigades, the garrisons of Taviers and Franquenay, and twenty battalions and a dozen triple-barrelled cannon around Ramillies, in support. Less sensibly, fifty more squadrons were deployed near Autre-Eglise on the French left, where broken and marshy ground around the Little Gheete effectively precluded their active employment.

All morning the French watched idly whilst Marlborough's eight columns deployed along the ridge of Jeuche and the plateau of Jandrenouille. On his right the Duke placed almost all his English formations, both horse and foot – twelve battalions and fifty-four squadrons under Lord Orkney. The mass of the Allied foot, backed by heavy batteries, filled the centre; on the left, facing the cavalry plain, General Overkirk drew up the sixty-nine squadrons of Dutch and Danish cavalry, with the Dutch Guards and a pair of field guns on their extreme flank. Shortly after one o'clock the batteries open fire.

It is doubtful whether Marlborough had a full plan already conceived, but he was evidently aware of the opportunities the terrain and the enemy's dispositions offered. His first orders were for the troops on his extreme flanks to advance on the enemy – the Dutch Guards to take possession of the two villages on the French right flank, Orkney and the redcoated battalions to press ahead over the Little Gheete towards their left. These probing attacks would hopefully test Villeroi's intentions and resolve.

And so it proved. The Dutch Guards made good progress on the left, driving the French and Bavarians out of both villages, inducing the French commanders to send twenty-one squadrons, including fourteen squadrons of dragoons under M. d'Aubigny, and several regiments of foot from their right centre to the support of their unfortunate colleagues. Simultaneously, on the distant right flank, Orkney and his battalions began to descend towards the Little Gheete. This movement, in its turn, served further to disrupt Villeroi's battle-line, for the Marshal was under strict instructions from Louis XIV to pay special attention to that part of his front that would receive the first English attack. Soon more brigades of foot were moving northwards. All this Marlborough noted with satisfaction, for he had already singled out the French centre around Ramillies for his master-blow. It was almost 3.30 pm.

The Duke realised he could use just a token force to contain the French left behind the Little Gheete and, concealed by the convenient dip, transfer most of the formation on his own right to build up a redoubtable strength for the blow in the centre. But two obstacles stood in way of this plan. First Lord Orkney, who had fought his way (French reinforcements notwithstanding) to the very outskirts of Autre-Eglise, proved very unwilling to fall back to his original position as Marlborough's master-plan now dictated, and it took nine visits by aides-de-camp, and lastly by Cadogan himself, to induce him to relinquish his grip. Only when the English battalions had returned to their ridge near Foulz could the full transfer movement commence.

Before this was ready to be executed, however, the Duke's attention was drawn by anxious officers to a highly dangerous situation developing on his left centre. As General Schulenburg began to move the Allied centre forward towards Ramillies, Overkirk ordered his squadrons to advance on their flank. This challenge was at once accepted by the sixty-eight remaining squadrons of Villeroi's right centre – and soon the plain south of Ramillies was filled with wheeling cavalry, as forty-eight Dutch squadrons and the twenty-one Danish attacked the Maison du Roi. The latter, as a French observer noted, had left over-large intervals between their squadrons, and this proved to be to their disadvantage. Marlborough, observing the conflict, sent aides post haste to summon eighteen squadrons from his right via the dip, but whilst their arrival on the scene was still awaited, the Duke and his staff rode over to join Overkirk. They discovered a major crisis. The Maison du Roi, despite the presence of Dutch squadrons on their flanks and rear thanks to the intervals, charged home with magnificent fire and discipline, and routed the Dutch right wing. Giving way, the Dutch horsemen placed in dire peril the flank of Schulenburg's infantry, although the steady fire of four battalions earned them a brief respite to reform.

Marlborough never hesitated – being instantly aware that this situation must be remedied – but at once summoned a further twenty-one squadrons from the distant right. Forward he spurred with his attendants, sword in hand, to lead two successive Dutch charges in the mêlée. This bold, even foolhardy, action by the Captain-General helped win time for the arrival of the transferring cavalry from the right wing – but it almost cost him his life. In one of the eddies of combat he was knocked or fell from his horse and, still worse, this coincided with a French advance. For a time it seemed that the Duke would be killed or at least taken prisoner, but the Dutch rallied to his aid, and he was able, despite his 57 years and cumbersome jackboots, to run several hundred yards to the shelter of the muskets of a neighbouring friendly battalion of Dutch-paid Swiss mercenaries, where he temporarily mounted an aide's horse. Even then his personal peril was not over. The Duke's spare charger was hurried forward, and as he was mounting this a cannon-ball passed between his legs as he swung up into the saddle – and killed his equerry, Colonel Bringfield, who was holding the stirrup. However, the cavalry crisis was now averted as first the eighteen and then the further twenty-one fresh Allied squadrons crashed into the fray, and overbore the Maison and their supporting squadrons with an overall superiority of force amounting to five to three. The French right wing began to swing back, pivotting on Ramillies.

Marlborough now sensed his opportunity. Summoning several British battalions from Orkney's silent right, which stood with its forward line of formations atop the ridge, the Duke began to build up forces for the coup de grâce against Ramillies. Villeroi and his staff, meantime, were anxiously awaiting the renewal of Orkney's onslaught on their left flank, and never thought to send their fifty useless squadrons southwards to assist their own right – but then the dip in the ground completely disguised the progressive dismantling of Orkney's command, and the crucial transfers already noted.

The fight for Ramillies was bitter, but with the collapse of the French right wing the battle was virtually won. Soon after 5 o'clock the Allied cavalry reformed in a new line facing north, and began to roll up the French line remorselessly. This advance was timed to coincide with a new, and decisive, onslaught against Ramillies and its death-dealing batteries. As Churchill has pointed out, this wheel by about 100 Allied squadrons – already part-spent by fierce combat – was a remarkable feat worthy of a special place in the annals of cavalry achievement. It proved decisive. The disordered French, striving to form a new line to face the advancing horsemen, found themselves hopelessly obstructed by their own tent-lines and waggon-trains behind Ramillies. Too late Villeroi ordered his fifty squadrons of the left wing to intervene – they melted away to the north – and soon the whole French army, the would-be avengers of Blenheim, was dissolving into a mass of fugitives leading for Judoigne.

Each side had lost some 5,000 casualties, but the French had lost more – their cohesion and reputation. But Marlborough had no time to assimilate this information – he at once plunged himself into the organisation of the pursuit. Ramillies is unusual for its day in this respect – for pursuits *à l'outrance* were rarely attempted. The Duke himself did not pause to rest until he reached Meldert, some twelve miles from the battlefield. During the pursuit, Villeroi and the Elector of Bavaria narrowly avoided falling into the hands of the English cavalry.

If the immediate, tactical pursuit of the French after Ramillies was a notable feat, so was the strategic follow-through. Fortress after fortress and city after city of the Spanish Netherlands fell to the Allied army – no post seemed capable of withstanding the whirlwind. 'We now have the whole summer before us,' exulted the victor, 'and with the blessing of God I shall make the best use of it.' This he proceeded to do: Louvain, Vilvorde, Brussels (the capital), Alost, Gavre, Bruges, Ghent, Damme, and after sieges, Menin, Ostend and Dendermonde, fell in turn to the Allies. The result was the conquest of the greater part of the Spanish Netherlands in a few short weeks. Not until Napoleon's pursuit of the Prussians after Jena-Auerstadt, exactly a century later, would a similar military achievement be brought off. The surrender of Ath on 2 October brought this *annus mirabilis* in Flanders to a close. Marlborough's reputation was now firmly secured – and so was that of the Allied cavalry he had led to victory.

APPENDIX B
The Cossack

The word 'Cossack' is an adaptation of the Russian *Khasak* – literally 'free' or 'freebooter'. The Cossack peoples were mainly of Tartar origin and came from settlements in the Caucasus, Black Sea and Caspian regions, including the area of the Don river. Since the fifteenth century these wild horsemen had played a role in Russian history, and the rulers of Muscovy, and later the Tsars of Russia, had granted them land-rights and tax exemptions in return for military service, for which every Cossack male was liable. Led by their *Hetman*, Cossacks proved ideally suited for reconnaissance, raiding and outpost work, but their notorious in-discipline, treacherous tendencies, and blatant disregard for authority precluded their incorporation in the formal lines of battle of Russian eighteenth-century armies. Peter the Great's experiments in giving them a more formal role and status did not prove very successful, and indeed some of the Cossack peoples proved a thorn in his side. In 1709 Charles XII of Sweden hoped to inspire a revolt amongst Mazeppa's Cossacks – vainly in the event – but Peter never wholly trusted these fiercely independent peoples who never fully recognised his authority as Tsar.

The Cossack was generally armed with a lance, sabre, pistol and sometimes a carbine or musketoon. They wore fur caps, voluminous cloth or animal-skin jerkins, baggy breeches and soft-leather boots. They were organised into sothias, or bands, each of which possessed a venerated chorigoy, or standard. They often rode to the sound of drums. In action the Cossack usually fought as an individual rather than as a member of a team. They operated in swarms or clouds of horsemen, and were particularly adept at picking off stragglers and fugitives. They were not of much use against formed bodies of either horse or foot – and as often as not would flee if faced with determined resistance – at least in the early eighteenth century. In later generations regular formations of Cossacks would be incorporated into the regular Russian forces, and their general competence increased to include standard cavalry roles. Less popularly, Cossacks would also be used by future Tsars as internal security troops and 'bully-boys' in much the same way as Louis XIV employed dragoons. The Cossack still serves in the modern Russian Army, and played as doughty a role in the defeat of Hitler's Wehrmacht in the Second World War as their predecessors had done against Napoleon's Grande Armée in the later months of 1812.

NOTES

1   From 1643 to 1715.
2   See G Bodart, *Militär-historisches Kriegs-Lexicon, 1618–1905*, Vienna and Leipzig, 1908.
3   D G Chandler, *The Art of Warfare in the Age of Marlborough*, Staplehurst, Spellmount, 1994, p. 29.
4   Marquis de Santa Cruz, *Réflexions Militaires*, 4 vols, Paris (nd).
5   Maréchal de Puységur, *L'Art de la Guerre*, 2 vols, Paris, 1748.
6   Gouvion St Cyr (1764–1830). See D G Chandler (ed.), *Napoleon's Marshals*, London, 1987 & 1998, pp. 118–37.
7   At full strength, a squadron required 150 cavalrymen.
8   Dragoons were mounted on horseback, but also carried muskets. They could, therefore, operate as cavalry and infantry in both roles.
9   Napoleon once suggested that the cavalry '. . . represented the legs and the eyes of an army; the infantry and artillery are the body and legs'.
10 *Camisards* were French rebels against authority.
11 Hence cavalrymen being unpopular by being posted to houses.
12 A soldier received about 8d a day (less 'off-reckonings'). See D G Chandler, *Marlborough as Miltary Commander*, Staplehurst, 1995, p. 72.
13 D Defoe, *An Enquiry into Projects*, London, 1697, p. 134.
14 F Quarles (1592–1644), *Epigrams*, London (nd).
15 Wandering explorers without 'fixed abodes' – widely blamed for thefts.
16 See R E Scouller, *The Armies of Queen Anne*, Oxford, 1966, p. 83.
17 Tassets were worn on armour on the upper legs and knees.
18 Volunteers willing to lead forward on a very dangerous attack or storming.
19 Hussars were fully accepted as regular light cavalry from around the 1760s.
20 A type of oboe used to play military music.
21 An estimate of two-thirds of regimental cuts could be suggested. See D G Chandler, *The Art of Warfare in the Age of Marlborough*, Staplehurst, 1990 (first published 1974).
22 Brigadier-General Richard Kane (1666–1736), formerly of the 18th Regiment of Foot.
23 Marlborough insisted on an advance no faster than a careful mid-trot.
24 Prince Louis II of Bourbon (1621–86) was very famous.
25 The League of Augsburg extended from 1686 to 1697, to include the First Grand Alliance to the Peace of Ryswick.
26 The Battle of Landen (or Neerwinden) was fought on 29 July 1693.
27 Marshal Camille d'Hostun, Comte de Tallard (1652–1728).
28 The Battle of Malplaquet (11 September 1709).
29 See G T Denison, *A History of Cavalry*, London, 1913.
30 The Battle of Ramillies (23 May 1706) was perhaps Marlborough's greatest cavalry success in the War of the Spanish Succession.

CHAPTER VI

The Foot

Infantry Variations 1689–1713

As today, the training that troops received was vital to their battlefield performance. As we have just seen in the last chapter, King Louis XIV's cavalry was excellent, although the French foot were still training according to drill books of the 1630s and tended to remain old-fashioned, fighting five ranks deep and still using a large of proportion of pikes. The greatest years of France's martial reputation under le Grand Condé, le maréchal Turenne and le général Luxembourg may have been slowly slipping away in the 1690s, but they had generally experienced half a century of success. The infantry of the English Army, however, rapidly improved during this period, but that meant William of Orange then had to improve his Dutch foot.

This too was achieved by improvements to their weapons and to their tactical fighting skills. By 1703 the Dutch and British foot had completely withdrawn the pike, and most regiments were trained in three-deep lines for battle. Many of the Dutch muskets were not marvellous for monetary reasons, but Marlborough's men were equipped with the 'King William musket' and, even better, with the 'Brown Bess' as we shall see. They also had the benefit of determined, professional officers. Brigadier-General Richard Kane (1666–1736) was deeply involved in retraining the English Infantry. Wounded while fighting as a captain in the 18th Foot (Royal Irish) at the huge siege of Namur in 1695, arguably William III's most important victory of his European wars, Kane was a major at Blenheim, and many years later in the late 1730s he recalled his memories of those days.

> Every one will allow that it is absolutely necessary that the Troops should be brought under one Method of Discipline: that when His Majesty King George II shall be pleased to order them together, or a General Officer is to receive them, they may perform a graceful Exercise. And when the're 20 battalions on one field they might answer each other in their Firings with all the Regularity imaginable: but then they are not to keep popping by single Platoons.

Proper training was vital. Prince Waldeck commented in 1686: 'I wish that

93

those troops . . . were as disciplined as they are brave. M.de Marlbrouck has much trouble with them.' Marlborough saw to it that training and discipline were instilled into them.

Victory on the battlefield has always been the product of many inter-connected influences and factors, and it would be presumptuous to claim that one particular requirement for success was invariably or even generally more significant than another. Considerations of numerical and material strength, of states of morale and standards of leadership are almost always relevant, and few military historians would challenge the claim of realistic and effective training, designed to make the best use of the available weaponry, to be included on such a list. Yet it is often very difficult, the further one goes back into history, to gain a clear impression of exactly how engagements were fought and decided at the formation level. Learned authors devote much space to the strategic skills and grand tactical gambits of their favourite 'Great Captains', and even more atten-tion to their charisma, their strengths and foibles; it is unfortunately all too rarely that they find time to descend to the detail of minor tactics.

The contrast in the martial fortunes of William III and his military and diplomatic successor, John Churchill, has never been difficult to portray. Dutch William 'became renowned for his skill in making the best of defeats rather than for any capacity for winning victories',[1] whilst Marlborough shares with Field-Marshal Montgomery the unique dis-tinction, amongst British commanders, of never having suffered a serious military reverse while serving in the highest command positions. The 'Old Corporal . . . never fought a battle which he did not gain nor laid siege to a town which he did not take.'[2] Doubtless, William's and Churchill's styles of leadership were very different, as were their personalities, but the troops they respectively led between 1688 and 1697, and between 1700 and 1712, were in many respects much the same. It is equally true that no French marshal faced by Marlborough (at least until 1709 when Villars assumed command in Flanders) measured up to the ability of Luxem-bourg, le tapissier de Notre Dame, and yet the French troops of Louis XIV cannot have differed very markedly over the two generations. However, although the contrast in leadership is clearly very important to any attempt to explain the varied martial fortunes, it is also suggested that certain tactical developments or rather refinements took place between 1688 and 1713 within the English and Dutch forces which throw some fresh light on the main issue. If it could be demonstrated that William's infantry fought the French less successfully than Marlborough's battalions for essentially tactical reasons, then a further partial explanation for their contrasting performances may be entertainable.

Throughout history the development of new tactics has as a general rule lagged behind improvements in weaponry. Moreover, it is a tenable hypothesis that it has often been patently the most successful military powers that have tended to lag behind in adopting new ideas, proving the most prone to military conservatism and the most resistant to proposals of military change. The urge to rethink, reform and remodel has often been stronger in a country that has undergone military tribulation than in one with a long-established record of victory. In the late seventeenth century the gradual transition from the traditional matchlock musket and pike combination to the flintlock musket fitted with socket bayonet was a development in weaponry shared by most West European armies which had far-reaching implications where the handling of infantry in battle was concerned. But the armies of Louis XIV, after almost half a century of nigh unsullied success and martial predominance on the European scene, seem to have proved less willing to adopt tactical changes designed to make the most of the new possibilities than did their Anglo–Dutch rivals. Thus, if this can be reasonably established on the basis of contemporary evidence, a second point of some possible significance may emerge.

Primary sources for such an investigation, whether documentary or printed, present certain difficulties to the researcher. In every age – not least our own – it is necessary to regard official contemporary governmental pronouncements with the traditional 'pinch of salt' or scepticism, if not with downright suspicion. To cite a single example, concerning the establishment of a reasonably reliable date for the effective change-over from the pike-matchlock combination to the flintlock and socket bayonet – a matter of central significance to the main hypothesis under consideration – it is extremely dangerous to assume that action was taken within even a decade of the official recommendation. Thus, when James II formally ordered the re-equipment of the 4th Foot (today the King's Own Royal Border Regiment) with the snaphance firelock in the year 1685, this did not, it would appear, lead to a speedy issue of the improved weapon. Indeed, as Colonel Cowper, the historian of the King's Own pointed out, 'there is ample evidence that orders to rearm the army were not carried out, and in 1704 the arms of the Regiment were reported to be all of 24 years old'[3] – dating, therefore, from 1680.

It is consequently very difficult to even hazard an informed guess as to when the English army was completely re-equipped with the improved weaponry, and even more so to arrive at any conclusion as to the date by which any degree of consistency was achieved in tactical training methods. In an age when Regiments were still very much regarded as their Colonel's possessions and financial investments (or, more often, their financial liabilities), a few of the wealthier commanding officers bought better weapons for their men to suit their whims, and similarly adapted the training they ordered their Majors to supervise according to their personal preferences. There is considerable evidence that numbers of drill-books which claim 'appointment to His Grace the Duke of Marlborough for use in the Regiments of Foot' were in fact little more than optimistic literary effusions by enthusiasts and cranks who hoped that their unsponsored recommendations might eventually earn wider recognition and adoption.

It would be equally fallacious to believe that the publication date of a particular drill-book bore any relation to the military tactical practices in use that year. Very often the evidence they present is retrospective, and consequently needs handling with circumspection. Thus *The Military Discipline; or the Art of War*,[4] published in 1689, must be cautiously regarded as – at least in part – a description of the methods in use as much as ten to twenty years earlier, a fair indication being provided in this case by the fact that it is labelled as a 'second edition', although embellished, the anonymous 'Captain J S' assures us, 'with many additions and corrections'. Instances of bare-faced plagiarism can also be cited. The Chevalier Folard, for example, claimed to have discovered in the French Royal Library an early seventeenth-century German drill-book, which was subsequently copied word for word (in translation) by the supposed French authority Lostelneau, whose *Le Maréchal de Bataille*, first published in 1647, was regarded as the standard authoritative work, the very epitome of 'modern' French military thought and tactical practice, until almost the 1690s. Considerable care, therefore, has to be exercised in placing reliance on such authorities.

Nevertheless, despite these obstacles and pitfalls, it is possible to infer a number of supportable conclusions from such sources by cross-checking their claims against the evidence of unbiased chroniclers with no particular axe to grind, and from prosaic but essential material as the arms-issue records of the Board of Ordnance and other day-to-day contemporary documentation.

As a starting-point, it is necessary to establish the type of tactics in use during the campaigns of King William III. The Allied army that fought in the Low Countries with such scant success between 1689 and 1697 was the product of two semi-distinct traditions or sources of military development. On the one hand, William was the Captain-General of the Dutch forces which he had commanded since the crisis of 1672. There is some evidence that his period of command saw great improvements introduced in the Dutch infantry arm. The famous statesman de Witt had shamefully neglected the Dutch land forces during the years leading up to the crisis of 1672, and there is little surprise that their showing in that year left something to be desired. By 1690, however, a great improvement had been achieved. William's major opponent, Marshal Luxembourg, declared that Prince Waldeck '. . . has every reason to be proud of his infantry'[5] on the basis of their showing at the Battle of Fleurus. His good opinion was corroborated, from the Allied side, by the Count of Mérode-Westerloo:

You cannot conceive the difference there was in the Dutch infantry during this war, compared to that of the year 1672, when my father was sent to their aid. At that time they were truly miserable troops, and the King of England has himself told me that it was after the methods, exercise and good order of my father's fine and good regiment that he formed his infantry, reforms which the Rhinegrave had begun to work upon before his wounding at Maastricht and subsequent death at Petersheim. Nevertheless, the Prince of Waldeck deserves the real credit for perfecting this transformation.[6]

The type of drill and tactical exercise employed by Dutch infantry during the Nine Years War is probably reflected in the first military publication following the Glorious Revolution of 1688, namely *the General Exercise ordered by his Highness the Prince of Orange to be punctually observed by all the infantry in service of the States General of the United Provinces . . .* etc., reprinted in English translation in 1689.[7] From this document it would seem that the generality of troops in the Dutch pay were still armed in the habitual proportion of one pike to five matchlock muskets, except for the grenadiers who are mentioned as being armed with the 'firelock and dagger' (or plug-bayonet). Subsequent drill-books issued in 1690 and 1696,[8] although designated 'by Their Majesties' Command' respectively* are practically identical with the earlier publication, expanding certain aspects and referring to the 'bayonet' and not the 'dagger'. None of these sources, however, describes the actual tactical forms adopted, and for these we have to look elsewhere.

This is where we meet the second military tradition represented in William's armies after 1688, namely the French-based military exercise as employed by James II's army immediately before the Glorious Revolution. In this context, two volumes are of distinct importance: *Le Major Parfait* by F Demorinet, a manuscript in French inscribed in another hand 'this did belong to King James. I had it from Coll. Grahame', and dated 1686;[9] and the second edition of Robert Morden's *Military Discipline* of 1689. Both these sources give considerable amounts of detailed information on tactical forms, and may cautiously be accepted as reflecting between them contemporary (or nearly so) French, English and Dutch practice, as so many of the drill and exercise sequences are identical to those published in the *General Exercise* of 1689.

Demorinet includes the following description of battalion fire-action:

The best way of firing is by ranks when it is desired to fire in line, parallel to the foe. To do this, and to fire without embarrassment, it is

---

* The variation of title is due to the dual monarchy of William III and Mary II which lasted until Queen Mary's death in January 1695.

best to fire at the halt without making any move except that needed to make the first five ranks kneel on the ground; and the sixth is that which makes first its fire, the fifth then doing the same and the rest consecutively.[10]

In other words the battalion drew up six deep, pikes in the centre, musketeers on the flanks, the grenadier company (if any) drawn up a little apart on the extreme right. Fire was then given in the manner described. Morden, in *Military Discipline*, distinguishes between several types of fire. Under the heading 'Directions of the several ways of firing' he lists methods employed 'in keeping the ground', 'of firing to the rear', 'of firing to the flanks', 'of firing the street way', etc., which demonstrate a considerable degree of tactical flexibility within certain limits. For example:

> In keeping the ground: this way of firing may be performed either by two ranks at a time, or three ranks; the first kneeling, and the second stooping, or else thus. 'Musketeers make ready all' . . . 'the first five ranks kneel', 'the rear rank Present, Fire', 'Fifth rank stand up, present Fire!'[11]

When the battalion made fire 'gaining ground', each rank would fire in turn, starting with the first, which would immediately thereafter 'file off to the right and left into the Rear'. These regulations also describe the 'reduction', whereby the musketeers formed three instead of six ranks, the rearward files moving into the intervals to their front to form a compact body. 'Grenadiers' (sic) were divided into three groups, one taking post at each extremity of the battalion line, the third drawing up before the pikes in the centre. Most of these basic methods of fire and movement are also to be found described in the historical sections relating to the methods used in 1688 and 1697 of Puységur's famous *Art de la Guerre* published after the author's death in 1748, so the link with the predominant French techniques of the period is fairly established, at least circumstantially.[12] Indeed, the publisher of *Military Discipline* refers in his Preface to 'the most useful parts out of Mr. Mallet, a Book dedicated to the King of France'. These tactical concepts also remained the standard French practice until at least 1708, if Puységur is to be credited, and only the rude shocks administered by such heavy defeats as Blenheim, Ramillies and Oudenarde shook French complacency and inspired changes along the broad lines of methods already employed by their Anglo–Dutch opponents. The older methods, although well-suited to the characteristics of battalions equipped with matchlocks and pikes in a proportion of 5:1, did not exploit sufficiently the higher firepower potential of units equipped with the next generation of weapons, which most armies, including the French, possessed in fair numbers by 1703.

It is noteworthy that in none of the late seventeenth century drill-books so far cited is there any mention of the flintlock musket fitted with socket bayonet, the replacement of the proportion of pikes by firearms, or of the employment of fire by platoons. There are, however, some indications that such weapons or methods were at least being experimented with on a small scale, or under development. The socket bayonet was probably invented by Vauban in 1687, although General Mackay is sometimes credited with this innovation in 1689, shortly after his defeat at the Battle of Killiekrankie at the hands of Dundee, where the royal troops, after giving fire, were overwhelmed by the charging Highlanders '. . . before our men could come to the second defence, which is the bayonet in the musle [sic] of the musket'.[13] Clearly the socket bayonet was a considerable improvement on both its predecessors – the plug and ring varieties. Some socket bayonets were certainly issued to French Guards formations in 1688, but general re-equipment with the weapon was only completed in the first years of the eighteenth century.

English grenadier companies appear to have received socket bayonets as early as 1689 in certain instances,[14] but it was not until 1702 that the 'ancient and puissant pike', which Marshal d'Artagnan deemed 'the Queen of Weapons', was officially superceded and withdrawn. Even then the rate of replacement was very uncertain, and we find the Board of Ordnance advising five colonels under orders to cross the Irish Sea that '. . . this is not to hinder you carrying your pikes to Ireland in case muskets be not time enough delivered to you'[15] – clearly a case of demand outstripping supply.

As for the flintlock musket, limited supplies of an early version, the 'snaphance', were available from the seventeenth century if not earlier, but the matchlock remained the standard English Army firearm well into the 1690s in a proportion of at least 3:2.[16] The basic reason would seem to have been one of economy, governments preferring to continue to issue outdated but available weapons rather than incur the expense of procuring large numbers of improved replacements. Thus the flintlock 'fusil', although well known in England long before 1660, was not widely issued to troops before 1704, when 'the new musket and bayonet' was issued to the line companies as well as to grenadiers.

The very first English troops to receive the 'fusil' would appear to have been the North British Fusiliers (raised in 1678), whilst the reign of James II saw the raising of the Royal Fusiliers (1685) and another formation that became the Royal Welsh Fusiliers three years later. These units seem to have been the only ones in the English Army to receive a complete consignment of flintlocks before 1689, despite King James's declared intention of implementing the wholesale 'adoption of flintlock muskets with all despatch possible within the confines of the appropriate funds'.[17] In the last phrase indubitably lay the rub.

It seems that the regiments of the United Provinces and other continental armies were generally more fortunate in this respect than the English for, following the Glorious Revolution, William was so horrified by the obsolescence of English arms that for three years he authorised the importation of every type of surplus snaphance from Holland and Germany in the most haphazard fashion, although many of these weapons in turn proved unsatisfactory, having rotten stocks or rusted barrels. Only from 1691, when the King entrusted the Gunmakers Company of the City of London with supervising the quality control of future overseas purchases, did the situation materially improve. As late as 1697 the Storekeeper of the Ordnance was still arranging payment for large quantities of Dutch firearms needed to equip English regiments. We can therefore conclude that a fair proportion of William's English troops continued to use pikes, matchlocks and snaphances until at least 1697, but that the majority of Marlborough's men were re-equipped with flintlock-fusils and socket bayonet by 1704.

Even this broad conclusion requires modification where bayonets were concerned, for as late as 1706 Lord Kerr proved incapable of procuring the socket variety from a niggardly and cost-conscious Board of Ordnance, which replied to his repeated requests for sufficient bayonets to replace the withdrawn pikes as follows:

All regiments raised since the disuse of pikes have provided bayonets as they do swords and belts at their own charge . . . few of the officers agree on the sort of bayonet fitt to be used, or on the manner of fitting them to the muskets, as may appear by the various sorts there are of them in the Army.[18]

Indeed, it would seem that varieties of weaponry remained on issue to British regiments, based upon availability and the whims of individual colonels, for a considerable further period, and only in the 1720s was a genuine degree of standardisation achieved with the issue in quantity of the first genuine 'Brown Bess' tower muskets to replace the King William land-musket of various types. Nevertheless, on balance, it would appear that Marlborough's infantry were somewhat better equipped than William's soldiery.

There is also considerable evidence that Marlborough's battalions had a more sophisticated tactical system than either William III's, or the French armies. It is almost impossible to trace the real origins of the platoon-firing system with any certainty. Le Blond, writing in the 1750s, considered that 'Fire by platoon . . . has long been in use amongst the Dutch; there is some evidence that its invention is due to them, and that they furnished the model for the other nations of Europe which have copied it'.[19] This conjecture is supported to some extent by the enquiry made of William

1. John Churchill, 1st Duke of Marlborough (c1690, as a younger man)

2. William III, probably painted after his victory in Ireland at the Battle of the Boyne

3. Louis XIV, the Sun King

4. An allegorical portrait
of Queen Anne c1704

5. Prince Eugene
of Savoy

6. Louis Duras, Earl of Feversham commanded royal forces at Sedgemoor

7. James II

8. Sebastien Le Prestre, Marshal Vauban

9. Camille d'Hostun, Marshal Tallard

10. Lord Cutts by R Williams after William Wissing

11. Comte de Mérode-Westerloo commanded Tallard's 2nd Line Cavalry at Blenheim

12. William Cadogan by Louis Laguerre

13. Henry of Nassau, Count Overkirk

14. Contemporary depiction of the Allied assault on the Schellenberg.

15. Donauwörth from the Schellenberg slopes

16. The plain of Höchstädt. Looking east from the French position to the Nebel Stream

17. Looking east, Unterglau from across the Nebel Stream

18. The Duke of Marlborough at Blenheim

19. The column of victory in the grounds of Blenheim Palace

Blathwayt, Secretary-at-War, by the Earl of Marlborough (newly appointed to command the English troops sent over into Flanders in 1689):

> I desire that you will know the King's pleasure whether he will have the Regiments of Foot learn the Duch [sic] exercise, or else to continue the English, for if he will I must have it translated into English.[20]

This at least shows that the English forces up to that date were not following the Dutch form; as we have already seen, it is far more probable that they had hitherto copied French concepts in view of the close association with France during the reigns of Charles II and James II. However, the Dutch claim to have originated the platoon-firings is not unchallenged, and there is a school of thought that believes that firing by platoons dates back to the Swedish armies of Gustavus Adolphus. It would certainly appear that a form of this tactic was employed at Breitenfeld (1631) where Hepburn's Scottish Brigade served with distinction. 'the first time that platoon firing had been done ... it utterly confounded Tilly's army',[21] but it would seem that Charles XII's Swedish veterans had changed or reverted to a substantially different form of fire-drill by 1708.

There were many variations of platoon-firing, and it is clear that the system developed over a considerable number of years rather than appearing all at once. It was certainly known to William III, but to what extent it was adopted in his time is uncertain. Marlborough and his generals thought particularly highly of it, and actively encouraged its widespread adoption throughout their infantry in place of all other firing methods, and accordingly the description that follows, based upon Brigadier-General Kane's celebrated *Exercise for the Foot* can be said to represent the standard English usage.[22] The change-over to the superior weapons already described would also suggest an increased efficiency for the method in the early eighteenth century. In the first place, the battalion or regiment took the field and drew up into line in a predetermined order of companies. The Colonel's company and that of the second-in-command invariably formed the centre of the line, whilst the remaining ten companies deployed to the left and right of the central nucleus in strict order of seniority of their captains. The grenadier company (which habitually marched at the head of the formation when in column of the route) meantime divided into two equal bodies, one, under the captain, remaining on the extreme right of the line, the second, commanded by the senior lieutenant of Grenadiers, taking post on the extreme left. The whole battalion then reduced itself from six ranks to three, closing up to half distance (one and a half pace intervals) in the process.

The major or adjutant next proceeded to ride down the front, dividing the twelve line companies (though not the Grenadiers) into four 'Grand Divisions', and each of these groups in turn into four equal platoons. Thus a thirteen-company battalion was reorganised into a total of eighteen platoons – sixteen of them in the four 'Divisions', and two more of Grenadiers on the extreme flanks. This division into ad hoc platoons was only employed for fire-drill and actual fighting; on all other occasions the company was the administrative unit.

Next, the senior officers re-divided the platoons into at least three 'firings' – or groups of six platoons apiece. The Grand Divisions were of no significance in this respect, for the platoons told off for each separate 'firing' were interspersed down the whole line in a carefully prearranged order so as to achieve continuity of fire from every part of the battalion line. Each platoon would then load or check their priming before moving into close order (one foot intervals) whilst the sergeants took up their supervisory positions in the intervals between them. The company officers took post either in front of the sergeants or four paces to the rear of the line; the colonel stationed himself and his drummer some seven paces in front of the colour party (placed exactly in the centre); the lieutenant-colonel positioned himself some ten paces *behind* the line (so as to be in a position to see everything and be ready to take over command in the event of the commander being killed or wounded), the major and adjutant moved out onto the extremities of the regiment. The remaining drummers meantime drew up behind the centre, the right and the left wings in three groups.

The battalion was now ready to advance against the enemy. All knapsacks, tentpoles and other impediments would have been sent to the rear. 'If we win the Day, they will be safe; if not, 'tis no matter what becomes of them', comments Brigadier-General William Kane. On the colonel's order, the line then marched steadily forward until it came to about sixty paces from the enemy, whereupon it halted.

On the order 'First Firing, Take Care!' (or a ruffle on the drums), the six platoons of the first firing and the *whole* of the front rank made ready to fire. The first rank knelt, whilst the remaining two ranks of the dispersed platoons of the first firing marched into close order and 'locked'. To do this each man placed himself with his left shoulder towards the enemy, and placed his extended left foot close behind the rearward-pointing right foot of the soldier to his front. The effect of this was to ensure that every man's musket-barrel at the present was clear of the soldier in front. This sensible precaution was not practised in the French Army, where the men in the files drew up immediately behind one another. This meant that at most only three ranks could fire – the first kneeling, the second crouching, the third standing upright, when a battalion volley was ordered – whilst the damage to French heads and collar-bones caused by the fierce kick of their discharged pieces caused considerable comment in contemporary medical circles. But this is to digress slightly.

On a further order (or a flan on the drums), the troops of the first regiments in the early eighteenth century were habitually trained to discharge their pieces one platoon at a time in a pre-set order, thus producing a rippling fire effect down the line. Many officers, however, including both Kane and Captain Robert Parker, came to regard this as a procedure more suited for Hyde Park or the review-ground then the battlefield, and insisted that all the six platoons of the first firing should discharge their pieces together on the colonel's single order. As they were not responsible for timing the exact moment of their platoon's discharge, this enabled the platoon officers to devote all their attention to supervising their men, ensuring with the aid of their spontoons and the sergeant's halberts or half-pikes that all the musket barrels were properly aligned, pointing at the enemies' stomachs.

Immediately after the first 'firing', the platoons concerned would open order march and start to reload, whilst the second and third firings took up the shooting in turn if the commanding officer so ordained. If the enemy still held his ground, the process could be repeated indefinitely, and a well trained battalion could get off two sets of three firings in a minute. It should be noted that the 'Third Firing' was slightly different from the earlier ones in that the grenadier platoons on the flanks wheeled slightly inwards to pour their fire into the mass of the enemy battalion, whilst the two central platoons aimed exclusively at the centre of the enemy's line in the hope of disabling their commanders.

Captain Robert Parker has left a description of a fire-fight between the Royal Regiment of Foot of Ireland and an equivalent unit in the French service at the Battle of Malplaquet (1709), which clearly shows the advantages conferred by the English firing system over that preferred by their opponents. It also reveals the inaccuracy of the muskets of those days if we consider the number of casualties suffered by each side in this representative action.

We continued marching slowly on, till we came to an opening in the wood. It was a small plain, on the opposite side of which we perceived a battalion of the enemy drawn up, a skirt of the wood being in the rear of them. Upon this Colonel Kane, who was then at the head of the Regiment, having drawn us up, and formed our platoons, advanced gently towards them, with the six platoons of our first fire made ready. When we had advanced within a hundred paces of them, they gave us a fire of one of their ranks: whereupon we halted, and returned them the fire of our six platoons at once; and immediately made ready the six platoons of our second fire, and advanced upon them again. They then gave us the fire of another rank, and we returned them a second fire, which made them shrink; however they gave us the fire of a third rank after a scattering manner, and then retired into the wood in great disorder: on which we sent our third fire after them, and saw them no more. We advanced cautiously up to the ground which they had quitted, and found several of them killed and wounded . . . We had but four men killed, and six wounded: and found near forty of them on the spot killed and wounded.[23]

Here, if ever, was a test-case of the platoon firing system. Parker goes on to attribute the success to the heavier one-ounce musket balls favoured by the English at this period and to the fact that 'the French at that time fired all by ranks, which can never do equal execution with our platoon-firing, especially when six platoons are fired together. This is undoubtedly the best method that has yet been discovered for fighting a battalion; especially when two battalions only engage each other'. Nevertheless, some 600 British bullets only accounted for forty opponents – although presumably many French/Irish wounded capable of walking evacuated into the woodland and were not included in Parker's estimate.

As has already been remarked, there were considerable numbers of variations of this method in use at different times and places. Besides the 'rippling' fire within the firings, many commanding officers chose to extemporise a 'fourth Firing'. This was done by reserving the fire of the entire first rank, the kneeling men being ordered to 'drop their Muzzles to the Ground', whilst the second and third ranks fired over their heads at their appointed moment. The front rank's fire could then be given when the colonel considered it best. This never applied to the two centre platoons, however; they invariably fired all three ranks together, the reason being the security of the colonel who had to move smartly to and fro to avoid being injured by these two platoons' volleys.

To summarise the advantages conferred by the platoon-firing system described above, it should be pointed out that these were principally threefold. First, the sub-division of formations into platoons greatly facilitated the degree of fire control that could be maintained by the officers and NCOs; this in turn led to more accurate shooting and better discipline than was possible when a complete rank – or even three ranks – fired off all at once, as was the favourite practice in the French forces. Secondly, the three or more firings ensured that the enemy was under concentrated and almost continuous fire once the action opened; there was no let up, and the psychological effects of this on the recipients at under 100 yards range should not be underrated; furthermore, the 'fire by line' school were only too well aware that fire by ranks was extremely difficult to make continuous, but their retention (in some cases at least) of five-deep formations undoubtedly wasted a great deal of fire potential. Thirdly, one third of a British battalion would always be loaded, and thus ready to deal with any sudden emergency; at no time would the formation – or any single sector of it – be wholly unprepared, for at least one platoon in every three all down the line would be reloaded at any given moment.

One further practice shared by England and many other continental powers (though not France until the 1740s) linked with fighting their infantry battalions deserves notice – namely the attachment of two light field pieces (usually one-and-a-half and 3-pounders) to each battalion for the provision of close fire support. This was not an innovation on the part of Marlborough personally, although he probably improved its implementation. Once again it was almost certainly a Swedish development of the 1630s, for Gustavus Adolphus had attached 'leather-guns' to his brigades for this kind of purpose. In the English armies similar measures were adopted from c.1650, and James II certainly attached two 3-pounders to each of the seven battalions camped in Hyde Park in August 1686, entrusting them to the grenadier companies. Furthermore, there is clear evidence that William III took similar measures in support of his infantry in 1693, if not earlier. Whatever their true origins, the effectiveness of these tactical methods is hard to refute. Although the French clung obstinately to the earlier forms of tactics until about the time of Malplaquet, we find in 1706 King Louis XIV specifically ordering Marshal Villeroi '. . . to pay special attention to that part of the line which will endure the first shock of the English troops'.[24] Clearly the English battalions had made their mark. Ultimately, the French realised the need for reform, and introduced a very similar system. Puységur, who fought at Blenheim, writes of the introduction, in about 1711, of 'par division un feu continuel'[25] – in other words, one form of the platoon-firing system.

The drill-books that have survived from the Marlburian period reflect the new methods very clearly. The *New Exercise of Firelock and Bayonet appointed by His Grace the Duke of Marlborough to be used by all the British Forces* by an Officer of Her Majesty's Foot Guards, London, 1708,[26] is of importance on several counts. In the first place it confirms beyond all doubt that the pike had disappeared several years earlier. Secondly, it reveals a significant simplification in words of command and, far more important, in the length of the Exercise of the Evolutions. In the days of King William, the basic evolutions had comprised no fewer than 121 separate 'motions', as the drill-books of his day bear witness; now, a little over ten years later, these have been reduced to fifty-five. This simplification could only be for the better, and probably underlies the improved efficiency – and rate of fire – of the British infantry. A human touch is to be found on the final fly-leaf, where a *cri-de-coeur* of so many authors, ancient and modern, is recorded. 'The author being in the country when the sheets were printing, there are some mistakes – which the reader is desired to mend with a pen.'

The Officer of the Foot Guards does not go into detail about the tactical methods employed, but useful evidence in this direction is to be found in *Captain John Foster – His Book* (1712), where we find the following under the heading: 'A Method how to draw up a battalion fit to receive an enemy':

Divide them into fifteen platoons (including Grenadiers), making three fires, six for the first, six for the second, the Grenadiers on left, right and the centre platoons for the third, taking all firings from left to right.[27]

In other words, at this time the fire was often delivered by a scatter of platoons firing in a predetermined order, rather than always by complete divisions or 'firings' at a time. It is clear from this source, and from *The Exercise for the Horse, Dragoons and Foot Forces, G.II R.* (2nd edition, London, 1739)[28] (indubitably compiled by soldiers of Marlburian experience), that battalions still paraded six ranks deep, but invariably 'reduced' to three for action. But one other interesting point in Captain John Foster is his reference (on the whole commendatory) to 'The Evolution to that explained in King William's *Book of Exercise*', which seems to show that the older drill-books were still in at least partial use.

It is thought that sufficient evidence has been produced to show that the infantry firing methods – and weapons – of Marlborough's day were superior to those of King William, and to those of the French Army until after 1709. Here, in all probability, resides one secret of the greatly improved success enjoyed by British arms on the battlefield during the first eight years of the War of the Spanish Succession. The methods evolved during this period – and probably earlier – remained in vogue for almost fifty years, for we read in General Wolfe's *Instructions to Young Officers etc.* that 'the firing of the infantry shall begin by platoons, followed by that of sub-divisions, then by grand-divisions as they approach nearer and nearer to the enemy'.[29] It was not until the staggering reverses suffered by General Braddock at the hands of Indians and French *colons* in 1755, and of later commanders at the hands of the American rebels, that a fresh look was taken at tactical method. Just as the French 'fire-by-line' system of their great years, 1643–97, induced a reluctance to adopt changes in weapons and tactics in their forces, so in turn did the victorious British become stereotyped in their ideas. Here, surely, lies one of the major lessons of military history – the crucial necessity of continually adapting military methods to meet new circumstances.

NOTES

1   The *Encyclopaedia Britannica*, Vol. XXIII, p. 617.
2   Captain R Parker (ed. D G Chandler), *Memoirs of the most remarkable Military Transactions…1683–1718*, London, 1968, p. 125.
3   L I Cowper, *The King's Own: The History of a Royal Regiment*, Oxford, 1936, Vol. I, p. 468.
4   R Morden, *Military Discipline; or the Art of War…*, Cornhill, 1689 (MoD Library).
5   Add. Mss 9723 (Blathwayt Mss), folio 7 (BM).

6   Le Comte de Mérode-Westerloo (ed. D G Chandler, London, 1968), *Mémoires*, Brussels, 1840, p. 68.
7   Ministry of Defence Library (Central & Army), London.
8   *The Exercise of the Foot, with the Evolutions*, London, 1690 (2nd edn, 1696).
9   Add. Mss 4655 (Harl.) (BM).
10 *Ibid.*, folio 43.
11 Morden, *op. cit.*, p. 70 & ff.
12 Maréchal de Puységur, *L'Art de la Guerre…*, Paris, 1748, Chapters 6, 7 & 9–11.
13 H Mackay, *Memoirs, Letters and Short Relations*, Edinburgh, 1833, p. 52.
14 See Cowper, *op. cit.*, I, Appendix, p. 469; Puységur, *op. cit.*, I, p. 72.
15 Add. Mss 745–65 (Harl.): 'Summary of Arms in Use 1687–91' (BM).
16 State Papers 44/172 (PRO).
17 Cited in R Held, *The Age of Firearms*, London, 1957, p. 111.
18 H L Blackmore, *British Military Firearms 1650–1850*, London, 1961, p. 42.
19 M le Blond, *Elemens de Tactious*, Paris, 1758, pp. 405–6.
20 Add. Mss 9723, folio 7 (BM).
21 L Weaver, *The Story of the Royal Scots*, London (1915), citing Harte, *Life of Augustus Adolphus*.
22 R Kane, *Discipline for a Regiment of Foot upon Action…*, London, 1745, pp. 405–6.
23 Parker, *op. cit.*, pp. 88–9.
24 J Pelet and F de Vault, *Mémoires militaires relatifs à la succession d'Espagne sous Louis XIV*, Paris, 1850, Vol. VI, p. 19.
25 Puységur, *op. cit.*, I, p. 152.
26 Published by J Morphen, near Stationers' Hall, London, 1708.
27 Add. Mss 29477 (Hume Papers relating to Dulwich College), folio 107 (BM).
28 Published by J Bagshot, London (1st edn 1728; 2nd edn 1739).
29 2nd edn, published by J Millan, London, 1780, p. 55.

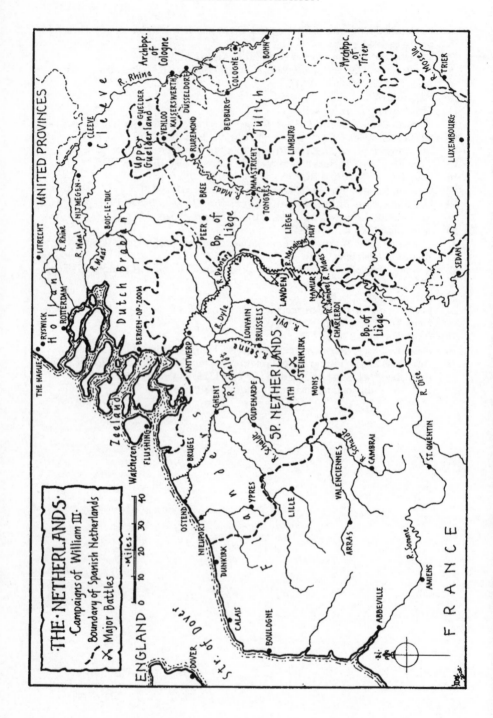

CHAPTER VII

The Guns

Field Artillery Trains 1689–97

King Louis XIV used to have the inscription 'Ultima Ratio Regis' (the final argument of the King) cast on his cannons. At this period the artillery were kept and controlled separately from the Horse and the Foot. This system had begun in the 1400s when kings kept their bombards as part of the 'royal wardrobe' – closely guarded in case any of their over-powerful magnates became a challenge. Gunners too were perceived as 'different' – private 'gentlemen of war' – as civilians with a martial function hired by the king for their specialist skills. When the British Parliament reduced the power of the monarch it was determined for economic and administrative reasons to keep these arrangements and the artillery remained 'away' from the rest of the army – hence the blue uniforms for the gunners rather than the red or scarlet which had become the basic English military uniform coat colour.

Gunners, and for very similar reasons the Engineers too, were controlled by the Ordnance officials. The Master-General of the Ordnance was a high official, but rarely had much contact with the senior commanders of the cavalry and infantry. Only when Marlborough merged the forces into a composite army around 1715, were the Foot, Horse, Guns and Trains fully combined administratively and tactically for war. However, they still retained 'marks of difference'. The artillery were proud of not having any formal colours because their cannon were for them the equivalent, but from 1695 there was a special standard placed in a socket on a gun-carriage. There was also a special drum-carriage drawn by six horses with two drivers which carried two very large drums played by one gunner-drummer.

The guns were difficult to move because of their weight, and as a result the march of an army was effectively controlled on campaign by the speed of the heaviest gun. As Serjeant Millner of the 18th Foot noted in his *Compendious Journal . . . 1701–1712* (1733), the true start and end of each campaign should be calculated from the dates the train of artillery set out from, or returned to, winter quarters, 'it being the metropolitan ensign of any army in time of war'.

The position of the English field artillery trains serving with William III's forces in Flanders during the Nine Years War was in many respects somewhat anomalous, and was to remain so until the founding of the Royal Regiment of Artillery in 1716.

The trains were probably the most significant part of all armed forces of the day, both in terms of the vital roles they fulfilled on campaign, and the disadvantages their inevitable presence within the armies conferred on the conduct of active operations. On the one hand, no general could risk the chances of a field engagement without the presence of most of his guns; on the other, nor could any serious siege be undertaken without the assistance of the heavy cannon. As Marlborough wrote urgently to Cadogan, charged with escorting the Great Convoy of guns and munitions from Brussels to Lille in August 1708: 'For God's sake be sure you do not risk the cannon.'[1]

Serjeant Millner, of the Royal Regiment of Foot of Ireland, stated in his *Compendious Journal* that he calculated the duration of campaigns from the time the train left winter quarters to the date of its return, 'it being the metropolitan ensign of any army in time of war'.[2] These two statements – albeit drawn from the history of the War of the Spanish Succession – serve to demonstrate the conviction of contemporary soldiers, from the highest to the lowest, that the trains had a large – even determinant – part to play in the conduct of warfare.

At the same time, however, the artillery trains of the period attracted storms of vilification and complaint from serving soldiers. The major objection was usually to their bulk and the slow rate of progress over the execrable roads of Europe, that they imposed on the rest of the army. William III's English train of 1692, for example, comprised thirty-eight brass cannon of varying sizes, and at least 240 four-horse waggons of munitions and ordnance stores (not to mention further vast numbers of baggage and supply waggons), and this was a relatively small affair by the standards of the time.[3]

Siege trains were inevitably far larger and slower; the one taken by Marshal Luxembourg to besiege Mons in 1691 included no fewer than 130 guns, 177 howitzers, and forty-four mortars.[4] William III's heavy train will be described later, but it was considerably smaller, while Marlborough's 'Great Convoy' of 1708 required 16,000 horses to draw its eighty heavy guns, twenty siege mortars, and 3,000 assorted munitions and stores waggons, and stretched along thirty miles of road in all.

Nevertheless, it should be noted that these siege trains normally moved separately from their parent armies, being called up from the rear once a particular siege had been settled on. And whenever possible they were moved by water in river barges or canal boats. Despite this, even the comparatively small trains of field artillery accompanying the infantry and cavalry columns could hopelessly hinder schemes of bold manoeuvre, and in unseasonable weather could bring all operations to a halt until conditions improved.[5]

Only a very few generals (such as Marlborough in May 1704) were prepared to abandon their larger pieces in order to gain superior mobility. Other causes of complaint stemmed from the fact that the guns and their attendants belonged to an entirely separate service – the Board of Ordnance, an institution that will be examined later in this chapter. The personnel – part military, part civilian – were on the whole better paid and clothed[6] than their envious and critical colleagues in the Horse and Foot, but this did not prevent acrimonious disputes within the complex organisation of the trains, whilst their record in action, particularly during the early stages of the Nine Years War, was often far from distinguished. They were constantly being accused of arriving late into action, though this was largely due to their being relegated to the rear of the army with the baggage trains. To sum up, it can be asserted that most commanders and their armies regarded the artillery trains as a considerable burden, although no doubt an indispensable one.

The purpose of this chapter is to examine the artillery services in existence under William III, with a view to explaining the gradual improvement in both organisational efficiency and general reputation that was accomplished between 1689 and 1697. The artillery trains that served with so much distinction under Marlborough in the succeeding war enjoyed a deservedly fine reputation, and often this is largely attributed to the Duke's personal intervention and influence as Master-General of the Ordnance (from 30 June 1702). While there is no denying that many reforms are directly due to his influence, the contributions of his immediate predecessors, in laying the sound foundations for later achievements, are often overlooked. This chapter, therefore, sets out to examine the record of William III's trains, taking into consideration the basic organisation (in England and Flanders) of the artillery services, the problems they were faced with, and the success with which they were tackled, with a view to establishing the point that the considerable improvement achieved in the Williamite trains was the unstated premise behind the even greater success of those serving under Marlborough.

At the outset, it is necessary to establish the condition of the trains William inherited from James II, to illustrate how truly abysmal the situation was. It was not so much a question of a lack of higher organisation (indeed, the true inception of the 'modern' Board of Ordnance dates from the Royal Warrant of 1683), but one of poor performance in the field and a general lack of *esprit de corps*.

The only occasion when James's train was put to the actual test of battle was at Sedgemoor in 1685. It was hardly an impressive performance. When Monmouth's rebels attacked the royal camp at Westonzoyland in the early hours of 6 July, the civilian drivers of the artillery teams immediately fled, and it was only thanks to the staunch activities of Dr Mew, Bishop of Winchester (who harnessed his coach-horses to the abandoned cannon) that the guns were brought into action at all. Their success in silencing Monmouth's three Dutch-served pieces was even then due more to the adaptability of some infantry soldiers who manned the guns – a Sergeant Weems of Dumbarton's Regiment later received a special grant in recognition of this service,[7] and we may premise that the gunners had followed the drivers into the misty darkness.

It is clear that Feversham held his gunners in low esteem, and even used their officers for odd staff tasks for, after the battle, the Master-Gunner, Henry Sheres, was moved to complain that he had been expected to carry out the functions of 'Secretary of War, Governor of Carriages, of Sick and Wounded, and a Commisary of Provisions', and that there had been 'no deference for the artillery as [is] practised in other armies.'[8] Three years later, with William of Orange's landing imminent, a new train was ordered into the field on 15 October 1688, comprising twenty-six guns in all, but it never went into service.[9] Following the Glorious Revolution, many of its senior officers disappeared from the establishment, but several junior officers entered William's service, including 'Engineer' Jacob Richards, 'Chief Bombardier' George Brown, and 'Captain of Pioneers' Holcroft Blood, all destined to play important parts in the developments in the artillery in later years.

Owing to the war in Ireland (1689–90), the proportion of the train sent to support the Dutch forces in Flanders was not at first very large, and no Warrant, giving details of what was sent across the Channel before 1691, seems to have survived. The odd letter has, however, suggesting that the showing of the Prussian and Hanoverian gunners was not very impressive. Reporting to Prince Waldeck on 27 June 1689, Colonel Goor reported that, despite the capture of Kaiserswerth:

> I must warn Your Highness that our artillery is very badly served. God knows what trouble I had to bring forward our batteries – although the Brandenburgers have been more advanced [exposed] than we – I waited two nights without advancing the trenches to await our batteries. Perhaps they need a man like the Captain who served the battery at Dusseldorf.[10]

William III was soon to echo these sentiments. He described his English artillery officers as 'ignorant, lazy and cowardly, and a week's easy work rendered the guns unserviceable',[11] and set about retrieving the situation by bringing in Dutch officers from Holland – including John Wynant Goor himself, summoned from Ireland to supervise the artillery in Flanders by Blathwayt's letter of 21 March.

112

This brief sketch must suffice to illustrate the general condition of the native artillery down to 1691. It was not, however, unique in its deficiencies. There was clearly room for improvement in all departments in the forces. On 18 September 1689 we find Waldeck reporting that 'the English suffer from sickness, temperament, nonchalance, wretched clothing and want of shoes', though 'the Earl of Marlboroy [sic] does his best.'[12]

To understand the organisation and standing of the English artillery during this period, it is necessary to describe certain aspects of its parent body, the redoubtable Board of Ordnance. This institution was virtually an independent organ of the State, and dated its modern format from the 'Instructions for the Government of our Office of Ordnance', issued on 25 July 1683,[13] and subsequently repromulgated with minor alterations by, in turn, James II,[14] William III and Queen Anne.

The Board was headed by the Master-General of the Ordnance, always a very important personage, assisted by five 'Principal Officers', most of whom, like the Master-General himself, were appointed under the Great Seal, their commissions bearing the signature of the Secretary of State.[15] Beneath these officials clustered a number of lesser luminaries, or 'Under Ministers' and 'Attendants', perhaps 160 in all, divided into fourteen categories, of which the most important were the 'Treasurer of our Ordnance' and the 'Secretary to the Master of our Ordnance', both of whom were often included in later lists among the 'Principal Officers' from 1685 onwards.

The scope of the Board's authority was truly vast, and included the provision of cannon for the Navy as well as for the Army (indeed, the first Master-Gunner of England was Captain Richard Leake RN), together with the thousand and one stores to make their employment effective.[16] Other defined duties were the provision of all engineering services, and the maintenance and repair of fortresses and barracks (these were the particular responsibility of the Surveyor-General), the finding of transport for the trains (under the Wagon-Master-General), the training and certificating of gunners (the Master-Gunner of England's charge), as well as the manufacture or supervision and testing of a whole range of weapons.

The Master-General was also responsible for myriad minor duties, from providing candles for Chelsea Hospital to arranging salutes of cannon and other celebrations on august occasions. For example, Colonel Richards was reimbursed to the tune of £30 on 2 November 1695 'on account of fireworks for His Majesty's Birthday in St James's Square or otherwise'.[17] The jealousy with which the Board guarded such minor prerogatives is illustrated by its protest in July 1708 to Boyle, the Secretary of State, who had been incautious enough to order the firing of the Tower ordnance in celebration of the victory of Oudenarde without prior consultation with the Master-General – who was, of course, the victorious general in Flanders – or, in his absence, with the Principal Officers.[18]

The powers vested in the Master-General and his officers were impressive. They were in no way subject to the normal military or naval authorities (except insofar as trains in the field were under the de facto command of the commander-in-chief), and indeed were only subordinate to the Treasury, the Auditions of Imprest for Accounting, and the Secretary of State for the issue of military equipment.[19] The Board also had a separate financial estimate before the Commons every year – and vast some of the nominal sums voted came to be. For example, for the year 1694, voted on 20 December 1695, the sum was £210,773–4s–5d for the 'extraordinary charge of the Office of Ordnance in relation to the land forces' (not, it should be noted, including expenditure for the Navy).[20]

Other powers of the Master-General included the direct commissioning of his Department's subordinate officers, and it is interesting to note that they were forbidden to buy or sell their commissions. This was a unique provision in the English forces of this period, and it is also interesting to record that this wise provision was abandoned by Louis XIV in 1703, when all offices in the French artillery services were put up for sale – and even made inheritable if the *droit de reversibilité* was paid.[21] It is possible, therefore, to surmise that this partly explains the rapid decline in the standards of the French artillery that set in from 1704.[22]

The most important of the 'Under Ministers' of the Ordnance from our point of view was the Master-Gunner of England (who received £190 p.a.). Under the general supervision of the Lieutenant-General of the Ordnance, he was charged with the following duties:

> To profess and teach his art at our under gunners in the exercise of shooting and great ordnance, mortar pieces, etc. in such publick places as by the Master of our Ordnance shall be allotted and appointed for that purpose, and there to exercise them once a month in winter and twice every month in summer . . .

He was also responsible for the certification of proficient gunners (receiving a handsome fee in return), for keeping a list of all gunners in pay, and for maintaining a register 'of all our great guns as well brass as iron belonging to any of our ships, forts, castles, blockhouses or garrisons'.[23]

This office was held by Sir Henry Sheres from 1688, and in October 1696 he was succeeded by the worthy George Brown Esq. The Master-Gunner was assisted by three mates (on £45–10s p.a.), a Firemaster (£150 p.a.), his mate (£80 p.a.), four Fireworkers (£50 p.a. each), two Proof-Masters (£20 p.a. a piece), and a peacetime establishment of sixty gunners (at 1/– and later 2/- a day).[24] In time of war, this number quadrupled, and additional classes of 'practicioner gunners' and mattrosses were added. This officer, then, was responsible for the training of the professional gunners, and had further duties relating to the preparation of trains for service overseas.

There do not appear to have been many major structural changes in this Board of Ordnance under Marlborough as Master-General (1702–12). There are, however, indications that he considerably improved its overall efficiency, by implementing all of James II's reforms (some of which had largely fallen into disuse after 1697, for want of any real army or artillery requirement), by keeping a close eye on the perquisites of junior officers and abrogating some of their privileges, and by encouraging his deputies to accept responsibility for decisions during his absences at the front.[25] Thus the Board seems to have operated in much the same way from 1683 to 1713, with only variations in efficiency truly distinguishable. The really vital changes that took place during this period related to the organisation of the trains in the field, and we must now turn to consider this subject.

The means by which a train of artillery was called into existence appear to have been applied consistently. The first step was the issue of a Warrant, signed by the Secretary of State on behalf of the monarch, and addressed to the Master-General or his deputy, warning him of the coming requirement. Thus, on 27 February 1691 we find Nottingham instructing the Lieutenant-General of the Ordnance, Sir Henry Goodricke (Schomberg being absent in Ireland), that a train is 'to be made ready' for Flanders, comprising eight brass demi-culverins[26] ten brass sakers, twenty brass 3-pounders, four 8 inch howitzers and two small petards.[27]

The same Warrant indicated the probable price of such provision: £2,114 for casting the pieces (if necessary), £39–6s–8d for the specified 560 rounds of case-shot[28] and £275–18s for 11,200 cannon-balls. It also mentioned that such a train would require '600 horses for Guns and Tin Boats', besides '200 waggons with 600 horses for stores', and a detachment of forty gunners and eighty matrosses. As time passed, further Warrants were issued to make good losses or expand the train's scale; for example, the 'Addition to the Flanders Train' of 5 March 1693/4, signed by Shrewsbury,[29] requiring the new Master-General, Henry, Viscount Sydney, to find sixty more cannon (thirty sakers, ten demi-culverins, twenty 3-pounders) and four howitzers 'to be forthwith provided and sent into Flanders for our future service'. The executive document, issued next day by Sydney, addressed to Colonel John Wynant Goor, is of the greatest importance at the organisational level, and we will return to it.[30]

The size of the demand was probably due to the losses sustained at Steinkirk (1692) and Landen (1693). On the first occasion, it would seem that the English artillery lost some eight cannon (though accounts differ), as well as several ammunition waggons.[31] On the second, Lieutenant-

Colonel Jacob Richards records that the Allies 'left the field, their artillery and what baggage they had with them, and retired over a small river that was in their rear . . .'[32] Richards gives no details of how many guns were lost, but most authorities cite eighty-four as the likely figure, although none indicates how many of these were actually of the English train. All the same, it appears very probable that overall losses on these two occasions fully justified the Issuing of the Warrant of 5 March 1693/4.

Fortunately documentation has survived that shows how accurately (or otherwise) these Warrants were executed. In a 'certified and true copy', dated 5 April 1692, all thirty-eight cannon demanded by Nottingham are listed in their correct quantities, although there is no mention of the howitzers.[33] The same document lists Richard Jacobs as Lieutenant-Colonel of the train under Colonel Goor, its commander, and Mr Meesters, the Controller (both Dutchmen, it should be noted). It would seem that the greater part of the original train reached Brill by mid-June, after suffering a great gale that drove six ships ashore.

There is also corroborative evidence regarding the implementation of the 'Addition' of the next spring but one. In his 'List of the English Artillery which was in the camp in the years 1694,5,6,7 in Flanders with the loadings of ye waggons, etc.'[34] Colonel Jacobs mentions the ten demi-culverins, thirty-six sakers, twenty 3-pounders and six howitzers (the surplus balance of sakers and howitzers presumably being the serviceable survivors of the debacles of 1691 and 1692). From this evidence, we can assert with reasonable confidence that William III's Board of Ordnance proved capable of meeting royal requirements at least in these instances. However, it must be added that it is well established that the Flanders front received the first priority in both William's and Marlborough's wars, in terms of both personnel and equipment, and that the same record of proficiency was not to be found in, for example, Spain (from 1703). Nevertheless, the Board was functioning capably as far as the supply of guns to Flanders was concerned, and that is our particular interest.

It is clear that the same procedures for producing a train for field service were in vogue in the succeeding reign. Thus, the 'Warrant for Holland', dated 14 March 1701/2 was the genesis of what became (in part) the 'Blenheim Train', calling for fourteen sakers, sixteen 3-pounders and four howitzers to be dispatched. This was subsequently reinforced by further Warrants dated 8 February 1702/3, 17 January 1703/4 (stores only), and 16 June 1704.[35] No distinctions, therefore, can be drawn in this respect.

A word must be inserted here concerning the siege trains of the period. All the pieces cited above have been of light calibre, and are consequently to be deemed field artillery (although the term was not used at the time). The heavier pieces required for siege warfare were kept separate from the ordinary army trains for reasons that have already been mentioned.

However, it is relevant to give details of William III's Siege (or 'Sea') train of 1693 for purposes of comparison.

In fact, the basic raising procedure differed not one jot. A Warrant of 28 February 1691/2 ordered Goodricke to create a second, heavier train, 'to be in readiness to be put on board such ships as shall be provided, to be employed in such service as we shall think fit', consisting of fourteen 24-pounders, sixteen 18-pounders, eight guns of 12, six of 6 and ten of 3 pounds, as well as eight 13 inch mortars, two of 10 inch and two 8 inch howitzers – some seventy-six pieces in all.[36]

It was to be commanded by Colonel Sir Martin Beckman, and its personnel as listed numbered 466 officers, soldiers, specialists and civilians, including the Master-Gunner of England, ninety-two gunners, as many mattrosses, and a tin-boat detachment, although specific provision was made for only 200 horses (the huge balance required to be made up, no doubt, by local contract). Only the 13 inch mortars were shipped straight to Ghent in 1692 – the rest being reserved, presumably, for sundry proposed sea expeditions. It was not until a further Warrant, dated 6 May 1693, was issued that the remaining guns (and a further ten of small calibre) actually reached Flanders. We may surmise that these were the pieces that reached Ostend with the Duke of Leinster on 1 September, which Richards subsequently saw 'within a small league of Ostend' on the 6th, when he 'met a great number of Well boats in which was all our Sea Trains and all the Stores of Warr belonging thereunto which were going to Nieuport'.[37] In view of what follows, it is appropriate to note that this siege train does not appear to have been organised into companies.

It is now necessary to examine the field train of 1693 in rather more detail, for this formation was in an important sense the prototype for those of the next fifty years.[38] The feature that distinguished it from all its English predecessors was its organisation on a *regimental* basis, in the sense that its components and personnel were deliberately and officially divided between a staff, four companies of artillery, and an unofficial one of 'Bridgemen or Tin-boat men'. Hitherto, this had never been the practice in the English trains, as an examination of the Ordnance establishments for Charles II, James II or the first years of William III will show.[39] In these instances, there was no formal attempt to organise the trains into sub-units, everybody of whatever rank or calling being set down in a single, lengthy list headed by the commander of the train and ended by the humble 'boys', sumpter men and drivers.

But now in the train of 1693, we suddenly find a far more sophisticated, handier and potentially more efficient organisation. It would seem that the trains were at last beginning to shed their hitherto predominantly civilian aspect and assume a more military appearance – a vital step towards the full recognition of this destined to lead to the creation of the Royal Regiment of Artillery in 1716.

117

At the head of the 1693 train we find a staff of twenty-six officers, civilians of officer status, clerks and assistants, including the 'Kettle-drummer, John Burnett' and 'his coachman, John Humphreys'.[40] As with the trains of 1691 and 1692, the four chief officers are the same – Colonel Goor in command, Mr Meesters as Comptroller, with Lieutenant-Colonel Jacob Richards as second-in-command, and Major John Rymond Schlundt (another Dutchman) as Major, aided by Daniel Cottin as Adjutant, and Ralph Wood as Quartermaster. The rest of headquarters consists of the Paymaster, Waggon-master, Auditor, Commissary of Horses (Daniel Coenen), a Chaplain, Surgeon, and Provost – most of them with their assistants.

Next we find the four Companies of Artillery, and by comparing two sources, we are able to form an accurate picture of their composition. The Warrant of 6 March 1692/3 gives the personnel; Jacob Richards' Journal (and the Ordnance lists of 30 March) provide the material.[41] Each company comprised a Captain, two Lieutenants, two Gentlemen of the Ordnance (in whose charge the guns were, except in battle), four sergeants, thirty-six gunners, four corporals of matrosses and fifty-six matrosses apiece – or five officers (two of them civilians), eight NCOs and ninety-two other ranks.

The First Company (Captain George Leslie) included ten demi-culverins and two sakers, and had attached to it the 'warning-piece waggon', a signal gun used for sounding alarms or other signals, such as the daily 'setting the watch, and seventeen waggons carrying sixty barrels of powder, six bundles of match, 1,090 round and 220 'partridge' (i.e. canister) shot, six hair-cloths and eleven ball boxes.

The Second Company (Captain Abraham Decock) escorted eighteen sakers with eighteen waggons, ninety barrels of powder, nine bundles of match, 1,280 round and 280 of 'partridge' shot, eight cloths and ball-boxes. The Fourth (Captain Leonard Vanderstam) was entrusted with the twenty 3-pounders, which were distributed to the infantry brigades before battle,[42] ten waggons, fifty barrels of powder, five bundles of match, 1,670 rounds of ball and 200 of 'partridge', five hair-cloths and five boxes.

The howitzers were placed 'in care of the firemaster' accompanied by eight waggons, but were not formally listed as a company, though his command probably comprised ten fireworkers and a dozen bombardiers, besides a deputy. The 'Tin-men' on the other hand had a quasi-official organisation, with two captains, one lieutenant, four corporals, fifty private men ('ten included to be English watermen'), a master tinman and two assistants, escorting fifty tin boats, each on its own special waggon.

In addition, the train of 1693 conveyed large amounts of ammunition and other stores for the craftsmen, who made up the remainder of the specialist personnel (carpenters, wheelwrights, smiths and collar-makers) and for the army as a whole – this being an important ancillary duty of the trains.[43] This involved a further eighty waggons for the Infantry carrying eighty barrels of powder and 6,400 spare flints, *inter alia*, twenty for the cavalry and dragoons, ten more for hand grenades, twenty-one filled with entrenching tools, nineteen with 'hand tools' (spades, picks, axes, etc.), one waggon per artificer with special stores, four in reserve for spare kit (including nails and lanterns), not forgetting sixty 'Tumbrells laden with ammunition for regiments in English pay' (containing a total of 180 powder barrels, 240 barrels of ball ammunition at 16 and 18 to the pound, sixty bundles of match, and 30,000 flints), and lastly 'Two waggons', one containing the Church tent and the Guard tent, the other the marquee and other tents for the officers' mess, a total of eleven tents, 800 yards of rope 'to surround the park', seventy pickets and two large mallets.

In other words, the train took with it 240 waggons of munitions (only seventy of them being directly concerned with the artillery as such), along with a further fifty-two waggons of specialist stores and the thirty boat-waggons, and comprised a total of 675 officers and men, besides drivers and boys.[44] With no fewer than 982 barrels of gunpowder habitually in the Parks, it is hardly surprising that harsh penalties were imposed for the least infringement of bounds within its vicinity, such as befell Mattross Berry Blackbourne, who was whipped by the hangman and branded on the hand and discharged for stealing powder 'by cutting small slits in some of the barrels'. This exploit might have cost him his life.[45] Enemy incendiaries caught near the trains were burnt to death – as happened, on one occasion, in 1692.

This type of train organisation – especially the company organisation of the artillery component – was henceforth standard practice for the field trains (although not, it would seem, for the siege trains). The greatly reduced 'Peace Train', instituted in May 1698 (originally four companies strong, but within six months all but disbanded by a penny-pinching Parliament), retained the same broad lines,[46] and with the outbreak of the War of the Spanish Succession, the first 'Holland Train' sent to Flanders by Queen Anne (ordered 14 March 1702) at an estimated cost of £70,973–13s–9d, consisted of a staff and two companies (each with three officers, six NCOs and fifty other ranks), plus (for the first time actually described as such) 'a Company of Pioneers' – two sergeants and twenty pioneers, and 'a Company of Pontoon Men' – namely a Bridge-master, two corporals and twenty pontoon men.[47]

This train was equipped with fourteen sakers, sixteen 3-pounders and four howitzers. It was subsequently considerably expanded (for example, in 1703, by the addition of six demi-culverins, but still retaining a two-company organisation). Thus, it can fairly be claimed that Marlborough received his artillery organisation ready fashioned from the later years of the previous war, and was not concerned directly with even the minor improvements in the first Holland Train of 1702 – his appointment as

Master-General only dated from 30 June of that year, though no doubt he was consulted about likely alterations.

As will be seen from the final section of this chapter, which is devoted to the specific problems and difficulties of actual service in the field, Marlborough's contribution affected many points of detail that eased the day-to-day working of the trains. This is not to belittle his efforts or beneficial influence, but the assumption must be made that he worked on firm foundations, inherited from his predecessors of 'King William's War'.

As will have become apparent, every field train comprised three main sections: the artillery, the engineers and specialist workers, and Ordnance stores. Each will be considered in turn, highlighting some of the problems associated with effective operation, and suggesting what reforms were implemented in an attempt to ameliorate them.

The first problem was common to all parts of the train, and lasted well into the eighteenth century. This was the constant friction between the military, quasi-military and civilian personnel. This curious mixture was to be found in all the branches. Some of the 'fighting' officers of the artillery and not a few of the engineers were serving officers drawn in from the line infantry regiments, and they tended to be scornful of colleagues holding the Master-General's commissions. Many disputes arose over relative status and authority. Indeed these extended to the highest officer in the Ordnance, for it required a special royal pronouncement to fix the Master-General's status as 'the most junior of our Lieutenant-Generals' in 1683.[48]

Secondly, there was considerable trouble between these elements and the civilians who dominated the supply and transport echelons as well as the specialist services. The drivers of the waggons were probably the most intractable. As most of them were recruited locally with their horses and carts, there is some excuse for this, but they represented a real martial hazard. The drivers at Steinkirk clearly emulated their colleagues at Sedgemoor – Richards recalled that the ammunition waggons were lost at the close of the day 'through the fears and neglect of the carters' whose panic led to 'some ammunition waggons [being] overset which we ourselves afterwards burned'.[49]

Controlling these unreliable elements seem to have driven long-suffering Colonel Goor to near despair, for we read:

> that a representation be made to his Lordship [the Master-General] of the want of a Comptroller upon the place to look after the civill part of the Train in Flanders, Colonel Goor now absolutely refusing to concern himself therewith – that some fitting person may be sent over for want thereof his Majesty's affairs suffer daily.[50]

If we may judge from the pictorial representation of Wynendael (1708) at Blenheim Palace, it would appear that the same problems were present under Marlborough – the tapestry clearly depicts a recalcitrant driver being 'encouraged' by an infantry sergeant wielding a spontoon!

All these civilians were not, of course, subject to military law, though doubtless rough justice was meted out to them on many occasions. And even the men who helped to serve the guns in action do not appear to have been properly attested. Thus, Matrosse Blackbourne (whose case has already been referred to) escaped with his life after tampering with the powder 'because he had never had [the] Articles of War read to him, and his design was only to load his pistol'.[51]

The only effective remedy for this type of problem would be the militarisation of the services, but this was not achieved in either William's or Marlborough's day. However, the fact that Marlborough was often in a position to pay his unwilling drivers for their services in gold (as on the Blenheim march of 1704)[52] helped to secure greater efficiency and, at least to a limited extent, willingness.

On the other hand, the personnel of the trains – at least in the officer echelons – in many instances proved remarkably adaptable. There was much interchanging of roles, though what the true effect of this on specialist efficiency must have been is open to conjecture. Holcroft Blood, son of the Crown Jewels robber, was serving as 'commander of the King's Company of Engineers' and as 'Second Engineer of England' in 1696, but by 1704 had become Marlborough's senior gunner before Blenheim, and eventually reached the rank of Brigadier-General, with an infantry regiment of his own to boot.[53]

Jacob Richards himself led a similarly chameleon-like existence, being listed sometimes as a gunner, and sometimes as an engineer. The same was true of the officers of Marlborough's trains, as the celebrated case of Captain Richard King illustrates. Originally an officer of the Royal Scots Fusiliers, at the siege of Menin in 1706 he served in turn as controller of the train, conductor of the artillery, supervisor of rations and munitions; then, as an engineer, he directed trench-making before commanding the breaching battery in action. To cap it all, he then reverted to his original infantry role at the conclusion of the siege – all in the space of thirty-one short days![54] There must have been a considerable amount of ready talent available in the trains.

The problems of the artillery can be divided into two main types – those of movement and those of employment in action. With guns weighing at least three tons each, drawn by long strings of horses harnessed in tandem, and with difficult civilian drivers to contend with, it is amazing that they made any progress at all. Even in fine weather, movement was beset by difficulties. On 25 August 1692, for example, Richards recorded that 'the soile is the richest in these parts [near the Scheldt] so that the roads were not able to beare the great weight of our artillerie, which made our march very tedious and was the reason that the army was engaged before we could come up with them'.[55] (This proverbial lateness was the army's greatest complaint against the artillery.) In wet conditions, movement of the trains became hell on earth. The same informant gives a description of one such day which is worth quoting in full as it gives such a clear picture of what the gunners faced:

> The artillery was stirring before day but it was six of the clock before they got of the grownde being a verry wet morning. We marched off first the Dutch and Spanish followed ... The wether proved extremely wet and the Way so verry that the Army had cut our march. We lost our Guide for some time and when he came he turned us backwards [we can imagine with what an accompaniment of confusion and cursing] to Otibreigne a verry soft way. The entrance into the village for about 200 paces was not passable. We made the artillery to halt for above four houres, being forced to cutt a new way wh. we made of straw and fascines. We had then a great Hill to get up and bad way so that severall guns stuck, but the night comeing on we were forced to lye by the way on a great Hill. Most of the Dutch guns and all our waggons was left on the other syde of the Defile... Mr. Van Hill came from the King to order us to get up the pontoons (but it was impossible), if not to march up very early and joine the Army.

Eventually the trains did rejoin the main force, but only after being diverted next day along another route, 'wh. they did but it proved very bad ffor the Army had marched that way before'. Even then the tale of tribulation was not complete, for 'it was late before we gott our baggage, the Hanovers having cutt our way'. Still, in the end they reached camp, understandably thankful: 'We werre not a little glad after so fatiguing and tedious a march.'[56]

Until equipment could be redesigned and the guns made lighter, there was little that could be done to reduce this type of problem. Marlborough, however, made one valuable contribution when he insisted on the adoption of a light, two-wheeled cart with springs for much of the train transport. This was drawn by two horses and proved much handier than the huge six-wheeled, eight-horse 'tumbrills' used by many of his Allies and opponents. We know, for example, that Tallard's massive convoy of 6,000 waggons (of which 600 carried munitions and powder) took eight days to get through the relatively short passes in the Black Forest in July 1704.[57] Marlborough's 'Great Convoy' of 1708, on the other hand, covered the seventy miles between Brussels and Menin via Soignies, Ath and Pottes in six days (6–12 August) – an average of almost twelve miles a day. This was highly commendable considering the size of the siege train convoys. In this respect, therefore, Marlborough may well have achieved some improvement.

In action, the guns proved difficult to deploy, and often almost impossible to 'bring off' after an unfortunate engagement – hence the loss of material suffered at Landen and Steinkirk. However, they could be well sited, and the withdrawal of the infantry from the latter battle was materially assisted by a well placed battery. 'Our cannon was so advantageously posted that they [the French] thought it not discretion to come fforward and so we parted ffor this cause . . .'[58]

The showing of William's siege trains at Namur (1695) was of course justly celebrated. Marlborough, however, was the greater user of the guns. Many contemporaries mention the care with which he personally supervised the siting of the batteries, for battle and siege alike. Under his inspiration, the toiling gunners could occasionally bring off the virtually impossible, as for example at Blenheim, when Colonel Blood managed to deploy ten guns forward over the Nebel at the height of the battle to check the successful advance of Marsin's cavalry,[59] or at Malplaquet, where the Allied right passed its guns through Taisnières Wood despite heavy opposition, to emerge on the French side of the obstacle and inflict grave harm on Villars' massed squadrons drawn up in reserve.[60] In the handling of the guns in action, therefore, Marlborough had no contemporary peer, but it should be noted that the concept of attaching light guns to the infantry brigades dates from William's wars (copying earlier Swedish masters) and not from Marlborough's campaigns per se.[61]

The Engineers of the train were drawn from two sources – the Surveyor-General's Department of the Board of Ordnance, and from the infantry regiments. Throughout the period under consideration, it was an all-officer organisation, the labour being provided by the local 'boors', with some assistance from the handful of pioneers included in the train. They suffered all the difficulties faced by the gunners concerning transport, but their record in siege warfare was generally good. Their prestige – like that of the artillery officers with whom they often interchanged – rose considerably over the course of the wars, but most particularly under Marlborough, for he paid special attention to ensure that both categories received their fair share of honours, rewards and bounties after a successful engagement.[62] This was an improvement on previous practice, when all too often 'there was no deference for the artillery', even under William III.

Moving to the side of the trains concerned with Ordnance stores, we have already described the large quantities of ammunition, match, flints, etc. conveyed with the guns for the support of the rest of the army. This was a vital, if often abused, service. The greatest problem was the uncertainty over which stores were issuable at public charge, and which were liable to repayment from unit resources (that is, by stoppages of pay and deductions from the 2d a day 'off-reckonings'). This problem was frequently met in the early eighteenth century, when the change-over of weapons was taking place, the Ordnance stalwartly refusing to issue free bayonets in lieu of the free-issue pikes which were being withdrawn on the rather specious grounds that the former was a type of sword, which had always been issued only on repayment terms.[63]

The leading representatives of the Ordnance Stores present in the trains in the field were the Commissaries of Stores and (from 1703) the two Controllers of Army Accounts.[64] The inclusion of these last-mentioned officials led to the avoidance of many abuses and anomalies, and reflects another improvement largely instigated, or at least encouraged, by Marlborough, who insisted on 'value for money', as well as equipment and stores of sufficient quality.[65] So, once again, we are bound to acknowledge Marlborough's patient concern with details of administration, the cumulative effect of which was a great improvement in the overall situation of the troops he led.

Finally, we must touch on one of the most intransigent problems of all – the provision of adequate transportation for the trains. The Ordnance had the only 'permanent' organisation – such as it was – in this field. The Waggon-Master General (on £100 p.a.) was responsible for providing the main transport facilities for the artillery components of the trains, being represented in the field by Waggon-masters, Conductors of Horses and the Commissary of draught-horses. In reality, however, official sources could only provide the merest shadow of what was required, so that the greater part of the trains, like the rest of the army and its supply services, had to rely largely on local contracting to make good the deficiencies.

Occasionally, outright impressment of country horses and carts was tacitly permitted, so desperate was the need. A shortage or non-arrival of horses at the outset of a campaign could hold up the whole campaign. Richards notes on 25 April 1693 that 'the Gunnes were fitted up and all the pontoons fixed for a march, wanting nothing now but Colonel Goor with the Contractors' horses and waggons, as also Mr. Fletcher with our recrute stores from Rotterdam . . .[66] Three weeks later (18 May) saw the arrival of the tired Colonel 'and the greatest part of our horses and waggons so that now our traine will soon be fixed for the first orders that may come.'

It is significant that so illustrious an officer as the train commander himself should have deemed it necessary to supervise this transport procurement – it gives some indication of its importance and difficulty. Continual assessments were being made of the transport facilities afforded by various areas likely to see the passage of the armies. In one such surviving document of 1692, it was regretfully noted that the District of Liège – currently under French contribution – might well afford the foe a total of 2,353 waggons and almost 14,000 local pioneers, whilst 'Flanders could provide us with 4–500 waggons which would serve to transport that which is coming from Brussels'.[67]

Many other aspects of this problem could be described, but it will suffice to note an observation written in King William's own hand in his *Memorandum on Military Matters*, dated 6 December 1689. Under the heading 'Artillerie and what depends on it', the King has jotted down 'contracts for wagens and horses. To send for Flanders'. Many of Marlborough's despatches, printed in Murray, similarly show signs of his grave preoccupation with supply, and several times we find Cadogan, Quarter-Master General, sent on such missions. Writing to Lord Raby on 20 September 1703, he records:

> I have been till now on the road of all posts, being employed to find horses in the country for drawing the cannon from Liège to Limburg; those whose business it properly was having so wholly neglected it that there wanted above 1,000, which with much ado I have got at last and sent away to Liège . . .[68]

If it is true that armies could operate over only such distances as they could carry their bread, it is equally clear that they could only conduct effective operations against such places as could be reached by their guns. In both respects, the key was the availability or otherwise of horses, drivers, waggons and fodder.

From an examination of this evidence, taken all together, it can fairly be asserted that William III's later trains were far better organised and run than his earlier ones, and that the improvement in organisation eventually incorporated laid the foundations for the establishment of the Royal Regiment of Artillery. It is also quite clear that Marlborough's subsequent work was largely concerned with matters of significant detail rather than of major reconstruction, but that the effect, based on the earlier efforts of Williamite artilleryists was to improve still further the standard of effectiveness and martial esteem of 'our Trains in Flanders', however great and numerous the remaining errors and difficulties.

NOTES

1   G Murray, *Letters and Despatches of the Duke of Marlborough*, Vol. IV, London, 1845, p. 144.
2. J Millner, *A Compendious Journal . . . AD 1701–1712*, London, 1733, p. 75.
3. Stowe Mss 444, folios 8–12 (BM).
4. de Beaurain, *Histoire Militaire de Flandres*, pp. 63–4.
5. As, for example, in 1707, when 'it was late July before the artillery could be raised from the ground', R Parker (ed. D G Chandler), *Memoirs*, London, 1968, p. 67.

6. See WO:47:18 under 11 January and 7 March 1695. Gunners' uniforms cost £7–15s a suit (£4–5s for matrosses) to the infantry soldier's £1–19s–6d (1693) – Grosse, *Military Antiquities*, Vol. II, p. 9. A gunner drew 2s a day to the private's 8d.
7. Young and Adair, *Hastings to Culloden*, London, 1966, p. 250.
8. Quoted by Dalton, *English Army Commission Lists and Registers*.
9. WO:55:424, No.13 (PRO); also Nos 14 and 15a.
10. SP/8/5, folio 42 (PRO).
11. Quoted in R E Scouller, *The Armies of Queen Anne*, Oxford, 1966, p. 179. The first train sent into Ireland (1689) was destroyed through negligence on 12 August 1690, when General Sarsfield surprised it in camp in a daring raid. (See Dalton, op. cit., Vol. III, p.64, Note 44.)
12. Add. Mss 9723, folio 28 (BM).
13. Ordnance Warrant WO:55:536 passim (PRO). See Appendix B for a list of Master-Generals.
14. WO:55:342, folio 16, dated 8 March 1689; WO:55:342, folio 291, dated 30 June 1702. James II's earlier amendments are quoted in full in Cleaveland, *Royal Regiment of Artillery*, London, 1881, pp. 83–91.
15. See Clode, *The Military Forces of the Crown*, London, 1689, Vol. II, pp. 186 & 204–5.
16. See *Inter alia* Ordnance issue scales, dated 8 November 1688 in WO:55:424, No. 14.
17. WO:47:1.
18. See CSP for the Reign of Queen Anne (1702–14), p. 477.
19. Clode, *op. cit.*, Vol. II, pp. 204–5.
20. Cleaveland, *op. cit.*, p. 133.
21. Napoleon III and Colonel Favé, *Etudes sur lapassée et l'avenir de l'artillerie*, Paris, 1863, Vol. IV, p. 23.
22. See Mérode-Westerloo (trans. & ed. D G Chandler), *Mémoires*, London, 1968, p. 172 for observations on the conduct of the French artillery at Blenheim.
23. Fully listed in Cleaveland, *op. cit.*, pp. 76–7.
24. WO:55:536 – Warrant of 25 July 1683 and subsequent amendments.
25. See Scouller, *op. cit.*, pp. 35–43 & 173–83.
26. See Appendix B for a description of the calibre, range and weight of these pieces.
27. WO:55:124, folio 20.
28. 'Tin cases to be filled with the King's shot' cost 5½d each for demi-culverins; smaller cannon seem to have used 'parchment cartridges' at 2s–5d a dozen. WO:14:17, folio 167.
29. WO:55:424, folio 23.
30. Stowe Mss 444, p. 10.
31. Stowe Mss 444, entry dated 3 August. Most accounts place the Allied net loss at ten guns.
32. *Ibid.*, folio 14(b), entry dated 29 July 1693.
33. *Ibid.*, folio 8(b)1–12.
34. *Ibid.*, folios 13–22.
35. WO:55:424, Nos 36, 40, 46 & 48.
36. *Ibid.*, No.21 *passim*.
37. Stowe Mss 444, entry dated 6 September.
38. Given in full in Cleaveland, *op. cit.*, pp.126–8.
39. It seems to have been French practice, however. See St Rémy, *Mémorial de l'Artillerie*, 2 vols, Paris, 1693, Amsterdam, 1701, Vol. II, p. 229 *et seq.* for their

use of 'Brigades', each with ten guns. The Dutch seem to have had a similar organisation since 1678 – 'compagnies'. See J W van Raa *Het Staatsche Leger* (1702–15), Vol. viii, The Hague, 1953–9, p. 230.

40. The drum-coach became the 'colours' of the artillery, the 'standard' being attached to it. First mentioned in the Train establishment of February 1691.
41. This information is derived from WO:55:421, Nos 23 & 24, and Stowe Mss 444, folios 13–22.
42. Under 16 June, Richards records that 'this evening our small pieces of cannon were sent to their respective brigades with all their appurtenences as also all ammunition for each brigade, not to be touched but in time of service'. This practice, then, did *not* originate with Marlborough as is sometimes stated, but existed before the Battle of Landen.
43. See Stowe Mss 444, folio 22 for Colonel Richards' summary of transport and stores.
44. Stowe Mss 458, 'Journal for 1693' under 14 June. See also Cleaveland, *op cit.*, p. 15.
45. Cleaveland, *op. cit.*, pp. 144–6. See also Stowe Mss 444, folio 23 *et seq.* for details of the train of 1796.
46. WO:55:424 No. 36, dated 14 March 1701/2.
47. Cleaveland, *op. cit.*, p. 132.
48. Stowe Mss 444 under 3 August 1691.
49. WO:47:18, folio 431 (PRO).
50. Stowe Mss 444 under 16 June 1693.
51. See Note 45 above.
52. See Biographical note in Parker, *op. cit.*, pp. 5–10.
53. J W Fortescue, *Historical and Military Essays*, London, 1928, pp.177–8.
54. Stowe Mss 444 under 24 August 1692.
55. *Ibid.*, under 31 July & 1 August 1692.
56. Mérode-Westerloo, *op. cit.*, p. 160.
57. Stowe Mss under 3 August 1692.
58. See Parker, *op. cit.*, p. 38.
59. *Ibid.*, p. 89.
60. See Note 42.
61. Cited in H L Blackmore, *British Military Firearms*, London, 1961, p. 42.
62. See, for example, the Blenheim Roll, reproduced in Dalton, *op. cit.*, Vol. V, pp. 1–73.
63. Treas. 1/84/35 and Clode, *op. cit.*, Vol. II, pp 668 *et seq.*
64. Hence his genuine concern for the men's clothing.
65. Stowe Mss 458 under entries dated 25 April and 18 May 1693.
66. KWC SP/81/3, folio 93.
67. C.S.P. (Dom.) 1689–90, p. 347 (& SP/8/6) (PRO).
68. Strafford Papers – Sloane 3392, dated 20 September 1703.

Appendix A

A Specimen Train of Field Artillery Analysed in Detail: William III's Flanders Train of 1693

Staff	Pay (per diem)	Equipment
Colonel Johan Wynant Goor and his clerk	£2 – 0 – 0	
William Musters, Comptroller, and clerk	3 – 0 – 0	
Lt. Colonel Jacob Richards	1 – 5 – 0	
Major John Rymond Schlundt	16 – 0	
Adjutant Daniel Cottin	8 – 0	
Quarter-Master Ralph Wood	8 – 0	
Paymaster	12 – 0	
His assistants, John Silvister and Edm. Williamson	7 – 0	
Waggon-Master Charles Ball	10 – 0	Two waggons carrying one Church Tent, one
His assistants, Godfrey Frank and Francis Ellis	8 – 0	large tent for Guard to the Train, Marquee for
Auditor Charles Watkins	6 – 0	officers of the Guard, nine more tents, 800 yds
Commissary of Horses Daniel Coenen	8 – 0	of rope, 70 pickets, two large mallets
Chaplain John Carpenter	8 – 0	
Surgeon John de Quavre	8 – 0	
His assistants, John Grele, Robert Shemer and one post vacant	10 – 0	
Provost John Hill	3 – 0	
His assistants, Matthew Browne, James Gold and Charles Hartley	7 – 6	
Kettle-Drummer John Burnett	4 – 0	One Drum-Carriage mounting two drums
His Coachman John Humphreys	3 – 0	with banners.

Bridgemen or Tin-Boat Men

First Captain William van Erp	6 – 2
Second Captain Thomas Glendall	6 – 2
Lieutenant Thomas Morrice	4 – 0
Four Corporals @ 2/6	10 – 0
50 private men, 'ten included to be English watermen', @ 2/–	5 – 0 – 0
Master Tinman	5 – 0
Two assistants @ 3/–	6 – 0

Forty tin-boats on as many flat-waggons; one spare waggon

Engineers

Two field forges

Five engineers @ 5/–: John Bodt, John Manclerc, Isaac Cock, Michael Richards, Daniel Shevrard	1 – 5 – 0

Fire-Masters (Howitzer crews etc.)

4 Howitzers

Chief Fire-Master John Doling	5 – 0
Fire-Master and Petardier John Lewis Schlundt	6 – 0

Four groups of two waggons, each carrying one barrel powder, half bundle match, 18 shells, six 'partridge', one hair cloth and one ball-box

Ten Fire-Masters @ 5/–:John Chanternell, John Churdes, Albert Borgard, Olaus Hulk, Henryck Lunenburg, John Suit, Erick Schiller, John Spicker, William Hendricke, John Bleckenback	2 – 10 – 0
Twelve Bombardiers @ 2/6	1 – 10 – 0

One 'warning-piece' waggon. Spare howitzer carriage

Ordnance Stores

80 waggons of infantry ammunition, each carrying 5 barrels of fine powder, one bundle match, 5 barrels of ball, 800 flints, one hair-cloth, one ball-box

Two Commissaries @ 8/–: Matthew Smallen, Robert Welsh	16 – 0
Four Clerks of Stores @ 4/–: Thomas Edwards, Hermaine de Weess, Thomas Fletcher, John Bourden	16 – 0

129

Staff

	Pay (per diem)	Equipment
Transport and Craftsmen		
Conductor and Plumber	4 – 0	20 waggons for cavalry and dragoons carrying same munitions except for 5 barrels of carbines and pistol shot and 1,000 flints
28 Conductors @ 3/–	4 – 4 – 0	
Two Conductors and Coopers @ 3/–	6 – 0	
Master-Carpenter	6 – 3	
Two mates @ 3/–	6 – 0	60 'tumbrells' of munitions for Regts. in
20 Private men @ 2/6	2 – 10 – 0	English pay; each holding 3 barrels powder, 4 of ball, 1 bundle match and 500 flints.
Master-Wheelwright	4 – 0	
Six Smiths @ 2/6	15 – 0	
Master Collar-Maker	4 – 0	10 waggons carrying 384 grenades apiece in boxes of 24.
Six Collar-Makers @ 2/6	15 – 0	
Master Tent-Maker	4 – 0	4 waggons of spare equipment.
Assistant	2 – 6	5 waggons of craftsmen's stores – one per artificer
Pioneers		
Lieutenant Robert Guybons	4 – 0	21 waggons of entrenching tools, and 19 more filled with hand-tools for the army.
Four Sergeants @ 2/–	8 – 0	
54 Pioneers @ 1/2	3 – 3 – 0	

Artillery

First Company
Captain George Leslie ... 0 – 12 – 0 ... 10 Semi-Culverine and 2 Sakers
Lieutenants: ... Five groups of three waggons, each group
  1st, George Spencer ... 8 – 0 ... carrying 10 barrels powder, one bundle match,
  2nd, Andrew Bonnet ... 7 – 6 ... one barrel 'fine priming powder', 186
Gentlemen of the Ordnance: ... roundshot, 36 'partridge', one 'hair-cloth'.
  1st, Edward Grove ... 5 – 0 ... Two waggons (for sakers), carrying barrels
  2nd, Thomas Rushall ... 5 – 0 ... powder and one bundle match, 160 roundshot,
Four Sergeants of Gunners @ 3/– ... 12 – 0 ... 40 'partridge', one ball-box.
36 Gunners @ 2/– ... 3 – 12 – 0
Four Corporals of Matrosses @ 2/6 ... 10 – 0
56 Matrosses @ 1/6 ... 4 – 4 – 0

Second Company
Captain Jonas Watson ... 0 – 12 – 0 ... 18 Sakers
Lieutenants: ... Nine groups of two waggons, each group
  1st, John Buttensten ... 8 – 0 ... carrying 10 barrels powder, one bundle match,
  2nd, William Bousfield ... 7 – 6 ... 160 roundshot, 36 'partridge', one hair-cloth
Gentlemen of the Ordnance: ... and one ball-box
  1st, John Hillibon ... 5 – 0
  2nd, William Bousfield ... 5 – 0
Four Sergeants of Gunners @ 3/– ... 12 – 0
36 Gunners @ 2/– ... 3 – 12 – 0
Four Corporals of Matrosses @ 2/6 ... 10 – 0
56 Matrosses @ 1/6 ... 4 – 0

131

Third Company
Captain Jonas Watson

16 Sakers	0 – 12 – 0	
Eight groups of two waggons, each group		
carrying identical munitions to those listed for		
2nd Company.		

Lieutenants:
1st, Daniel de Young — 8 – 0
2nd, Peter Gelmuyden — 7 – 6
Gentlemen of the Ordnance:
1st, Joseph Durden — 5 – 0
2nd, Samuel North — 5 – 0
Four Sergeants of Gunners @ 3/- — 12 – 0
36 Gunners @ 2/- — 3 – 12 – 0
Four Corporals of the Matrosses @ 2/6 — 10 – 0
56 Matrosses @ 1/6 — 4 – 4 – 0

Fourth Company
Captain Leonard Vanderstam

20 three-pounders *either*	0 – 12 – 0
One waggon for two guns, each carrying 10	
barrels powder, one bundle of match, one hair	
cloth *or* (alternately) 334 roundshot, 40	
'partridge' and one ball-box	

Lieutenants:
1st, Albert Briulis — 8 – 0
2nd, Abraham Butler — 7 – 6
Gentlemen of the Ordnance:
1st, Joseph Lamotte — 5 – 0
2nd, William Gunn — 5 – 0
Four Sergeants of Gunners @ 12 – 0 — 2 – 8 – 0
36 Gunners @ 2/- — 3 – 12 – 0
Four Corporals of the Matrosses @ 2/6 — 10 – 0
56 Matrosses @ 1/6 — 4 – 4 – 0

Summary of Stores:

70 artillery waggons; 298 barrels of powder; 36 bundles of match; 1,000 demi-culverin roundshot*; 3,600 saker roundshot*; 2,000 3-pdr. roundshot*; 40 howitzer 'partridge-shot'; 41 ball-boxes; 37 hair-cloths.

170 waggons army munitions: 684 barrels of powder; 160 bundles of match; 640 barrels of musket balls; 85 barrels of carbine shot; 15 barrels of pistol shot; 100 hair cloths; 100 ball boxes; 114,000 spare flints.

* Additional rounds (above numbers quoted for the waggons) were carried in 'lockers of the Cannon' or ready-use chests; e.g. 7 roundshot and 6 case per demi-culverin

Richards noted that as much again was held in arsenals behind the front or 'in ships'.

Appendix B

A. List of the Master-Generals of the Ordnance, 1682–1725

1682–1688	George, Lord Dartmouth
1689–1693	Frederick, Duke of Schomburg
1693–1702	Henry, Viscount Sydney (later Earl of Romney)
1702–1712	John, Duke of Marlborough
1712	Richard, Earl of Rivers (d. August)
1712–1714	James, Duke of Hamilton and Brandon
1714–1722	John, Duke of Marlborough
1722–1725	William, Earl of Cadogan

B. Specifications of English Artillery Pieces, 1689–1697 (Selection) All Brass

Name	Poundage (ball)	Weight of barrel	Length of barrel	Point-Blank range*
Demi-cannon	24 pdr.	5,600 lbs	12 ft	160 paces
Culverin	18 pdr.	4,500 lbs	11 ft	180 paces
Demi-Culverin	9 pdr.	2,000 lbs	10 ft	174 paces
Sakers	6 pdr.	1,500 lbs	9 ft	160 paces
Minion	3 pdr.	800 lbs	7 ft	120 paces

* 'The Shot of a gun, level'd in a direct line without mounting or sinking the Muzzle.'

Information drawn from *A New Military Dictionary* (London: 1702)

NB Sources conflict on certain details but these figures seem 'average'.

C. *Specimen Artillery Trains – English (1693), French (c.1700) and Dutch (1701)*

a) English Train of 1693	b) French Train of c.1700	c) Dutch Train of 1701
I. Staff		
Colonel Goor and his clerk	Colonel	Kolonel O. van Verschner
William Musters, Comptroller and Clerk	Lieutenant-Colonel	Luit. Kol A. van Mijill
Lt. Col. Jacob Richards		Controullers-General
Major John Schlundt	Major	Majoor
Adjutant Daniel Cottin	Aidemajor	Geswindschieters
Q.M. Ralph Wood	Meréchal des logis	Officieren van het Brugwegen
Paymaster and 2 Assts.		Lager
Waggon-Master and 2 Assts.	Vaguemestre	(no information)
Auditor	Agent	
Commissary of Horses	Le Greffer	(no information)
Chaplain, John Carpenter	Aumonier	
Surgeon and 3 assts.	Chirugien	
Provost John Hill and 3 assts.	Prevôt and 5 archers	
Kettle drummer John Burnett		
His coachman John Humphreys	Le Bourreau (executioner)	
II. Specimen Artillery Company		
Capt. George Leslie	Captaine	Two Kapiteen-en-jongen
Two lieutenants	Lieutenant	Two luitenant-en-jongen
Two Gentlemen of the Ordnance	Sous-lieutenant	Two ordinaris meester-vuurwerkers and 2 assts.
Four sergeants of gunners	2 sergeants	

36 gunners	3 caporaux	4 bombardiers het kond-ukteurs der nuurwerkers
Four Cpls of Matrosses	5 anspessades	3 Onderluitenants
56 Mattrosses	47 cannoniers	25 konstabels
		21 konstables
		One Korporaal van de Timmerleiden
		10 Timmerlieden
		4 Korporals van de handlangers
		62 handlangers

NB The Dutch organisation was considerably more comprehensive than the English or French.

III. *Specimen Specialist Company* (unofficial in English trains until 1702)

5 engineers	Capitaine	Waggenmeister
Chief-firemaster and Asst	Two lieutenants	Two Luitenants-Waggenmeisters
10 firemasters	Two sous- „	Two van de conducteurs „
12 bombardiers	Four sergeants	One adjudant
2 commissaries	4 caporaux	One kwartermeister
4 clerks of stores	8 anspessades	1 schrijver
1 conductor and plumber	94 artificiers	4 wachtmeesters
28 conductors		3 specialists
2 conductors and coopers		45 conducteurs.
Master carpenter and 2 mates		
20 private men		
Master-wheelwright and 6 mates		
Master-collar-maker and 6 mates		

Master tent-maker and Asst.
Lieutenant of Pioneers
4 sergeants of pioneers
54 pioneers

IV. *Specimen Bridgemen Company* (unofficial in English army until 1703)

No information

Two Captains
One lieutenant
Four corporals
50 private man (of whom
  10 to be Eng. watermen)
One Master-Tinman
Two Assistants.

One Kapiteen
Two luitenants
6 Korporals
2 blislagers
6 timmerleiden
60 pontgasten.

Sources: a) English: WO 55/424 No. 23.
b) French: St. Remy, *Mémoires d'Artillerie* (Amsterdam: 1702) Vol. I p. 32 *et seq.*
c) Dutch: Het van Raa, Band VII pp 250 *et seq.*

CHAPTER VIII
Fortification and Siegecraft
The World of de Vauban and van Coehoorn

Although relatively simple matters for 'my uncle Toby' and 'Cpl Trim' in Laurence Sterne's *Tristram Shandy*, the developments and complicated details of fortifications and sieges require careful consideration by the modern reader as well as the learning of new vocabulary of technical terms. This was the age of the great Frenchman, Marshal Sebastien le Prestre, Seigneur de Vauban (1633–1707), who was claimed to have built some thirty-three fortresses and conducted fifty-three sieges during his career. His only rival was the Dutchman, Menno van Coehoorn (1641–1704), who won King William III's only costly victory at Namur in 1695. Marlborough, in the midst of planning his great march to the Danube, remarked that he was 'most affected' with great sadness to hear of the death of 'Father Coehoorn' on 17 March 1704.

From the earliest historical times soldiers have used fortifications to strengthen important positions and to support their field armies. The evolution of the art of fortification has, therefore, been continuous and inevitably reflects the developments in weapon technology and the Art of War. In particular, the increasing range and destructive power of artillery weapons have compelled military engineers to adapt and repair permanent fortifications to meet the new conditions, while improvements in field guns and in the accuracy and rate of fire of small arms have prompted alterations in the design and method of constructing field defences. As the eighteenth-century soldiers used to say, 'trumps were spades'.

The incidence of siege warfare during the Nine Years War was not so marked as Fortescue and other historians have claimed – at least not in the Netherlands region, which saw the most significant actions of the struggle. If minor investments are excluded, only nine important sieges can be listed, and two of these were in fact bombardments, and this situation compares with the thirty-five or more major operations during the succeeding War of the Spanish Succession. Nevertheless, siege warfare played an important part in the campaigns of William III for reasons which will be analysed below, and if there were only nine sieges in almost as many years, it should also be appreciated that the same period saw only three important land battles and two actions. This chapter sets out to place siege warfare in its contemporary setting, and to provide an evaluation of the engineering services of the period and their techniques, with special reference to the efficacy or otherwise of William's English and Dutch engineers.

The sources for this study are as follows: for the history of siege warfare itself comparative use has been made of the main contemporary chroniclers of the day, most especially Edward d'Auvergne's volumes for the English point of view, and de Beaurain and de Quincy for the French. All these works are very biased, and need careful treatment. Contemporary accounts of major sieges include de la Colonie (very valuable for Namur), Captain George Carleton (somewhat suspect), Robert Parker (sound), and a number of Memoirs by Villars, Berwick and Feuquières of varying usefulness.[1]

For the techniques of siege warfare enormous amounts of material are available. It is impossible to discount the contribution made by, or attributed to, Sebastien le Prestre de Vauban. According to Fontenelles, Vauban in his lifetime improved 300 fortresses and built thirty-three, was present at 140 'actions de vigueur' and conducted fifty-three sieges, thirty of them under the royal eye.[2] Yet, despite the mass of publications bearing Vauban's name, modern scholars deny that he wrote anything on siege warfare with an eye to publication,[3] and assert that most volumes that appeared under his name were forgeries, wrong attributions, or pirated versions of the supposedly secret instructions the great engineer drew up for restricted circulation amongst the French high command, and for the military education of the young Duke of Burgundy.[4] All the same, it would appear that his *Traité des Sièges et de l'attaque des Places*, published in many editions, many of them at The Hague, was indeed the synthesis of his opinions, and indubitably had very widespread currency as the standard work in its field well into the nineteenth century.

Of almost equal importance, and undisputed authenticity, are Surirey de St Rémy's two-volume *Mémoires d'Artillerie*, completed in 1696 and published in Amsterdam in 1702, dedicated to the Duc de Maine. Vauban's Dutch rival, Menno van Coehoorn, was another influential writer on the subject.[5] However, there seems to have been no important English author-engineer, although the Stowe Mss include various manuscripts by the famous Richards family, including fragments of draft treatises.[6] Works of this nature, together with such minor *opuscula* as Marshal Boufflers' *Observations on the Siege of Furnes*, do not add greatly to the sum of knowledge.

On the organisation of engineer services during this period, the Ordnance Papers at the PRO provide a wealth of detail.[7] The tome by Colonel A Allent provides the basis for the French system,[8] whilst van

Raa's *Het Staatsche Leger*, Band VII is invaluable for information about the Dutch.

Fortresses fulfilled three major functions. First, they served as frontier fortifications intended to inhibit, or at the very least delay, an invasion by an enemy army. For the successful carrying out of this role, much depended on their being sited at carefully selected places on important waterways or mountain passes to enable them to control local traffic whether by land or water. It was equally important that they should be built in mutually supporting series, presenting a succession of obstacles to an opponent, and enormous amounts of time and treasure were expended by the French on their triple-line defending the North-Eastern frontiers, and on their imposing Meuse–Moselle–Rhine complex, whilst the United Provinces paid equal attention to their Barrier.

The second role of fortresses was to serve as magazines and supply depots for the field armies. Much seventeenth-century campaigning was carried out from series of pre-stocked arsenals, and the provision of rear-facilities of this nature was obviously of importance. Similarly, fortresses often served as a place of refuge for a defeated force pending recovery and reinforcement.

Thirdly, fortresses were inevitably the centres of local civil-military government, controlling the neighbouring countryside. In this role, their governors and intendants were expected to levy the requisite taxes, either in specie or in kind, to build up the resources in their storehouses to the requisite level. Frontier fortresses were also used as bases for raiding parties – sent out either to place an adjacent enemy area 'under contribution', or to disrupt a foe's convoys or siege operations elsewhere.[9]

Of course fortresses had always carried out these roles to a greater or lesser extent, but one reason for their greater significance in the later-seventeenth and eighteenth centuries was that the art and science of defensive engineering had progressed much faster than contemporary developments in gunnery material and techniques; hence, a certain imbalance had grown up, and the better-designed fortresses of a Vauban and a Coehoorn could often put up a disproportionate degree of resistance.

A second reason for the significance of fortresses was the attitude of governments and generals in tending to prefer time-consuming siege operations to indulgence in other forms of military operations. It was widely, if often erroneously held that siege wars were relatively humane in respect of the degree of civil suffering and the scale of military casualties involved. Secondly, the material progress of a war could be measured in terms of fortresses and cities lost and won, and the eternal preoccupation of governments and commanders with the requirements of supply also encouraged a widespread indulgence in sieges and the operations in support or in relief of them, as it was a matter of no inconsiderable importance to provide one's forces with a fertile region – preferably an enemy one – for the period of winter quarters which followed every campaign. And clearly, no commander could be so fool-hardy as to bypass or ignore enemy fortresses near his line of operations lest their garrison sally out to attack his vulnerable convoys, without which he could hardly hope to keep in the field, let alone conduct a major siege with the mass of material and munitions required.

So much, then, for the roles played by fortresses in the warfare of this period. We must next consider the specific influence they exerted on the Netherlands campaigns of 1689–97. Apart from operations attendant on the action of Walcourt (25 August 1689), and the considerable defeat sustained by the Allies the next year at Fleurus (1 July), the main emphasis of the struggle during the first two years of the war was on the Rhine front, where three sieges of note took place, two of them ending in Allied successes (namely Kaiserswerth, June, and Mainz, July–September 1689) and one in failure (the loss of Philippsburg to the French in October 1688).

The Netherlands only became the main focus of attention from early 1691, with the arrival of William III from Ireland to take over command from the unsuccessful Prince Waldeck and to integrate English formations in the Allied army. This was the signal for the opening of a war of attrition destined to last six years. Neither Dutch nor French national security was seriously endangered during this considerable period; it was more a question of a struggle for prestige, intended on the one side to consolidate the cohesion of the First Grand Alliance and to induce France to accept an equitable peace, and on the other to disrupt the Allied coalition and influence neutral opinion (particularly Sweden) in the hope of persuading William III to accept a mediated settlement that would leave France's recent gains practically intact. Louis XIV was essentially on the defensive strategically from 1690 onwards. Provided they held together, therefore, the Allies could hardly lose the war in any sense; but they might throw away the peace if they allowed themselves to be divided. It is against this background that subsequent events in Flanders should be evaluated.

The French were not tardy in seizing the initiative in 1691 by appearing before the important barrier-fortress of Mons (15 March), which they promptly besieged, both Louis XIV and Louvois being present in the trenches, together with Vauban. This caught William unawares: his army was not assembled, and consequently he foresaw 'extraordinary diffi-culties'[10] in relieving the garrison. Desperate Spanish promises of assist-ance proved as unproductive of waggons and fodder as William had anticipated, and as a result nothing could be done to prevent the fall of the city on 10 April, following an investment of only twenty-six days. The end was hastened by the French threat (aimed at the prosperous citizenry of Mons rather than the garrison) that a fine of 100,000 crowns would be levied for each day of resistance after the opening of the trenches. The

142

populace accordingly compelled the garrison to open negotiations on 8 April, and the capitulation became effective two days later.[11] This represented a grave military and diplomatic setback for William's plans and prestige. The Governor of the Spanish Netherlands, Gastañaga, was made the scapegoat, being replaced by the Elector of Bavaria, but William was never able to retrieve the initiative that year. By adroit manoeuvring he prevented the French from taking Hal or Liège, although they bombarded the latter, but these were only negative achievements, not positive or constructive. All that William could console himself with at the close of the year was the knowledge that the barrier had held without Mons, but on the debit side Sweden had made an offer of mediation in the war, Münster refused to send forward her contingent of troops, and Saxony became wholly uncooperative. Such were the effects of the loss of Mons.

Worse was to follow. Although the naval success at La Hogue ruled out the likelihood of a French invasion of England or Ireland (18 May and 2 June 1692), the next year's climax was the French siege of Namur (25 May to 30 June) and its fall despite the presence of the vaunted Coehoorn within the walls. William's desperate attempts to force battle on Luxembourg, and thus raise the siege proved unavailing, partly because of torrential rain over the critical period, and once again the citizenry of the beleaguered city induced the Duke of Barbançon to capitulate to Vauban. A month later William forced a battle on the French at Steenkirk and although the outcome can only be represented as a draw tactically, on the strategic level it was undoubtedly on Allied success as his casualties dissuaded Luxembourg from moving against Liège – the loss of which, with its grenade and bomb manufactory, would have been a serious blow to William's cause. Once again, then, the year ended in an atmosphere of stalemate, and William's political foes attempted to make capital out of Steinkirk by representing it (erroneously) as a major defeat.

The campaign of 1695 similarly hinged on the security of Liège. Owing to renewed unwillingness by the German states to honour their obligations, the French were able to take the initiative once more with a considerably stronger field force. Marshal Luxembourg could move from Namur in one of two directions: either towards Liège by way of Huy (and beyond Liège lay only Maastricht before the United Provinces) or by moving north he could threaten to ravage Brabant, attacking Louvain and Brussels. William had to cover both possibilities as best he might, and by placing his army at Parcq, equidistant between the two threatened sectors, he hoped to be able to avert both dangers. Unfortunately, the need to send off large detachments to strengthen Liège (under Count Tilly) and to levy contributions (under Württemburg) considerably reduced his fighting strength, so that when William moved to counter the French siege of Huy (commenced 6 July) he was again considerably weaker than his opponent.

Huy surrendered without even making a determined defence (13 July) and at the subsequent battle (Landen, 29 July), William sustained a definite defeat. As in 1692, however, this setback ultimately aided rather than hindered the Allied cause, for once again Luxembourg was dissuaded by his losses from moving on either Liège or Brussels, and William received a six-week breathing space to re-order his forces. In the end, all the French could do in exploitation of their victory was to besiege and take the strategically unimportant town of Charleroi on the Sambre, which only fell on 11 October. Ultimately, therefore, both the Grand Alliance and the Barrier stood the strain. The French could not win the war.

In 1694 the initiative at last began to pass to William. From his position at Rousselaere, he covered the siege of Dixmude near the coast, a project crowned with success (15 July). This operation was little more than a ruse, however, to distract the attention of the Dauphin and the ailing Luxembourg from the key Meuse sector, where William was planning a coup. This was suddenly executed by the Duke of Holstein-Ploen, who descended on Huy and retook it after a short siege (12–19 September). This success safeguarded the approaches to Liège once more, and more than offset the failure of General Tollemache's descent on Brest in June.

There followed William's *annus mirabilis*. The siege of Namur is well documented both by myself and other writers in several books, but brief mention must be made of the supporting and attempted relief operations associated with it. William entrusted the covering army to Prince Vaudemont, and despite various alarms, he ultimately proved more than a match for Villeroi, Luxembourg's successor. Vaudemont successfully eluded a French trap (13–15 July), prevented them from taking Nieuport on the Channel coast, but was unsuccessful in attempting to prevent the fall of Dixmude and Deynse (28 and 30 July), where Allied garrisons cravenly surrendered without offering even a token resistance. Villeroi's march on Brussels, and heavy bombardment of that unfortunate town (13 August) was an error of judgement, as the siege of Ath on the Dender river would have yielded far better results as a diversion to the proceeding siege of Namur, in which the French army proved powerless to intervene. William weakened the forces before Namur to join Vaudemont near Waterloo, and thus placed himself half-way between Namur and Brussels, but Villeroi dared not attack him, so strong were the field defences constructed by the Allies.[12] In the end, Villeroi withdrew baffled, leaving Namur to its fate (it capitulated on 5 September). This was the highlight of William's military career, and the repercussions of this success assured him of German and Parliamentary support for the rest of the war. After this setback, Louis XIV desired a speedy end to hostilities.

The war would last two more years, both of them dominated by tortuous negotiations. Militarily, 1696 was a non-event; William's plans to besiege Dinant or Charleroi were frustrated as was the French plan to mount a naval raid on the British Isles. Politically, the Alliance suffered a severe setback with the defection of Savoy, which signed a unilateral peace with France. This might have proved fatal to the Grand Alliance in any year before 1695, but coming in 1696 its effects were less damaging. It released Marshal Catinat and his army from Piedmont, however, and this enabled the French to pull off something of a final coup in 1697, when Catinat besieged Ath (16 May), covered by the army of Marshal Boufflers. Anticipating peace, many of William's allies had not sent up their contingents promptly, and so were too weak to prevent Ath's fall (5 June). This proved the last major event of the war.

It is hoped that this brief resume of the fighting in Flanders will have demonstrated how the various campaigns were dominated by half a dozen key fortresses, which changed hands several times. In general terms, the situation supported the Earl of Orrery's assertion that 'wee make warre more like foxes than lyons, and you have twenty sieges for one battel'.[13]

This continuing emphasis on siege warfare was not accompanied by any marked advances in the organisation of the engineering services themselves. Even in France, the great Vauban's pleas for a properly constituted field company system failed to elicit any response, although he did succeed in regularising the senior, static appointments (1690). Under the Directeur-Général des fortifications (Vauban) there was a hierarchy of regional Directeurs des fortifications, ingénieurs-en-chef (in charge of each major fortress or sub-region) and lastly ingénieurs ordinaires. But when the armies took the field, numbers of engineers were gathered into ad hoc brigades; it was generally allowed that they enjoyed officer status, but no clear system of corresponding ranks was evolved. Consequently, many engineers were granted reformed infantry positions to provide them with some measure of military standing, but this was patently unsatisfactory.[14]

As in other armies, there was no real other rank organisation to support the sapper officers. There was from 1671 a *compagnie des sapeurs* attached to the Regiment Royale d'Artillerie, and this was eventually supplemented by the raising of three companies of *mineurs*, namely those of Mesgrigny (1673), specialists in mining, Goulon (1679) experts in artillery work, and Esprit (1695), specialists in building fortifications, but the establishments and status varied considerably almost from year to year, and after 1697 the second and third were wholly absorbed into the artillery organisation. Indeed, no part of the engineering service was ever truly independent from the Grand-Maître's authority, for the Artillery was responsible for their financing and the provision of all forms of sapper equipment. In the field, therefore, so insignificant was the size of the sapper contingents, that much use had to be made of impressed or contracted peasant labour.[15] At the height of the Nine Years War, Vauban had some 600 engineers on active service employing them in teams or brigades of a dozen or so, but after Ryswick he found it difficult to retain even 300 in employment.

Much the same situation was true of the English and Dutch engineers. In the former case, William III's sappers were mostly minions of the mighty Board of Ordnance, although many of the more junior engineers were often regimental officers drafted into the service for a limited period. On the Board, all matters pertaining to military engineering came under the responsibility of the Surveyor-General, one of the five 'Principal Officers',[16] but much of the executive authority was vested in 'our Principal Engineer' by the Warrants of 1683 and 1689, who was charged with training up 'Inferior Engineers', designing and building new fortifications, and the conduct of any sieges.

> In the time of action, or when there is intention of forming or laying a siege against any place, he is to have a draught or ground plot of the place if possible, if not, to take a careful draught and to see where the attack or attacks are most advantageously to be made, how the circumvallation and contravallation (if need be) is to be laid out and designed, and to direct and see the breaking of ground, planting of batteries, making of platforms, conducting of trenches and mines, and to have such Engineers and Conductors as will be necessary to see them carried on and executed, to be constantly moving from one attack to another to see that all possible expedition be made, and so to divide the Engineers under him that they may relieve one another, and never to suffer (as far as his authority extend) any single person to be wholly entrusted with any work or an attack without he be well assured of his ability and capacity to undertake and discharge such a service.[17]

The Principal (or Chief) Engineer received a salary of £300 p.a., was assisted by a Second and Third Engineer, often described as 'of England', paid £250 and £150 p.a. respectively, and there were also varying numbers of 'ordinary engineers' and of 'Young menn to be Bredd up in the Art and Knowledge of Fortifications &c'. It is impossible, however, to distinguish these senior personnel from those of the artillery, for time and again we find engineers being appointed to artillery posts and vice versa. To cite a single example, William Holcroft Blood, 'Second Engineer of England' in 1697, was commander of Marlborough's guns at Blenheim seven years later.[18] On some occasions, one individual would be called upon to perform a double function: thus Colonel John Wynant Goor 'doubled' as Chief Engineer and Commander of the Train sent over to Flanders in 1692.[19]

146

It is notable that William generally appointed Dutch officers to the highest appointments in the English trains – Goor himself, William Musters, Martin Beckman and Johanen Schlundt among them. This would seem to reflect upon the inexperience of English officers, although in due course the Richards brothers and William Blood and John Armstrong would qualify for high posts.

A peculiar and obscure body of sappers was the 'King's Company of Engineers' – a group of twenty-eight officers in all under a 'Director and Commander-in-Chief' – which apparently was not under the authority of the Ordnance but was responsible directly to the King. As many of its members also held positions in the Ordnance, it may have been some form of holding unit or cadre for trained engineers, but it is never mentioned after 25 March 1700.[20]

From existing lists of personnel serving with the various trains, it would seem that on average five or six engineers (paid 10/– or 5/– a day) were included on the strength, although on one occasion, the train for the 'Summer Expedition' of 1693, no fewer than eleven are listed. These officers were never accorded formal military ranks before 1697, and this led to difficulties over the division of prize-money. William III made a ruling on this matter on 16 December 1692 by which every engineer, heedless of grade or seniority, was to receive fifteen shares – or a Captain's portion.[21] After the Peace of Ryswick the 'Peace Train' included six engineers, designated for the very first time as 'Captains', together with four 'sub-engineers'.[22] But at no time before 1697 is there any mention of any other rank structure in support of the engineers, who presumably relied upon the 'boors' for the greater part of their labour force; in that year a Company of Pioneers is mentioned for the first time as such, although for some time there had been an appointment as Captain of Pioneers on the Ordnance lists. Thus there is scant evidence to support any claim that the English engineering services were remodelled in any significant way under William III. They remained a vague and indistinct adjunct of the Board of Ordnance throughout the period of the Nine Years War.

We must next turn to describe some features of the contemporary forms of siege warfare. These had become almost standardised in outline by 1688, although of course the details of each operation varied a great deal. For a besieger, the basic requirements for success were a commanding superiority of numbers over the opponent (not only in terms of the garrison but also as regards any field force the enemy might try to employ to raise the siege), mathematical and engineering knowledge of a high order, and the patient application of a number of highly specialised technical skills. For the besieged, survival of the crisis demanded patient courage, an active defence, a sufficiency of men, munitions and rations, and a compliant civil population. Few sieges were pushed to the extremity of a general storm, however, for the conventions of the day frowned upon such excesses, and in any case rendered them unnecessary by devising a protocol of surrender after a siege had reached a certain point.

The mechanics of later seventeenth-century siege warfare are nowhere better described than in Vauban's *l'Attaque des Places*; for additional illuminating detail, recourse can be made to Surirey de St Rémy's slightly less well known work. 'La résolution des Sièges est une affaire de Cabinet',[23] comments Vauban. The decision had to be taken well in advance of opening operations, as there were truly vast preparations to be undertaken. Thus the French prepared for the siege of Mons (1692) throughout the preceding winter, and William III was at pains to complete his preparations for the second siege of Namur by late February 1695.[24] According to Vauban, a besieging army needed to number ten times the garrison for safety, and be at least 20,000 strong initially if preliminary works of circumvallation were to be undertaken. To assist in the work he suggested rounding up 15,000 local peasantry and 3–4,000 carts with their horse-teams.

St Remy takes as his average an army of 32,000 foot and 18,000 horse, aided by 10,000 peasants, and estimates that for a period of forty days some 3,300,000 rations would need to be collected, and some 720,000 issues of forage.[25] As for munitions, he calculated that at least 40,000 rounds of 24-pounder shot, 16,000 of lighter calibre, and at least 9,000 bombs would be required, together with 40,000 grenades and 30,000 musket shots. Such a fire programme required 792,750 pounds of powder, besides a reserve of a further 150,000 pounds. An ideal siege train, he calculates, should comprise 110 cannon (including fifty pieces of 33-pounder or 24-pounder calibre) and some forty mortars. In fact, such provision was quite frequently surpassed; thus at Mons the French fielded 130 cannon, 177 howitzers, forty-four mortars and eight *pierriers*.[26] Before Namur, William III fielded 147 cannon and sixty mortars. Other types of siege materials increased the complexity of administrative requirements. St Remy lists, *inter alia*, 55,000 pounds of lead, 36,000 lengths of match, sixty gun platforms, and 550,000 feet of assorted timber, as well as 4,000 baskets and 18,000 tools. The collection and movement of such vast quantities of stores and munitions needed much organisation, and the financial backing for such enterprises took considerable arrangement, although details of this aspect are sadly lacking.

Once these preliminary arrangements were complete, the army would set off for its objective, leaving the siege train and the heavier convoys to follow at their slower pace. On many occasions, feint operations would be mounted against a distant sector of the front to distract the attention of the enemy field forces – as in 1694, when the Allies besieged Dixmude as a cover for their main intentions against Huy. Alternatively, an attacker might contrive to move off before the opponent was in a position to take the field, as was the case in 1691 when the French descended on Mons in the second week of March.

The phases of a major siege followed a conventional pattern, although the details of their timing and duration obviously varied every time. Occasionally, when there was a possibility that treachery would deliver a town, an immediate *coup de main* might be attempted, but in the great majority of cases the full ritual had to be gone through. In his *Traité de la Défence des Places*, Vauban gives a timetable for a siege, amounting to a total period of forty-three days from first investiture to capitulation.[27]

The first stage was the blockade, usually conducted by the cavalry, who set up posts on all roads leading into the fortress in the hope of preventing any last-minute reinforcement of the garrison. These measures were not always effective: writing to the Prince de Vaudemont on 3 July 1695, William reported 'M. de Boufflers entered yesterday evening with two regiments of dragoons, whose horses he has since sent away . . . which is most annoying for the presence of M. Boufflers there will change the aspect of affairs.'[28] This incident occurred *after* the establishment of the blockade (1 July).

Next the town would be fully invested. As the bulk of the besieging troops made their appearance, they and the conscripted peasantry would be put to work to effect a complete isolation of the target. This often entailed the construction of lengthy lines of contravallation – entrenchments facing the town and forming a continuous belt around it, preventing even cross-country communication with the outside world for the citizens and garrison, although the occasional messenger could find a way through at night. These positions would be supplemented if there was serious danger of an enemy field force making an attempt to raise the siege by lines of circumvallation, a second line of positions looking outwards; the different camps, magazines and parks of the besiegers would be established within the area thus enclosed. Vauban would allow up to nine days for the completion of these extensive works,[29] but in fact at Namur in 1692 only took three before passing on to the next stage – the opening of the trenches – but this was due to exceptional circumstances. Three years later, Coehoorn required ten days (1–11 July) for this task.

Meantime, the bulk of the besieger's cavalry would be serving as a screen watching for any sign of reaction from the enemy's main forces. Once the investment was completed, up to two-thirds of the infantry and some light guns would march to join the horse, and form a complete covering force, whose tasks were to meet and defeat any enemy attempt to interfere with the progress of the siege, and also to forage and build up the reserves of supplies required by the army. This was a vital function if a successful outcome was to be obtained; in 1691 and 1692 Luxembourg in person commanded the observation forces during the sieges of Mons and Namur, and in 1695 William entrusted the task to Prince Vaudemont, frequently joining him from the siege lines when danger from Villeroi's army appeared imminent.

Before the investment had been completed, the officer in charge of the siege would have conducted a number of close reconnaissances of the town's defences to decide upon the sector for the main and subsidiary attacks. When the defences comprised both a town enceinte and a citadel, as at Namur, it was customary to attack the town first as the easier objective, before proceeding against the very kernel of the defences. The main reason for this seems to have been the need to progressively reinforce the covering army from the besieging forces. As the weeks went by, the chances of an enemy relieving army making an appearance became steadily greater, and consequently the investors were usually keen to take the town and thus make possible a considerable reduction in both the area of lines they were holding and in the number of troops required for the further prosecution of the siege against the smaller, though probably stronger, citadel. All troops superfluous to this reduced requirement could be transferred to the covering force, thus increasing its battle-power in the event of any overt challenge.

There followed the second major step in the progress of the siege – the opening of the trenches. To avoid sustaining crippling losses in a direct assault over the glacis, it was necessary to draw near to the main defences by digging approaches and three parallel trenches to give cover from direct and enfilade fire. To confuse the defender as to the main line of attack, several sets of trenches would be started, but the price was great duplication of effort and material, especially as out-works had often to be neutralised in the first instance. Batteries of mortars and howitzers would be established to bombard the enemy defences and unsettle the gun-crews.

The defender did not passively watch his fate creeping towards him. Although Vauban was against rash sorties, he was in favour of counter-mining and limited night raids by the garrison to damage the besieger's works and delay his progress. An active defence was considered a prime necessity in gaining time, and thus improving the chances of relief.[30] For his part, Coehoorn was far more aggressively minded than Vauban, and the Dutch expert was quite a few times guilty of premature sorties and, conversely, assaults.

With the completion of the third parallel, the time had come for the establishment of the main breaching battery. The great 33- and 24-pounder cannon would be dragged forward during a dark night and placed in prepared positions, often no more than 200 yards from the main enemy defences, often much less. Before the guns could be safely positioned, it was necessary for the attackers to gain possession of the covered way and of the demi-lune or ravelin set in a ditch to protect the scarp wall. Vauban allowed nine days for the sapping to the area of the counterscarp (eighteen from the investment), and up to eighteen for the capture of the covered way and its neighbouring defences.

St Rémy advocated the establishment of three breaching batteries, each containing eight large guns. He was most precise about the dimensions of the battery positions, which must be strong enough to withstand enemy fire. An eight-gun battery required a position sixty paces in length (flanks excluded) and about eighteen feet thick to exclude enemy shot. The embrasures were to be two feet wide on the inner side, and nine feet on the exterior. To construct such a position in twelve hours required 110 soldiers working hourly shifts and forty-five more building fascines. The position would require 390 nine foot by nine inch fascines for the front walls, and 160 twelve feet by nine inch for the embrasures. These were to be dug into the ground leaving no more than three feet above the surface. A further 800 smaller fascines (five to six feet high), prepared by the cavalry, would be used in the flanks, and there was a requirement for 1,840 six-foot picquets.

Few periods of military history can have been more dominated by siege warfare than the late seventeenth century. No doubt the Earl of Orrery was exaggerating when he wrote in 1677: 'We make warre more like Foxes than Lyons; and you have twenty sieges for one battel',[31] but the trend definitely existed in his day.

Without exception, all the great commanders found themselves frequently involved in siege warfare. Some commanders deliberately set out to avoid battle under any but the most favourable circumstances. Their number included such notable soldiers as Marshal Luxembourg during the Nine Years War, although he also had a record of notable field successes to his credit.

Other leaders might deplore the need to spend so much time and matériel in the tedious toils of siege warfare, but all were frequently compelled to indulge in the practice. For the rest, many lesser commanders welcomed the opportunity of disguising their lack of initiative or military ability behind the convenient cloak offered by the need to indulge so frequently in such static and relatively predictable operations. As Daniel Defoe sarcastically remarked in 1697:

> Now it is frequent to have armies of 50,000 men of a side standing at bay within sight of one another, and spend the whole campaign in dodging – or, as it is genteely called – observing one another, and then march off into winter quarters.[32]

The basic design of permanent fortifications

The art and science of defensive engineering made considerable progress under the inspiration of such influential figures as Vauban, Coehoorn and

Rimpler. Each expert founded a 'school' of followers and imitators, and developed his own specialities of design, but in almost every case these improvements were merely variations on a theme. Although details might differ considerably, the broad aspects of design remained common to all; they shared, for instance, the concept of a polygonal trace or ground-plan; similarly, most of the component parts of a defensive scheme were used by every nation, although regional variations certainly existed. As Coehoorn himself wrote, 'Is it not a wonderful thing that in a whole Age (1588–1700) there should be such small improvement made in the Art of Fortification?'[33]

Throughout history, fortifications have been designed to perform certain functions, although the order of priority and emphasis amongst them has frequently shifted, reflecting changes in weapon capabilities and the methods of construction. Perhaps the most important concept since the onset of the age of gunpowder has been that of producing a maximum of effective firepower; certainly in the later seventeenth and early eighteenth centuries it was axiomatic that the approaches to all sectors of a fortress should be swept by converging fields of fire, both cannon and musketry. Acting upon this assumption, every position and outwork had to be carefully designed to permit the freest use of all the defenders' weapons and the maximum degree of mutual support.

A second principle was the function of protection – for garrison, citizenry and real estate within the perimeter. This was partly a question of designing defences strong enough to withstand the effects of shot, bomb and shell, and partly of compelling the hostile batteries to operate from as long a range as possible. The former consideration was very much a question of design. The towering walls of medieval castles had given place to squat, immensely thick bastions and curtain walls, let down into the ground, as engineers strove to reduce the destructive power of the increasing numbers of cannon becoming available by opposing to them stone-reinforced positions of rammed earth and deep ditches.

The second desideratum was obtained by adding ever more outworks in closely related series in order to push the enemy's batteries farther and farther away from their ultimate target. As cannon became more numerous and (marginally) more powerful and effective, so defensive systems became increasingly complex, as one ring of outworks was super-imposed upon another until the point was reached in the eighteenth century when fortresses were ringed with several successive layers of defences.

A third object in the design of fortifications was the obstruction of the enemy foot-soldier's approach by means of both fire and physical obstacles; his arrival at hand-to-hand grips with the garrison was to be delayed for as long as possible. Every day that passed increased the possibility of relief by a friendly field army – or the exhaustion of the attacker's patience and resources – although as we shall note on a later page, the desirable length of a sustained resistance was clearly defined and in many ways curtailed by contemporary customs and regard for the 'laws of war'. Security, however, was lax. 'There are presently few places in Europe,' observed Vauban, 'of which there are not plans; most are even engraved; and although these plans are often inexact one should not refuse to use them . . .'[34]

The outermost part of the vast majority of fortresses was the glacis, an area of ground between 200 and 400 yards wide entirely encircling a town or fortress. The glacis was often carefully sloped gently upwards towards the main defences, and was completely devoid of all forms of cover and inequalities of ground so as to provide the garrison's sentries with a clear view, and the guns with an ideal killing ground. In some instances the outer edge of the glacis was protected by a ditch, but many engineers, including Vauban, discouraged this practice as likely to interfere with the effectiveness of sorties as well as providing the enemy with a ready-made source of cover for use as a *place d'armes*. Sometimes the glacis was dispensed with – as when a fortress was placed on top of a hill.

The inner edge of the glacis merged into the covered way – the first regular outwork. This also ran all the way around the fortress on the outer side of the main ditch. The covered way usually comprised a circular access road and parapet provided with a firestep, from which musketeers could engage an advancing opponent. This was generally an earthen construction strengthened by palisading.

From the rear of the covered way dropped the counterscarp wall, the outer face of the ditch – a steep bank occasionally revetted with bricks or stone. Sometimes let into its face were counterscarp galleries, fire positions commanding the bottom of the ditch and the foot of the facing scarp walls. Ditches varied in width and depth according to the size of the positions beyond or within their area which would usually have been constructed with the earth dug out from them. Vauban advocated a width of ninety-five feet and a depth of between eighteen and twenty feet (below the ground level of the fortress interior).

There were three varieties of ditch: dry ones, which would be provided with a deep trench running down the centre to obstruct assaulting troops and intercept enemy mining attempts, and wet ditches of two kinds, namely those filled with still water (which represented a health hazard in those days of primitive sanitation and disease prevention), and those holding moving water as at Namur (which presented the difficulty of erosion and the danger of flooding at intemperate seasons of the year). Nevertheless, this last kind was regarded as the best form of obstacle as it was very difficult for an attacker to bridge it under fire.

Many dry ditches contained a *fausse-braye* or earthen rampart running round the foot of the rampart, but these were becoming obsolescent by the late 1690s. Within the ditch area were also situated numbers of further outworks of growing complexity, all designed to protect this or that part of the main position. These included *ravelins*, *demi-lunes* and *tenailles*; sometimes there would also be *caponnières* let into the angles of the ditches to command the foot of the ditch; to protect major gateways into the town or fortress, vast crown-works and horn-works were often constructed abutting the glacis.

The scarp (or inner-wall) of the ditch was almost invariably faced with stone, and adjoined the main curtain wall with its projecting bastions. Both the *courtine* (or curtain) and the bastions were relatively low structures – projecting about twelve to fifteen feet over the edge of the glacis, but this height associated with the depth of the ditch made them into considerable obstacles. Their real strength lay in their thickness, many measuring perhaps as much as sixty-six feet at the foot, tapering to some thirty feet at the level of the gun-platform. Curtain walls were somewhat less strong, but nevertheless still redoubtable enough, many parapets being up to twenty-four feet thick. They were constructed of rammed earth, and were usually provided with sloping outer faces in an attempt to minimise the damage done by the impact of cannon balls. These faces were habitually sown with wiry turf (Vauban particularly recommended *four de Bourgogne*), or osier saplings, in order to bind the earth together with the roots. Of course these were not permitted to obstruct lines of fire, but were burnt or cut down periodically.

Bastions projected forward from the main trace in order to achieve patterns of flanking fire with neighbouring positions for the guns placed upon their respective platforms. They presented a number of faces towards the glacis – normally two but the angle of the apex and the precise shape of the flanks linking them to the rampart of the *courtine* led to much contention between the rival schools of engineering. The distance separating bastions was often calculated on the musket-range of the day, but this was not invariably the practice.

Within the bastion was situated the gun-platform, protected by a strong parapet provided with a firestep and pierced with wide gun embrasures. A popular practice was to add *guérites*, or small watch towers, at the apex of the bastions or at intervals along the curtain walls to serve as observation posts, but these were later superseded, especially in France, by *tours bastionnées* of two or more storeys (a speciality of Vauban's later years), which were designed to hold the guns as well. Along the summit of the rampart ran a *chemin des rondes*, paced by the sentinels. Finally, behind the bastions would run a military road to enable the garrison reserves to reinforce a threatened sector, with staircases running up to the ramparts or earthen slopes up to the gun-platforms.

Preparations for a siege

Any important siege involved the collection of large numbers of men and animals and huge quantities of munitions, rations, forage, stores and waggons, together with all possible information about the town to be attacked, the size of its garrison and the morale of its citizens. These preparations were hard to conceal from enemy agents, and Vauban deplored the common lack of security surrounding such projects. He advised that a besieging force needed to be at least ten times the estimated size of the garrison, and in any case no less than 20,000 strong if the construction of lines of contra- and circumvallation was envisaged. St Rémy believed that 32,000 foot and 18,000 horse, supplemented by 10,000 peasants, were sufficient for most operations. The average for the major fortresses would seem to have been in the region of 50,000 to 60,000 which accords closely with St Rémy's estimate.

Siege trains usually did not accompany the armies in the field, but remained in rear ready to move ponderously forward when required. As might be expected these were vast organisations. In 1693 William III ordered a seventy-eight-gun heavy train to be prepared against 'this summer expedition', comprising twenty 24-pounders, as many coehoorns, eighteen sakers, and ten 13-inch, and as many 10-inch mortars. Commanded by Colonel Sir Martin Beckman, this train had an establishment of eighty-seven assistants of officer status (including fourteen engineers), thirty bombardiers, twenty-six conductors, twenty-two bridgemen, 100 gunners and as many matrosses, sixty-one craftsmen and ninety-six drivers – almost 550 officers and men in all if we include boys. Most siege trains were very slow-moving and, with their myriad attendant waggons, filled many miles of road. Whenever possible, they were conveyed by water.

Although Vauban was explicit in his opinion that no fortress, however well defended, could hope to hold out for an indefinite period, he was equally insistent that no fortress should be lost prematurely by default. In *La défense des places* he gives explicit instructions on the proper composition of staffs and garrisons, and the exact weapons and stores the governors should lay in against the evil day. Basing his calculations on the number of bastions a fortress possessed, he provided exhaustive lists for fifteen different sizes of towns (but excluded the needs of the civil population as irrelevant to his particular survey). A six-bastion fortress, for example, needed to be garrisoned, armed and stocked on the following scale to stand a forty-eight-day siege:

(Garrison, peace): 1,200 infantry, 100 cavalry and a skeleton staff
(Garrison, war): 3,600 infantry, 360 cavalry and 200 staff; 120 gunners, 80 bombardiers, and 40 miners.

Weapons: 60 cannon, 30 mortars, 60 wall-muskets; 3,000 spare muskets.

Shot: 24,000 cannon-balls, 15,600 bombs and grenades.

Powder: 340,000lbs, besides 419,240lbs of lead and 300,000 lengths of match.

Rations: *inter alia* 3,495 *sentiers* (235lbs each) of grain and rice, 5,051 boxes of onions, 1,424 quintals (112lbs each) of beef, 480 quintals of mutton 'for sick or wounded officers', as much of veal for wounded rank and file, 385 quintals of cheese; 8 quintals of plums 'for the sick', 275 *muides* (280 pints each) of wine, 825 *muides* of beer and 108 more of *eau de vie*, 'for distribution at a rate of two small tots a day'.[35]

How far this represents an 'ideal' rather than a practical state of affairs it is difficult to assess. In 1691 it would seem that the Dutch garrison of Namur (8,800 strong) was equipped with sixty-two 24-pounders and twenty-eight lighter guns and mortars, besides 442,736 pounds of *luspolver* (loose powder) and 64,000 made-up charges; 41,137 shot were available for the 24-pounders.

The progress of a siege – as conducted by both the besiegers and the garrison

With certain exceptions, the prosecution of sieges had become a highly ritualised affair by the late seventeenth century. Although there were unique features in each operation, there were also certain fixed conventions which both besieger and besieged generally observed. Unless treachery could be counted on to open the gates, a commander usually had to undertake the performance of a regular siege in all its stages.

The lengths of sieges varied enormously. Many factors might account for the duration besides the size of its garrison, the state of the town's defences, or the presence of disaffected elements. The morale of the defenders could be a decisive factor. It was not unknown for the attitude of the civil population to overwhelm a weak governor. At Mons, in 1691, Louis XIV hastened the conclusion of the siege by threatening to levy a fine of 100,000 crowns from the prosperous citizenry for each further day the city's resistance continued; the result was a capitulation after only twenty-six days. Nevertheless, a great many sieges fit into the forty- to sixty-day range, which partly supports Vauban's dictum that a defence of forty-eight days' duration was respectable.

Vauban's timetable for the capture of a well-appointed and resolutely held six-bastion fortress provides an interesting commentary on the 'standard' proceedings of a normal siege, however much practice might vary from precept in matters of detail.

To invest a place, collect material, and build lines	9 days
From the opening of the trenches to reaching the covered way	9 days
The storm and capture of the covered way and its defences	4 days
Decent into and crossing of the ditch of the *demi-lune*	3 days
Mining operations, siting of batteries, creation of a fair breach	4 days
Capture and exploitation of the *demi-lune* and its defences	3 days
Crossing of the main ditch to two bastions	4 days
Mining operations and siting of guns on the covered way to making a practical breach	4 days
The capture of the breach and its supporting positions	2 days
Surrender of the town after the capitulation	2 days
Allowance for errors, damage caused by sorties, a valorous defence	4 days

Total: 48 days[36]

This was only intended to be a rough guide to help commanders estimate what they were up against, and if complications could be expected, further days were to be added to allow for the capture of outlying hornworks, redoubts, etc. Against these Vauban balanced the effects of mounting casualties and worsening conditions in the town. Much digging of 'parallel' and 'approach' trenches was involved.

Up to the present, it may have seemed that a siege unrolled with remorseless precision whilst the governor and garrison of the place under attack helplessly watched enemy trenches creeping towards them. If the governor was a man of spirit, however, nothing was likely to be further from the truth, for the prosecution of an 'active' defence could cause a besieger, however strong numerically, much anxiety and no inconsiderable delays. Vauban describes a number of counter-activities open to the defence. First amongst them came sorties, sub-divided into 'external' and 'internal', designed to set back the progress of the siege. Second in the defender's repertoire came the construction of counter-approaches. Allies encountered considerable difficulties owing to this type of operation at the siege of Namur (1695): the capture of French outworks protecting the Porte St Roche sector was particularly protracted for this reason. Thirdly, a defender could make great use of mining.

The types of operations a relieving army might attempt to compel the besieger to abandon his enterprise were as follows. First, this might be achieved by marching up with a superior army and forcing a direct confrontation. These attempts seem to have achieved their purpose comparatively rarely. William III for instance, proved completely incapable of saving Namur in June 1692 thanks to Luxembourg's shadowing. If direct confrontations were not possible, a foe might resort to a war of supply. Such operations were intended to intercept and destroy the besieger's support convoys. Or again, a relief force might resort to extreme measures to force a way through a besieger's lines in order to deliver urgently needed material to the garrison or reinforce it. The creation of a major diversion by means of a sudden descent on some important and distant enemy fortress, to induce the besieger to draw off a large part of his army to deal with the new threat, was a fourth possibility. The French used a sudden descent against Brussels, capital of the Spanish Netherlands, in an attempt to save Namur in August 1695. The attempt proved abortive.

Normally, military moderation was the rule. A final summons would be despatched when the main breach was ready, but as often as not the defending commander would forestall his besieger by hoisting a white flag and requesting the opening of negotiations.

Such then, in outline, were the main forms and conventions of siege warfare. Small wonder if kings and commanders lavished rewards on their engineers-in-chief who brought such complex operations to a successful conclusion. Louis XIV gave Vauban a gift of 40,000 crowns for capturing Namur in 1692; on other occasions he awarded him captured cannon and wide estates. William III lavished promotions and honours on Coehoorn after his recovery of the same fortress for the Allies.

Chronology of a Specimen Siege
NAMUR 1695

Investment	– 1 July
Lines completed	– 10 July
Trenches opened	– 11 July
Outworks taken	– 24 July
Town surrendered	– 4 August
Citadel isolated	– 28 August
Outworks taken	– 30 August
Citadel breached	–1 September
Final capitulation	–5 September

This success cost William III an estimated 18,000 casualties, and Marshal Boufflers 13,000 (including 5,000 prisoners of war). The siege had lasted sixty-seven days (compared to only twenty-six days when Vauban captured Namur in 1692).

NOTES

1 Including de la Colonie, *Chronicles* and Parker, *Memoirs*. See also Chandler (ed. & tr.), *Military Memoirs of Marlborough's Campaigns* (London, 1998).

2 Fontenelle, *Oeuvres de Vauban*, Vol. I, No. xxxiv (Paris, nd); Blomfield, R, *S le Prestre de Vauban* (London, 1938), p. 52 & seq, and Rothrock and Hebbert (eds), *Vauban* (Ann Arbor MI & London, 1982) passim.

3 Vauban, *Traité de l'Attaque; de la Défense des Places; on Mines* (Paris, 1668; London, 1779, 1792)

4   Vauban, *Mémoires pour server . . . des sièges* (Paris, 1699) and *Projet d'une Dime Royale* (Paris, 1707).

5   van Coehoorn – see Chandler, D G, *The Art of Warfare in the Age of Marlborough*, pp. 278–82 and Savary, T, *The New Methods . . . of Baron van Coehoorn* (London, 1705) passim.

6   See *JSAHR*, Vol. 81, No. 325 (Spring 2003), Hebbert, F J, 'Maj Gen John Richards (1667–1709)', pp. 8–30; Stowe Mss 444, 453, 458 (BM Addn Mss). See also Hebbert, 'The Richards Brothers', *The Irish Sword*, Vol. XII, No. 48, pp. 200–11.

7   Ordnance Papers (PRO), WO/55,539, WO/47/22, WO/47/17 & 55/422. See also Tomlinson, H C, 'Guns and Government', *RHS* No. 15, passim.

8   Allent, A, *Histoire du Corps Impérial de Genie* (Paris, 1805).

9   See Vauban, Traité de la Defense des Places (Paris, 1776), passim; also Rothrock, G A, (ed. & tr.), *A Manual of Siegecraft and Fortification* (Ann Arbor MI, 1968), pp. 156–62.

10 Childs, J, *The Nine Years War and the British Army 1688–1697* (Manchester, 1991), pp. 156–62; *Archives . . . de la Maison d'Orange-Nassau*, 3rd series, p. 169.

11 Childs, *op. cit.*, p. 162 on the Siege of Mons; see *Archive van A Heinsius*, Vol. II, p. 34, and Van'T Hoff, *The Correspondence of John Churchill . . . and Anthoine Heinsius . . . 1701–1711* (Utrecht, 1951), Introduction, passim.

12 Villeroi, *Campagnes de Flandres en 1695 Archive*, Vol. II, p. lvii.

13 Orrery, Earl of, *A Treatise on the Arte of Warre* (London, 1627), p. 15.

14 Allent, *op. cit.*, p. 363.

15 Ambert, J, *Esquisses de l'armée française* (Brussels, 1849), p. 229.

16 Chandler, *The Art of Warfare . . .*

17 Porter, W, *History of the Royal Engineers* (London, 1889), p. 50.

18 Porter, *op. cit.*, p. 80, and Cleaveland, T, *Notes of the Royal Engineers* (London, nd), p. 159.

19 WO/124, p. 20 (PRO).

20 Porter, *op. cit.*, p. 61.

21 Add Mss 9326 f 42 (BM).

22 Cleaveland, *op. cit.*, p. 240.

23 Vauban, l'Attaque, p. 1.

24 *Correspondentie*, Series II, Vol. 3, pp. 341–9; also Childs, op. cit., pp. 264–301.

25 St Rémy, *op. cit.*, Vol. 2, Ch. 1, passim.

26 de Beaurain, *Histoire Militaire de Flandres*, Vol. 1, p. 63.

27 Vauban, *Défense*, p. 52 – 4 and Rothrock, *op. cit.*, pp. 140–1.

28 Add Mss 21,498, No. 2 (BM).

29 Vauban, *Défense*, p. 52 and passim.

30 Ibid., pp. 126 – 8 on 'How to Make Successful Sorties', and Rothrock, *op. cit.*, pp. 126–7.

31 Orrery, *op. cit.*, p. 5 (bis).

32 *An Essay under Projects* (London, 1697), p. 135.

33 Savary, *The New Method of Fortification* (London, 1705), p. ii.

34 Vauban, *l'Attaque*, p. 30.

35 Ibid., pp. 45–101.

36 Vauban, *Défense*, pp. 51–4.

CHAPTER IX

Supply

Logistical support in war

For our period there are two important writers about logistics: Professor G Perjes, *Army Provisioning Logistics and Strategy in the second half of the 18th Century* (Budapest, 1970), and R E Scouller, *The Armies of Queen Anne*, which is a full study of the administrative and organisational aspects. William III certain worked hard on logistics – the art of moving and quartering troops – or supplying and maintenance of men, horses and the myriad items required for wars. However, organisation of supplies for an army was a speciality of Marlborough's, and possibly because of his attention to small detail the ordinary soldiers nicknamed him 'Corporal John'.

It has been calculated that an area needed to be capable of supporting a population of thirty-five people per square kilometre if it was to be able to provision an army operating without benefit of magazines. This calculation is based on the assumption that such areas were self-supporting with locally grown grain stocks being available. A study of regional population distribution in the seventeenth and eighteenth centuries reveals that only five areas of Europe had such a population and the implicit agricultural yield, namely parts of France and the Rhineland, the Spanish Netherlands, Westphalia and Lombardy. It comes as no surprise, therefore, to discover that these were the major theatres of war throughout our period.

For a six-month campaign, an army of 60,000 men would require, in terms of bread alone, almost 43 million kilograms, and few indeed were the areas of Europe capable of bearing such a burden without facing local destitution, starvation and depopulation.

The intention of this chapter is to examine several administrative aspects of late seventeenth-century English military affairs with a view to determining the nature and extent of the deficiencies that were revealed, the effects these exerted on the conduct of military operations, and what steps (if any) were taken to improve the general situation. Whenever feasible, comparisons will be drawn with procedures adopted in the light of experience during the wars of Queen Anne. In this way, it may prove possible to gain some impression of how far administrative problems lay at the root of the generally undistinguished performance of English arms in Flanders during the reign of her predecessor.

Sound, centralised administration and properly coordinated methods of supply are vital for the effective conduct of war in any age or generation, and when we study the haphazard, chaotic and slipshod manner in which these matters were carried on during the Nine Years War, it becomes a matter for considerable amazement that anything was achieved in the field at all. Without a doubt military administration constituted the Achilles' heel of every English army at this period. Success or failure often lay in the ability of the Crown's servants to extemporise some sort of short-term solution to the problems that repeatedly returned to plague them. Behind most of them, as we shall see, lay the perennial inadequacies of war finance and the lack of any true system of national coordination from the top.

The science of logistics can be defined as being concerned with all matters pertaining to the movement, quartering, maintenance and supply of the forces of the Crown both at home and abroad. For our purpose only the first two will be treated, and it will be convenient to examine each of these fields in turn.

William III's personal awareness of the multiplicity of logistical difficulties facing the English army can be illustrated from a list written in his own hand in the late days of 1689. This document, which would seem to be a series of jotted-down notes arising from points under discussion at some conference, mentions problems of recruitment, remounts, clothing, tentage, 'artillerie and what depends on it', land conveyances, provisions, abuses prevalent in sea transportation and pay, and lastly the need for a 'regulation for the hospital'.[1] Here, on a single sheet, lies a survey of almost every important aspect of logistics.

Possibly the greatest single problem William encountered in trying to impose some sort of order amidst the military chaos, and a legacy of almost thirty years of Stuart neglect, was the proliferation of responsible authorities and vested interests at departmental level. It is often difficult to distinguish clear limits to spheres of responsibility, for many fields involved several administrative organisations, and almost every one of them had a finger in most pies.

The Board of Ordnance was an authority almost completely independent of army control (except in respect of actual command in the field), with responsibility for providing a mass of services and materials of war, ranging from the cannon themselves to the pontoon trains, the manufacture of arms, the building of barracks, and the provision of certain amounts of wheeled transport for the trains. The Ordnance was in fact a quasi-independent department of state, responsible only to the monarch, the Lord Treasurer and the Secretary of State, its organisation, privileges and duties being based upon Charles II's Warrant of 1683 as redrawn during the reign of James II.[2] A second group of powerful authorities were the Commissioners of Transport and Victualling, responsible for the movement of troops overseas and for feeding them while on ship, and accountable only to the Admiralty and (to a lesser extent) to the Secretary of State.

Where the supply of fuel and provisions in kind to troops on land was concerned, the Commissariat come into its own, a civilian organisation closely supervised – one almost might say obstructed – by the Treasury, and dependent upon the endeavours, well-meaning or fraudulent, of a score or more of contractors. Equally hamstrung by the Treasury was the department of the Paymaster-General, always chronically short of funds, but nonetheless charged with the duty of issuing pay to the Regimental agents once the Muster-Masters' reports had been approved by the Commissary-General of the Muster.

Similarly the supply of medical equipment and medicines remained the jealously conserved prerogative of the Physician to the Forces, the Surgeon to the Forces and the Apothecary to the Forces, forever wrangling among themselves over demarcation disputes, not to mention the Commissioners for Sick and Wounded who assumed vague responsibilities for the persons of wounded soldiers evacuated home, and for inspecting chests of medicines prior to their dispatch to units. Lastly, there was the baleful influence of the Treasury – already mentioned several times – which ruled everybody by virtue of the Lord Treasurer's control of what paltry sums of specie there might be available for issue, and his power to veto any proposed contract. Commanders in the field were always dependent on this plethora of clashing and often competitive principalities and powers, bodies over which they had no control and upon which they could not bring much pressure to bear. Much more might be said on this subject, but it will be touched upon again when we turn to consider such machinery as existed for the coordination of all these diverse and conflicting authorities.

The methods by which transportation was arranged for the movement of troops and their equipment were on the whole very unsatisfactory. It is necessary to differentiate between movement over land and water as different authorities and systems governed each. To take sea transport first, we come across numerous examples of mismanagement and sheer fraudulent exploitation. From the days of Elizabeth I, acting on the order of the Secretary of State, the Commissioners of Transport had been responsible for 'the hiring of the transports, provision of food, payment of the troops prior to embarkation, and mustering and disembarkation on arrival'.[3] From sundry lading tables included in King William's Chest, it would appear that the official calculations of the amount of shipping required to move a given force was to allow three gross tons burthen for each cavalry trooper and his mount, and about thirteen hundredweight per infantry soldier. Thus, to move 22,926 foot, 1,538 dragoons and 4,853 horse (or 29,317 men and 10,697 quadrupeds to include 1,000 allocated to the staff and the artillery) from various English ports to Ireland in 1690, called for shipping totalling 50,341 tons. But variations are frequent; in 1692, for example, we find fodder for horses being apportioned at four tons apiece (including hay) and the troops at one and a quarter to the ton.[4] The types of abuses practised were fairly stereotyped. Agents would pack men on to transports heedless of the official restrictions, and pocket the spare hiring money if they could escape detection. Even for the comparatively short sea trip from the Hook to The Hague, conditions aboard cannot have been very alluring. Private Deane of the 1st Foot Guards, crossing to Flanders in 1708, described his experience as 'continual destruction in the foretop, the pox above board, the plague between decks, hell in the forecastle and the devil at the helm ... labouring under many inconveniences, having only the bare deck to lie upon, which hardship caused abundance of our men to bid adieu to the world.'[5] Unscrupulous masters would similarly turn a pretty penny by withholding the rations they were supposed to provide, not that the demand for salt pork and biscuit was likely to be excessive during the winter crossings. In consequence not a few lives were lost.

Another hazard of the transport service was obviously delay. On the one hand, the sailing of shipping to bring back troops from Ireland might be held up by the late arrival of part of their victuals for the voyage. 'Mr. Greggs our Correspondent at Whitehaven, by his letter of the 29th past [1690] acquaints us that all the provisions for the troops of Guards that are to be brought from Carrickfergus, would be shipt by tomorrow – except the beer, which would take up to two days more ...'[6] Bad weather or unfavourable winds might equally delay a troop move. 'I thought fit to acquaint you,' wrote Colonel George Ramsay to Secretary Blathwayt from the Leigh Roads, on 17 February 1691, 'that ye forces ordered by His Majesty to be transported to Flanders have been embarked now these fourteen days, but ye wind hath been and is yet at East and South-East soo that we could not saile ...'[7] Not all the inconvenience was the fault of the weather or of the shipping agencies and the masters. As always, the government proved very slow in paying for services rendered. One Captain Greenhill reported that he hoped that sufficient shipping would be soon available at Exmouth to transport the Earl of Bath's Regiment from Guernsey to Ostend, '. . . tho' the masters are hardly to be persuaded to go on that service, notwithstanding our assuring them of ready pay and giving them Protections, and that they are to have convoy.'[8] Doubtless the masters had heard such promises before, and did not think that the risks of being caught by a French privateer were worth dubious promises of hard cash, exemption from the press-gangs for their crews, and a naval escort.

Shipping was a fairly costly business, although details varied enormously. In 1703, for example, store ships were hired for sums ranging between 10/– and 50/– per ton per month, and by 1711 the Commissioners were contracting for transport at £4 per man including bedding and necessaries.[9] It would appear, however, that by this date some improvement had taken place in the serious matter of overcrowding, for the scale had become 1¼ tons burthen for each soldier. Of course most of these charges were ultimately deducted, like clothing and weapons, from regimental funds, but a certain number of 'free' passages were provided for new recruits travelling to join units already serving overseas.

The movement of troops on land within the United Kingdom was under the overall control of the Secretary of State, although the Secretary at War could on occasion order the movement of troops from garrison to garrison. Abroad, all moves naturally came under the control of the Commander-in-Chief, the Secretary at War (when accompanying the King) and the Quartermaster-General. Many such orders still survive in the Public Records dealing with both reigns and it would be pointless to quote examples here.[10] To expedite the issue of orders moving troops into winter quarters, other general officers would on occasion be authorised to sign the documents in the absence of the commander-in-chief and his immediate deputies.

Great difficulty was always experienced in producing sufficient army and regimental transport for the munitions, provisions and stores without which the armies in the field could not function. From 1688 there were three types of train: permanent trains supplied for general service; trains organised locally on a semi-permanent footing; and hired or pressed transport. In a telling passage, Walton attributed the army's general shortcomings in this field to 'the fatuous ignorance of the British officer, the indolence or indifference of the British soldier, and the helpless inexperience of both'.[11] In an attempt to produce a measure of order during the Irish campaign, William III made the Commissary-General responsible for all aspects of transportation on land, but this proved of little use – through a general lack of adequate administrative machinery – except to provide a scapegoat on whom to blame all subsequent shortcomings.

The Ordnance, of course, remained in a world of its own under the overall supervision (for transport) of the Commissary-General; the responsible officials – civilians of course – were the Controller of the Train, the Waggon-Master and the Commissaries of draught-horses. When any of these officials were absent, conditions often grew worse than ever. A desperate Minute of the Ordnance in 1695 reads:

That a representation be made to his Lordship of the want of a Comptroller upon the place to look after the civill part of the Train in

Flanders, Colonel Goor now absolutely refusing to concern himself therewith – that some fitting Person may be sent over for want whereof his Majesty's affairs suffer daily.[12]

There is some evidence of the raising of semi-permanent trains; in April 1690 one such was raised for service in Ireland,[13] and similar measures were lately adopted for the increasing numbers of troops being sent into Flanders. The precise organisation of these units is somewhat unclear, but an excellent plan for a permanent train of 200 waggons, employing 800 horses, and divided into two divisions with a proper establishment, and dating from as early as the 1670s, survives in the British Museum but it is uncertain whether it was ever put into practice.[14] It is safe to assert, however, that the only really organised transport services came under the aegis of the Ordnance, but their responsibility was confined to their own trains; the responsible officer was the Lieutenant-General of the Ordnance, acting through the Waggon-Master-General. For all other types of transport – bread waggons, ammunition waggons, carriages for the sick, baggage conveyances and the bulk of the artillery horses – each commander had to fend for himself from army down to battalion level. Abuses were therefore likely to creep in.

The means by which these vehicles were provided were somewhat haphazard. Much reliance was often placed on local hire on contract, whereby a local owner would agree to supply so many carts and horses or pack-animals for such and such a distance or period of time at a fixed price of hire. When such voluntary efforts failed to produce the requisite 'lift', recourse was made to requisition (first officially countenanced in 1691). The army area would be carefully assessed for its transport resources, and then a varying proportion would be impressed for service at fixed rates payable by the government. In 1692 for instance, the district of Liège was assessed as being capable of providing 2,533 waggons and almost 14,000 local pioneers, and it was further estimated that 'Flanders could . . . provide us with 4–500 waggons which would serve to transport that which is coming from Brussels.'[15]

There seem to have been no true scales of transport entitlement during William's reign. In Marlborough's time there is evidence that he strove to provide four waggons per battalion for the march to the Danube,[16] but in 1707 the rate seems to have been fifty carts per 10,000 men[17] – of course, the Ordnance trains were not included in these calculations. Finding sufficient horses was a perennial problem, and in September 1703 we find Cadogan himself, Marlborough's Quartermaster-General, 'being employed to find horses in the country for drawing the cannon from Liège to Limburg; those whose business it properly was having so wholly neglected it that there wanted above 1,000, which with much ado I have got at last . . .'[18] At least 2,000 horses were required for the waggons and guns in 1704. General officers had set entitlements for personal waggons, but frequently exceeded them, and in 1708, shortly before Oudenarde, we find orders being issued restricting Lieutenant- and Major-Generals to two waggons and one coach apiece – clearly with a view to expediting the march of the army.[19] The same source strictly enjoined that the sutlers should travel in rear of the trains, any being found near the advance guard 'shall be plundered', and laid it down that no regiment was to send back a detachment to 'hasten by force' the progress of its own baggage. These details are significant in revealing the types of troubles that could beset the waggon trains on the march.

Convoys were frequently very large and slow-moving, imposing considerable delays on the march, and quite often becoming the objects of attack. Before the siege of Namur in 1692, for instance, the French Intendant of Hainault amassed 6,000 waggons. Tallard's march to the Danube in July 1704 was reputedly accompanied by 8,000 conveyances[20] – or so a participant claimed – and the ammunition convoy that travelled from Ostend to succour the besiegers of Lille in 1708 numbered 600 vehicles.[21] Given the bad state of the roads of Europe, adverse weather could gravely delay movement, as in early 1693, when an Allied relief column vainly tried to reach besieged Furness, taking four days to complete each normal day's marching distance.[22] Examples are not lacking of operations centring on convoys; their interception and destruction was an early form of 'strategic interdiction'. Thus in 1692 we learn of the Allied garrison of Charleroi sallying forth to destroy twenty waggons of French flour in the Pass of Slenrieu in an attempt to hinder the siege of Namur, and the even more celebrated engagement in 1708, when La Motte tried to destroy General Webb's convoy en route for Lille at Wynendael, also springs to mind.

All in all, the provision and administration of transport provided generals with grave anxieties during these wars. The cost bulked large on the annual estimates. In 1692 the estimated charge of 'transports' (probably sea as well as land) for the campaign of 1697 was placed at £200,000;[23] that for 1695 is even more explicit, putting the charge for 'carryages for the Foot in Flanders', at £11,800, and claiming a further £28,316–10s–6d for 'bread waggons' for some 56,000 men in pay.[24] By 1703 the costs for Flanders in these respects had risen to £18,259 and £39,822 for the support of 40,000 men (besides a further £5,880 as a half share in the support of the 'augmentation'), out of a total military budget for the theatre of £670,000 – or approximately one tenth of the cost.[25] The reasons for this increase are the steady devaluation in the value of money and the great insistence that Marlborough placed on acquiring transport on a regularised basis in order to retain the sympathy of the local populations. We can hazard a guess that in William's time unauthorised commandeering was more widespread – and often connived at for want of any adequate machinery to supervise hirings.

We must now turn to the second aspect of logistics currently under review – namely the subject of quartering. It will again be necessary to distinguish between practice at home and on the Continent. Once more the tale is one of sad neglect and half-measures where the United Kingdom is concerned. As Fortescue wrote, 'There were few barracks . . . and the soldiers were scattered in small detachments in scores and hundreds of ale-houses . . . [and] municipalities and inn-keepers fought bitterly against the inclusion of troops within their borders.'[26] Regular barracks were few and of very poor quality throughout both reigns; an interesting definition of what was meant by the term at this period is to be found in *A Military Dictionary*, published in 1702.

> A hut like a little cottage, for soldiers to lie in the camp. Once only those of the horse were called barracks, and those of the foot, huts: but now the name is given indifferently to both. These are made, either when the soldiers have no tents, or when any army lies long in a place in bad weather, because they keep out cold, heat or rain better than tents, and are otherwise more commodious. They are generally made by fixing four strong forked Poles in the ground, and laying others across them; then they build the walls with wattle, or sods, or such as the place affords. The top either thatched, if there be straw to spare, or covered with planks, or sometimes with turf.[27]

Responsibility for such unattractive sounding living-quarters technically lay with the Board of Ordnance, but it was not until 1697 that much building took place. In that year Parliament voted £25,000 for barrack construction in Ireland, where presumably the hostile attitude of the populace discouraged the more usual forms of billeting that will be described below. And in 1715, presumably for the same reason, funds were voted for similar work in Scotland. Conditions within these hovels remained very poor – with beds, fuel and rations often in pitifully small supply thanks to the inadequacies of the Ordnance and the Commissariat. The best standard aimed at was the provision of a room 18 feet by 17 feet for five beds, one of which was to be issued for every two men – if the regulations were applied.[28] Small wonder that a season in barracks could result in many deaths. In one notorious case, one third of the garrison of New York perished in a single winter.

Barracks, however, were still rarities in our period; most recourse, therefore, was had to billeting the troops locally. This had long been a great bone of contention. The Petition of Right (1627) had complained for the way in which officers:

> . . . compel many of Your Majesty's subjects to receive and lodge them in their own houses, and both themselves and others to

contribute towards the maintenance of them, to the exceeding great disservice of Your Majesty, the general terror of all, and the utter undoing of many of your people.[29]

Various Acts of Parliament were later passed to prevent the compulsory billeting of troops on unwilling civilians, and attempts were made to confine such practices to 'victualling houses, taverns and ale-houses' in England, and additionally to 'brewers, butchers and chandlers' in Ireland. But between precept and practice there remained a world of difference, and under James II 'free' quarters had been demanded from publicans, and private citizens imposed upon were only afforded 8d a week compensation for the presence of the 'brutal and licentious soldiery'. Small wonder that safeguards against such exploitation were included in the Bill of Rights and the Mutiny Acts. Many stringent efforts were made to restrict billeting thenceforth to 'inns, livery-stables, victualling houses, and all houses selling brandy, strong waters, cyder or metheglin by retail to be drunk on the premises, and in no other, and in no private house whatsoever.'[30]

The effects of such a system were often deplorable. It inevitably led to units being split up into small detachments over a wide area, making any form of training or adequate supervision impossible. The troops, always desperately short of pay, frequently had recourse to violence and barefaced looting in order to survive. All the faults were by no means on their side alone. Hard inn-keepers – that other criminal class – ensured that only the dingiest outhouses were placed at the soldiers' disposal, and ruthlessly, if realistically, restricted their supply of drink and victuals to the precise amount they could pay for. Semi-starvation, sickness, brawling and indiscipline were often endemic.

Considerable numbers of troops were still billeted on technically 'willing' ordinary citizens. Careful steps were taken to regulate the practice. On the application of the Commissary-General, the local sheriffs and JPs issued orders for billets on a minutely prescribed scale of charges to safeguard both householder and unwelcome guests. Private soldiers, for example, were to be charged 4d a day for such a billet, and officers of dragoons below the rank of captain were to pay 1/– for small beer, hay and straw in addition to accommodation. All bills thus incurred were to be cleared before the troops were paid, the regimental officers being held responsible for this on pain of having their own arrears debited for any outstanding sums. In Anne's reign, threats of cashiering were rife.[31] But of course as often as not there was no pay forthcoming at all, so the practice of leaving behind certificates was tacitly approved by authority, for a few hundred government creditors more or less could make little difference or extra inconvenience – except for the hapless holders of such certificates who would be extremely fortunate to see them redeemed at face value.

Moreover officers – heedless of possible penalties – often conveniently 'forgot' to issue any certificates at all.

An even more unscrupulous government measure was to connive at the practice of allowing a billet to buy out the soldier by paying him 5d a day in quit of all demands other than a roof over his head – which really amounted to little less than protection-money against barefaced pilfering. Such malpractices inevitably caused immense ill-feeling against the army in the country at large, and did nothing to redeem the service's reputation. Heartrending pleas from local authorities were sent up to London for justice. One such, sent by the Mayor of Portsmouth in April 1697, recalled that the town had subsisted Gibson's Regiment for a whole year, but that the unit was now in the process of embarking for foreign service without paying off any of its debts, and pointed out that the town 'cannot provide another Regiment with money or other necessaries', being by now far too poor.[32]

The central government continually strove to regularise the system of quartering troops, but the insuperable barrier was ever the shortage of ready money and the lack of a genuine desire to provide the forces at home with a fair deal. And even when attempts were made to build inadequate barrack accommodation of the type already described – as in 1697 – the provision was restricted to that required for 5,000 infantry within the United Kingdom (plus tentage for 6,000 more and 4,000 horses),[33] although it must in fairness be noted that this was at a time when the size of the army was in the process of being drastically reduced.

When the army was overseas and on active service, the men had to take quarters as and when they came – in tents, under hedges or in a house if they were fortunate. The troops enjoyed much more scope for scrounging and liberating, although the more concentrated billeting made some form of control more practicable. The pious Blackadder blessed 'the Lord for his mercies to me. I have got accommodation here of a cottage, though,' he ruefully adds, 'it is like to be pulled down about my ears by soldiers searching for wood and straw.'[34]

Responsibility for quartering on campaign lay fully on the Quarter-master-General and his assistants. This officer habitually rode half a day's march ahead of the army with the brigade-majors, and selected suitable camp-sites, or apportioned the houses of a town between headquarters and the regiments. The Brigade-Majors then briefed their quartermaster or other regimental representative, and the men squeezed themselves into their respective sectors of the town as best they might after attending the trooping of the colours to fix the regimental rallying point firmly in their minds. Marlborough's staff perfected the measures for selecting suitable camp-sites to a highly developed art, as is evidenced by Captain Parker's description of the march to the Danube in 1704:

As we marched through the country of our Allies, commisars were appointed to furnish us with all manner of necessaries for man and horse; these were brought to the ground before we arrived, and the soldiers had nothing to do but pitch their tents, boil their kettles, and lie down to rest. Surely never was such a march carried on with more order and regularity and with less fatigue to man and horse.[35]

Such painstaking care for administrative detail was, however, the exception rather than the rule. Camp-sites were carefully laid out along principles that need not detain us here, and on occasion, as before Ramillies in May 1706, the QMG's party could run almost into the arms of the enemy.

When the campaigning season was over and the troops entered winter quarters, careful considerations of strategic placing, as well as administrative aspects as regards supply and forage, determined the towns and villages selected. An injudicious choice of locations might afford a better-placed opponent with a considerable initial advantage at the opening of the next campaign. Throughout William III's wars in Flanders, the French regularly succeeded in taking the field several valuable weeks ahead of the Allies. There was always much squabbling over winter quarters – not only between regiments, but also between nationalities; everybody not unnaturally wished to secure the best areas that were going and to palm off the worst on somebody else. One of the very few occasions when Marlborough's diplomatic patience actually snapped was in October 1710, when dealing with criticisms levelled at his quartering arrangements. 'It is grown too much the fashion,' he flashed back, 'to canvass and reflect on what I do without any consideration of the service.'[36]

Once the troops were ensconced within their quarters, the toll of bad sanitation, boredom and as often as not semi-starvation, began to reap their grim harvest. Sickness in quarters was universal, and its ravages are evidenced by many reports by Commissaries of the Musters when they inspected the regiments the following spring. The number of sick revealed by an inspection of the Flanders garrisons carried out between 22 and 27 April 1692, shows great variation between regiments. The worst-hit unit was the Danish regiment of 'La Reine', which was reported as having ninety-one sick and four men unaccountably absent, leaving only 342 men to parade – or a sickness rate of over 25 per cent. The 'best' regiment, on the other hand, was Colonel Graham's, which fielded 692 men with only four sick and another nineteen absent, in other words less than 1 per cent. In all, the consolidated survey shows that a total of 1,659 were absent through sickness (and a further 2,034 from other causes), and a total of 47,182 men ready to march.[37] Thus the incidence of incapacitating illness was not particularly severe in 1692, but from another source it becomes perfectly evident this was an exceptionally good year, and that many more men had been ill over the winter and recovered. 'It is astonishing,' reported this official on 27 April, 'that in all the places of Flanders the sick have dropped in the past two weeks; but you can still see it on the soldiers' faces that a great many have been ill.'[38]

It is interesting to compare the figures of 'wastage' suffered before the opening of the campaign of 1692 with the official casualty figures (so far as these can be trusted) issued at its close: namely 7,794 killed and wounded besides 295 missing (English, Allied and Dutch figures included).[39] It might seem, therefore, that at least one man was sick or a deserter during the winter period (though presumably an unknown proportion of the ill caught up with their units later) for every two casualties sustained in action later the same year. This possibly gives some indication of the ill effects sustained – either directly as in the case of the sick, or indirectly (through encouraging desertion) as a result of the inadequate measures taken to assure the troops of adequate food and accommodation between October and March.

So far, we have examined the worst shortcomings revealed in the logistical field in the realms of transportation and quartering; on a future occasion the study must be extended to incorporate maintenance and supply, and the attempts to improve the overall direction of all matters pertaining to logistics at governmental level. It is difficult to show in conclusive terms how far these inadequacies and confusions are accountable for the varying fortunes of the English armies in Flanders, but perhaps enough has been disclosed to indicate that the underlying conditions of military administration were very haphazard and un-satisfactory. Confusion, inadequate supervision, clashing authorities, lack of money and of a general policy, would seem to sum up the situation prevalent in William's day; the following generation saw some amelioration of conditions and a few real improvements, but most of these were to prove sadly transitory.

Strategic types of logistics

The sixty years between 1688 and 1748 form a watershed in the history of the development of warfare. More scholarly attention has tended to be paid to the periods of the Thirty Years War and the earlier parts of the reign of Louis XIV on the one hand, and to the events of the main Frederickan era, the American War of Independence and the ensuing Revolutionary and Napoleonic Wars on the other, than to the intervening years. Of course the achievements of Marlborough, Prince Eugene and Marshal Saxe have been analysed and re-analysed in a number of notable works, and new attention has been drawn to the struggle in the Spanish Peninsula in the early eighteenth century, but few works have devoted more than a few pages or at best a chapter to a close examination of the development of the art of war in these generations.

It is extremely difficult to judge the great commanders of any age and the martial proclivities and fluctuations of the major European powers unless they can be set clearly against their military backgrounds. All too often these action-filled years are cursorily dismissed as being of little interest, or branded as a period of 'limited warfare', barren of significant developments – and yet in fact they saw the laying of important tactical foundations for succeeding generations.

Professor Nef declared over fifty years ago that '. . . no Age is more in need of re-examination than the 100 years which began in England with the outbreak in 1642 of the Civil War and in France with the accession of the infant Louis XIV in 1643. These 100 years were of immense importance in the general history of Europe and of the European colonies . . .'[40] The scope of this present volume does not exactly coincide with the century Nef referred to, and only attempts to deal with a very circumscribed aspect of even the military affairs of that period, but it does hope to contribute something to aid the comprehension of military events.

This study has been deliberately restricted to an examination of the tactical organisation and handling of the European 'teeth arms' of the late seventeenth and the first half of the eighteenth centuries. That is to say, its four main sections deal with the Horse, the Foot, the Trains of Artillery and the Engineer Services of the period, describing their representation, organisation, equipment, training and tactical employment. The treatment is not restricted to the examination of a single army alone: most attention is devoted to the English and French forces, which serve as controls, but comparisons are drawn with Dutch, Swedish, Prussian, Austrian, Russian and Turkish practices on a more limited scale to demonstrate regional differences and peculiarities. Thus it is hoped that something of an over-view of European military practice at the tactical level will emerge.

It is necessary to establish a number of basic strategic considerations affecting the conduct of military operations during the period under review. The century from 1650 to 1750 is often described as forming a period of 'limited' warfare, and of military mediocrity. These concepts require a little examination, for they can be misunderstood.

It is true that many of the wars that took place between 1650 and 1750 were relatively 'limited' in the way they were conducted – that is to say, that concepts of 'totality' were rejected as impracticable or inadvisable for one or more pragmatic or ideological reasons. The notorious Thirty Years War (1618–48) had been a 'total' struggle during the most devastating parts of its long course. It had been an ideological struggle fought over bitter religious issues between Catholic and Protestant populations; it had been a constitutional power struggle within the Holy Roman Empire, in which the Emperor's authority had been challenged by some of his princes; and it had become the scene of inter-dynastic rivalry, as first Sweden, and then France, had intervened for various motives in the war and broadened its scope to include a power-struggle by the Houses of Vasa and (later) Bourbon against the Austrian Habsburgs. This complex and prolonged war or series of wars had been conducted with a terrible and ruthless ferocity which had led to the depopulation of sizeable tracts of southern and central Germany. The loss of life proved grave, and in the years after the Peace of Westphalia there had developed an international reaction against such measures, and a demand for the avoidance in future conflicts of such extremes. This, then, was the basic psychological restraining factor behind the succeeding period of so-called 'limited' wars. However, there were notable exceptions. The ancient Habsburg–Ottoman struggle in south-east Europe continued to be waged spasmodically with most of its old religious animosity, and parts of the Great Northern War between Sweden, Poland and Russia were similarly waged with great ferocity. Even in Western Europe there were occasional barbaric episodes but at least they were rare enough to cause international outcries.

There were also important physical limitations on the conduct of war, which indubitably restrained the intensity of the waging of campaigns. The seasonal nature of campaigning was dictated by the appalling condition of European roads and waterways during some seven months in the year, and this in turn encouraged the prosecution of sieges or elaborate manoeuvres rather than attempts to achieve all-out victory. Mediocre generals preferred siege wars for a number of reasons. They were largely predictable – in terms of both course and likely outcome. They were economical in terms of movement and (they believed, often erroneously) in terms of casualties – and this was regarded as a practical as well as a humanitarian factor. And they offered something tangible (useful pawns for peace negotiations) in the event of success. Major engagements were unpopular for the opposite reasons: they were often hard to procure strategically; they were very expensive in terms of casualties – especially in view of certain developments in weaponry; and they were rarely predictable.

But by far the most significant limitation on the fighting of wars was bound up with logistics. It has been convincingly demonstrated in recent years that the war *aims* of the major combatants were rarely limited. Perhaps they were not so 'total' as the concepts of 'unconditional sur-render' demanded in the world wars of the last century, but they were far-reaching enough in their demands for reallocation of frontiers and territories, and armies were steadily growing in size as governments increased their administrative organisation. In one vital respect, however, the powers failed to rise to the challenges they set themselves: they never proved capable of solving the basic problem of supplying their armies effectively whilst in the field.

This was the factor that caused what Professor Perjés has termed 'the crisis in strategy'.[41] The development in the size of field armies will be treated in some detail below, but here it is sufficient to mention that whereas early-seventeenth-century field forces had rarely exceeded 40,000 men, by the end of the first decade of the eighteenth century individual armies in excess of 100,000 men were not unknown. Generals often argued in favour of smaller forces, for they became increasingly aware of the problems posed by the need to subsist the larger armies that the ambitions of their masters forced upon them as they strove to outbid the claims of rivals to hegemony in Europe and overseas. The period of so-called 'limited war', therefore, was dominated by much aggressiveness on the national level, only thinly disguised by a veneer of rationalism. Surprisingly, perhaps, there was no great upsurge in population sizes or agricultural productivity to underpin this military expansion, except in the cases of the United Provinces (of a short-lived nature) and of England. France's population was actually declining a little at the turn of the century, and the overall growth of Europe's peoples was only very slight. What had changed dramatically was the improvement in the means and methods of state administration – which made it possible to mobilise, equip and marshal more and more men in pursuit of national objectives. It did not, however, make it commensurately easier to feed them – and there lay the rub. As Guibert declared, the overall decline in the standards of the art of war during the eighteenth century in France was in large measure due to the imprudence with which Louis XIV and his minister, Louvois, had inflated the manpower of France's armies which caused them to become clumsy and largely unmanageable masses.[42] The expansion in army sizes, therefore, was due far more to political causes than to social, economic or purely military factors. Political ambitions came to outstrip the means of production. Larger armies could be collected, but the means of supplying, transporting and commanding them remained inadequate to the challenge.

The basic problem, simply stated, was that the quantities of food needed to feed these larger armies could not be obtained on the spot. Neither the populations nor the levels of agricultural productivity were large enough to maintain, even for a brief period, so vast an accretion of men and horses. Armies, their increased sizes notwithstanding, still functioned along single lines of operation. There was little idea of moving, and subsisting, in a number of widely separated columns in order to spread the burden over the roads and countryside more evenly, before concentrating to fight. Such concepts would hardly be encountered before the French Revolution and the Napoleonic *corps d'armée* system. Consequently, the only means of subsisting armies that marched, as well as fought, in concentration, was to collect huge quantities of food and fodder in magazines and depots before the opening of a campaign – and to pass forward the supplies to the moving armies by means of convoys operating in their rear. Armies had used convoys to some extent in every age, of course, but never on the scale now required – and neither the administrative machinery nor the logistical experience necessary to satisfy the new demands existed; nor did roads of a type suitable for the weight and volume of traffic now envisaged. Small wonder, therefore, that many campaigns were conducted with what seemed to be deadening slowness and lack of decisiveness. Only the very greatest commanders of the age – Luxembourg, Marlborough, Eugene, Villars, Saxe and Frederick – proved occasionally capable of transcending these logistical limitations, and thus returned something of pace, colour and decisiveness to the conduct of warfare.

The sheer bulk of provisions required was staggering. Most armies tried to issue each man a kilogram of bread a day, but on account of extra rations issued to officers, and the need to feed waggoners and expert craftsmen accompanying an army, a force of 60,000 men might require all of 90,000 rations a day; Puységur calculated that 120,000 soldiers required 180,000 bread rations – and Dupré d'Aulnay, perhaps the most skilled logistical expert of the mid-eighteenth century, laid down the principle that it was always necessary to allow rations on a scale one third greater than the nominal strength of an army,[43] just to allow for the surplus entitlements of the French officers and general staff.

Professor Perjés has calculated every aspect of the problem of supplying an army with bread. On the basic assumption that 60,000 men required 900 quintals or hundredweight of bread a day (made from 675 quintals of grain or flour), at least sixty ovens operated by a staff of 240 bakers would be needed to undertake the baking of four days' rations. Armies habitually marched for three days and halted on the fourth, which was needed for rest and re-supply. To build a single oven called for 500 two-kilogram bricks, so to supply the basic requirements for sixty ovens called for sixty carts of bricks, and it required several days' work to establish an efficient bakery and the necessary stores around it. The fuel problem was even more dramatic. To fire the sixty ovens seven times a month required all of 1,400 waggon-loads of fuel (a single baking called for 200 loads). The milling of flour also presented daunting logistical problems: local mills were often targets for enemy interdictive action, so armies had to carry grinding equipment with them – still further enlarging the trains; on occasion commanders are known to have issued small hand-mills to regiments – as did Marlborough in 1705.

Some idea of the basic problems involved in feeding an army on campaign in our period may be gained from consideration of statistics of this kind. Unless a force could build up large quantities of milled flour at convenient points prior to entering on campaign, its operational freedom could be severely restricted. Only rarely were such resources available in advance – although most armies attempted to build up some reserves during the winter season (for example this formed a perennial duty for the French intendancies along the frontiers) – and this of course tended to restrict the scale and scope of operations. Although recourse was often had to wholesale requisitioning of supplies and transport in friendly or hostile areas alike – and many were the outcries of outrage that such actions provoked – the areas capable of supporting large numbers of men even if the local inhabitants went largely without were limited, as we have already noted. Only in those rare instances of an army being in a position to pay its way was anything approaching local cooperation whole-heartedly given. One such case was Marlborough's march to the Danube theatre from the Netherlands in 1704 – when it was noted that the local people vied with one another to bring supplies to the collecting points, for the Duke's quartermasters were paying good English gold at fair prices. But this was regarded as a wonderful novelty: in most cases, local populations regarded the presence of *any* army, whether friend or foe, as an unmitigated disaster, and prayed with fervour for it to march away elsewhere.

Given these difficulties, Marlborough's proud claim that during his period of command, '. . . everything has been so organised, and there has been so little cause for complaint, that all know our army in Flanders has been regularly supplied with bread during the war . . .'[44] is of no little significance.

However, if reserves were to be built up in advance, much reliance had to be placed on civilian contractors. No country possessed a formal procurement executive as such until the mid-eighteenth century, so much recourse had to be made to civilian entrepreneurs. This system was open to abuses from both sides: contractors were occasionally fraudulent and corrupt – mixing sand with the grain and resorting to other nefarious practices; but at the same time many governments were extremely remiss in honouring their agreements to produce payment. The English army dealt with contractors through the agency of Commissioners of Supply and Transport, appointed by the government; and acting through field commissaries. The bulk bread contractors of the early eighteenth century in Flanders included such names as Solomon and Moses Medina, Mynheer Hecop, Vanderkaa and Machado, most of them Spanish or Dutch Jews. The last-named, together with Solomon Abraham, were amongst the less scrupulous, and had to be carefully watched. But if the English army in Flanders was generally well supplied with necessaries, the same cannot be claimed for other armies – for example the English and Dutch forces serving in Portugal and Spain. Thus, in 1704 King Pedro of Portugal was induced to replace Salvador Segundez – as chief contractor – by Messrs. Gomez. This achieved nothing, as Segundez had control of the sources of supply, both bread and meat, such as they were in that semi-barren land, and proceeded to hold his successors to ransom. After one month of the autumn campaign that year, shortages steadily grew, and sometimes the army was three days without basic rations – which effectively immobilised General Fagel's forces.[45] Difficulties of this sort were common throughout Europe. Only when the French government came to rely upon the brilliant logistical skills of d'Aulnay did they begin to set their supply system in order. Prior to the mid-eighteenth century, they had placed reliance on the Intendants to find rations for the armies, but the development of central procurement – at least to a certain degree – proved an enormous advantage.

If feeding the troops posed enormous problems, that of finding fodder and forage for the horses – tens of thousands of which accompanied every army – was equally difficult. An army of 60,000 men would have at least 40,000 horses accompanying it. In the campaigning season – the exact length of which was dictated equally by the state of the roads and the availability, or otherwise, of fodder – such an army needed to find 10,000 quintals a day; in time of winter quarters, this dropped to about 5,000 quintals of solid feed – oats and straw. To convey such quantities called for some 1,000 carts in summer, and perhaps 500 in winter.

It was rarely attempted to convey such bulky quantities during the spring and summer, and all armies relied on local requisitioning – but local reserves of the period were once again not always equal to the task. Oats were only provided for the first and last months of a campaign, and for the period of winter quarters. At other times, continuous recourse was had to 'Grand Foragings', which might need anything from 4,000 to 10,000 troops to carry out at any one time. The best periods when the grass was lushest were first the main spring months and next the six or so weeks before the harvest. Less abundant supplies were available in early summer and late autumn. In spring it was estimated that horses needed two weeks of grazing to 'purify' themselves after the inadequate feeding of the winter months. In April 1710 the Hungarian patriot leader, Rakoczi, wrote that no operations could yet be undertaken '. . . before grass, for the army horses are depressed and look down upon the ground.' Thus another limitation on the waging of effective campaigns becomes apparent.[46] Foraging was as perennial a chore as baking.

'Grand Forages' were in any case elaborate affairs, calling for minute organisation and control – for it was during them that the ever-present danger of desertions reached its peak. Almost as many troops were therefore employed as guards and patrols as were involved in cutting the grass. On each occasion sufficient forage would be gathered for four or five days.

Few generals could break away from these deadening routines. Prince Eugene of Savoy, *pace* many historians, was insistent that his armies should operate from pre-stocked magazines. During his Italian campaigns of 1701 and 1702, he was particularly insistent on the establishment of suitable depots in the Frioul and Tyrol; in 1707 it was partly dissatisfaction with the supply arrangements – and his unwillingness to rely on the British Fleet as a source of major supply – that led to the abandonment of the siege of Toulon; and the following year, it was his 'conventional' concern for convoys and lines of communication that led him to oppose Marlborough's grandiose scheme, after Oudenarde, for an invasion of France along the coast (drawing supplies from the Fleet through Abbeville), and caused him to insist on the siege of Lille instead.

Some countries proved more adept than others at measuring up to these problems. The French, as the Earl of Orrery percipiently noted as early as 1676:

> ... with great prudence attack places in the beginning of the Spring, when there is no army to relieve them; and in the Summer, when the whole confederacy is in the field, they are usually on the defensive, and cover what they have took [sic]; and in my weak judgment they do at least as much by their always providing well to eat, and by their entrenched encamping, as by their good fighting, which questionless is the most hopeful and most solid way of making war.[47]

The French 'pounce' on Namur early in 1692 is a good example. Surprisingly, for in other respects the Ottoman Turk lagged in many of the martial skills and sciences, the strategy of the Porte was also realistic. Count Raimondo Montecuccoli noted that they operated from well filled magazines, and only when forage was available, seeking short, sharp wars and deliberately courting battle by invariably seizing the initiative and invading. His views were corroborated by de la Colonie, the seasoned Bavarian campaigner who observed:

> The Turks in all preceding wars against the Empire had always given battle on the first opportunity. If they lost the day, they immediately retired and made off to their homes. If victory declared itself in their favour, they would then make an extremely rapid advance, not employing themselves as is the custom in Europe in discussing camping grounds and strategy, for they believed the only way to make war upon the Christians was to strike a blow as rapidly as possible.[48]

Although he considered most of their huge armies, the Janissary Corps and the *sipahis* apart, as 'a mob', . . 'ignorant of all discipline . . .' and remarked cuttingly on the disorder of their encampments, he nevertheless admired the simplicity of the Tartar ration system.

Each of these nations are fed in a different fashion. That of the Tartars, perhaps has the merit of at least being the most convenient in form, the only provisions carried by their soldiery being cheeses made of mares' milk ... When required for use the Tartars scrape a little into a pannikin of water, stir it up with their finger, and swallow the mixture, which is as white as milk and constitutes their only nourishment. If we could all exist on such food, what a deal of trouble would be spared the world in general![48]

However, the 'Old Campaigner' believed in rather more elaborate self-help where supplies were concerned. Writing of the Battle of Belgrade in 1717, he reveals he

... had taken the precaution of seeing my canteens were well filled with provisions, including plenty of wine. ... I have always taken care to do this, finding it to be of the greatest use on all occasions ... but never more so than upon this day, for after the battle everyone suffered from hunger, and still more from thirst, and my officers of rank who had not shown the same forethought were much relieved to find that I had the wherewithal to minister to their needs.'[49]

Logistics, then, played a vital, even determinant, part in strategy. Some commanders, like Vendôme, tried to ignore the implications; that officer even ordered on one occasion that he was not under any circumstances to be troubled with matters pertaining to the supply of his men. Others became totally dominated by these problems – and achieved little in consequence. As in so many matters, it was Gustavus Adolphus of Sweden who had pioneered the seventeenth- and eighteenth-century system of logistics. Although his armies were smaller and therefore handier than their successors, he developed an integrated system of pre-stocked magazines, compact supply trains and well-organised services, and preached the advantages of orderly requisitioning over the traditional methods based upon indiscriminate looting and devastation. By the early eighteenth century, the formalised warfare of the day had become almost wholly based on an elaborate and ritualised system of logistics that sacrificed both range and mobility. This was the period of the 'rolling magazine', and of inter-related systems of fortified depots and defended lines of communication. Baggage and supply trains became ever larger as armies grew and as officers demanded the presence of more comforts in the field. Requisitioning became closely controlled, administered when-ever possible through municipal and provincial authorities under terms often formally defined by treaty. Battles became rare; military movements sluggish and often aimed against hostile lines of communication and bases rather than armed forces per se. In other words, 'War became an appendage of logistics', and Frederick II of Prussia would be moved to remark that 'the masterpiece of a successful general is to starve the enemy'. Wellington starved out Massena's troops in front of the Lines of Torres Vedras in 1811.

Thus, there is justification in talking about a 'crisis of strategy' in the late seventeenth and for much of the eighteenth centuries. Wars became 'limited', but not really because the war aims were restricted; indeed, an examination of many of the struggles of the period reveals the opposite. In 1672 France set out, quite simply, to destroy the United Provinces. The Spanish overseas empire had fallen apart, and the Dutch and Swedes fell into major decline by the 1720s; France and Turkey forfeited much of their former paramountcy whilst new major powers – England, Russia and Austria – moved to the centre of the world stage. These were not matters of a few frontier adjustments here and there – they represented major shifts in the balance of power, and the wars that led to these adjustments were fought with the intention of imposing a solution on the enemy rather than in seeking an accommodation or compromise with him. Yet these wars were undoubtedly 'limited' in a very real sense – namely in the restricted ability of armed forces to carry out the grand strategic or political aims ordered by their rulers and governments. Schemes of vast manoeuvre and rapid decision were beyond their scope. Campaigns and even wars were therefore largely controlled by logistical factors: an army was only operationally viable for areas over which it could carry its bread. Magazines of pre-stocked supplies were essential, but this reliance placed obstructions on the freedom of strategic movement. No army dared to advance more than a week's march from its latest magazines. Then it had to halt to establish a new depot, resite the ovens, and bake a fresh bread supply. And of course the likely presence of enemy fortresses in the vicinity still further impeded freedom of action. A general was ever aware of the vulnerability of his lines of communication – and these could be interdicted by enemy raiding parties unless all fortresses were either reduced by siege operations or at least carefully masked. Small wonder, then, that so many campaigns became dominated by formal siege warfare.

It has been calculated that the average campaigning season might last six months. But this period of time was never open for an uninterrupted advance, and unless a decisive battle could be forced at the very outset of a campaign (Ramillies in May 1706 is a rare case in point), there would be inadequate time for any truly effective follow-up or exploitation of the success gained. Normally a battle situation took several months to procure, and a victorious commander would be fortunate if he had 100 days left for pressing his advantage. But no fewer than seventy of these days would be taken up by basically administrative considerations. The twenty-four-hour halt every four days for foraging and issuing bread used up some twenty-five days; the need for regular rest days accounts for a further sixteen days; and when due allowance has been made for the resiting of magazines closer to the army, and the time taken in securing these moves, we find a mere thirty days left for true military advances. Few days' marches averaged above ten or twelve miles, so the maximum operational range for a successful army, which had won a battle by mid-campaign and thus earned the initiative, works out at a probable distance of between 300 and 350 miles. This would not in fact be achievable, for it presupposes the absence of any enemy fortresses to impede the line of march or threaten the extending communications behind the advancing army and also the absence of continuing resistance by the defeated army. As a result, it was physically impossible for a victorious army to defeat its opponent's main force and then occupy a substantial area of hostile territory before the onset of the next season of winter quarters during which the defeated foe could recover both his morale and his strength.[50] Small wonder that many wars became matters of elaborate manoeuvre.

Such then was the nature of the 'crisis in strategy'. The armies of the period were too preoccupied with problems of supply to be able to achieve a truly total victory. Even Marlborough's acclaimed march to the Danube in 1704 in fact covered little more than 250 miles – and all of the route was through friendly territory. The French could not intervene on the Neckar river to create a diversion because, the marshals declared, they could not operate there without first establishing magazines. After Ramillies the whole campaigning season lay ahead of the victorious Duke – and the result was the dramatic clearing of the French and their allies out of almost the whole area of the Spanish Netherlands. But opportunities of this sort were only rarely experienced. Limitations of space and time, and of manoeuvrability, hedged in even the most gifted of commanders with pressing and daunting difficulties – and this fact accounts for the inde-cisiveness of so many of the campaigns in our period. The situation had thus been reached in which decisive victory could only very rarely be won by the field armies of the day: they had become too large to be truly operationally viable. The results were long-drawn out wars of attrition until the processes of mutual exhaustion led to a pacification.

So much for this consideration of strategy in the early eighteenth century. As will be appreciated, this is a vast subject which deserves full examination in a volume on its own; all that we have had space for here, however, is the briefest sketch of some of its salient features, in order to place the studies of individual arms which make up the body of this study in some sort of strategic context, however inadequately treated.

NOTES

1 CSP (Dom), Vol. I (1689–90); and KWC, SP/8/6, dated 6 December 1689 (PRO).
2 Add Mss 19,519 and Harl. Mss 6334 (BM). Also Ordnance Warrants 55/536 (PRO).
3 C G Cruikshank, *Elizabeth's Army*, London, 1946, p. 31.
4 KWC, SP/8/8, folio 68 (PRO).
5 J M Deane, *A Journal of the Campaign in Flanders, MDCCVIII*, London, 1846, p. 4.
6 SP/63/353, folio 17 (SP Ireland, William & Mary) (PRO).
7 *Ibid.*, folio 32.
8 *Ibid.*, folio 18.
9 SP/Mil/41/3, folios 129 & 130 (PRO): reference tonnage ratio, see CSP (Dom), Anne II, p. 58.
10 KWC, SP/8/12, folios 29 & 30 (PRO); Add. Mss 23642, folios 16, 17, 18, etc. (BM).
11 C Walton, *History of the British Standing Army, 1660–1770*, London, 1894, p. 699.
12 WO:47:18, folio 431 (PRO).
13 *London Gazette*, April & May 1690.
14 Add. Mss 28082, folio 97 (BM).
15 KWC, SP/8/13, folio 93 (PRO).
16 G Murray, *Marlborough's Letters and Despatches*, London, 1845, Vol. I, p. 371.
17 *Ibid.*, Vol. III, p. 468.
18 Letter from Cadogan to Lord Raby, dated 20 September 1703, Strafford Papers, Add. Mss 22,196, folio 8.
19 Add. Mss 23642, folio 26, Tyrawly Papers (BM).
20 Mérode-Westerloo, *Mémoires*, Vol. I, p. 287.
21 W S Churchill, *Marlborough: His Life and Times*, London, 1947, Vol. II, p. 446; R Parker, *Memoirs of the Most Remarkable Military Transactions*, Dublin, 1746, p. 152.
22 Walton, *op. cit.*, p. 234.
23 SP/8/14, folio 122 (PRO).
24 SP/8/15, folio 110 (PRO).
25 R E Scouller, *The Armies of Queen Anne*, London, 1966, p. 204.
26 J W Fortescue, *The Last Post*, London, 1928, p. 20.
27 *A Military Dictionary*, London, 1702, p. 8.
28 H Gordon, *The War Office*, London, 1935, p. 148.
29 C M Clode, *Military and Martial Law*, London, 1874, Vol. I, p. 20.
30 Scouller, *op. cit.*, p. 165.
31 *Ibid.*, p. 165.
32 Add. Mss 33278, folio 69 (BM).
33 Commons Journals, Vol. XII, quoted in Clode, *op. cit.*, p. 221.
34 A Crichton, *The Life and Diary of Lt-Colonel John Blackadder*, Edinburgh, 1824, p. 407.
35 Parker, *op. cit.*, pp. 95–6.
36 SP/Mil/41/3, folio 121, dated 11 October 1710 (PRO).
37 KWC, SP/8/13, folio 90 (PRO).
38 *Ibid.*, folio 85 (PRO).
39 SP/8/13, folio 97 (PRO).
40 J U Nef, *War and Human Progress* (2nd edn), Harvard, 1950, p. 147.

41 Perjés, p. 51. He also cites in support the views of H Delbrück, *Geschichte der Kriegskunst*, Vol. IV, Berlin, 1920, p. 343.
42 H de Guibert, *Essai Générale de Tactique*, London, 1772, Vol. II, p. 6.
43 Puységur, *op. cit.*, Vol. II, p. 62; and D d'Aulnay, *Traité générale des subsistances militaires*, Paris, 1744, p. 116.
44 *Parliamentary History*, Vol. 6, p. 1088.
45 See D Francis, *The First Peninsular War, 1702–13*, London, 1975, pp. 99–100.
46 *Archivum Rackoczianum*, Vol. I, p. 229, cited in Perjés, *op. cit.*, p. 15 (footnote).
47 The Earl of Orrery, *A Treatise on the Art of Warre*, London, 1677, p. 139.
48 De la Colonie (ed. W C Horsley), *Chronicles of an Old Campaigner*, London, 1904, pp. 414–18.
49 *Ibid.*, pp. 442–3.
50 See Perjés, *op. cit.*, pp. 35–51 for a full analysis of this hypothesis.

CHAPTER X
Casualties

Military casualties were terrible in this period. Medical methods were hardly better than those used by the Romans. Of the wounded, only one in five could hope for recovery. These were bad odds! The Great Duke did whatever he could to help the wounded. Once the awful and bloody Battle of Malplaquet had ended (1709), Marlborough ordered his staff to help the wounded for both the Allied and enemies. A truce was announced, and the French were encouraged to collect their fallen and administer succour. On this and several other occasions we see evidence of Marlborough's humanitarian side – to modern, more cynical eyes a contradictory trait in those trained to cause death and destruction. Frederick the Great too, in his *Instructions to His Generals* of 1747, ordered them to 'think also of the poor wounded of both armies. Especially have paternal care for your own and do not be inhuman to those of the enemy'.

Hard times and suffering were not only the lot of the soldiery and poor. Princess Anne, soon to be Queen, lost seventeen children, and her only son who survived infancy, Prince William of Gloucester, died from smallpox in August 1700. Marlborough himself was broken hearted when his promising and only surviving son, Lord Blandford, died from smallpox at Cambridge in early spring 1704. Children also died in the field. At the Battle of Blenheim, Marshal Tallard, when taken prisoner, had just learnt of the death of his young son during the engagement. High and low could be summoned by death for many reasons. Indeed, William III was not destined to see the completion of his plans. His health had been giving considerable alarm for several months, and on 21 February 1702, while out riding, his horse stumbled on a mole-hill and threw him. He sustained a broken collar-bone and was very shaken. He died on 8 March. 'The King is dead. Long live the Queen!' *'Regina est!'*

Few subjects in later seventeenth- and early eighteenth-century military history are more intriguing – and yet more baffling – than the study of the statistics relating to great battles and sieges. These more or less 'bloody solutions of the crisis' (in Clausewitz's overworn phrase) form the focal points of every war, and Sir Winston Churchill tells us that they can be regarded as the 'principal milestones in secular history'.[1] Yet it is extremely difficult for the student to obtain even a reasonably accurate impression of casualty rates sustained. However, it may be possible at least to arrive at some approximate conclusions by means of a judicious comparison of available evidence and one or two other methods of objective approach to the problem.

Any comparison of the two wars waged in Flanders between 1689 and 1715 must start from two basic assertions, which should be examined at some length. First, it should be demonstrated that the thirteen or so years of the Spanish Succession War were considerably more active in overall military terms than the nine years of the preceding struggle. Secondly, it must be factually established that the level of Allied success was vastly greater in the second conflict than in the first. A quick study of some objective figures should suffice to establish these hypotheses, though of course they will not in any way explain the reasons for the contrast.

First let us examine the course of the Nine Years War (1689–97), and try to acquire a statistical picture of the major military events. As a pre-liminary step it is necessary to lay down our terms of reference. Broadly speaking, I have adopted the complementary approaches of Dr Gaston Bodart and the American Quincy Wright.[2] For the purposes of this study, I intend to ignore military manoeuvrings as such – as productive of relatively few casualties apart from deserters and stragglers, if those categories of martial flotsam can justly be considered under that title – and concentrate on four types of major military engagements: the battle (graded 1 to 3 according to the severity of losses sustained), the action (similarly graded 4 to 6), the siege, and finally the eighteenth-century military speciality, the forcing of defended lines.

During the Nine Years War, the Flanders theatre witnessed three major battles, two actions, one major crossing of the lines and five sieges – a total of eleven major events, or an average of approximately 1.2 'engagements' per year of hostilities. These bald facts do not reveal a very dynamic or action-packed series of campaigns, and when we turn to examine the subsequent conflict, we find a dramatically different picture. During the War of the Spanish Succession, as fought in the general 'Cockpit of Europe' area, there were once again three major battles (the only point of consistency between the two struggles in statistical terms), six actions, two celebrated passages of defended lines, and no fewer than twenty-nine sieges[3] – a total of forty major military events, or an annual average of just over three engagements. Of course, such arbitrary averaging out of events over the whole period really needs considerable qualification, for in point of fact two years of the earlier struggle (1694 and 1696) saw no sizeable operations in Flanders, whilst a further four saw only a single action apiece.[4] Similarly, four years of the Spanish Succession War (1701, 1704,

1707 and 1713) passed relatively passively in the Flanders region, but none of the remaining nine years included less than two major operations and no fewer than four separate years contained five or more apiece. Therefore, if we deduct the years of inactivity in both cases, the operational average changes to 1.5 operations per 'active' year for the Nine Years War, and 4.5 for the Spanish Succession struggle – highlighting still further the contrast in the scale of energetic operations in the region.

It may be useful to interpose at this point a brief analysis of the probable reasons for this contrast in activity – although of course it is a subject that merits far more comprehensive investigation. The main fact that I believe must be grasped is the totally different atmosphere of the two conflicts, which was itself largely due to the inter-action of the immediate and long-term aims of the respective governments and commander-in-chief, and the relative levels of military ability of the soldiers entrusted with the implementation of these policies.

Let us first examine the Nine Years War from this point of view. I believe the relative inactivity of this struggle was as much due to Louis XIV's lack of any definite war aim for the Flanders region, and to Marshal Luxembourg's adeptness at avoiding unwanted engagements, as to any military incapacity on the part of William III, who had most definite war aims in the theatre, and an almost painful eagerness to get to grips with his opponent, but unfortunately lacked either the physical or moral means of gaining the true initiative. This observation requires some qualification. If Louis XIV was generally complacent about the situation on France's north-eastern frontier, at least after his capture of Namur in 1692, his most brilliant commander of that epoch would seem to have felt considerable frustration at the royal directives he received urging him to avoid battles. A glance at the table of contents of the celebrated work of de Beaurain reveals such passages as 'defensive strategy enjoined' (1690) and 'ordered not to court battle' (1691), and it is interesting to note that his trio of great victories over the Allies all took place in the years when the Duke was serving as 'commander-in-chief separate from the King' – namely in 1690, 1692 and 1693.[5] Otherwise, once his forces had captured Mons and Namur, the French monarch was content to have his armies rest upon their laurels, attempting little in terms of further aggrandisement, and complacently safe within the famous triple line of fortresses that Vauban had by that time practically brought to a state of completion.

If Louis XIV was generally pleased to 'let sleeping dogs lie', nothing could have been further from William III's wishes. Unfortunately his notable moral courage and determination did not prove sufficient to make up for the lack of general material support from England, the United Provinces, and his other Allies, whilst the King did not personally possess sufficient military talent to be able to outwit the great Luxembourg, and his subordinate commanders, such as Solms and the aged Waldeck, were either very mediocre or past their prime. Consequently, William never really had the chance to seize the true initiative – at least until 1695. All Allied efforts to wrest a battlefield advantage over their opponents foundered, and without such preliminary successes in the field there was no chance for William to tackle the French fortress barrier. As a result, the war dragged on with little attempt to reach a genuine decision, with complacency and calm aloofness on the one side and near-desperate frustration and inability on the other.

It is against this rather apathetic background that we must place William's one startling achievement – the recovery of Namur in 1695; the furore this feat produced at the time (it inspired numberless odes, panegyrics and heroic poems, as a glance at the Catalogue of the British Museum will testify) was as much due to the fact that it was wholly contrary to the established, rather dreary pattern of the war, as to any really startling military merit displayed in the associated operations. But this episode proved the sole excitement over the last four years of the struggle in Flanders. Indeed, we can assert that this inconclusive and drab type of conflict was true about all fronts in the Nine Years War. Further consultation of Wright's exhaustive tables reveals that although seven major states were involved in the war, there were only a total of twenty-five battles (all fronts). For the War of the Spanish Succession, on the other hand, although it lasted four years longer and involved nine major states (if we include Bavaria), there were no fewer than 105 battles.[6]

Of course 'Marlborough's War' was fought under wholly different conditions. Although Louis XIV was once again on the strategic defensive – attempting to retain the Spanish inheritance in Europe and overseas – the tenor of events is far more dramatic, as we have already demonstrated. Not only was Marlborough by far the best commander produced by either side (Eugene is his sole rival), being endowed with a great gift for enforcing his will upon his opponents (and, generally speaking, upon his Allies too), supported from home and the United Provinces far more comprehensively in terms of men, money and munitions than William had ever been, at least until 1710, but his skill as a battlefield commander in the Netherlands enabled him to wrest the initiative in campaign after campaign (although there were exceptions, as in 1703, 1705 and 1707, the 'lean' years that seemed always to precede and follow the 'fat' years of great achievement). Thereafter he was in a position to tackle the great systems of French fortresses, although it must of course be noted that he fell from grace and command before he was in a position to finally open 'the road to Spain through France',[7] his avowed Grand Strategy.

Turning to the second assertion we made at the outset, it is very easy to prove the relatively high degree of success enjoyed by the Allies in Flanders between 1701 and 1713, compared to that enjoyed – or rather endured – in the earlier war. Of the eleven major military events of the period 1689 to 1697, only two operations went wholly satisfactorily for the Allies – namely the initial combat at Walcourt (surprisingly omitted by the conscientious Bodart), and the second siege of Namur, and it was only in the latter that William III played any direct part. This represents a degree of Allied success of only 18.2 per cent. In the subsequent war, however, the Allies gained the advantage no fewer than thirty-one times out of the total of forty engagements and sieges. This represents a success rate of 77.5 per cent overall; it is also revealing to note that Marlborough was personally associated with twenty-four of those successful operations (or 77.6 per cent), and was in no way connected with the nine setbacks which took place either before his arrival in the theatre or following his disgrace.

The fact that Marlborough's successes included no fewer than eighteen sieges between 1702 and 1711 makes another explanatory comment necessary. At first sight, the fact that he fought only three great battles and two actions in Flanders – as against such a redoubtable number of siege operations – might seem to challenge the widely held view that Marlborough was pre-eminently a 'battle-seeking general'. We must be wary, however, of over-hastily readjusting our opinion. Mostly the evidence *does* in fact support the established view, no matter what the figures may appear to indicate. From first to last, Marlborough was genuinely seeking 'the bloody decision', but for reasons largely beyond his control, he was all too often thwarted in his search. We should place besides his three battles in Flanders the four different occasions when he was frustrated of the desired action, although in three of them the situation was highly favourable and the chances of victory as certain as they ever can be. On the fourth occasion (1711), he was forced to refuse Villars' challenge owing to shortage of numbers and material due to Allied parsimony immediately prior to his dismissal by Queen Anne. Generally speaking, however, the basic reason for the failure of the battle to materialise on the three earlier occasions (the Heaths of Peer, 1702; Waterloo, 1705, and Seneffen, 1707) was largely Allied obstruction based on their fear of sustaining heavy casualties. On at least two of these occasions, Marlborough could have forced their hand, but so great was his unselfish ability to view the interests of the Grand Alliance as a whole, that he was prepared to throw away practically ideal situations and thus incur the slurs of his enemies and detractors, rather than strain the never-robust cohesion of what must have been some of the most selfish, short-sighted and bigoted nations ever to join together in an international alliance.

This statesmanship caused Marlborough to take militarily less satisfactory decisions, and in order to 'play along' with his conventionally minded and cautious Allies, he more or less willingly undertook the lengthy list of sieges associated with his campaigns in Flanders. This was one reason for the number of Marlburian sieges. There are, of course, other equally important ones. First, there was the indubitable difficulty of forcing action on unwilling adversaries, in an age when organisation and tactics were either still very rudimentary or formalised to a deadening degree, which gave every possible advantage to a defender holding a strong and carefully chosen position. Although part of Marlborough's genius lay in his ability to 'snatch' battles from unlikely situations, as at the Schellenberg and before Blenheim in 1704, and above all before Oudenarde in 1708, he was not always able to force his opponents' hand, and with the probable exception of Ramillies and Malplaquet, the French were for their part consistently eager to avoid trying conclusions with 'Monsieur Malbrouck' – and with good reason we may add!

Then secondly, it was militarily imperative that the French fortress barrier should be destroyed or at least neutralised before Marlborough could undertake his avowed design of reconquering Spain for the Habsburg claimant by way of a march on Versailles. He could not afford to leave the enemy garrisons, or the remnants of French field armies operating under the cover of these *points d'appuis* a free hand, firstly because this would expose all of the reconquered Spanish Netherlands and even the United Provinces to enemy raids, devastation and 'contribution', and secondly because this would also dangerously expose his lines of communication as he pressed on into France.

In an age when the bulk of any army could not be trusted to forage for themselves for fear of mass desertions, almost total dependence was placed on pre-stocked magazines and lengthy convoys, which at times comprised several thousand waggons. These last were clearly vulnerable to enemy attack, especially if they had to pass through country where enemy garrisons still lurked. One notable French 'interdiction' raid which illustrates this type of hazard – though thanks to Major-General Webb's staunch fight with the escort it proved a complete failure – was General de Lamotte's attack on the Allied convoy at Wynendael in 1708, during the siege of Lille. The same period also provides an illustration of the French carrying out wasting raids as diversion when they launched an attack against Brussels in an attempt to draw off the main Allied army from the trenches around 'the greatest city of France.'[8] For these reasons, then, Marlborough had no real option but to undertake siege after siege, and as he never could afford enough men to simply blockade the French fortresses, the long-awaited advance into the heart of France was continually postponed, and in fact never materialised. In other words, siege warfare on an extensive scale was practically unavoidable in a river – and town – dominated area such as Flanders.

At this point we must leave these rather generalised considerations of the campaigns in Flanders, and turn to make an examination of casualty figures sustained there, seeking any valid distinctions between those suffered in William's operations and those borne by Marlborough's men. Figures relating to the English force have been worked out covering all aspects of warfare for the periods 1690–9 and 1700–9. From these, it would appear that in the earlier period the British Isles lost a total of some 19,000 killed and wounded, out of a total number of 133,250 troops put into the field – or just about 14.26 per cent overall (alternatively .35 per cent of the whole population of 5,475,000); for the second period, the total loss is placed at 37,950 killed and wounded out of a grand total of 258,300 – or about 14.7 per cent.[9] If correct, these figures would seem to show only half a per cent rise in casualty proportions over the greater part of the two wars we have under consideration. At first sight this may seem surprising, considering the far greater range of activities indulged in during the Spanish Succession War, but no doubt the higher proportion of Allied successes (especially in Flanders) partially accounts for this, for as a general rule the victor suffers less than the vanquished, though this was certainly not true at Malplaquet, whilst quite a few sieges also exacted a heavier toll of life and limb from the besiegers – even if ultimately successful – than from the besieged. Nevertheless, William III's whole series of battlefield failures were somewhat more costly when taken together as a percentage of the total strength than Marlborough's battle-field victories.[10] The figures we have quoted of course take no account of Allied losses over the same period – and I have not been able to discover similar estimates for the Dutch, Imperialists, Danes, etc. (who undoubtedly suffered proportionately heavier casualties than the British at both Ramillies and Malplaquet), or for the French and Spaniards. These, it can be hoped, will materialise as research continues.

However, no military historian would deny that the whole business of casualty figures is fraught with inconsistencies, pitfalls and unjustifiable generalisations. It is not difficult to see where the problems lie, although it is virtually impossible to overcome them all. In the first place, there is no officially standardised way of calculating casualty figures even today, and if that is the case, there is even less reason to suppose anything but an even worse situation for the seventeenth and eighteenth centuries. This does not so much refer to figures of the killed, for 'stone dead hath no fellow', and qualitatively we are on firm ground even if quantitatively much remains in doubt. But we can draw no such meagre comfort for figures of the wounded, for here there is an almost insuperable qualitative problem as well. Some authorities apparently regard 'wounded' as men laid 'hors de combat' – out for the count and needing carts or ambulances after the battle; others include anybody hit with anything – be it but a clod of earth winging by – and blithely include lightly and walking wounded within this category, this clearly adding a vast number of men to their statistics. Unfortunately, they have all too rarely – in past or present – cared to detail their exact terms of reference. When we go on to consider 'prisoners' the situation is equally obscure; do such statistics only refer to 'hale, hearty and whole' captives, or do they include the incapacitated as well? If the latter, as is probably most usually the case, have the calculators avoided the pitfall of adding such wounded prisoners into their totals twice? And so on. Such problems are hardly capable of definitive solution, and if the argument is still raging over such a comparatively recent battle as the Somme,[11] what chance have we of reaching more accurate figures for Steenkirk or Malplaquet?

Many historians place great reliance on primary sources – or contemporary evidence – in their attempts to reach objective truths, but this can be just as problem-prone as any other approach when dealing with casualties. For various reasons, contemporary evidence is very suspect. In the first place, there is the very human temptation to minimise one's own losses for purposes of prestige or propaganda, in the ancient 'I may look a sight but you just ought to see the other fellow' tradition of gamesmanship (if we can interpolate such a whimsical concept into an historical thesis).

In the early eighteenth century there was a second, more mundane, reason for such barefaced subterfuges as falsifying casualty returns, especially at battalion or regimental level. Commanding officers were often tempted, not so much by a becoming sense of modesty, as by a very real financial consideration, from revealing the true extent of their losses on the battlefield. At the time such matters as pay and supplies were wholly calculated on a daily per capita basis, and it accordingly behoved a colonel to represent his unit as being as nearly up to strength as possible – or to the extent he could get away with. Checks by the staff were superficial to say the least; on the morrow of a battle each regiment would be paraded for inspection, but there is plenty of evidence that the staff assistants counted only the first rank and then multiplied by the depth. In an age when regiments still habitually paraded six ranks deep, it did not take much cunning on the part of the sergeants to conceal a considerable number of gaps 'in the brown'. Such 'paper-men' or 'dead-pays', as they were called, feature prominently in our national literature, particularly in the recruiting field where the rackets were identical, from Sir John Falstolf's palmy days to the equally grafting period of Sterne's Uncle Toby, or George Farquhar's Captain Plume and Sergeant Kite.[12] Doubtless, such dishonesties are as old as military history, but this does not assist the serious student.

Thirdly, there was the great difficulty experienced by contemporaries in obtaining accurate estimates of enemy strengths and losses. This, too, led to many miscalculations which slip by at the time and are subsequently repeated again and again by later historians in the grand old tradition of 'history never repeats itself but historians repeat each other'. Two notable examples of this are the sources relied upon by no less a personage than the Duke of Luxembourg when estimating William III's casualties at Steenkirk. A despatch to Versailles, dated the 'Camp of Hoves, 4th August, 1692', runs (in part) as follows:

Milord Lucan spoke yesterday with the Governor of a young Scottish lord, who came from Brussels to find his body on the battlefield. The Governor told him into his very ear in a low voice and in confidence that the English and Scots had lost 3,000 on the field of battle and that these two nations had more than 3,000 wounded.

A little later in the same document we find that the noble Duke is still open to suggestions on this ticklish matter, for we read:

A French wine-waiter in the service of M. Overkirk told one of my guards that they had lost over 10,000 men – and I think that is at least so.[13]

But when, a few days later, it comes to the matter of revealing his own losses to the parsimonious 'Roi Soleil', Luxembourg sees fit to write:

The loss suffered by the King's army was between 6 and 7,000 men killed and wounded; that of the foe was a third higher, without including the prisoners.[14]

In point of fact, the French commander was being extremely fair and even accurate by the lights of the time. Some far more blatant exaggerations could be cited even though his estimates of enemy casualties clearly and optimistically miss every time – Bodart puts the respective losses at 8,000 Allies and 7,000 French respectively, but I trust the point about the haphazard sources of information employed, and the consequent room for misinformation or misrepresentation, has been adequately made.

If contemporary sources need to be handled with caution, so do the calculations of later experts. It is extremely easy for a modern historian to give an entirely fallacious impression about an engagement by quoting technically accurate and yet wholly misleading statistics. Steenkirk, again, provides us with an interesting case in point, and the culprit is none other than the worthy Bodart himself. According to this reputable source, the Allies lost seven generals, 450 officers together with 8,000 other ranks – or 6,600 killed and 1,400 wounded – which are reasonably dependable figures, the abnormally high death rate being due to the extreme ferocity of the fireflight at literally point-blank range. However, he then goes on to claim that this loss represents 12.8 per cent of the Allied army (63,000 strong), which is mathematically sound enough but historically gives completely the wrong impression of the battle, for nowhere does he mention that *only* the Allied advance guard and a few nearby supporting units were engaged at all – a total of twenty-six infantry battalions (twenty-three English, three Danish) and three dragoon regiments, or some 15,000 men in all. But it was these unfortunate 15,000 that bore the brunt of the casualties, and thus over 50 per cent of their number went down killed or wounded, justifying Walton's comment (for 12 per cent battle casualties were a commonplace) that 'the battle is, for the number engaged, one of the most bloody on record.'[15] This, surely, is almost a classic example of how figures, wrongly used, can lie, not that the excellent Bodart had the least desire to deceive.

Of course there are steps an historian can take to check the reliability of his sources of information. Obviously he can compare sets of figures, and try to draw inferences from their points of similarity and dissimilarity; he can study the detailed analyses of such fine scholars as C T Atkinson.[16] Even better – if he is fortunate enough to find them – he can seek out completely objective contemporary documents which can throw a lot of light upon their less reliable brethren. We are quoting Steenkirk a great deal, but at least it provides a thread of continuity from argument to argument. After the battle, we find in the Treasury Dispatch Book a request for twenty remounts for Berkeley's (3rd Dragoon Guards), twenty-three for Godfrey's (4th Dragoon Guards) and thirty-six for Galway's (later disbanded) – or a total of seventy-nine horses. As cavalry played a very minor part in this engagement, 'the severest ever fought by infantry',[17] these figures suggest a loss of perhaps twenty troopers killed and as many wounded – a horse providing so much larger a target. This impression is largely borne out by a document included in King William's Chest which claims that Berkeley's lost one officer and six men killed and five troopers wounded besides twenty-three horses, whilst Godfrey's lost eight men killed, six wounded and twenty-six horses.[18]

So far these figures tie up well with the Treasury document, but this second source then goes on to reveal that Galway's Regiment – disbanded in 1698 – lost only one trooper killed and an officer and six men wounded. Why then, does the unit need as many as thirty-six remounts? Of course there may have been a howitzer shell exploding amongst a large group of held horses (though this is pure surmise), which would account for such a loss of quadrupeds, but to say the least it sets the historical sleuth a-sniffing! Similarly, the same source lists Langston's Regiment – officially disbanded in 1692 soon after the battle (24 August 1692, in fact) for 'such heavy losses'[19] – as having suffered merely one officer and ten troopers killed, two more wounded and twenty-six horses lost. If these figures are true, why was the regiment disbanded? Unless it already was at a strength of barely half a troop, which is improbable. Nevertheless, such information can be extremely valuable, none more so than the document in the War Office volumes dated 14 December 1709, which lists by regiments the number of recruits needed to bring them up to strength for the next campaign – listing twenty-one units and calling for drafts totalling 3,234 infantry.[20]

Finally, to reach conclusions on the relative expenditure of life, limb and blood in the two wars mainly under consideration, we must assess a vast amount of conflicting information which is best tackled in tabulated form. It would seem that there is not in fact a great deal to differentiate between the two wars' respective rates of loss, although, predictably, William's proportionate battlefield losses are considerably greater than Marlborough's. As for the sieges, the story is much the same: some great towns won for a song; others, like Namur or Lille, taking as great a toll as a major battle.

To conclude, I would like to quote a passage from *Tristram Shandy*, referring to the Battle of Steenkirk.

'There was Cutts,' continued the corporal, clapping the forefinger of his right-hand upon the thumb of his left, 'there was Cutts', Mackays', Angus', Graham's, and Lever's – all cut to pieces; so had the English Life Guards been too, had it not been for some regiments upon the right who marched up boldly to their relief and received the enemy's fire in their faces, before any one of their own platoons discharged a musket.'

'They'll go to heaven for it,' added Trim.

'Trim is right,' said my Uncle Toby.

Would that all problems relating to late seventeenth-century warfare could be equally definitely and simply resolved.

NOTES

1   W S Churchill, *The Life and Times of the Duke of Marlborough* (2nd edn), London, 1947, Vol. II, p. 381.
2   See Q Wright, *A Study of War*, 2 Vols, Chicago, 1942, Appendix XIX, Tables 22, 24 & 26.
3   They include Antwerp (1706) and Hondeschoote (1708) as sieges.
4   The earlier sieges include the two in Flanders in 1694 and 1696.
5   See de Beaurain, *Histoire militaire de Flandres*, Paris, 1775, Vol. I, *passim*.
6   Wright, *op. cit.*, Table 35, p. 644. See also J Childs, *The Nine Years' War* (1991) and *Warfare in the Seventeenth Century* (2001).
7   Mérode-Westerloo, *Mémoires*, Brussels, 1840, Vol. II, p. 68.
8   Churchill, *op. cit.*, p. 424.
9   Wright, *op. cit.*, Table 54, p. 660.
10 King William III's casualties can be put at 26%; Marlborough's overall losses at 10.8%.
11 See *RUSI Journal*, February 1966, p. 69.
12 Shakespeare, *King Henry IV*, Part I, Act 3, Scene 2; Lawrence Sterne, *Tristram Shandy*, London, 1759, and George Farquhar, *The Recruiting Officer*, London, 1906.
13 de Beaurain, *op. cit.*, p. 208.
14 *Ibid.*, p. 209.

15 C Walton, *A History of the English Standing Army, 1660–1700*, London, 1894, p. 2.

16 C T Atkinson, article in *SAHR Journal, op. cit.*, p. 200 on Steenkirk.

17 J W Fortescue, *History of the British Army*, London, 1899, Vol. I, p. 369, and *Treasury Dispatch Book*, Vol. VI, p. 36.

18 SP/8/12, folio 117 (PRO).

19 C Dalton, *English Army Lists and Commission Registers, 1661–1714*, Vol. III, p. 221.

20 WO IV, Vol. IX, dated 14 December 1709.

Part Two

Now all the youth of England are on fire,
And silken dalliance in the wardrobe lies;
Now thrive the armourers, and honour's thought
Reigns solely in the breast of every man:
They sell the pasture now to buy the horse,
Following the mirror of all Christian kings,
With wingèd heels, as English Mercuries.

Shakespeare, *King Henry V*, Prologue

CHAPTER XI

'The Old Corporal'

A Preliminary Report

On 8 March 1702 Anne Stuart ascended the throne, and was crowned on 23 April. Her bosom friend, Sarah, Lady Marlborough, was appointed to three high posts, including Mistress of the Robes. Marlborough was made a Knight of the Garter, Captain-General and Master of the Ordnance; and he was also soon to become a Duke. It was indeed 'a sunshine day' for the Churchills, their children and nearest friends.

It is said that 'behind every great man there stands a woman', and John Churchill was blessed, and in certain ways bedevilled too, with rather more than his share of 'fair intriguers'. No fewer than five important ladies played vital roles in his life at various times. But for his elder sister, Arabella – who became the mistress of James, Duke of York – John might never have emerged from the West Country. Made a page at court and then appointed a junior officer in the Guards, he soon made his mark at the Restoration Court of King Charles II. Young John risked an early fall by 'sharing' one mistress, Barbara Villiers, Duchess of Cleveland, with the King, by whom she became pregnant, and he received a gift of £5,000.

The third and most important woman in John Churchill's life was Sarah Jennings (correctly Jenyns). Although both families were against the marriage, the young people made up their own minds in 1678 and the pair proved devoted lovers. They so longed for each other's company that Sarah once wrote to a friend that, upon his returning from the wars, 'my Lord pleasured me with his boots on'! Despite Sarah's waspish wit, haughty bearing and ability to scold furiously, they were popular at court and enjoyed the trust and support of many powerful people.

Most powerful among their friends was the Queen herself, the special friendship between Anne and Sarah dating from 1684. They privately called themselves 'Mrs Morley and Mrs Freeman' for long years, and exchanged confidences and innermost thoughts. The intimacy became strained when Sarah achieved her first royal position, but had collapsed by 1710 after Queen Anne found another more homely friend in Abigail Masham, her bedchamber-woman. Queen Anne was not a very dynamic person, and not strong in health; she was not noted for her intelligence, and could be stubborn, and during her last years she turned more and more to Mrs Masham. Sarah was removed from court and Mrs Masham's 'friends' now had the sovereign's ear and could influence her.

In one way or another, these five important women effectively raised and then ruined the First Duke Marlborough. By 1713 he had lost all his posts and dramatically fallen from favour. A more detached analysis may ascribe this as largely due to extreme Tory politics, but one must not forget the stubbornness of the Queen, and who 'helped' her decide to entrust the nation to Harley and Bolingbroke.

On one occasion as his long life drew towards its close, Marlborough is reputed to have paused before his portrait by Kneller, painted when he was still a young soldier, and to have made the rather sad remark: 'that was once a man.'[1]

For his physical appearance we have only to glance at this somewhat later portrait by Kneller, painted in 1706, and to supplement it with Colonel Goslinga's description, written a few years later. The Duke, he wrote:

> is a man of birth; about the middle height, and the best figure in the world: his features without fault, fine sparkling eyes, good teeth, and his complexion such a mixture of white and red as the fairer sex might envy; in brief, except for his legs, which are too thin, one of the handsomest men ever seen.

The impact of his deeds and personality proved even more irresistible to his contemporaries, both for good and ill, than did his personable presence. His first major biographer, Thomas Lediard, recorded with wonderment (and a little exaggeration, but only a little):

> ... that in twenty campaigns, ten of which were successive, he passed all the rivers and lines he attempted, took all the towns he invested, won all the battles he fought (this often with inferior, rarely with superior force) was never surpriz'd by his enemy, nor charg'd with one action of cruelty, was ever belov'd by his own soldiers, and dreaded by those of his Enemy.

To his rank and file, he was 'the Old Corporal'. One of them, Corporal Matthew Bishop, enthused that 'the known world could not produce a man capable of more humanity, and all honour was due to him, for what he promised he would perform'.[2] As was the case with Erwin Rommel in the Western Desert 1942, this respectful admiration was not restricted to his own side alone. Marshal Vendôme, for example, summoned to take over command from Villeroi after the disaster of Ramillies in 1706, noted with disquiet at French Headquarters at Valenciennes that 'everybody here is only too ready to raise their hats at the mention of Marlborough's name'. The fact that the French army paid the Duke the oblique honour of adapting an earlier folk song dating back to the days of Simon de Montfort and the Albigensian Crusade, and marched to war singing somewhat ruefully, '*Malbrook se va t'en guerre, Mironton, Mironton, Mironton*',[3] provides a further indication of his pervasive prestige.

Duke John's charisma extended far beyond the purely military environment which witnessed his greatest achievements. Anne Stuart, as both Princess and Queen, had the utmost faith in her 'Mr Freeman' – the mode in which she preferred to address him in private correspondence, signing herself with the *nom-de-plume* of 'Mrs Morley' – over a period of some forty years, and only latterly did her disillusion with the waspish Duchess Sarah and the increasing influence of Marlborough's High Tory opponents over a lonely, ageing and ailing woman come to mar the relationship. Emperors, Margraves and Princes hastened to pay him compliments, and – the younger ones at least – to seek positions in his entourage. Electress Sophia, 'the Old Strumpet' as history has slightly unkindly dubbed her, recalled of his visit to Hanover in late 1704, that she '. . . never met anyone pleasanter, nor more courteous and obliging. He is as good a courtier as he is a brave soldier', although this encomium promptly aroused Sarah's jealousy of 'that ridiculous creature' as she thereafter called poor Sophia.

Of course his political foes in England had other, less flattering names for him, including 'King John II', a reference to his repeated but vain efforts to be appointed Captain-General for Life. But even one of the most bitter of his critics, his erstwhile protégé, Henry St John, later Viscount Bolingbroke, is reputed to have said of him that 'He was so great a man that I forget that fault', and the same political foe was also secretly commissioned by Duchess Sarah, years after her husband's death, to compose the celebrated panegyric describing Marlborough's martial achievements that is carved on the pediment of the Column of Victory at Blenheim Palace – a masterpiece of concise and beautifully expressed Augustan English, which, Sir Winston Churchill has avowed, 'would serve as a history in itself were all other records lost'.

Any attempt to assess or summarise John Churchill's standing as a military commander must necessarily take as its starting point the man himself. A commander's character and personality, as well as being influenced by the strains of warfare, equally place a stamp on his particular brand of generalship, and this was particularly true under the conditions of early eighteenth-century warfare when a Commander-in-Chief habitually issued orders direct to his regimental colonels.

If the behavioural scientists are to be believed, the essential nature of a man is largely formed in childhood and adolescence. The genteel poverty and confused political atmosphere of his earliest years at Asche House in Devon indubitably left their mark.[4] His father's social pretensions and strong Royalist sympathies were clearly passed on to his eldest son, born in 1650 sixteen months after the execution of King Charles I. From his father, the young Churchill learnt to revere the established church of the realm and the House of Stuart, to conceal his personal political feelings, and to be extremely careful in all matters pertaining to money. Several of these traits we shall in due course return to.

We know relatively little about his mother's influence. Apart from the fact that she opposed her son's proposed marriage to Sarah (largely on financial grounds), and that she was decidedly 'peevish' when her daughter-in-law lived under her and Sir Winston's roof in 1680 (though Sarah must have been a redoubtable member of the family, even in youth),[5] Elizabeth Churchill remains in the shadows. John's maternal grandmother, on the other hand, was evidently of the strongest character and puritanical in outlook, and doubtless applied the rod of discipline to the young boy when his father was lost in his genealogical research and his mother was wholly absorbed with the care of the rest of the family. There seems to have been little softness in Lady Eleanor Drake.

His schooling appears to have been conventional for the day if somewhat dislocated by the family's frequent moves. However, the transition from the strict penury of Asche House and the intellectual discipline of St Paul's School to the 'jovial times' and permissive atmosphere of the Court of Charles II must have been a considerable shock to the adolescent youth's system. Certainly he seems to have made the most of his opportunities, both courtly and amorous. His long liaison with Barbara Villiers, Duchess of Cleveland, whose 'langorous eye bespoke the melting soul', and whose favours he riskily shared with his monarch on what seems to have been a 'shift and shift about' basis, gained him no little experience of life, several exciting adventures, and some not inconsiderable gifts of money. The fact that he was not wholly transformed into a voluptuary courtier must be in large measure ascribed to his earlier upbringing. He had learnt from the earliest years to keep his own counsel and not to be taken in by appearances, and these qualities were to serve him well on many a long campaign in later years.

Two reasons may be suggested for his choice of a military career. First, the influence of Sir Winston Churchill, the sometime Captain of Royalist Horse, probably provided the original incentive. Secondly, the continued poverty of both John and his family after the Restoration must also have played a part. A young courtier with no money and even slenderer prospects could hope for no better way to improve his fortunes than to adopt the profession of arms – and earn preferment and possibly an heiress by gallant behaviour at the cannon's mouth. Of his poverty there can be no question: he relied on the gifts of the Duchess of Cleveland to procure his early steps in the army, and it was only after five years of marriage to Sarah that he could afford to buy a house of his own.

Thus by his early twenties we have a young man already worldly-wise and experienced by the standards of his day, with two duels behind him, yet also noticed for his basic common sense, willingness to learn, confidence in his own judgment, and his general good humour (rather than sense of humour, for to his life's end John Churchill seems to have been of a rather staid and serious temperament). His marriage to Sarah Jennings in 1678 proved a genuine love-match, and although it can be argued that his tempestuous and opinionated spouse did his career more harm than good in the end, there can be no doubting how much store he placed on his family life and home. His qualities as a husband and father were severely tested over the years – but some of the most likeable aspects of the man are those that relate to his life-long love for both Sarah and their children. It is clear that not all his frustrations on active service stemmed from ineffective allies and obstructive Dutch deputies when we read, of one return from the wars, that 'My Lord pleasured me twice with his boots on'. And in 1702 he wrote from the seat of war that her letters were 'so welcome to me that I could not forbear to read them ... even if I was expecting the enemy to charge me'. The family story held sadness as well as joy. The death of his son and heir in 1703 left a lasting scar, and that of his favourite daughter, Anne, in 1716, hastened the collapse of his own health. His last years were also overcast by Sarah's devastating rows with her surviving and equally contentious daughters.

From these general points drawn from his early life, we must pass to consider specific character traits which affected his skills as a general. First we must examine his ambition, for Churchill was driven by a ruthless demon from earliest manhood. He was avid throughout his life for wealth, power and social position. Fortunately for both himself and his country, his dreams were to a great degree matched by his talents, and although he suffered many disappointments and setbacks, and had to wait until his middle years for the realisation of most of his ambitions (he was 53 before he secured international recognition as a soldier), he was tireless throughout his life (until the last decade, perhaps, when ill-health and a touch of disillusion appeared) in his quest for fame, rank and riches. In pursuit of his personal interests he could be unscrupulous – as his desertion of James II in 1688 bears evidence. Long years of close association with the convolutions of Stuart politics inevitably bred a complex personality with a strong instinct for personal survival. His continued contacts with the court-in-exile of James and his son were as much a matter of insurance as one of convenience. It made him a hard man to trust. On the other hand he could also display a strong streak of altruism and unselfishness – as his long loyalty to Queen Anne, which survived the cooling of their friendship until 1713, or his refusal of the twice proffered position of Viceroy of the Spanish Netherlands in his genuine concern for the interests of the Second Grand Alliance, provide incontrovertible evidence. He became both a Duke and a Prince of the Holy Roman Empire, yet the passion for pre-eminent position (as well as political stability) could move him to press repeatedly and ill-advisedly for the award of the Captain-Generalcy for life during the years between 1709 and 1712.

This ambition was often concealed behind an urbane and polished exterior. His charm and outward gentleness were legendary in his own time. On occasion he could revert to straightforward flattery – as during his visit to Altranstadt in 1707 when he assured Charles XII of Sweden of his desire to serve under his command to learn the last refinements in the military arts. It is recorded of him that he never issued a harsher rebuke than to send a message to the culprit to the effect that 'My Lord Duke is surprised . . .' The published correspondence, however, does occasionally give a sharper expression of phrase, and his private letters to Heinsius often reveal his unadorned feelings. Yet he could refuse a request with considerably more grace than many examples of his courtesy to his enemies, especially when vanquished or wounded, as after Malplaquet. His gentleness extended to the rank and file; he would give occasional lifts to tired and sweaty foot-soldiers in his coach,[6] he was ever concerned for their welfare, and yet was genuinely surprised and elated when they responded with marks of affection – as at Elixhem in 1705 when he was cheered by his cavalry. '. . . This gave occasion to the troops with me to make me very kind expressions, even in the heat of the action, which I own to you gives me great pleasure, and makes me resolve to endure anything for their sakes.'[7] This mutual confidence and esteem formed one vital ingredient of victory.

When occasion demanded it, however, he could be utterly ruthless. On 16 July 1704 he coolly wrote to Godolphin as his army ravaged Bavaria: 'We are doing all the mischief we can to this country, in order to make the Elector think of saving what he cannot reach; for as we advance we burn and destroy; but if this should not make him come to a treaty, I am afraid it may at last do ourselves hurt for want of what we destroy'.[8] However, he wrote to Sarah at much the same time that the destruction '. . . is so uneasy to my nature that nothing but an absolute necessity would have obliged me to consent to it'. Yet as a general he was prepared to burn 400 villages in the name of 'cruel necessity'.

This aspect of his personality contrasts markedly with the image of the solicitous and cosmopolitan Milord who could ease his path through matters personal, diplomatic or military with the same patience, deft courtesy and smooth urbanity – whether he was dealing with the touchy Württemburg in 1690, the cantankerous Baden in 1704 and 1705, the critical Goslinga or the mercurial Charles XII. A few were wholly untouched by his charm – including General Slangenberg; others refused to let it sway their judgment or ambitions – such as Robert Harley, and (latterly) the unscrupulous Henry St John. The majority of men, however, and not a few women, were deeply impressed by his manifest courtesy, poise and sound common sense. Yet it is possible that he was – his soldiers apart – rather admired than loved. As Professor Trevelyan aptly described it, 'the flame of his spirit served for light not warmth'.

And yet this same commanding figure also had the reputation of being the meanest of men where money was concerned. One reason for this has already been suggested in the impecunious circumstances of his youth, but whatever the explanation there is no doubting that this meanness existed. Not all the stories can have been apocryphal, and there was no lack of them, whether pertaining to his military or private life. In an age when generals were expected to keep open house for their subordinates, the Duke avoided entertaining in the field whenever possible. It is true that he was a man of simple habits, but he went to some pains to arrange to 'drop-by' his generals' quarters at appropriate times of day. 'There in my presence they were regulating the marches,' wrote Lord Ailesbury of a visit to headquarters in early 1704, 'and my lord asking what general officer would be, of the day, as they term. And then asked if such and such had a good cook, as that they should treat him at supper after the marches . . .'[9] He was similarly averse to spending good guineas on hiring suitable accommodation for part of the winter season, if an alternative could be discovered. Early in 1709 he persuaded a Dutch general to take a modish and sizeable residence at The Hague, and then moved into half of it with his suite as a largely uninvited and certainly non-paying guest. All great men have their quirks of character, and Duke John was no exception. But if he hoarded his guineas he was equally careful with his men's lives – a trait of which they thoroughly approved. And he could be generous – with Sarah and the family always – and occasionally he is known to have paid for the promotion of some deserving but impecunious junior officer.

His personal courage – both moral and physical – was also firmly established from at least the Maastricht episode of 1672 if not earlier. Yet he was certainly never over-confident or unduly sanguine. We see him set out for almost every campaign 'with a heavy heart', burdened with the sense of responsibility and strain that are the inescapable concomitants of high command. He was frequently very depressed and even physically ill over the days immediately preceding battle – as before both Blenheim and Oudenarde. His comments after the latter battle reveal how aware he was of the risks he undertook in crossing the Scheldt that July day – but he was aware that 'nothing else would make the Queen's business go well. This only made me venture the battle yesterday; otherwise we did give them too much advantage.' His personal interventions, sword in hand, in the cavalry engagements at both Elixhem and Ramillies, stand testimony to his continued gallantry in action.

Given his age on first assuming high command, Marlborough must have been endowed with a remarkably strong constitution to have survived so well the rigours of ten successive campaigns with barely a break. We know that he relied upon hard riding every day to keep himself fit, and the abstemious side of his character and his preference for simple living on campaign were undoubtedly of assistance. By any standards he was remarkably tough for a middle-aged man. At Ramillies he spent fifteen hours in the saddle planning and controlling the battle; he led at least two charges, was 'rid over' and almost captured once, and narrowly avoided being killed by a cannon-ball – and yet was still capable of pursuing the enemy for twelve miles before at last snatching a few hours' sleep on the bare ground, wrapped in his general's cloak, which with typical thoughtfulness (and perhaps a cunning awareness of the opportunity for a theatrical gesture) he invited the critical Dutchman, Goslinga, to share.

On the other hand he was frequently the victim of severe migraines and 'dizziness in my head'. It is clear that these attacks were often brought on by the relentless strains of politics and war, and always lurked in the background at times of maximum crisis and stress – as, for instance, before Oudenarde. In the end these headaches may have led to the series of strokes that killed him in 1722. There is also some evidence that on occasion he suffered from insomnia; the utterly calm and composed aspect of the Duke on days of battle – so admired by his soldiers – was partly a deliberate act and reveals his great degree of self-control. He appears never to have vented his rage on any human being, but most probably his bottled-up emotions, suspicions and 'silent rage' were a major contributory factor to his migraines. His chaplain, Dr Hare, noted that 'The Duke does not say much, but no one's countenance speaks more'. By 1710 he was becoming 'sensible of the inconvenience of old age', and during his last campaign he was mentioning 'frequent and sensible remembrances of my growing old'. By that time he was over 60, and it is notable that his capabilities, both mental and physical, were still so unimpaired.

It seems distinctly improbable that he was venal – as his enemies so often strove to prove. He certainly took pleasure in the legitimate perquisites attached to his high rank and station (it is estimated that in his hey-day he was worth £60,000 a year in the values of the time), and indubitably collected every penny he considered his fair due from the percentage on the sale of commissions and other offices in his gift; but it is nonsense to assert that he sought 'to prolong the war in order to further his advantage'.[10] He and his Duchess were the victims of 'scurrilous pamphlets and malicious invectives' (Parker); the 'little mercenary scribblers' and even the great Jonathan Swift certainly did their best to sully his name and bring him down.

On the other hand, there was a little fire beneath all the smoke of party and factional vituperation. As we have seen, he was fully aware of the value of his services to Queen and country, and was determined to gain his fair share of recognition, honours and monetary rewards. This is understandable. But it was one thing to maintain a clandestine correspondence with St Germain and Versailles as a means of gaining political and military intelligence and of dispensing a little fallacious or out-dated information in return, and yet quite another to make use of these channels to make it clear that he expected a *douceur* of several million gold *livres* in return for good offices in helping to secure an amelioration of peace terms at the conference table – as happened in 1708 and 1709 – or again to seek Louis XIV's personal guarantee for the security of the Marlborough fortune – as happened in 1713.

Indeed it is clear that his sense of pride and personal integrity were capable of adjustment to meet the needs of the hour. If a little flattery and sinuosity are acceptable and even amusing in his handling of Charles XII in 1707, it is difficult to reconcile the scourge of the French army with the abject lordling who could plead on his knees for his wife's continued employment about the Queen in 1710. But then Sarah was as redoubtable in defeat as in victory, and her spouse had to write to her from the seat of war that same year, 'I beg you will not remove any of the chimney pieces' – as the fiery Duchess set about vacating her grace and favour apartments at St James's Palace. Yet this same man was capable of long and genuine friendships with such men as Godolphin and Cadogan, and was in his wife's view tolerant and forgiving to a fault where others were concerned. As the Duke wrote to Godolphin, he had a great belief in 'patience that overcomes all things'. In sum, here was a most complex and multi-sided personality that in effect baffles final analysis. If, as was most certainly the case, there was both good and bad in the man, all that we can say is that the gold far outweighed the dross.

As a general, Marlborough proved equally skilled in waging conventional and unconventional eighteenth-century warfare. He proved adept at forcing four major battles and two important actions on evasive foes and unwilling Allies alike, but on fully twelve other occasions for one reason or another he found himself thwarted of determinant action. For this was an age when governments frowned upon the losses inseparable from a major battle. Little daunted by royal or republican limitations (the States-General placed Field Deputies at his side with power to veto the employment of Dutch troops), the Duke proved equally skilled at the more acceptable but infinitely more tedious business based upon wars of sieges and elaborate chess-board manoeuvring – forcing strong lines a number of times with great finesse and minimal loss of life, and capturing over thirty major fortresses including Lille (1708), Mons and Tournai (both 1709), not to forget Bouchain (1711), perhaps his masterpiece as a manager of siege warfare as well as his swansong as a commander in the field. Like Prince Eugene, he firmly believed in the importance of forcing major battles as the most direct means to reduce the foe's military capacity and thus his will to resist. As he wrote in 1703, a single battle was worth many sieges. At the same time he was acutely conscious of the political problems underlying the vast and rather unwieldly Alliance he had been called upon to lead, and in the interests of international unity and amity he refrained from pressing his views to the uttermost. With Napoleon, he was aware that 'war, like government, is a matter of tact'.[11]

These strictures notwithstanding, his achievement was remarkable by any standard. To bring off so much required a full mastery of the perennial problems affecting seventeenth- and eighteenth-century warfare: the seasonal nature of campaigning, their 'stop-go' nature dictated by the atrocious roads of late autumn, winter and early spring, and the eternal problem of finding sufficient food and forage for man and beast. There were also immense financial and recruiting difficulties to overcome, governments proving very chary at finding gold, and populations regarding the military profession as only slightly preferable as a calling to that of public hangman. Somehow all these pitfalls were circumvented, and year after year Marlborough was able to lead his multi-national armies (for native-born Englishmen and Scotsmen formed but a small proportion of his commands) to success after success.

This military achievement is all the more amazing when we consider the all-embracing nature of Marlborough's responsibilities and activities. Besides commanding the Grand Alliance's largest army in the field for ten campaigns, he was virtually 'manager' of the Queen (through the medium of the termagant Sarah) and the inspiration and sometime controller of a number of her ministries (through the agency of his staunch friend, Sidney Godolphin, Lord Treasurer). At the military level, he bore grave responsibilities for all levels of activity from grand strategy to minor tactics and logistics, and it is to his showing in these respects that I wish to devote the rest of this chapter.

At the level of national policy formulation, he had to contend with often selfish and clashing interests of politicians, statesmen and nations, but with little more official standing, to cite Sir Winston Churchill's apt description, than an 'informal chairman of a discordant committee'. Working through the 'Winter committee' at home and his ceaseless visits to Allied courts abroad, somehow he managed to maintain the common cause, whose main aims were to curb the seemingly insatiable ambitions of Louis XIV and gain a fair division of the Spanish inheritance and thus maintain some semblance of a European balance of power. As 'grand strategist' he also had to dissuade possible newcomers from entering the struggle – hence the rapid dash to Altranstadt in 1707. All things considered, Duke John kept the original objectives well in view, but in one respect he committed a crucial error, by lending active if largely tacit consent to the Austrian Emperor's and the Whig party's insistence that it was possible and desirable 'to conquer France through Spain', he doomed the Grand Alliance to the maintenance of as costly and ultimately as futile a war as that faced by Napoleon in the Peninsular War a century later.

Marlborough too had early hopes of achieving peace through Spain and Italy. Following the disasters of 1707, however, the chances of victory in Spain became increasingly remote, and Marlborough stands charged with not pressing his private grave doubts on this subject. The Allies would have been wise to cut their losses after Almanza, and close down the Spanish front. Instead they insisted on reinforcing failure. Marlborough – for understandable political and diplomatic reasons – never spoke out, and to that extent he must bear a measure of responsibility. The Spanish front proved a devastating drain on Allied resources of men, material and money, and was largely responsible (indirectly at least) for enabling the Bourbons, against all the odds, to weather the last years of the war in Flanders and thereafter win a more favourable peace at Utrecht and Rastadt than had seemed conceivable four years earlier.

In assessing Marlborough as a strategist, we find a man with a rare grasp of the broad issues and problems involved. From the start of the war, he could see the struggle as a whole, and if his judgment of the Spanish front was blurred after 1707, he proved remarkably prescient and competent in other areas. Few, if any, contemporaries shared this attribute, and so non-existent was the general appreciation of the rudiments of strategy that in 1704 it was possible for serious politicians at Westminster to declare that he had 'stolen the army' when he left the Netherlands for the Danube. Marlborough's 'over-view' (if such it may be termed) is well exemplified that same spring by his willingness to detach four prized English battalions from his army in Flanders for service with Rooke's fleet in the Mediterranean on the very eve of his own risk-taking march.

As a strategist – or planner of campaigns to achieve the declared aims – Marlborough generally proved far-sighted and inspired. In 1704, despite all the attendant difficulties, he appreciated the importance of transferring aid to Austria if the Alliance was to survive. Thereafter, he appreciated that ceaseless pressure exerted against the strongest sector of the French frontiers in the Netherlands and Flanders area would serve to bleed France white (in much the same way as the Germans planned to use the Verdun offensive of 1916), and thus compel Versailles to accept a dictated peace. By late 1711 this object had all but been achieved when circumstances – and the skill of Marshal Villars – intervened.

Passing his ten campaigns in review – eight of which were wholly waged in the 'Cockpit of Europe' – it is difficult to escape the conclusion that the Duke was often at his best in a strategically defensive role. His first two campaigns, together with those of 1704 and 1708, were largely fought to neutralise enemy gains and retrieve lost ground. His offensives – as in 1705, 1707, 1709 and 1710 – tended to lead to less dramatic results, but that of 1706 reveals his greatness in exploiting an unanticipated battle success to the very limit. Unfortunately a similar opportunity after Oudenarde had to be abandoned in favour of a more prosaic and conventional approach – namely the siege of Lille. But in judging Marlborough's showing it cannot be stressed too much that he never enjoyed true freedom of action. His Allies proved late in reporting – as was the case with Baden in 1705 – or insisted on mounting irrelevant campaigns – for example the Austrian attack on Naples in 1707.

The French problem was diametrically opposite to his own. If the Duke had to carry his Allies with him and frequently accept compromises in order to ensure their cooperation, the proud marshals rarely dared to change or even vary a plan without time-consuming reference to Versailles.

The Duke was also unique in his appreciation (for his time) of the strategic significance of sea-power in support of a continental war. He never subscribed to the emerging 'blue water' school of thought, but adhered to William III's concept of a continental approach to European and naval strategy. His experiences aboard the fleet in his early career, and the influence of William III, had convinced him of the value of a navy deployed in support of a large native army fighting in Europe, employing such operations as coastal raids, the capture of bases (particularly in the Mediterranean) and the threat of landings to distract enemy resources. If this policy had its failures (Cádiz in 1702 and Toulon in 1707), it also had its successes with the fortuitous capture of Gibraltar (1704) and the deliberate taking of Minorca five years later, which firmly established Allied naval control over the Western Mediterranean. His abortive plan for exploiting Oudenarde in late 1708 further demonstrates his ability to marry up naval and military forces in single enterprises, and so do the emergency arrangements made to support the siege of Lille. His influence over naval matters was exercised for many years through his friendship with Prince George of Denmark, Lord High Admiral, and his youngest brother, Charles Churchill.

In the realm of 'grand tactics' – or the planning and general control of engagements once a genuine battle situation had been procured – Marlborough had few contemporary peers. After discovering the foe's circumstances with the aid of his spy network, Marlborough used forced marches and surprise to confound their schemes time after time. 'If they are there, the Devil must have carried them – such marching is impossible!' was Marshal Vendôme's reaction to news of the Allied approach to Oudenarde from Lessines in July 1708. The Duke also had a sure eye for ground, and on a number of occasions he used concealed valleys and re-entrants to spring tactical surprises on his opponents. He was capable of devising unusual orders of battle, massing strengths on certain sectors and denuding others, and he proved highly skilled at controlling the fluid encounter-type of battle represented by Oudenarde as well as set-piece engagements such as Blenheim. At all stages of a battle, the Duke was insistent that infantry, cavalry and cannon should cooperate closely in what today would be termed combat groups. At the same time, he invariably made a point of keeping a strong force of cavalry in reserve ready to deliver the *coup de grâce*, or (it never proved necessary) cover a retreat. The action developed from probing attacks to stronger onslaughts on selected points, designed by means of relentless pressure to draw in the remaining enemy reserves, and, ideally, to induce the foe to weaken the sector chosen for the main attack. Then, after containing the induced amalgamations of enemy troops with a minimum of his own forces, the Captain-General would assemble a decisive superiority of force opposite the predetermined point, and unleash his devastating blow. The enemy line once sundered, the battle was *ipso facto* won, but it still remained to convert the foe's defeat into rout. Marlborough was unusual in his belief in immediate pursuit when feasible. After Ramillies the follow-through was relentless; after Blenheim, however, the pursuit was delayed for a day by the need to cope with the mass of wounded and prisoners; after Malplaquet there were no fresh troops available.

A major problem was the imposition of overall control over a battle area that might be several miles in extent, with the scene almost wholly obliterated by the dense clouds of black-powder smoke. Marlborough was famed for his ability to overcome the problems of distance and obscurity, and for his knack of appearing at critical points to rally the men as if guided by superhuman knowledge. His secret was the use of carefully selected aides-de-camp, and running footmen, who were trained to report on what was taking place on every sector using their own judgment. These 'eyes' served the Captain-General well on many an occasion. If he had a fault as a grand tactician, it was that he became a trifle predictable in his general preference for delivering the *coup de grâce* against the enemy centre, although on three occasions he attempted out-flanking manoeuvres, as at Oudenarde with success. Using this knowledge, Villars was able to make the Allied victory at Malplaquet exorbitantly costly, although he proved incapable of averting a defeat.

Marlborough's interest and skill also extended to minor tactics. He insisted upon the use of cavalry as a shock-force, and employed massed squadrons, advancing at a fast trot, to clinch all of his victories. For the 'poor Foot', he imposed a strict training programme carried through during the winter months, and standardised the earlier platoon-firing system in three-deep battalion formations, a method which conferred advantages of fire-control, preparedness and continuity based on five-deep formations, firing rank after rank or in massed (and often inaccurate) volleys. He thus encouraged the adoption of the basic modern infantry tactics of 'fire and movement', a significant development based upon the Duke's appreciation of the changes wrought by the replacement of pike and matchlock by the more deadly and flexible combination of socket-bayonet and flintlock musket. Similarly, as Master-General of the Ordnance he paid special heed to the siting of his guns, awkward monsters of up to three tons deadweight apiece, and even encouraged his perspiring Ordnance officers to resite them in the heat of battle, as at Blenheim. The fortunate coincidence of his two posts – Captain-General of Horse and Foot and Master-General of the Ordnance – made possible a unique degree of cooperation between all arms on the battlefield, another major factor in achieving victory.

The Duke also lavished special attention on all matters appertaining to military administration and supply. These aspects were often the greatest source of weakness in eighteenth-century armies, the former being paid scant attention, the latter entrusted to hard-pressed (and sometimes corrupt) contractors. Marlborough instituted few innovations (although he did introduce a light, two-wheeled cart for the supply trains), but by rigid supervision he made the system work as well as could be expected. During his period of command, the troops in Flanders rarely went hungry or unpaid, and such administrative masterpieces as the march to the Danube in 1704, in which he brought an army of eventually 40,000 men over a distance of 250 miles and produced them before Donauwörth fit to fight an immediate, gory engagement, bear testimony to his skills in this respect. Whether the situation required a complete switch of lines of communication, or the issue of spare boots or of hand-mills to the infantry, no detail was too insignificant for the Captain-General's attention. The result was a gratified and trusting army, ready to make exceptional exertions at the Duke's request. They regarded him as 'ever watchful, ever right' and endowed with a 'peculiar excellency' as a general. 'The Duke of Marlborough's attention and care was over all of us,' recorded Matthew Bishop.

Marlborough's basic strengths as an administrator were the following. First, he was ever aware that wars are concerned with human beings. His humane attitudes have frequently been mentioned, and need no further elaboration here. Second, he was able to distinguish the essentials in an administrative problem. At the same time, and thirdly, he had a minute eye for detail. Fourthly, he had a distinct gift for making existing systems work well or at least adequately; he on the whole eschewed innovations, and thus avoided much confusion. It is true that the administrative systems he inherited were often inefficient and extremely rudimentary, but close supervision of the responsible authorities kept such bread contractors as Solomon and Moses Medina and Vanderkaa up to the mark, or revealed the fraudulent practices of the less scrupulous who included Mechado and Solomon Abraham. At the same time, he tried to gain them a fair deal in terms of government payments of contracted sums – not always successfully, however. Fifthly, he appreciated the importance of well trained and well disciplined officers as the very basis of an efficient and battle-worthy army.

Little of all this would have been possible had not Marlborough developed a sure gift for choosing reliable subordinates. A handful of men enjoyed his unbounded trust: William Cadogan, Quartermaster-General, unofficial chief of staff, was the vital *éminence grise*. When he fell into French hands in 1706, an exchange was arranged with record speed, and when he sustained a serious neck-wound in 1710, the Duke wrote to Sarah: 'I hope in God he will do well for I entirely depend upon him', adding, on a slightly more prosaic but heartfelt note: 'His wounding will oblige me to do many things by which I shall have but little rest'. Others included Adam Cardonnel, the Duke's secretary, who conducted much of the crippling load of diplomatic correspondence which pursued his master, both in campaign and out; and Henry Davenant, his financial agent. He was equally well served by his heads of arms and services, who included such men as Holcroft Blood, senior gunner, and John Armstrong, senior engineer, not to forget such aides as the remarkable Richards brothers.

He was equally fortunate in the great majority of his subordinate generals, both English and foreign. Lords Cutts and Orkney, and Generals Overkirk, Fagel and Goor represent these two categories. But above all it was the special relationship with Prince Eugene of Savoy, who shared four of the ten campaigns with him and played a vital part in three of the four great battles, that underlay so many shared successes. They knew each other's minds exactly, shared most tenets as to how wars should be waged, and accorded each other an absolute trust which no slanders or friction could undermine. Contemporaries likened them to the Castor and Pollux of mythology. Well might Marlborough declare, 'I love that Prince'. It was no more than the truth. On the other hand the Duke also had to bear the hesitant Baden and jealously obstructive Slangenberg, who proved resistant to his acclaimed charm and courtesy and effectively compromised several major operations.

I opened this chapter with some indications of Marlborough's contemporary standing. I close it with a few remarks on posterity's reaction. Marlborough has attracted much criticism. According to Sir John Creasey, 'There are few successful commanders, on whom fame has shone so unwillingly'.[12] This was particularly true of the Victorian era, when Lord Macaulay unleashed his righteousness to indict the Duke on serious charges of moral turpitude – stressing his youthful indiscretions, the desertion of James II, his reputed betrayal of plans in 1694, and above all his alleged venality. More recent historians, Sir Winston Churchill, G M Trevelyan and C T Atkinson, not to forget Major R E Scouller and Dr Ivor Burton, have sprung to Marlborough's defence, but inevitably some stain has remained on his reputation. It is only just to judge a man within the context of his times, and if Milord Duke occasionally stooped to unscrupulous practices, he was no worse than the great majority of his contemporaries, and few of the world's great men of action have ever enjoyed wholly unimpeachable reputations. Today, the moral atmosphere perhaps makes it easier to reach a more balanced judgment than was possible either in the nineteenth century, or even in the 1930s of the twentieth. Sir Winston's celebrated volumes remain unsurpassed[13] – and possibly unsurpassable – as the overall biography of his great ancestor, but he makes no attempt to conceal his family loyalty. Wholly objective history makes for dull reading, but in certain respects it is necessary to be as wary of Churchill's warm eulogies as of Macaulay's strident denunciations.

Military men have had fewer doubts about his standing. We know that Napoleon, although he never included the Duke's name in his list of the seven greatest commanders of all time, studied the campaign of 1704 with admiration. Later, at St Helena, he described Marlborough to Surgeon Arnott of the 20th Foot as follows:

> He began talking about English armies, and particularly praised the Duke of Marlborough whom he described as 'a man whose mind was not narrowly confined to the field of battle; he fought and negotiated; he was at once a captain and a diplomatist'.[14]

Equally interesting is the Duke of Wellington's reply, when asked whether he thought Napoleon or Marlborough the greater general. He replied:

> It is difficult to answer that. I used to say that the presence of Napoleon at a battle was equal to a reinforcement of 40,000 men. But I can conceive of nothing greater than Marlborough at the head of an English army. He had greater difficulties than I with his allies: the Dutch were worse to manage than the Spaniards or the Portuguese. But, on the other hand, I think I had most difficulties at home.[15]

More recently, Field Marshal Montgomery described the Duke as 'a military genius, capable, when given the chance, of transcending the contemporary limitations of warfare ... Marlborough absorbs the attention of the military historian as the giant of his times.'[16]

The 282 years since Marlborough's passing have seen immense changes in both world and military affairs, and yet in certain respects the present day has more in common with his generation than with the more immediate past. Both periods have been typified by a limited rather than a total approach to the conduct of warfare, although for vastly different reasons, but both share basic humane considerations. How Marlborough faced up to the limitations imposed upon his conduct of war, and still achieved a notable degree of success, is one fruitful field for study. Another, equally significant, is his failure to 'win the peace' by dint of military achievement alone. A third relevant field for reflection is the problems Great Britain, and above all the Duke, faced in keeping the members of the Second Grand Alliance in some form of concert – for no period has been more influenced by the convoluted problems of international agreements and associations than our own. Marlborough's skill at first creating, and then preserving the Alliance until his dismissal was a great achievement by any standards of diplomacy. And above all we can learn a great deal from the Duke's superb skill, of leadership and of man-management, his power to inspire and, to borrow Napoleon's phrase, 'speak to the soul'.

What, then, should we conclude was the achievement of Marlborough? His reputation rests more on his record as soldier and statesman than as a politician or courtier – that much is evident. His wholly unsupportable burden of responsibility – military, diplomatic and domestic – eventually led to his personal eclipse and downfall. Indeed, his fall was in large measure due to his failure to secure his political base. As a commander, he was an experienced and dedicated professional rather than a brilliant amateur. He was the product of half a century of military experience – and pupil, successively, of Turenne, Prince Waldeck and William III – rather than a human phenomenon of the type of Napoleon. For ten consecutive campaigns he had produced 'the constant display at their highest of those qualities which are necessary to victory', with the occasional brief lapse caused by illness or fatigue. In the process, he raised the reputation of British arms to a level which had not been known since the Middle Ages, and inaugurated a period of British prominence, both in Europe and overseas. It is fitting to turn to Captain of Grenadiers Robert Parker for a last salute and tribute to this commanding figure.

> As to the Duke of Marlborough (for I cannot forbear giving him the precedence) it was allowed by all men, nay even by France itself, that he was more than a match for all the generals of that nation. This he made appear beyond contradiction, in the ten campaigns he made against them; during all of which time it cannot be said that he ever slipped an opportunity of fighting, when there was any probability of coming at his enemy: and upon all occasions he concerted matters with so much judgment and forecast, that he never fought a battle

which he did not gain, nor laid siege to a town which he did not take.[17]

It is therefore fitting that we should do honour to Duke John's memory in this, the 300th anniversary year of his great victory at Blenheim.

NOTES

1 S J Reid, *The Duke and Duchess of Marlborough*, London, 1914, p. 413.
2 M Bishop, *The Life and Adventures of Matthew Bishop . . . from 1701–11*, London, 1744, p. 194.
3 The French song expressed the hope that the Duke had died.
4 See D G Chandler, *Marlborough as Military Commander*, London, 1973 (3rd edn, 1995), p. 2.
5 *Ibid.*, pp. 3 & 312.
6 D Defoe, *The Life and Adventures of Mother Ross*, London, 1927, p. 54.
7 W C Coxe, *Memoirs of John, Duke of Marlborough*, London, 1820, Vol. II, p. 145.
8 *Ibid.*, p. 371.
9 T B Ailesbury, *Memoirs*, Edinburgh, 1890, Vol. 12, p. 570.
10 Mérode-Westerloo, *Mémoires*, Vol. I, p. 221.
11 D G Chandler, *Campaigns of Napoleon*, New York, 1976, p. 85.
12 J Creasey, *The Fifteen Decisive Battles*, London, 1948, p. 271.
13 W S Churchill, *Marlborough: His Life and Times*, London, 1967.
14 C Ray, *The Lancashire Fusiliers*, London, 1971, p. 72.
15 Stanhope, Lord, *Miscellanies*, London, 1872, p. 87.
16 B L Montgomery, *A History of Warfare*, London, 1956, pp. 295 & 311.
17 D G Chandler, *The Marlborough Wars*, London, 1968, p. 125.

CHAPTER XII

Donauwörth 1704

The march to the Danube

Marlborough was certainly well placed in English, and indeed European, high affairs. Now he was to make both his own and his country's military reputation. He began slowly but steadily. The first two years of his campaigns in Flanders were successful but not dramatically so. In early March 1702 he had sailed to The Hague, and started to tackle many national and international problems, both military and political. Due to his efforts the Allied Manifesto was completed in mid-May, neatly nullifying Louis XIV's instructions to his marshals to launch a pre-emptive strike action.

At first the French controlled part of Flanders, but steadily the forces of the Second Grand Alliance began to manoeuvre and fight more effectively. To Marlborough's chagrin there were no major battles. An ideal opportunity to inflict a major defeat was lost on 23 August near Hamont and Peer, where deft movement had the French trapped but the Dutch Deputies refused to allow their troops into action! As a result Marshal Boufflers and his army were able to escape. For the rest of the campaign, the Allies contented themselves with the capture of six important fortresses: Kaiserswerth on 15 June; Lüttich after a lengthy siege of 13 June–17 October; and the towns of Venlo, Stevenswaert, Ruremonde and Liège which fell on 29 October. There was one 'exciting' moment, however, when, on a boat journey on 7 November, Marlborough was almost captured. Although stopped by the enemy, an alert servant swapped two passports, and a crisis was succinctly averted. Despite the lack of field victories, Queen Anne was delighted by the overall events of the year, and on 15 December she conferred a Dukedom on Marlborough.

The following year, a new campaign began again in Flanders. To a background of renewed squabbles between the Allies, the new Duke captured Bonn, Huy and Limburg from 15 May to 25 September. However, Marlborough learnt that the French were now advancing deeply into Austria, and soon Vienna itself would be threatened. If that city fell, the Alliance might well collapse and with it, all of Marlborough's grand-scale plans, dating back to the days of William III, might fail. Political backing to counter this threat was minimal; the self-interest of both the Dutch and many English politicians boded ill for the future. However, an amazing new campaign and two major battles were in the making; and two Allied joint-commanders – the first Duke of Marlborough and Prince Eugene of Savoy – were going to save Vienna, and therefore save the war. By late 1704 they would be called the 'Twin Generals' throughout Europe. Great things were going to happen.

'My Lord, I never saw better horses, better clothes, finer belts and accoutrements,' declared Prince Eugene, as he completed his inspection of part of Marlborough's cavalry on 11 June 1704; 'but money, which you don't want in England, will buy fine clothes and fine horses, but it can't buy that lively air I see in every one of these troopers' faces.'[1] Never to be outdone in paying compliments, the Duke replied: 'Sir, that must be attributed to their heartiness for the public cause and the particular pleasure in satisfaction they have in seeing your Highness.'

The rule-defying march to the Danube was almost completed when the two leaders of the Grand Alliance first met at Gross Heppach, not far from the Neckar river. In an hour of deep crisis on the Danube front, the Duke of Marlborough had led a force of Allied troops from the Netherlands over a distance of more than 250 miles to assist the outnumbered and hard-pressed armies of the Holy Roman Empire. This, in itself, was an operation of major military importance – but, in the weeks that followed, even more stirring news was to be borne by spurring messengers to the capitals of Europe, whose destiny lay in the lands of the English general and his force of travel-stained redcoats.

The year of 1704 had opened with singularly threatening prospects for the member nations of the Grand Alliance – England, Austria and the United Provinces. Two years of expensive war against France, Spain and Bavaria had resulted only in minor successes on the Rhine and Meuse rivers, besides the acquisition of two small and dubious allies in Savoy and Portugal. For the 'Party of the Two Crowns',[2] on the other hand, 1703 had been a year of victory in North Italy and, most particularly, on the Danube, where the joint achievements of Marshal Villars[3] and the Elector of Bavaria[4] had created a direct threat to Vienna, the capital of the Holy Roman Empire and the 'Achilles Heel' of the Grand Alliance. The city had been saved from immediate capture by dissensions between the two commanders, resulting in the recall of the brilliant Villars and his replacement by the mediocre Marsin;[5] but, in the opening months of the following year, the initiative remained everywhere with the French and Vienna's fall was confidently expected at the courts of Versailles and Madrid. Rakosi's Hungarian revolt was already threatening the eastern suburbs and, on the Rhine, Marshal Tallard was preparing to march through the Black Forest with 36,000 men to reinforce the similar numbers of troops in the vicinity of Ulm under the command of Marsin and the

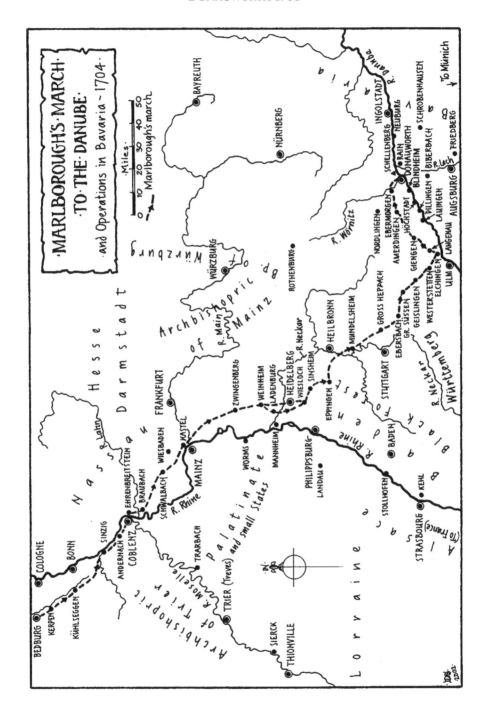

Elector. As soon as the spring floods receded, and the rivers and mud-roads of Europe became passable for marching armies, the union of forces would be effected and the march on Vienna resumed. The meagre imperial forces blocking the road to the capital would soon be brushed aside, their attention distracted by the threat of an offensive through the Brenner Pass by Marshal Vendôme's[6] strong army, at present in North Italy. To isolate the Danube front from any intervention by the Allied forces stationed in the Netherlands, Marshal Villeroi's[7] 46,000 men were expected to pin the 70,000 Dutch and English troops around Maastricht, while de Coignies protected Alsace against surprise with a further corps.

The sole forces readily available for the immediate defence of Vienna, in the early spring of 1704, were the 36,000 Imperialists under the uninspired command of Prince Louis of Baden,[8] stationed in the Lines of Stollhofen to watch Tallard at Strasbourg, and a weak force of 10,000 soldiers under Count Styrum[9] observing Ulm. Austria's dire peril was fully appreciated at the Schönbrunn – throughout the winter Count Wratislaw and other imperial envoys had pleaded with the English and Dutch governments for material assistance, but with scant success. Although the impending fall of Vienna would almost certainly entail the collapse of the Grand Alliance, the crises of Southern Europe seemed comfortably remote from Whitehall and the Court of St James's, where colonial and commercial considerations were more to the fore in men's minds, while the cautious and dyke-minded Dutch at The Hague were almost solely concerned with the problem of their own national security behind the fortresses of Flanders and the River Barrier.

Only a handful of enlightened statesmen, on each side of the English Channel, understood the crucial implications of the situation on the Danube. Foremost was the Duke of Marlborough. 'For this campaign I see so very ill a prospect that I am extremely out of heart,'[10] he wrote on 20 February to his wife, Sarah. In his 54th year, John Churchill was at the height of his powers, and the Marlborough fortunes were almost at the zenith owing to the influence of the Duchess Sarah[11] over Queen Anne. The Duke's reputation as politician, statesman and courtier already stood high. Ever since the Restoration of Charles II in 1660, Churchill had been at the centre of national affairs, first as page to the Duke of York, when his career was materially furthered by the benign and amorous influence of Barbara Villiers, and later as confidential adviser to James II, and in due course, to William and Mary, after overcoming their not unnatural suspicions that the Marlboroughs harboured Jacobite sympathies. Marlborough, nevertheless, was entrusted by William III with much of the negotiation preceding the Alliance of 1701 – and in this task the Duke earned golden opinions for his tact, courtly manners and wise states-manship. He was also widely regarded as a competent soldier; from his birth he had been brought up amid martial surroundings: his father, Winston Churchill,[12] had served with the Royalists during the Great Civil

War, and no doubt the future Captain-General learnt much from the old man concerning the right handling of cavalry in action. Commissioned into the Guards, Marlborough later served for a period with the fleet as a marine; he probably saw service at Tangier and was certainly present at the naval battle of Solebay in 1672 – and from these experiences he came to appreciate the importance of sea-power and the significance of the Mediterranean. In 1674 he was sent to serve under the great Marshal Turenne[13] in Flanders, where, besides earning a reputation for courage, he fought alongside many young French contemporaries whom he was later to meet under different circumstances on half a dozen battlefields. Back in England, Churchill was promoted Brigadier in 1685 and served as Lord Feversham's second-in-command against the Duke of Monmouth in the West Country, learning the need for good military administration, firm discipline and sound training – the factors that won the campaign that culminated in the Battle of Sedgemoor.[14] Four years later, he served again in Flanders under Waldeck alongside Dutch troops and, the next year, accompanied William III to Ireland, where he received his first independent command in an expedition against Cork and Kinsale. Thus Marlborough was by no means an inexperienced soldier when he was appointed to command the Anglo–Dutch army in the Netherlands, on the death of King William, shortly before England's entry into the War of the Spanish Succession in May 1702. His record as Captain-General during the first two campaigns of the war was good but not outstanding; for his genius was never given free rein by the obstructive Dutch field-deputies who accompanied the army and wielded the power of veto over the employment of the Dutch contingents. Only in 1704 – through force of circumstances and no little cunning – was Marlborough able to throw off these trammels and give full proof of his military capabilities.

It is not known when the Duke first decided to undertake a march to the Danube with part of the army in the Netherlands; for, in an age of lax security and conflicting loyalties, he was wise to keep his counsel to himself. It was only six weeks before his departure for the Danube that he first committed his plan to paper, writing on 29 April to his governmental colleague and confidant, Godolphin, the Lord Treasurer,[15] in the following terms:

> My intentions are to march with all the English to Coblenz and to declare that I intend to campaign on the Moselle. But, when I come there, to write to the Dutch States that I think it absolutely necessary for the saving of the Empire to march with the troops under my command and to join with those that are in Germany that are in Her Majesty's and the Dutch pay, in order to take measures with Prince Lewis of Baden for the speedy reduction of the Elector of Bavaria. What I now write, I beg may only be known to nobody but Her Majesty and the Prince.[16]

His purpose was to reinforce the Imperial forces and destroy the Franco–Bavarian army, before Tallard could bring his army to its assistance.

This scheme was extremely bold in the light of eighteenth-century military experience. The theoretical possibility of such a transfer was doubtless considered in many quarters during the preceding winter, but the political and military problems that stood in the way of success were so immense that it was universally declared impracticable. In the first place, it was very soon evident that the Dutch States General would never permit any weakening of the Netherlands forces – faced as they were by Marshal Villeroi's army – and, for all his influence, Marlborough was never in any real sense a 'supreme commander', but was continually dependant on the precarious support of the politicians of The Hague and Westminster. His first problem, therefore, was to overcome or by-pass Dutch opposition; and the only way this could be done was by reticence and guile. Besides this political difficulty, large contingents of the Allied army were made up of mercenary elements, hired from the rulers of the smaller states of Europe – Denmark, Hanover and Prussia[17] among them. These princelings were very sensitive to the trend of events; and the apparent prospect of Allied defeat discouraged them from honouring their agreements to supply men and munitions. Marlborough had to cajole, flatter and charm each ruler in turn to secure their unwilling cooperation in his projects.

To contemporary observers, versed in the recognised principles of warfare, the military dangers, inherent in a scheme of the type Marlborough was now secretly preparing, would also have appeared prohibitive. His line of march down the Rhine would necessarily pass across the fronts of two large French field armies, who were ideally placed to take Marlborough's army in flank. To add to this peril, from the moment the Duke left the region dominated by the Dutch General Overkirk[18] north of Coblenz until the time he reached the Margrave of Baden in the area of the Lines of Stollhofen, his march would be completely unsupported by friendly covering forces. Even if he were allowed to pass unhindered, his lines of communication along the Rhine would be hopelessly exposed to French interference; for Louis' generals controlled the left bank of the river in its central reaches. This risk accentuated another military problem – that of supply. Burdened by heavy guns and bulky waggons, eighteenth-century armies habitually crawled along the earth roads of Europe at a rate of not more than ten miles a day – and to execute the 250-mile march to the Danube would involve a high wastage of men and horses through exhaustion and disease; for adequate food and fodder would be extremely hard to procure. Faced by this combination of problems, it seemed highly improbable that Marlborough could reach the Danube with an intact army, fit enough to fight an immediate major battle. But the urgency of the hour demanded radical measures; and, as Marlborough made his last preparations, he wrote to Godolphin on 1 May: 'I am very sensible that I take a great deal upon me. But should I act otherwise, the Empire would be undone, and consequently the Confederacy.'[19] There was need to hasten; on 14 May Marshal Tallard[20] completed the operation of manoeuvring 10,000 reinforcements through the Black Forest to Ulm, neatly parrying Baden's clumsy attempt to intercept his convoy. The Franco–Bavarian drive on Vienna was clearly imminent. Five days later, Marlborough's march began.

A combination of strategic deception and brilliant administration enabled Marlborough to achieve his purpose. His departure from Bedburg on 19 May, at the head of 21,000 men, excited little comment, for his declared purpose of campaigning along the Moselle was the logical sequel to the previous year's operations on the Meuse and Rhine. It was only when he reached Coblenz on the 26th and ordered his troops to cross over to the right bank of the Rhine the next day, pausing only to add 5,000 Hanoverians and Prussians to his strength, that anyone suspected a hidden intention. 'When we expected to march up the Moselle to our surprise we passed over that river by a stone bridge and then the Rhine over two bridges of boats,[21] wrote Captain Parker in his *Memoirs*. The first bluff was over, but Marlborough continued to dominate the situation and keep the enemy guessing. Marshal Villeroi was shadowing Marlborough with 30,000 men, and had taken up a defensive position on the Moselle; the French general was now forced to report to Versailles: 'There will be no campaign on the Moselle – the English have all gone higher up into Germany'.[22] Dutch anticipation of an immediate French counter-offensive against their weakened forces in the Netherlands proved illusory; for Villeroi deemed it his duty to continue to observe Marlborough's movements with 10,000 men: 'My forces will continue to cover the advance from the left bank of the Rhine.'[23] This left the Dutch perfectly secure; in any case, Marlborough was able to quieten any lingering anxieties by promising that he would return at once to the Netherlands if a French attack developed there, transferring his army in barges down the Rhine at a rate of eighty miles a day. Heartened by this assurance, the States General promptly voted him their full support.

The march continued, the French meekly following without making the least attempt to interfere with its progress. Now a second possible objective appeared on the horizon: an English incursion into Alsace towards the great city of Strasbourg. Marlborough was careful to heighten this illusion by ordering the Governor of Philippsburg to build bridges of boats across the river and by massing supplies in the fortress. Not only Villeroi, but also Marshal Tallard, was partially deceived by the preparations; and the latter postponed his main army's march to Ulm whilst he referred to Versailles for revised orders in the light of the new situation. This hesitation gave

Marlborough time to cross two major obstacles across his path – the Main river on 3 June and the Neckar four days later; and shortly thereafter the 'scarlet caterpillar' (as the Duke's distinguished descendant[24] Sir Winston Churchill has termed it) swung away from the Rhine towards the Danube; and at last the ultimate destination was clear to all. At the beginning of the month, Tallard had ordered his garrison at Tour-le-Seine to interrupt the Rhine traffic,[25] but it was now too late for the French to prevent the duke's arrival in the critical theatre. The most dangerous part of the march was safely over; the Lines of Stollhofen[26] and Baden's army were now close at hand, while a new series of communications, running from the expedition's financial base at Frankfurt down the Main to the friendly areas around Nuremburg and Nordlingen, replaced the previously exposed system based on the Rhine. During the latter stages of the march, moreover, Marlborough's army had been increased to 40,000 men by the late arrival of Danish and Prussian contingents. On 22 June these forces linked up with Baden's Imperialists at Launsheim; a distance of more than 250 miles had been covered in just over five weeks and Europe applauded a major military feat. Even more amazing, the transferred army was evidently in a state to fight immediately.[27]

The secret of the fine morale and first-class condition of Marlborough's army lay in the care the Captain-General had lavished on every detail of administration. Aided by a mere handful of assistants – Cadogan, the Quartermaster-General,[28] Cardonnel,[29] the Duke's secretary, and Henry Davenant, the financial agent – a comprehensive scheme of supply arrangements had been planned and implemented. To speed the march, all heavy impedimenta, including the larger guns, had been left in the Netherlands; the vital stores and lighter cannon were conveyed by river barges as far as possible, and then carried in specially designed carts. At Heidelberg, a new pair of shoes awaited every man, and ample gold was carried in the Military Chest for the purchase of local supplies. These measures were supplemented by a carefully planned march timetable, designed to confuse the enemy scouting parties and save the men from undue wear and tear. Captain Parker described it as follows:

> We frequently marched three, sometimes four days successively and halted one day. We generally began our march about three in the morning, proceeded about four leagues or four and a half by day, and reached our camping ground about nine. As we marched through the country of our Allies, commissars were appointed to furnish us with all manner of necessaries for man and horse; these were brought to the ground before we arrived, and the soldiers had nothing to do but pitch their tents, boil their kettles and lie down to rest. Surely never was such a march carried on with more order and regularity and with less fatigue to man and horse.[30]

In recognition of this genuine care for their well-being, the rank and file dubbed their leader 'Corporal John'; and the high morale engendered by his fine administration enabled Marlborough to make calls on their endurance that few other generals would contemplate. This feature of Marlborough's generalship contrasts strongly with Marshal Tallard's record: the French march to Ulm in May was carried through at a cost of one third of his army's effective strength through desertion and straggling.[31] But the Allied journey had not been without its difficulties – especially for the infantry and guns, which travelled two or three days' march behind the cavalry. Owing to torrential rain[32] several delays were experienced, and French spies reported that 900 sick had been left at Cassel. Nevertheless, such losses by the wayside were kept to a minimum, and Captain Blackadder's gloomy prophecy at the outset of the march that 'this is like to be a campaign of great fatigue and trouble'[33] proved over-pessimistic.

While the last stages of the march were being completed, Marlborough met the Margrave of Baden and Prince Eugene of Savoy at Gross Heppach on 12 June to concert plans for the destruction of the Elector of Bavaria's army. At the age of 50, Prince Louis[34] was the senior commander in rank and experience if not in years. A long record of distinguished service against the Turk had established his reputation as a fine soldier; but his outlook on warfare was wholly 'conventional', and he was cautious to a fault and a stickler for the observance of the proper formalities. Prince Eugene,[35] on the other hand, was not yet 41, but had enjoyed a meteoric career in the Imperial service, having been promoted general of cavalry at 26 and a commander-in-chief ten years later. In most ways, he shared Marlborough's disregard for the accepted conventions that favoured the siege at the expense of the battle, but was understandably unpopular with the crusty Baden. This created a delicate command problem; but, as usual, Marlborough's tact found a solution. To save the Margrave's face, it was agreed that the daily orders should be signed alternately by Baden and Marlborough – giving the impression of a joint command – although, in fact, it was clearly understood at Vienna that the Duke was senior commander, and secret arrangements had been made for the Margrave's removal from command should he prove fatally obstructive.

The three generals between them commanded a force approaching 100,000 men.[36] A plan was rapidly evolved. Prince Eugene was to return to the Lines of Stollhofen, with a force of under 30,000 men, to keep a close watch on Tallard's movements. This was a crucial duty; and, although Marlborough would have dearly liked to have Eugene at his side, he was aware that it would be safer to keep the troublesome Baden under his own eye. Marlborough's men, therefore, marched on to join Baden's Imperialists at Launsheim,[37] and thence the two generals set out together with 80,000 men to seek out the Elector of Bavaria and Marsin.

Meanwhile, feverish councils were taking place at Tallard's head-quarters in the city of Strasbourg. It was imperative that rapid action should be taken to save Bavaria; but the rigidity of the French command system laid it down that any variations from the original plan of campaign must be sanctioned by Versailles. As a result, Tallard was delayed for almost three weeks, awaiting Louis XIV's instructions. The Count of Mérode-Westerloo,[38] commander of the Flemish troops in Tallard's army, was openly critical of this delay. In his interesting *Memoirs*, which provide a valuable account of the campaign as seen from the French side, he wrote: 'One thing is certain: we delayed our march from Alsace far too long and quite inexplicably, for it was contrary to the usual diligence, promptness and vivacity of the French.' Louis' orders at last reached Tallard on 27 June; he was to advance, with a force of forty battalions and fifty squadrons, through the Black Forest to relieve the Elector, covered by Villeroi's slightly stronger army, which was to 'advance on Offenburg, observe the enemy, retain them in the Lines of Stollhofen, follow them into Alsace, or join Marshal Tallard if they move all their forces towards the Danube.'[39] Meanwhile, de Coignies'[40] corps would safeguard Alsace. On 1 July, at long last, the advance began. Mérode-Westerloo records:

> After making a feint-attack on the Lines of Stollhofen we left the fortress of Kehl and entered the Black Forest down the Kintezingerthal valley. Before we did so, M. Tallard formed us into battle-order . . .'[41]

Tallard's progress was almost pitifully slow: this was due partly to the poor condition of the cavalry, suffering from an epidemic of a mysterious 'German sickness'[42] partly to the lumbering convoy, 'made up of more than eight thousand waggons of bread, flour and biscuit', which the army had to escort through the difficult mountain passes; and not a little to the commander-in-chief's insistence on besieging the minor town of Villingen for six days with his entire army, instead of leaving a small covering force to mask its defences. In due course, the French were compelled to break off the siege on 22 July, when Eugene's shadowing army of 18,000 men appeared near Rothweil; for Tallard was misled concerning the strength of this Imperial force, and, in any case, was determined to avoid a battle before joining his allies. After seeing the convoy safely into Ulm, Tallard at last joined up with the elector and Marshal Marsin at Augsburg on 5 August. The French had taken thirty-six days to complete a march of only half the distance covered by Marlborough's men in an almost identical period of time.

Meanwhile, the Duke and the Margrave were endeavouring to force the Elector to make peace. The Allies were short of heavy artillery, and in consequence were unable to attack the main Bavarian camp at Dillingen.

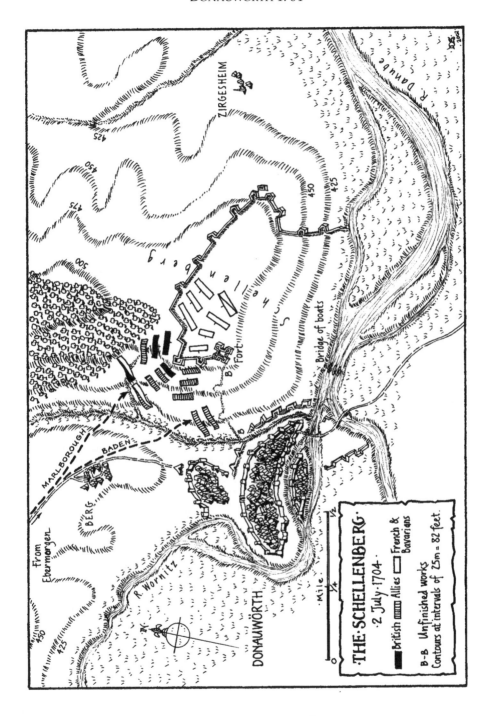

ZIRGESHEIM

R. Danube

Schellenberg

Bridge of boats

B. Fort

B.

From Ebermorgen

MARLBOROUGH

BADEN

BERG

R. Wornitz

DONAUWÖRTH

·THE·SCHELLENBERG·
·2·July·1704·

British ▬ Allies ☐ French & Bavarians

B–B Unfinished works
Contours at intervals of 25m = 82 feet.

Mile

Proceeding along the north bank of the Danube, they unexpectedly appeared outside the fortress of Donauwörth on the afternoon of 2 July – to the surprise of the local Bavarian commander, Comte d'Arco,[43] and his garrison of 10,000 men, who were hard at work modernising the ancient defences. Marlborough hustled the doubtful Baden into sanctioning an immediate assault, to be attempted in the first instance by a picked corps of grenadiers and volunteers totalling 6,000 men. The struggle began at 6.15 in the evening, and proved extremely bloody. One of the defenders, Colonel de la Colonie,[44] has left a graphic description of the desperate action for control of the Schellenberg Heights, the key to the position.

> The enemy broke into the charge, and rushed at full speed shouting at the top of their voices, to throw themselves into our entrenchments, the rapidity of their movements together with their loud noise was truly alarming, and as soon as I heard them I ordered our drums to beat the charge so as to drown them with our noise lest they should have a bad effect on our people. The English infantry led the attack with the greatest intrepidity right up to our parapet ... [which] became the scene of the bloodiest struggle that could be conceived. During this first attack we were all fighting hand to hand, hurling them back as they clutched at the parapet ... At last the enemy, after huge losses, were obliged to relax their hold, and fell back for shelter to the dip of the slope where we could not harm them. A sudden calm now reigned amongst us.

This apparent Allied repulse was deceptive: to hold the heights against the onslaught, d'Arco had drawn more and more men from the central portion of his defences, which linked the Schellenberg with the town of Donauwörth. It was against this weakened sector that Baden unleashed the Imperial cavalry backed by supporting infantry – and in no time these troops interposed themselves between d'Arco and the town. De la Colonie resumes the tale:

> At about 7.30 I noticed all at once an extraordinary movement on the part of our infantry, who were rising up and ceasing fire withal. I glanced around to determine what had caused this behaviour, and then became aware of several lines of infantry in greyish-white uniforms on our left flank. I verily believed reinforcement had reached us; no information whatever had reached us of the enemy's success to the left. So in the error I laboured under I shouted to my men that they were Frenchmen and friends.

He was speedily disillusioned, and by 8.30 pm the remnants of d'Arco's garrison were in full flight for the Danube, where many were drowned when a bridge collapsed. The town of Donauwörth surrendered soon afterwards.

This important success provided the Allies with a crossing-place over the Danube into the southern regions of Bavaria, and at the same time gave them a terminal and forward depot for their lines of communication running south from Nordlingen. But the cost had been heavy: the Allies suffered 6,000 casualties, and numbered among their slain eight generals and twenty-eight brigadiers and colonels; for their part the Bavarians lost 5,000 men or half their strength.[45] Had Marlborough listened to Baden and postponed the attack, the Allied death-roll might have been far longer; for without siege artillery a direct assault was the only course open to the Allies, and every hour's delay gave d'Arco more time to strengthen his defences and summon assistance. But as yet there was no sign of the Elector's main army. The decisive victory that was required to complete the campaign had still to be sought and won; and, at thus juncture, the fortunes of war temporarily favoured Marlborough's foes and placed his whole achievement in jeopardy.

NOTES

1   Dr Hare's *Journal*. See G Murray (ed.), *Letters and Dispatches of The Duke of Marlborough*, London, 1845, Vol. I, pp. 322–8.
2   'The Two Crowns' were France and Spain, aided by Bavaria and Cologne.
3   Marshal Claude Louis Hector, Duc de Villars (1653–1734).
4   Marshal Maximilian Emmanuel, Elector of Bavaria (1678–1734).
5   Marshal Ferdinand, Comte Marsin (1656–1706).
6   Louis Joseph, Duc de Vendôme (1654–1712).
7   Marshal François de Neuville, Duc de Villeroi (1644–1730).
8   Prince Louis Guillaume, Margrave of Baden (1655–1707).
9   Lieutenant-General Count Styrum.
10 To Sarah Churchill, 20 February 1704 (new style).
11 Sarah Churchill, long a favourite of Princess, later Queen, Anne.
12 Sir Winston Churchill (d. 1685), father of John Churchill.
13 Marshal-Général Henri de la Tour d'Auvergne, Viscomte de Turenne (1611–75), an excellent soldier of the earlier part of the seventeenth century.
14 5 July 1685.
15 Earl Sidney Godolphin (1645–1712), Marlborough's greatest friend.
16 See G M Trevelyan, *England Under Queen Anne*, London, 1965, Vol. I, p. 354.
17 See D G Chandler (ed.), *The Oxford Illustrated History of the British Army*, Oxford, 1994, pp. 53–71.
18 Field-Marshal Hendrik van Nassau-Ouwerkirk (or Overkirk) (1640–1708) of Holland.
19 See W C Coxe, *Memoirs of John, Duke of Marlborough*, London, 1820, Vol. I, p. 320.
20 Marshal Camille d'Hostun, Marquis de la Baume, Comte de Tallard (1652–1738), He was taken prisoner at Blenheim in 1704 and spent seven years captive in England.

21 R Parker, *Memoirs of the Most Remarkable Military Transactions from the Year 1683 to 1718*, London, 1747 (new edn, London, 1968). See also D G Chandler, *The Marlborough Wars*, London, 1968, pp. 5–133.
22 W S Churchill, *Marlborough, His Life and Times*, Vol. II, p. 273.
23 J J G Pelet and F E de Vault, *Mémoires militaires relatifs à la succession d'Espagne sous Louis XIV*, Paris, 1846–52, and see Vol. IV, pp. 470–2.
24 See D G Chandler, *Marlborough as Military Commander*, London, 1973, p. 129, and W S Churchill, *op. cit.*, Vol. II, p. 275.
25 An example of the Duke's talent for fooling Tallard on the great march.
26 Chandler, *Marlborough as Military Commander*, p. 132.
27 Dr Hare's *Journal*.
28 William Cadogan (1675–1726), eventually full General (1718) and First Earl. At Blenheim, he was a Brigadier-General as the Duke's Quartermaster-General.
29 Adam Cardonnel (d. 1716), the Duke's Secretary from 1692.
30 Parker, *op. cit.*, p. 31.
31 The French march was slower because of sickness. See Chandler, *Marlborough as Military Commander*, p. 157.
32 J M Deane (ed. D G Chandler), *A Journal of Marlburian Campaigns, 1704–1711*, Special *SAHR*, No. 12, 1994, p. 2.
33 A Crichton (ed.), *The Life and Diary of Lt-Col. John Blackadder*, Edinburgh, 1820.
34 See Note 9.
35 François Eugene de Savoie-Carignan, Prince of Savoy (1663–1739), a brilliant soldier against the Turks and the French, with Marlborough the 'Two Princes'.
36 At the town of Gross Heppach on 12 June 1704.
37 From 22 June 1704.
38 See Mérode-Westerloo, *Mémoires*, p. 158.
39 Between Lauingen and Dillingen close to the Danube.
40 Général Robert de Coignies (fl. 1704).
41 See Mérode-Westerloo, *op. cit.*, p. 158.
42 Possibly glanders.
43 Comte Jean Martin d'Arco (d. 1715), Chief-of-Staff of the Elector of Bavaria.
44 See W C Horsley (ed.), *The Chronicles of an Old Campaigner*, London, 1904.
45 See Deane, *op. cit.*, pp. 7–8.

APPENDIX

The storm of the Schellenberg above Donauwörth, 2 July 1704

The figures of casualties are complex, but useful information can be drawn from Col. Charles Dalton's vast information in his six volumes of *English Army Lists and Commission Registers* (London, 1892–1904 and revised in 1960). The most recent calculation has been in James Falkner's fine book, *Great and Glorious Days* (Staplehurst, 2002), pp. 29–48, which shows that the Allies lost 5,040 casualties (the British losing 1,287 men killed on that grim day). Marlborough had forty-five battalions in all nearby, and ordered 5,850 selected Allied grenadiers from the whole army to start climbing the slopes. They were backed by 8,000 troops (English, Dutch and Germans), and thirdly in the rear came seventeen squadrons of dragoons (including two English regiments).

As for Count d'Arco's force, he had in place seventeen battalions of Bavarians, five more French units, eight squadrons of dragoons, and sixteen artillery guns in all. Once the terrible storm was completed, the Bavarians and French must have lost at least 4,000 men, and many more had fled.

It was vital for the Allies to cross the Danube there, but Donauwörth had been won for a grim price. Winston S Churchill states that the senior commanders had lost killed or wounded, eleven lieutenant-generals, four major-generals, and twenty-eight brigadier-generals, colonels and lieutenant-colonels. Such numbers may be challenged, but two English regiments suffered the worst: the 1st Guards, and the two battalions of Orkney's Regiment. Sentinel John Marshall Deane was present there:

> Whereupon the Duke of Marlborough sent an order that eleavon regiments of English and Dutch should be ready imediately to goe upon the attacque, besides the Fforlorne Hope & the Horse & Dragoons to back them, namely: our battalion of Guards, my Lord Orkneys two battallions; Major Gen'll Ingoldsbyes and Coll. Merrediths regiment went on intire, beside the English Horse apoynted for that sarvice. But no sooner did our Forlorne Hope appear but the enemy did throw in their volleys of canon balls and

small shott among them and made a brave defence and a bold resistance against us as brave loyall hearted gentlemen souldiers ought to for there prince and country, and they being strongly intrenched they killed and mortyfyed abundance of our men both officers and souldiers.

As for the officers and souldiers of our own battalion I shall give you a particular account, as first viz:- Killed upon the spott; Coll. Blunt; Captaine West; Capt Rawley; Ensn. Peirson; and Quarter Master Bibbey West; Wounded:- Coll. Primrose; Comandant. Coll. Fferrers; Capt. Adams; Capt. Pocock; Ensn. Smith; Ensn. Rich; and Ensn. St. Denny; we had likewise in our regiment killed upon the spott and dyed of there wounds 172 private centinells, besides above a hundred that was wounded and recovered againe. Of the Sargeants:- 7 killed & 5 wounded; of the Corporalls 3 killed and 12 wounded; and our battalion sufferd so extremely I leave the reader to judge of the rest.

Dalton also claims that Orkney's two battalions, now 'the Royal Scots' and Meredyth's (the 37th Foot, later the Royal Hampshire Regt), suffered as badly as the 1st Guards at this attack. Orkney's (two battalions) lost nine officers killed and thirteen wounded; one serjeant and thirty-eight other ranks killed, and three serjeants and 103 ORs. Meantime, Meredyth's suffered at the Schellenberg, four officers killed and ten more wounded; one serjeant killed and three wounded; eighteen ORs killed and fifty-seven more wounded. The 1st Guards (according to Dalton) lost seven serjeants killed and eight wounded; seventy-five sentinels were killed and 127 wounded at the Schellenberg. As for officer casualties, six were certainly listed as killed and at least three more wounded. This shows why it is so difficult to agree the names in killed or wounded lists, but the names given on the Blenheim Roll (1705) are mostly acceptable as they list the bounties paid.

For the fuller record,here is the remainder of Deane's description of the Schellenberg:

In short both English and Dutch behaved themselves to admiration and the foraigners, give them there due, did stand like a wall and acted as became brave gentlemen and as duty combines a souldier at such a juncture, and severall generall officers they lost in this action and abundance of old experienced centinells. A glorious action it was to be sure for this vigourous and bold attacque held neare 3 hours but wth. Gods assistance we driving them out of there works and possessing ourselves of them. Our horse likewise persued and killed abundance of them driving severall hundreds of them into the river Danube, who there made there *exile* [scored out] exit. We still persued and cutt them down as long as there was any light left in the sky. We took that night and next morning 31 pieces of cannon and 1 mortar and 15 pontoone boats and some baggage but the enemy had before this action transported most of there valuable things over the river Danube.

The next morning being June the 22nd, our Generall sent a detachment from the army to the town of Danuwart wch. town immediately surrendered. Our horse that morning killed and took abundance of the enemy who ware skulking in holes not knowing wch. way to runn nor what to dow by reason the Duke of Bavaria had cutt of the bridge of boats that was made over the river.

CHAPTER XIII

Blindheim 1704

Now entertain conjecture of a time
When creeping murmur and the poring dark
Fills the wide vessel of the universe.
From camp to camp, through the foul womb of night,
The hum of either army stilly sounds,
That the fix'd sentinels almost receive
The secret whispers of each other's watch.

Shakespeare, *Henry V*, Act IV, Prologue

All of Europe was amazed to learn that Allied armies had managed to march through central Europe successfully from mid-May to early August 1704, and then had won a battle that affected the direction of the war. The situation was changing. Marlborough and the Margrave of Baden had won the battle of Donauwörth near the Danube and opened the way for a new strategy. Now they could swing deeply into Bavaria – the greatest friend of France. However, several more serious problems had first to be met and solved by the astute skills of Marlborough and Eugene.

It is strange that being such experienced diplomats the two men had never met before they did on campaign, and that they instantly forged such a close friendship and total trust. Classically handsome, Churchill was aged 54 in 1704 and he had never been in command in a major battle. The 'ugly' Prince Eugene of Savoy-Carignan was 41, thirteen years younger and since having been appointed by the Emperor in 1683 had already been involved in several successful actions and had won the celebrated Battle of Zenta, on 11 September 1697, when he was only 34. In earlier years, the Prince had wished to become a soldier in France, but Louis XIV refused his request, telling him to become a priest! The King considered him totally lacking in officer qualities. Le Roi Soleil was no fool, generally speaking, in spotting latent military talent and his remarks may have had something to do with Eugene having joined a clique of fashionable French 'perverts' whose delight was the wearing of feminine attire. After this the Prince had left France, and instead took his sword to the Austrian Emperor at Vienna where his military talents were spotted immediately.

Napoleon listed Eugene as one of the seven great generals of history, while Marlborough was not included. The Duke would win four great battles and two smaller victories, and conduct thirty successful sieges over ten years. Eugene was to continue commanding the Imperial Austrians, including at the famous victory of Belgrade in 1717, where he first won a siege and, two days later, a triumphal battle. He never married, was an adept courtier and a noted patron of the arts. The only setbacks in his splendid military record were the two defeats of Toulon in 1707 and Denain in 1712. Marlborough, of course, never lost a battle, but it is clear that Eugene assisted the Duke at the important victories of Blenheim, Oudenarde and Malplaquet. But there was no envy between them, and the ancient title of the 'Twin Captains' was certainly deserved. Now we must read on, about their deeds on 13 August 1704.

After the capture of Donauwörth, success began to elude the Allies. The Elector refused either to fight or negotiate, but kept his forces behind the strong fortifications of Augsburg, which were impregnable to Marlborough and Baden without the assistance of a siege train. Similarly, the city of Munich defied the Allied army. The Elector of Bavaria was soon informed by a smuggled message[1] that Tallard was on his way through the Black Forest; and this cheering intelligence reinforced his policy of inaction while the Allies impotently ravaged the Bavarian countryside, burning possibly 400 villages.[2] The crisis of the campaign was fast approaching, and the initiative appeared to have passed back to the French; if Marshal Tallard and the Elector succeeded in interposing their combined army between Eugene's small force (retreating along the north bank of the Danube) and Marlborough and Baden south of the river, the Duke's communications with Franconia would eventually be severed and all the Allied forces placed in a very critical position. In such disturbing circumstances, Marlborough's brilliant march to the Danube and forceful capture of Donauwörth might only result in a crushing disaster for the isolated and separated armies of the Grand Alliance in the crucial theatre.

This opportunity of total triumph, however, was to prove too much for the restricted abilities and imaginations of the Franco–Bavarian generals, faced as they were by the genius of Duke John and the fine quality of the men he led. Marshal Tallard was a soldier of great experience and considerable achievement, who, apart from his military career, had earned a notable reputation as a diplomat – serving at one time as French ambassador to the Court of St James's. He was famed for his courtly manners and hospitality; 'he would, on occasion, entertain anything up to a hundred officers during the first or second halt of a day's march,' wrote Mérode-Westerloo, 'keeping two mule trains laden with good things to eat – and wines too – at the head of the army for this very purpose.'[3]

This generosity contrasts strangely with Marlborough's parsimony: the Duke rarely entertained his subordinates on a lavish scale, and made a point of dining at their tables whenever possible. This strange streak in an otherwise extremely liberal character was doubtless due to the financial difficulties he had experienced in his youth. Little need be said of Tallard's military colleagues: Marshal Marsin was a competent mediocrity; Max Emmanuel, Elector of Bavaria, was a picturesque figure of considerable dash and ability, but also an unscrupulous opportunist who had deserted the Emperor and adopted the Franco–Spanish cause through motives of purely selfish aggrandisement. The Bavarian field forces were considerably weakened by detachments sent to protect the electoral estates, and the Elector's relationship with his French colleagues was frequently acrimonious. Marlborough's cordial friendship with Prince Eugene and his tactful handling of the Margrave compare very favourably with the strained relations in the enemy camp.

Following their union at Augsburg,[4] the Franco–Bavarian army set off for the Danube, intent on isolating Marlborough to the south of the river. Fortunately Marlborough's flexible military mind was equal to the new challenge. The crisis of the campaign had clearly arrived, and the first problem was to place Baden out of harm's way: his presence on a critical battlefield might well prove disastrous. Consequently, at a conference with Eugene on 7 August, Baden was persuaded to take 15,000 men to besiege the town of Ingolstadt[5] farther down the Danube. Prince Eugene returned to Höchstädt[6] to note every enemy move. On 10 August he sent an urgent dispatch to Marlborough from Munster, reporting that he was falling back towards Donauwörth.

> The enemy have marched. It is almost certain that the whole army is crossing the Danube at Lavingen. They have pushed a Lieutenant-Colonel whom I sent to reconnoitre back to Hochstadt. The plain of Dillingen is crowded with troops. I have held on all day here; but with 18 battalions I dare not risk staying the night ... Everything, milord, consists in speed and that you put yourself forthwith in movement to join me tomorrow, without which I fear it will be too late. In short, all the enemy is there ...[7]

Marlborough needed no urging; by a series of brilliant marches, he concentrated his army and converged his forces on Donauwörth, part crossing the Danube at Merxheim, the rest taking the direct road from Rain over the Lech river. During the 11th the link-up with Eugene was completed; but no effort was made to recall Baden. Meantime, the Franco–Bavarian army advanced methodically eastwards from Lavingen, not for one moment expecting to be concerned in a major battle; and, on 12

August, Tallard camped behind the small Nebel river near the village of Blenheim.[8] The same day, Marlborough and Eugene made a full reconnaissance of the French position from the church spire of Tapfheim, and moved their army forward to Münster – a mere five miles from the French camp. The 'Two Princes' – in direct contravention of the rules of conventional war – had made up their minds to risk everything in an attack timed for the next day. The night was spent in final preparations for the coming conflict.

Early the next morning, the Allied army was roused from its tents and put in motion towards the Nebel, marching in nine great columns. At six o'clock the first troops came within sight of the French cantonments. Mérode-Westerloo, who had been put in command of the cavalry on the right of the second line, had spent the night in a barn on the outskirts of Blenheim.

> I slept deeply until six in the morning when I was abruptly awoken by one of my old retainers – the head-groom, in fact – who rushed into the barn all out of breath. He had just returned from taking my horses out to grass at four in the morning (as he had been instructed). This fellow, Lefranc, shook me awake and blurted out that the enemy were 'there'. Thinking to mock him, I asked: 'Where? There?' and he at once replied 'Yes, there! There!', flinging wide as he spoke the door of the barn and drawing my bed-curtains. The building looked straight onto the fine, sunlit plain beyond – and the whole area appeared to be covered by enemy squadrons. I rubbed my eyes in disbelief.[9]

The Count soon recovered his composure, however, coolly ordered a cup of chocolate, and wisely instructed his servants 'to pack my kit with all speed, and to watch Marshal Tallard's retainers and do with my belongings exactly what they did with his'. Shortly afterwards, Mérode-Westerloo rode off to the camp, accompanied by his two aides-de-camp and no fewer than thirteen spare horses.

He found everything quiet.

> There was not a single soul stirring as I clattered out of the village: nothing might have been happening. The same sight met me when I reached the camp – everyone still snug in their tents, although the enemy . . .were already pushing back our pickets.[10]

The Count ordered his cavalry to mount, but was careful not to sound the general alarm.

> Soon everyone was on his horse, and I kept them all drawn up at the head of their tents – and then – and only then – did I see the first signs of movement in Blenheim village.[11]

Marshal Tallard was still in no way worried by these warlike demonstrations to his front. As late as seven o'clock, he penned a postscript on to his report of the previous day, and sent the messenger on his way to Versailles.

> This morning [13th] before daybreak the enemy beat the 'générale' at two o'clock and at three the 'assemblé'. They are now drawn up at the head of their camp and it looks as if they will march this day. Rumour in the countryside expects them to move on Nordlingen. If that be true, they will leave us between the Danube and themselves, and in consequence they will have difficulty in sustaining the depots which they have taken in Bavaria.[12]

The events of the next twelve hours were to prove this forecast singularly unfortunate. An hour later, Tallard decided he had better rouse his men, but it was only at ten in the morning, when Colonel Blood's batteries opened fire, that he fully realised he had a major battle on his hands.

The reasons for this miscalculation, and for the lack of awareness on the part of the French commander, are not far to seek. By the rules of eighteenth-century chessboard warfare, Marlborough and Eugene had been out-generalled; and the prescribed course for them to follow was a retreat along their lines of communication. In any case, Allied 'deserters' had confirmed this assessment of the Allied intentions; for Marlborough had been careful to plant corroborative evidence on the gullible Tallard. The latter further reasoned that his army was in possession of a strong natural position which would be costly to attack; and this made a battle even less likely in an age when economically-minded governments deplored heavy expenditure of almost irreplaceable manpower and material. Mérode-Westerloo wrote:

> Our right wing was on the left bank of the river Danube, with the village of Blenheim some two hundred yards to its front . . . In front of this village ran a small stream running from its swampy source a mile or so away to the left . . . The Elector and his men held a position reaching away as far as the village of Lutzingen where his headquarters were situated – with the woods stretching away towards Nordlingen to his front. Before this position was an area of marshy ground, a few hamlets and one or two mills along the little stream. Blenheim village itself was surrounded by hedges; and fences and other obstacles enclosed gardens and meadows. All in all, this position was pretty fair . . .[13]

Another advantage of the position was the long ridge set back at a distance of some 800 yards from the Nebel, connecting Blenheim with the village of Oberglau and then on towards Lutzingen. With both flanks secured, and with his army holding a position overlooking an area of marsh and stream, Tallard felt he had reason for confidence.

In addition to these natural advantages, Tallard possessed a slight superiority in overall numbers – 56,000 French and Bavarians facing 52,000 Allies – and a definite advantage in artillery – ninety cannon against sixty. His force consisted of seventy-nine battalions and 140 squadrons, while Marlborough and Eugene deployed rather more cavalry (160 squadrons) but only sixty-five infantry battalions.[14]

In spite of being surprised and forced to accept battle, Tallard was fortunate enough to be given ample time to draw up his battle formation, for, although Marlborough's left and centre were ready by ten o'clock, Eugene was delayed on the right by hills and wooded country, and was only in position after midday. The French commander used this respite to deploy his troops along the three-mile front. A strong garrison of infantry was placed in the village of Blenheim, with twelve squadrons of dismounted dragoons (whose mounts had died of 'German sickness') holding the interval between the village and the Danube. Slightly to the left and rear of Blenheim, he drew up eighteen battalions to constitute his infantry reserve. All the forces in the immediate vicinity of Blenheim were put under the command of the Marquis de Clérambault. In the open space between Blenheim and Oberglau, Tallard placed over seventy squadrons of his cavalry under General Zurlauben; these units were drawn up in a double line, supported by two brigades of infantry and several batteries of artillery. Marshal Marsin drew up fourteen battalions under General de Blainville[15] around the village of Oberglau; and beyond this strongpoint were arrayed the remaining sixty-seven squadrons of horse, while the left flank was held by twenty-nine battalions of the Elector's infantry in the vicinity of Lutzingen. Cannon were stationed at various points along the whole front.

These dispositions reveal Tallard's probable plan of battle. At first sight, the weakest section of his position was the area between Blenheim and Oberglau, held by virtually unsupported cavalry, drawn up at a considerable distance from the Nebel. Tallard hoped to lure Marlborough to cross the Nebel against this sector: while the Allies were struggling through the marshes, they would be caught in a cross-fire from Blenheim and Oberglau. The moment the survivors reached the firm ground beyond the Nebel, they would be attacked on each flank by the village garrisons and the infantry reserve; the *coup de grâce* would then be administered by the massed French cavalry, charging downhill into the already disordered ranks of the Allied centre, who would be flung back in ruin upon the marshes and stream.

If all its parts were implemented, this plan held a fair prospect of success; but the spyglass of the Duke of Marlborough had not failed to notice several grave errors in the French dispositions. Owing to the strained relations that existed between the respective commanders, the Franco–Bavarian army had, in fact, been drawn up in two practically independent wings, and not in a single, integrated battle-line. This would make it difficult for Tallard to support one flank with troops from the other. Marlborough also noted the perils and possibilities of Tallard's chosen 'killing-ground' in the centre; but he saw that, if the garrisons of Blenheim and Oberglau were firmly contained within their defences, the French centre would be dangerously exposed without hope of re-inforcement. It would probably be wrong to assert that Marlborough worked out a detailed plan before the opening of the battle; but, no doubt, his trained eye appreciated the flaws in the French position.

During the time the two generals were making their preparations, the rival forces stood in full view of one another. 'The two armies in full battle-array were so close to one another that they exchanged fanfares of trumpet-calls and rolls of kettle-drums,' recorded our Flemish cavalry commander; but very soon the batteries on both sides opened fire, 'whilst the French, following their usual deplorable custom, set fire to all the villages, mills and hamlets to our front, and flames and smoke billowed up to the clouds.'[16] To minimise the effect of the cannonade, Marlborough ordered his infantry to lie down in their ranks; and he in person rode from point to point, checking the siting of the artillery.

A little after 12.30, a galloper from Prince Eugene informed Marlborough that all was ready on the right; and Lord Cutts[17] at once advanced with the twenty battalions and fifteen squadrons of the Allied left wing against the village of Blenheim. His leading brigade held its fire until within sword's distance of the French palisades; but the French garrison repulsed the attack and killed the brigade commander, Lord Rowe.[18] The second brigade, however, scattered the counter-attack launched by three squad-rons of the crack French Gendarmerie cavalry; and, after pausing to lengthen his line, Lord Cutts launched a second assault. This, too, was driven back with heavy loss; but the French commander, the Marquis de Clérambault,[19] was so impressed by the fury of these onslaughts that he promptly ordered all eighteen battalions of Tallard's infantry reserve to enter the defences of the village. This was done without any reference to the commander-in-chief, and constituted the worst French error of the day. Mérode-Westerloo, as observer of the scene from the cavalry lines, wrote:

> The men were so crowded in upon one another that they couldn't even fire – let alone receive or carry out any orders. Not a single shot of the enemy missed its mark, whilst only those few of our men at the front could return the fire . . . to make things even worse, the village had been set on fire by the French troops and our poor fellows were grilled.[20]

By two o'clock sixteen Allied units were containing twenty-seven French battalions and twelve squadrons within the village, and Marlborough had secured his left flank.

Tallard, meanwhile, had been visiting Marsin at Oberglau, and was not therefore available to countermand his subordinate's rash and un-authorised squandering of the infantry reserve. The Marshal's attention, moreover, was fully occupied watching the almost unbelievable rout of eight squadrons of the Gendarmerie at the hands of only five English squadrons under Colonel Palmes.[21] This reverse, though slight in itself, shook the French commander-in-chief's faith in the ultimate victory of his army. Elsewhere the situation was favourable: away on the left, Prince Eugene's seventy-four squadrons and thirteen battalions were receiving a rough time from the numerically superior Bavarians, while the village of Oberglau in the centre was holding its own with ease.

Once Blenheim was safely masked, Marlborough was free to turn his attention to the Prince of Holstein-Beck's[22] initial assault on Blainville's defences. The garrison of Oberglau, issuing forth from their positions to rout them with the bayonet, severely checked the leading battalions. Foremost among the units engaged in this task were the 'Wild Geese', the regiment of Irish exiles serving in the French pay. The arrival of part of Tallard's first line of cavalry almost turned this check into a disaster for the Allies; but the exploitation of their initial success was badly handled, which gave Marlborough just sufficient time to lead up three reserve battalions and several batteries to rally the wavering line. While these stirring events were taking place before Oberglau, the first and second lines of the Allied centre were steadily crossing the Nebel and taking up new positions on the French side. Marlborough's centre was drawn up in a unique formation – four lines deep. The front line consisted of thirteen battalions (not including the ten already in action under Holstein-Beck); this formation was intended to cover the cavalry squadrons, formed up in two lines totalling seventy-one squadrons to the infantry's immediate rear. In reserve behind these mounted troops stood a further ten battalions of foot; and the command of the whole of the centre was entrusted to General Charles Churchill, the Duke's able brother.[23]

The crisis of the day took place at 2.15 pm when a French cavalry attack practically penetrated the right flank of Marlborough's centre. In some anxiety, Marlborough sent an urgent appeal for assistance to his comrade-in-arms, Prince Eugene, who was desperately engaged against twice his own number of the farther side of Oberglau. But so great was Eugene's trust in Marlborough's judgment that he at once detached a brigade of Imperial cuirassiers under General Fugger to the centre's assistance. These horsemen fell like a whirlwind on the flank of Marsin's second cavalry attack, and scattered it in confusion. Although the Prince of Holstein-Beck had been mortally wounded in the first assault, his men were heartened

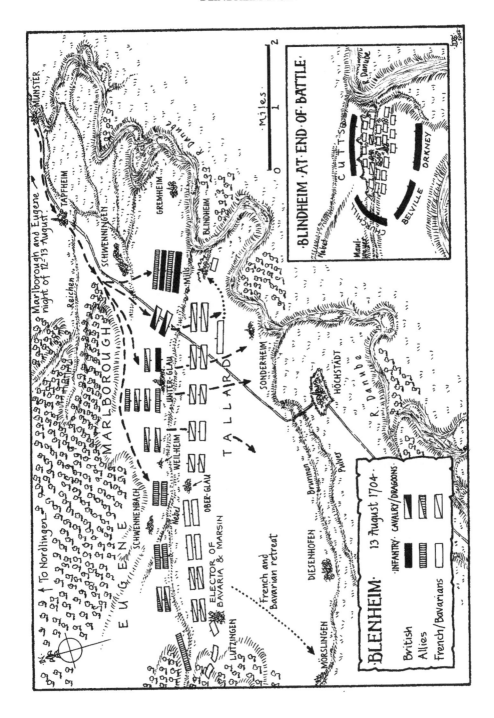

BLINDHEIM · AT · END · OF · BATTLE ·

CHURCHILL
CUTTS
BELVILLE
ORKNEY

Miles
0 1 2

Marlborough and Eugene
night of 12-13 August.

MÜNSTER
TAPFHEIM
SCHWENNINGEN
Reichen
GREMHEIM
R. DANUBE
BLINDHEIM
Mill
SONDERHEIM
HÖCHSTÄDT
R. Danube

MARLBOROUGH

UNTER-GLAU
WEILHEIM
Nebel
OBER-GLAU
SCHWENNENBACH

EUGENE

To Nördlingen

ELECTOR OF
BAVARIA & MARSIN
French and
Bavarian retreat

TALLARD

Brunnen
Pulver
DIESENHOFEN

MÖRSLINGEN
LÜTZINGEN

BLENHEIM·
13 August 1704·
·INFANTRY· CAVALRY/DRAGOONS·
British
Allies
French/Bavarians

243

by this reversal of fortunes, and once more returned to the attack against Oberglau; and by three o'clock Blainville's garrison had been forced back into the village's defences, where they were firmly contained. Tallard had now missed his last opportunity of victory, and Marlborough had surmounted the crisis of the battle.

The deployment of the centre continued with both its flanks secure; and, for the space of an hour, a lull descended on the battlefield. This is not surprising; for the entire line of both armies had been heavily engaged for more than two and a half hours. By four o'clock Marlborough's centre was firmly planted in the midst of the French line – its eighty fresh squadrons (nine had been transferred from Lord Cutts' wing) supported by twenty-three battalions and several batteries of guns. All Tallard could produce to face this imposing array were the blown and dishevelled remnants of his original sixty-eight squadrons, all of which had already been in action. In desperation, the French commander called for infantry reinforcements to sustain his horsemen; but, thanks to Clérambault's earlier folly, the only units available were nine battalions of raw recruits. In spite of their local superiority, Marsin and the Elector declined to send assistance from the left, on the grounds that they were too busily engaged trying to check Eugene's infantry, who were working their way round the Lutzingen flank.

The outcome of the battle in the centre was now practically a foregone conclusion. Mérode-Westerloo had done his best to retrieve the situation:

> I rode over to Blenheim, wanting to bring out a dozen battalions (which they certainly did not need there) to form a line on the edge of the stream supported by the cannons and the debris of my squadrons. The brigades of Saint-Second and Monfort were setting out to follow me when M. de Clérambault in person countermanded the move, and shouting and swearing drove them back into the village.[24]

Clearly that officer had lost his nerve during the excitements of the day, and would not admit his earlier error even at the eleventh hour. To gain a temporary respite, Tallard ordered his remaining cavalry to charge, and the Allied advance was checked for a short while. Major-General Lord Orkney,[25] however, was at hand to remedy the damage:

> I marched with my battalions to sustain the horse, and found them repulsed, crying out for foot, being pressed by the Gendarmerie.[26] I went to the head of several squadrons and got 'em to rally on my right and left, and brought up four pieces of cannon and then charged.

Marlborough's wisdom in placing infantry battalions in close support of his cavalry in the centre was now fully proved. By five-thirty the advance was again under way; the nine French battalions were decimated by close-range artillery and platoon fire, and the remnants of Tallard's squadrons vainly tried to check the tide with their pistols and carbines. It was soon over: the French recruits were overrun and died where they stood; the French cavalry was borne back by weight of numbers and completely broken, Mérode-Westerloo's horse being carried along 'some three hundred paces without putting hoof to ground' so tight was the press, until both mount and rider were hurled twenty feet down a ravine near the village of Sonderheim. Upwards of 3,000 French horsemen were probably drowned trying to swim the Danube. The crowning disaster for the French cause was the capture of Marshal Tallard by some Hessian cavalry as he tried to reach Blenheim; and, deprived of its leader, French resistance rapidly deteriorated. Away on the left, Marsin and the Elector decided the day was lost, and at once set about extricating their own units for a retreat towards Höchstädt, leaving the Blenheim garrison to its fate.

By six in the evening, General Charles Churchill[27] had completed the encirclement of the village. But his men were understandably weary, while the majority of the French garrison had hardly discharged a shot all day; and the twenty-seven battalions might well have fought their way out, had not their commander slipped off unnoticed in the confusion and drowned himself in the Danube. Leaderless, the French hesitated, affording Orkney enough time to bluff them into surrender.

> The firing of the cottages we could perceive annoyed them very much, and seeing two brigades appear as if they intended to cut their way out through our troops, who were very fatigued, it came into my head to beat a parley, which they accepted of immediately, and their Brigadier de Nouville capitulated with me to be prisoners at my discretion and lay down their arms.[28]

Unit after unit followed their example; but it was not until nine in the evening that the last regiments – among them the cream of the French Army – accepted the terms. The Regiment of Navarre ceremonially burnt its colours to prevent them falling into enemy hands; and, with this last act of symbolic defiance, the hard-fought Battle of Blenheim came to an end. Meanwhile, the troops of the Elector and Marsin left the field, almost unmolested.

It had been a glorious victory, at one stroke saving Vienna, reversing the tide of the war and establishing the reputation of John Churchill, first Duke of Marlborough, as the champion of the Grand Alliance and one of the great captains of history. The events of 13 August 1704, which had culminated in the capture of the French commander-in-chief and the destruction of two-thirds of his army, were to have immense repercussions throughout Europe. At a cost of 12,000 Allied casualties, Marlborough and

Eugene had inflicted a loss of 20,000 killed and wounded on the foe, and taken a further 14,000 prisoners of war along with sixty cannon, 300 colours and standards, and the entire contents of the French camp. For the first time in over forty years, the forces of Le Roi Soleil had sustained a major defeat, and thereby forfeited their claim to military predominance. The victory had been as much a vindication of the fighting methods of the Allies as a demonstration of the talents of their commanders. The proper use of fire and movement, the controlled platoon volleys, the effect of cold steel wielded by the cavalry, the careful siting of batteries, had all contributed to the downfall of the French Army, which obstinately clung to the outmoded tactics of a former age. Mérode-Westerloo summed up the case against Tallard's army when he wrote:

> The French lost this battle for a wide variety of reasons, For one thing, they had too good an opinion of their own ability – and were excessively scornful of their adversaries. Another point was their faulty field dispositions, and in addition there was rampant indiscipline and inexperience displayed in Marshal Tallard's army. It took all these faults to lose so celebrated a battle. [29]

But the chief credit for the victory was due to Marlborough's generalship: his firm control of the battle at its different stages, his personal intervention at the places of crisis, and his proven ability to weld a multi-national army into an integrated weapon of high morale and single-minded purpose, contrasted most markedly with Tallard's muddled leadership and weak authority. In Prince Eugene, the Duke was fortunate to find a kindred spirit, willing to cooperate to the full in accepting Marlborough's overall direction of the struggle. He was equally fortunate in his subordinate generals and in the calibre of the men they led. As Orkney, with true insular understatement, wrote after the battle: 'Without vanity, I think we did our *pairts*';[30] and that has also been the opinion of succeeding generations of soldiers and scholars.

The fruits of victory were impressive: the remnants of the Elector's and Marsin's forces limped away, passing over the Danube at Dillingen and Ulm, and eventually found their way back to Strasbourg, but only after losing a further 7,000 men through desertion by the wayside. The 'German sickness' continued to ravage the horses; from his personal equipage, Mérode-Westerloo lost no fewer than ninety-seven horses during this period through sickness, 'besides the thirteen that were killed or injured on the battlefield'.[31] The Allies followed up their advantage: before the end of the campaign both Ulm and Ingolstadt surrendered, and the whole of Bavaria fell into Allied hands. Advancing to the Rhine, the Allied army laid siege to Landau – the fortress guarding the approaches to Strasbourg – and, on 28 November, the garrison surrendered on terms. Probably more important than these territorial gains, the victory rallied the morale of the Grand Alliance, and many wavering German princelings were won over to support the Allied cause. The only dissident voice was that of Baden – furious at the trick that had deprived him of a share in the glory – but in due course he forgot his grievance amidst the general rejoicing.

All this, however, still lay in the future. As the evening shades of 13 August deepened into night and the sounds of battle and pursuit receded into the distance towards Höchstädt, a weary but triumphant Marlborough at last found time to scrawl his famous Blenheim message to Sarah on the back of a tavern bill:

> I have no time to say more but to beg you will give my duty to the Queen and let her know her army has had a glorious victory. Monsieur Tallard and two other generals are in my coach and I am following the rest. The bearer, my Aide-de-Camp Colonel Parke, will give her an account of what has passed. I shall do it in a day or two by another more at large.[32]

Five years were to pass before the French armies redeemed their reputation; and, for the first time for centuries, England had assumed the military leadership of Europe.

NOTES

1   On 14 July 1704.
2   See W S Churchill, *Marlborough: His Life and Times*, London, 1933, Vol. II, pp. 349–50.
3   See Mérode-Westerloo from D G Chandler, *The Marlborough Wars*, London, 1968, pp. 161–2.
4   On 4 August 1704.
5   At the siege of Ingolstadt, 11–21 August 1704.
6   On 7 August 1704.
7   D G Chandler, *Marlborough as Military Commander*, Staplehurst, 1995, p. 140.
8   The German place name Blindheim was wrongly spelled by English soldiers as 'Blenheim'.
9   See Mérode-Westerloo in Chandler, *The Marlborough Wars*, p. 166.
10 *Ibid.*, p. 167.
11 It is amazing how slow Tallard was to realise what was happening.
12 Several English 'deserters' had been sent into French headquarters. Tallard had been fooled – hence his message.
13 Mérode-Westerloo in Chandler, *The Marlborough Wars*, p. 164.
14 Estimates of numbers vary. W S Churchill's figures have been used.
15 The Marquis de Blainville would die of wounds during this battle.
16 Mérode-Westerloo in Chandler, *The Marlborough Wars*, p. 168.
17 Lt-General John, Baron Cutts of Gowran (1661–1707).
18 Brig.-General Charles Rowe (or Rue or Row) was killed earlier.
19 Lt-General Philippe de Pallnau, Marquis de Clérembault (d. 1704) was reportedly drowned in the Danube.

20 Mérode-Westerloo in Chandler, *The Marlborough Wars*, p. 169.
21 Colonel Francis Palmes. He later became a Major-General and died in 1716.
22 The Prince of Holstein-Beck was mortally wounded near Oberglau village.
23 General Charles Churchill (1656–1714) was 'General of the Foot' and, of course, Marlborough's younger brother.
24 Mérode-Westerloo in Chandler, *The Marlborough Wars*, p. 172.
25 Major-General Lord George Orkney, Earl of Hamilton (1666–1737) was destined to become the first British field-marshal.
26 This was part of the crack Household Cavalry of the French monarch.
27 D G Chandler (ed.), *A Journal of Marlborough's Campaigns* by John Marshall Deane, London, 1984, SAHR Special Publication No. 12, p. 11.
28 See Chandler, *Marlborough as Military Commander*, p. 148.
29 Mérode-Westerloo in Chandler, *The Marlborough Wars*, p. 174.
30 By Orkney – see Chandler, *Marlborough as Military Commander*, p. 149.
31 Mérode-Westerloo in Chandler, *The Marlborough Wars*, p. 181.
32 W S Churchill, *op. cit.*, p. 372.

CHAPTER XIV
Private John Marshall Deane

It was a rare find to discover the writings of a private soldier of the 1st English Foot Guards who had been through and described most of the Marlburian Wars, particularly the Battle of Blenheim. This discovery was made at Kingston-upon-Hull in 1953, and the author's name was only definitely proved in 1984. The details revealed in this chapter tell of events just before and during the great battle itself. However, it was very satisfying to have discovered the name and work of Sentinel John Marshall Deane, whose memoirs were near-completed to the campaigns of 1712.

There are currently some eighteen existing contemporary letters about Marlborough's Wars, and they originate from many different ranks and positions. Most of the authors were officers and several were clergymen, for the ability of ordinary soldiers to write was limited at this period. It is therefore important to examine the writings of an educated private soldier – our friend Sentinel Deane.

Fortunately for posterity, there were a number of soldier eye-witnesses to the Marlburian age whose letters, journals and chronicles, however incomplete, give us the image of the time – warts and all. They include General (later the first Field Marshal in 1736) George Hamilton, Lord Orkney KT (formerly 1st Foot, the Royal Scots), Lt-General Sir James Campbell KB (formerly Royal Scots Greys), Brigadier-Generals Robert Stearne and Richard Kane (both of the later 18th Foot, or the Royal Regiment of Ireland); Colonels Granstoune and St Pierre; the lugubrious Lt-Colonel John Blackadder of the Cameronians; Captains Robert Parker (of the 16th), the change-coat Peter Drake, and Andrew Bonwell of the Train of Artillery; not to overlook Lt Pope of Schomberg's Horse or James Gordon of Craichlaw; or again Dr Hare, the Duke's chaplain, and Chaplain Noyes. Even rarer are voices from the NCOs and the few available include Sergeants John Milner of the 16th, and John Wilson of the 15th . . . 'the old Flanderkin serjeant', and Corporal Matthew Bishop of the 8th. However, rarer still are the thoughts and perceptions of the rank and file, the humble 'hatmen' and 'troopers'. From these thousands we have the anonymous Royal Dragoon of Lord Raby's Regiment in Spain, and last but not least, we have Sentinel John Marshall Deane of the 1st English Foot Guards and his memories of Blenheim, and we respect him despite his bad spelling and old syntax.

'Personal narratives of the War of the Spanish Succession are so rare that any addition to their slender number is welcome . . .' Thus wrote C T Atkinson at the start of his Introduction to the autobiographical writings of an anonymous Royal Dragoon, published by the SAHR in 1938.[1] The rarity is illustrated by the fact that so many years have intervened before the discovery and positive identification of another, and possibly even more important, contemporary journal dating from Marlborough's Wars. It is further enhanced by the near certainty that its author, besides being a participant in many of the events he describes, was also – like Atkinson's Royal Dragoon – a voice from the ranks, albeit in this case a man of some education and reasonable (for the period) literary ability.

Contemporary accounts by Other Ranks are rare for any period before the twentieth century, and even today writings by senior commanders and commissioned officers far outnumber those by NCOs or private soldiers – at least in terms of published works. Inevitably, the farther back in time the military historian delves, the greater the problem of finding valuable contemporary sources, and yet these are vital requisites if any breath of life and immediacy is to be added to scholarly analyses of distant events. The early eighteenth-century wars which saw the emergence of the British Army to a place of central significance on the European and world scenes are certainly no exception to this rule. First-hand sources in English by serving soldiers of any rank that have survived and are known (although who can estimate how many more may still lie concealed or ignored) cannot number more than a dozen and a half.[2]

Private[3] John Marshall Deane, of Her Majesty Queen Anne's First Regiment of Foot Guards, whose Journal of the Campaign in Flanders AD MDCCVIII had been known since 1846, but whose previously available limited writings, restricted to the events of 1708, were regarded as of considerable interest by Winston Churchill, G M Trevelyan, C T Atkinson and other historians working on military aspects of Marlborough's campaigns and battles. Even more important than the intrinsic interest of the discovery is the new light Deane sheds on a number of issues. Although much that he has written has been long known from other sources and therefore has only corroborative value, and infuriatingly omits matters of minor everyday detail of a soldier's life which he takes for granted, there are several points of significant detail concerning military operations that emerge.

The discovery of the manuscript came about as follows. It was donated to the city of Kingston-upon-Hull's Museums and Art Galleries on 2 July 1953 by a Mr R C Holyday of Suffolk Chambers, Scale Lane (and was registered as Accession no. 62/53). How it came into Mr Holyday's possession is not quite certain, but it is thought that it was found in a house being demolished. It has been provisionally called 'the Hunter Manuscript',[4] for the name 'W Hunter' is to be discerned, written somewhat indistinctly, on the thick paper cover of later date enclosing the ninety-seven unnumbered pages of the *Journal*. Each page is unlined, but is ruled with double pen lines in red to mark off the margins until the end of 1708, and thereafter a rougher handwritten squirl is employed on each sheet for the same purpose. There are an unknown number of pages missing from the beginning (including the title page), from the end of 1708, and for the entries between 23 June and 11 July 1709, and from the end of the *Journal*, which concludes with the entry for 1 August 1711. As there is no title page, there is no indication of the name of the author. The pages are roughly sewn together inside the strong paper cover bearing Hunter's name, and sewn on top of the front and back halves, hiding the signature, are two pieces of vellum. These are cut from a report on the Vicar of Holy Trinity, Church, Hull, in 1685, to the effect that he was conforming to the Anglican rites, and from an Oath of Allegiance and Affirmation of the Anglican faith signed by Thomas Somerscales, Mayor of Hull, and other leading city fathers, dated 1725. This latter document provides some clue as to the possible identity of William Hunter.

In March 1976 Mr Arthur Credland, the Keeper of the Town Docks Museum at Hull, decided to initiate some enquiries about the manuscript. The Museum of the Brigade of Guards confirmed that there was no William Hunter on the list of officers belonging to the First Guards, and surmised that Hunter might have been the secretary to a senior regimental officer – or even the Adjutant of one of the Regiments with which the First Guards were often brigaded during parts of the Spanish Succession War. Regrettably, no lists of ordinary soldiers' names for the Marlburian period seem to have survived.[5] The National Army Museum was next approached and Mr David Smurthwaite examined the manuscript and wrote a short evaluation, reaffirming the possibility that the author could have been the secretary to a Guards officer, either a soldier or a civilian held on the ration strength, and mentioned that the only known writing by a private soldier of the Guards was John Marshall Deane.[6] He did not suggest that this might have been the author of the manuscript, however. In later correspondence early in 1977, David Smurthwaite discounted the idea that Hunter might have been a chaplain, and restated the possibility that the author might have been '. . . a secretary or a civilian serving with the commissariat but attached to the Guards'.[7] There the matter rested until 1982, when the transcript was passed to the Hon. Editor of the SAHR *Journal*, Michael Cane, who brought it to my attention. After a visit to inspect the manuscript, I reported on my preliminary findings to the Council, and they decided that an edited version of the 'Hunter Journal' (as it was still called) should be prepared for possible publication by the Society.

Accurate attribution of authorship continued to present a problem for some time. Searches of burial registers in Hull and Beverley in 1976 by Mr W Fost Walker found no mention of any William Hunter in the Holy Trinity records. Probate had been granted to a William Hunter of Beverley in 1685 (too early for our purpose), while another of the same name was buried in Beverley Minster in 1797 aged 76 (and thus could not have been the author of the *Journal*). Once it became clear that Hunter was not in fact the name of the author – but was probably its owner or transcriber, the mists began to clear a trifle. The *Journal* found in Hull would appear to be a fair copy of an original by the owner or a third party, not the original document.

The name William Hunter is comparatively common, but one tantalising possibility presented itself, although it has not been possible to establish positive proof. One of the most celebrated bearers of the name in the eighteenth century was the distinguished surgeon and anatomist who lived from 1718 to 1783. Like many another intelligent, cultivated and wealthy man of the Age of Reason, he was a person of broad interests. Instead of investing his wealth in land, this William Hunter built up a famous collection '. . . of coins, medals, manuscripts, books, paintings, medical specimens, minerals, fossils and natural history objects of his day, owning 30,000 coins alone . . . bequeathing them all . . . to his *alma mater*, Glasgow University.'[8] He was the brother of the famous surgeon, John Hunter (1728–93), whom the erudite Hunterian Society was founded to commemorate, and who certainly was interested in military affairs, being at one time Surgeon-General to the Army. He was also in correspondence with another celebrated collector of his day, Horace Walpole, and letters between the two men on numismatical subjects was included in the sale of the Strawberry Hill library in 1844.[9] It is also well established that the editor of the Deane extract dealing with the events of 1708 – until the present time the only known writings by John Marshall Deane – purchased the sheets from a bookseller, Mr Thorp of Piccadilly, on 9 October 1844, and was assured by him that the papers had come from the sale of the Horace Walpole collections.

It is possible, therefore, that the full Deane *Journal* (i.e. the 'Hunter' *Journal*) was in fact owned by William Hunter, who loaned part of it – or a transcript – to Horace Walpole, who forgot to return the sheets – hence their turning up as a job-lot in the 1844 sale. A comparison of the signature on the Hull manuscript with those on letters from the anatomist reveals that they are not identical – but then the writing on the former may be that of a clerk or librarian indicating the ownership. No such title, however, appears in Young and Henderson Aitkens (the massive *Catalogue of the Manuscripts in the Library of the Hunterian Museum*, published in Glasgow in 1908), although one item – 'Dr. William Hunter, List of Books lent' – reveals that he, like many another before or since, lost many volumes

'. . . by lending them to my Acquaintance', and resolved '. . . from this time to enter all lent Books in this volume.'[10] Might not one of his missing books have been the full Deane *Journal*, as well as the '1708 extract'? We shall never know, but it is intriguing to speculate. It is more likely, it must be admitted, that the owner was either the William Hunter who died in 1797 or the gentleman of the same name who was also buried in Beverley Minister on 24 August 1726, but checks on autograph signatures have proved inconclusive.

The positive establishment of the identity of the true author of the so-called 'Hunter' *Journal* occurred in October 1983. The editing of the section relating to 1708 stirred up memories of parts of the passages having been encountered before – and eventually reference to the works of Churchill, Trevelyan and Atkinson revealed quotations from the *Journal of the Campaign in Flanders AD MDCCVIII* by 'John Marshall Deane, of the First Battalion of the Foot Guards', as privately published in an edited version by the Rev. J Bathurst Deane[11] in Edinburgh in 1846. With the aid of the Inter-Library Loan Service, the then Senior Librarian at Sandhurst, John Hunt, was able to run a copy to ground at Liverpool University,[12] and my diagnosis was proved to be correct. Page after page were practically identical with the equivalent passages in the Hull manuscript, although there were considerable adjustments to punctuation, paragraph indentation and, in a few cases, to the order of certain phrases. However, it was clear that 'Hunter' was for all intents and purposes identical to 'Deane' throughout the 1708 passages. Even better, several pages missing in the Hull manuscript could be inserted by reference to the 1846 publication, which, as an additional bonus, included as an introduction an account of the seaborne expedition to Scotland which does not appear at all in the fuller version of Deane's work.[13]

The problem of identifying John Marshall Deane from amongst the serried redcoated ranks of the First Guards remains considerable. The frequent references to that elite formation – 'our Regiment' – its moves, adventures and mishaps (including the named officer casualties) in-dubitably establishes that Deane was a member – but in precisely what rank or capacity remains open to conjecture. However, there are certain clues, leading to a number of hypotheses. It is certain that he was not a commissioned officer. The lists published by Charles Dalton and by Lt-General Sir F W Hamilton produce only two officers with something approaching the same surname in the Brigade of Guards.[14] One – Ensign John Dene – can be dismissed at once: he was killed at Oudenarde and the fact that our chronicler mis-spells his name as 'Dean' in both versions of the *Journal* for 1708, and makes no reference whatsoever to any kinship, rules out any association. There was also another Ensign in the First Guards – one Alexander Deane. He is never mentioned in the *Journal*, but the Rev. John Bathurst Deane in his Preface suggests a possible relationship: 'It is just possible that the author of this journal whose hand-writing, and style of thought and diction, indicate a man of some education, might have been a relative of . . . [that] . . . officer, serving in the ranks as a volunteer.'[15]

Relatively few officers of the name Deane served anywhere in Marlborough's army between 1704 and 1711. There was a Captain John Deane[16] included in the lists for HRH the Prince of Denmark's Regiment of Foot (otherwise the 3rd of Foot or 'the Buffs') in 1708, who was 'out of the Regiment, 1714'. There was also a Lt-Col. Jno. Deane of the Queen's Regiment of Horse (later the 1st Dragoon Guards), and a Cornet of Horse of the same name appointed to Major-General Crowther's Regiment on 1 June 1712 – but there are no indications of any possible identity or relationship with our soldier of the First Guards.

Various other suggestions about Deane's identity have been made. Could he have been a chaplain? The list of Guards' Chaplains is incomplete for this period, and the author was evidently a man of some education. However, although he does evince interest in certain churches and monasteries he visited, and occasionally mentions French formations holding Mass,[17] there is no mention whatsoever of the holding of services in the English Army; and what chronicler-of the-cloth, however determined to preserve his anonymity, would have omitted mention – if only in passing – of the dramatic service under fire Marlborough ordered to be held amidst the cornfields at the head of every regiment on 2/13 August 1704?[18] Deane certainly makes occasional references to 'the Lord preserving us' and ends most annual sections with a valedictory grace, but these occasional passages do not, in themselves, '. . . seem to indicate a religious interest deeper than that which one would expect of any reasonably educated man of the eighteenth century.'[19]

Another suggestion is that he might have been a civilian attached to the First Guards, possibly in the commissariat. Again, this would explain the number of descriptions of misadventures befalling sutlers and convoys that crop up from time to time,[20] and the interesting reference to inflated local prices for food during the march to the Danube in 1704,[21] but as a future commander of some note was to remark, 'An army marches on its stomach' and every soldier is interested in his rations and pay next to the preservation of his skin. Moreover, the duties of regimental baggage escort would doubtless come round to each Company of Guards in turn, and Private Deane would take his share of such unpopular chores along with his comrades. A further hypothesis is that he might have been the civilian representative of the Regimental Agent – an important administrative official responsible to the Colonel of the Regiment for filling officer vacancies and other duties with financial implications.[22] This theory could explain the identity of the person for whom Deane was writing his *Journal*. 'Now Sr., to resume . . .' – such dedicatory references are frequently to be found. Moreover, Deane gives names of officer casualties at several of the battles he describes – but, perhaps significantly in challenging this line of thought, not *all*. Thus, in his account of Malplaquet, he gives the numbers of officers struck down but no names.[23]

No, it would seem that Deane was indeed, as his first editor elaborated in 1846, a 'gentleman centinel' serving in the ranks of the elite First Guards, and both content and proud to do so. His preface to the *Journal* for 1708 as published is important evidence in that it refers to 'our Company', and the conditions he describes himself suffering on board ship – the lying on the bare deck, 'the fateague of the devell', as he calls it, the purser swindling the troops of their due rations, and the celebratory 'glass or two of brandy' imbibed once he and his comrades had safely returned to Ghent at the end of their nautical adventure, do not suggest even the rank of 'Senior Soldier' let alone NCO.[24] On the other hand his references to the good behaviour of the Army as a whole at Oudenarde give a possible hint of his genteel origins: 'All the officers and *souldiers* . . . fought as became brave *gentlemen*.'[25]

This said, it would also be very unlikely that Private Deane's educational abilities were wholly ignored. From certain indications, it would appear that he had access to the periodic bulletins issued by Marlborough's headquarters – which the Guards habitually protected – and even to copies of certain of the Duke's letters (unless the passages alluded to were added later, after the publication of Lediard's *History of John* . . . which included many documents). It is therefore possible that Deane was employed at Regimental Headquarters as a Clerk or even keeper of a rudimentary form of War Diary. This would explain his knowledge of the details of marches, distances, dates and above all of the precise locations of Marlborough's quarters, for the security of which the Guards were responsible.[26] But he was no 'headquarters' lurker', and from what he writes it is quite clear that he took part in several of the actions he describes.

There are also a number of other problems associated with the *Journal* which require attention. First, the matter of dedication needs further discussion. The identity of 'Sr.' frequently alluded to will probably never be known. Of course if Deane wrote with a view to publication, this term might allude to 'the reader' – and at one point Deane does in fact employ that term.[27] It is clear that he was writing at many points of his narrative shortly after the events he describes, although it is equally evident that at certain places additions were later incorporated in the text – either by Deane himself or by his transcriber. Thus the reference to the Margrave of Baden's alleged involvement in the Battle of Speyerbach, which is included in the section dealing with 1704, is followed by the phrase, 'though Mortus Est'.[28] Above the line in another hand is the word 'mortuus'. This phrase was clearly an addition post-1707, the year of

Baden's death. Elsewhere, on many occasions, there are clear indications that the author was originally writing entries on campaigns soon after they happened, although he rarely speculates about future events except to express such sentiments as '. . . but we will not believe them' or '. . . since we have no news of them.'[29] Of course he may have been writing for his father or some other relative or patron, after the fashion of Captain Robert Parker, whose writings were only intended for his family and were published by his son after his death, and of the unknown Royal Dragoon, who wrote up his experiences in Spain for 'Son William' – adding the information '. . . I have beene abought a whole year in writing of this that you desired me to writ.'[30] Unfortunately, Deane does not give us so clear a steer.

Clearly, 'Sr.' was someone who had a particular interest in the doings of the First Guards, or Deane would not have taken so much trouble with details of his Regiment's officer casualties at the Schellenberg, Blenheim and Oudenarde.[31] He could not have been writing for either of Marlborough's immediate predecessors as Colonel of the First Guards, for Henry Sydney, 1st Earl of Romney (Colonel from 1689–90 and again from 1693–1704), reputedly the handsomest man of his time, died in 1704, whilst Charles, 2nd Duke of Schomberg (Colonel from 1690–3) had died in 1693. Colonel Sir Edward Henry Lee Bart., who was briefly Colonel for just one month (30 November to 31 December 1688) over the critical period of the Glorious Revolution, while the Duke of Grafton was temporally out of favour and over the actual abdication crisis of James II, appears to have lived until only 1705. And it is also possible, of course, that he was writing for some lesser luminary of the First Guards such as Sir Charles O'Hara, 1st Baron Tyrawley,[32] Lt-Colonel of the First Guards from 1689 to 1695, who only died in 1724 and who never served under Marlborough in person but fought in Spain; or another candidate for consideration, General Henry Withers,[33] Lt-Colonel from 1695 to 1722, who was, it seems, on campaign with Marlborough in 1704 and 1709. But then Deane would have been aware of this – and his *Journal* for 1709 gives not a clue to such a proximity of his patron. No, the odds are that our author was writing for a lowlier England-based officer or former member of the First Guards, and that the part of his manuscript dealing with 1708 one way or another came into the possession of the Walpole family or one of its associates or servants at an undisclosed date, and subsequently passed to the Rev. Deane through process of legal purchase in 1844. More than that we are unlikely to know.

Passing on to consider what the Deane *Journal* has to offer by way of contribution to our knowledge of the wars of Marlborough, inevitably much of what he has to tell us is corroborative rather than original. Many another has travelled the same dusty or muddy roads of Flanders and Germany – but Deane proves a remarkably accurate witness to the campaigns; only rarely has one to challenge his dates, descriptions or comments. From time to time, however, we come upon a gem of information that throws new light on old contentions, or contributes a genuinely new fact or point of view. Whilst it is interesting to read the details of the contemporary 'Great Tun of Heidelberg' and compare them with those of its successor (still surviving), this is a point of mainly tourist or general interest – as are his descriptions of castles, great churches and monasteries he passed along his foot-weary way. However, there are some important military contributions that add to our knowledge. One example is his definite identification of certain regiments as fighting in Blenheim village on 2/13 August 1704 – where certain scholars have thrown doubt upon their presence. Another is the detailed specifications he gives of the Lines of Brabant and the full descriptions of the great sieges of Lille, Tournai, Douai and Aire in the later chapters of the *Journal* (although it is a pity that his account of arguably the greatest of them all – Bouchain in 1711 – is unfortunately cut off in its early stages, the last pages of the diary being lost).

Of course, the relatively static conditions of siege warfare favoured the work of our enquiring and intelligent writer. Similarly, he gives us excellent ideas of those parts of the great battles he personally experienced, although naturally enough he has less if anything to say about those sectors farther away amidst the fog of battle except in the most generalised terms, and sometimes is understandably confused by events close at hand. This of course increases his claims to authenticity: had he appeared to be infallibly all-knowing, suspicions would have arisen in our minds that the *Journal* might be 'an old soldier's tale', written years later with the aid of numerous sources, rather than a participant's recollections written down almost before his aching feet had recovered from the latest day's march on campaign or his browned musket barrel had cooled from firing; but no one who reads Deane's account of Blenheim or the other great battles will get anything but a sense of true immediacy. He is clearly writing shortly *post facto* – but here and there he (or possibly the hand of a transcriber) adds a comment that is clearly of later date. He also gives us full details of partisan raids against the baggage trains and convoys (the lesser engagements that were nonetheless of great significance taken together), and paints some horrific pictures of atrocities. Possibly most important of all, he gives us information on *le grand chef*, John Churchill, First Duke of Marlborough. On the one hand, he reinforces our knowledge of 'the Old Corporal's' psychological hold over his rough soldiery, who would do almost anything to obey his ever-courteously conveyed commands: 'Milord Duke desires that the Foot shall step out.' On the other he performs a unique service through his precise knowledge of the whereabouts of Marlborough's quarters each night.

Often in his *Dispatches*[34] we find them dated 'at the Camp before Lisle' or some such generalisation. But Deane, through the 'hard duty' of the Guards in providing their Colonel's personal security force day after day, month-in, year-out, is far more informed than most other contemporary chroniclers on this point, and from his conjectured camp-table in the 1st Guards' Orderly tent he was in a position to check details of locations and headquarters' movements and cast an eye over the issued bulletins of the army, and even, very occasionally, we may guess he also sneaked a look when his superiors were otherwise engaged at some letters and old orders, from the Duke himself.[35]

All in all, our estimable private sentinel has a great deal to tell us and even if he usually does so in the rather deadpan, laconic phraseology that he considered proper to the task (and which probably indicates the limits of his abilities, considerable although these indubitably were for a soldier of his generation, rank and station), and even if he tantalisingly omits the myriad tiny details of everyday military life which he assumes are too trivial to merit the attention of his reader, still we are afforded a rare insight into a description of the great campaigns he shared with his admired Lord Duke and his devoted, multi-national army of mainly social misfits, wastrels and ne'er-do-wells. There is no doubt that John Marshall Deane's *Journal* is a significant contribution to the history of Marlborough's Wars as seen from the ranks. In this fact rests much of the *Journal's* fascination – and it is to be hoped that its value will be appreciated by many another reader.

There is one more aspect of this chronicle that merits attention. By reading between the lines it is often possible to observe Deane's development as man and soldier. In 1704 he marches to the Danube almost as a tourist, staring about him at new sights and sounds, which he hastens to record in his daily writings. Then the great battles – and the perils he shares in them with his comrades – begin to impose a serious attitude: thus his clear horror at hearing the screams of the wounded, burning alive amidst the blazing houses of Blenheim village, or the laments of the incapacitated left out in the open at Oudenarde.[36] Deane is very human, and whether it is the sufferings he shared on shipboard with his mates in early 1708,[37] or the sense of elation and euphoria as he takes part in a special forced march under Marlborough's appreciative eye, we sense his sentiments. But later, as one long campaign merges into another, and yet another, there are traces of war-weariness detectable. He becomes less charitable towards the 'boors', of his own side or the enemy.[38] He expresses bitterness over even minor setbacks, and attributes any enemy successes to treachery rather than professional ability.[39] His end of campaign summations become ever more fervent in their heart-felt prayers to the Lord for the rapid conclusion of a just peace. He thus shows something of the strain of at least eight successive campaigns (we do not know if he took part in the earliest operations of 1702 or 1703, or the last, disgraceful campaign of 1712 when the High Tory politicians – having engineered Marlborough's fall – forced his soldiers to rat on their Allies and leave the war prematurely in return for advantageous peace terms, because of the missing pages). But at no time does John Marshall Deane lose faith in his Captain-General, truly one of the greatest soldiers of his age and one of the most notable four (with Cromwell, Wellington and Slim) to have been produced by these islands since the invention of gunpowder.

'Oh, the brave music of a distant drum!' wrote Edward Fitzgerald in the *Rubáiyát of Omar Khayyam*.[40] Doubtless that has always been the reaction of civilians whom fate has placed in the possible proximity of warring armies – but how frustrating for the historians it would be were not the marching columns, creaking cannon and jingling and clattering cavalry occasionally brought within our comprehension through the writings of such contemporary warrior-chroniclers as Kane and Parker, Millner and Webb – and of course John Marshall Deane, who now at last takes his full place amongst their number.

Since at least 1846 some idea of his value has been recognised – if only in very limited form, but Deane only began to come into his own, albeit on a small canvas, in the first half of the twentieth century. Winston Spencer Churchill, in his great biography of his ancestor, uses our 'laconic' chronicler to illuminate the events of the campaign of 1708, which Deane describes in just summary as '... very long, tiresome, troublesome, mischievous and strange yet very successful,'[41] and warms towards the shadowy sentinel of the First guards, referring to him as 'our Private Deane'.[42] G M Trevelyan, in his famous trilogy on *England under Queen Anne*, also makes use of his – then but few – available pages.[43] And so, of course, ten years before them, had Christopher Thomas Atkinson. In the Bibliographical Note to his notable study of *Marlborough and the Rise of the British Army*, he writes: 'Private John Deane of the Grenadier Guards has left a short account of the campaign of 1708 which is interesting and curious and contributes a certain amount to our knowledge of the brief period which he covers.[44] Now thanks to a fortunate conjunction of circumstances, future students of the days of John, Duke of Marlborough, will be able to approach his greatest campaigns with the full aid of the almost complete recorded recollections of John Marshall Deane, self-appointed Chronicler of the British Army and its celebrated Captain-General. Posterity, too, should raise '... a glass or 2 of brandy ...' in salute to Deane's memory, inspiration and achievement.

July the 24th we marched and incamped at Stetzling; the 25th marcht & incampt at Ainling; the 26th and 27th halted. Still burning all round by the Emperers Order, and burnt in all neare 700 touns and villages.[45]

The 28th marcht and incampt at Scrobenhausen. The 29th marcht &

incampt at Salach, all this while in Byerland.[46] July the 30th we marcht leeving Reyne on our righthand and crossing the river Danube incampt at Hammelbay in Swaberland, all the small touns & villages behind us being burnt; and itt being agreed that Prince Lewis off Baden should invest and besiedge Ingoldstädt,[47] he was left behaind in Byerland with a good army enough, and on the 31st of July we marcht all along the Danube side and halted a while at Scholembergh hill and at last incampt at Steney. August the first, we beingg joyned this day with Prince Eujeane,[48] both our armies drew out to give the enemy battle but in 2 hours time we returned home to our camp againe. August the 2nd the Generall beete at 2 a clock in the morning; and there halted till a little light; and then marched and approached the enemy about 6 and as soon as ever the enemy gett sight of us they fired there great guns uppon us but we played none at them till toward 9 a clock in the morning.[49]

Monsr. La Count d'Tallard,[50] head Generall Ffelt Marshall, his head quarters was att Hoguestadt[51] and the Duke of Bavaria, Gen[erall], likewise, both of the enemyes army.

Prince Eujeane Comanded the right wing that day and made a bold attacque upon the enemy and the enemy did as bravely stand itt and so stoutly behave themselves that Prince Eujeane was forced to give way, but my Lord Duke of Marlborough hearing and seeing that tooke some certain squadrons of Horse and assisted Prince Eujeane and regained the ground that was lost, but abundance was killed on both sides on that wing.[52]

About 3 a clock in the afternoon our English on the left was ordered by My Lord Duke to attacque a village on the left full of French called Blenheim[53] wch. village they had fortifyed and made soe vastly strong and barackaded so fast wth. trees, planks, coffers, chests, waggons, carts and palisades that it was almost an impossibility to think wch way to gett into it; but how ever there was orders for [our] battalion of Guards; my Lord Orkneys 2 battalions Regiment – [scored out] & Brigadier Merrediths regiment and Lt. Genll. Churchills regiment and 1 regiment of Hanovers to attacque the village [of Blenheim] in which there was 26 battallions of the enemy, and each battalion as many men in it as a regiment of ours.[54] Yett we according to comand fought our way into the village wch. was all of a fire, and our men fought in and through the fire and persued others through it, untill many on both sides were burnt to death.[55]

Att length the enemy making all the force they could upon us forced us to retreate and to quitt the village having lost a great many of our men, but we rallyed againe, having received some fresh amunition, resolving to give the enemy another salute. So that asson as they perceived our designe they beate a parley and fired all there pieces up in the aire and Lt. Genll Churchill went to heare there conditions; which was to surrender themselves prisoners of warr, to his Grace the Duke of Marlborough. The village was sett on fire before we came to it by the enemy whereby they thought to have blinded our gunners, but great and greivous were the cryes of the maimed, and those suffering in the flames after we entered this village and none is able to express it but those that heard it.[56]

The battle went on from right to left very brave, the horse charging most furiously on both sides and I must say our confederate forces behaved themselves to a miracle being led on by brave and prudent generalls and comanding officers, having made lanes through them, cutting and hewing them to a degree, that it seemed rather a battle fought by the Divine hand then to be fought by men; driving severall squadrons of them in to the river Danube where they all perrished men and horse, and likewise abundance of them taken prisoners.

There Genll. and many other principall officers were taken in this battle and I will endeavour to give the best account I cann at the end of this particular journall. The number of prisoners taken are generally computed to be thirteen thousand thirty nine. As for those killed upon the spot I believe few or none can pretend to give that account being a thing seeming almost impossible; butt this I can and will affirm that the earth was covered in a manner for three English miles together wth. dead bodys of both armies soe that from any more such sights good God deliver me.[57] The French and Bavarians ware that day 6 [in fact four] thousand men stronger then we by reason Prince Lewis of Baden was left at Ingoldstadt to besiege it.[58]

The battle being over; and the feild our own, we lay upon our armes that night[59] and the next day being the 3rd of August the whole army marcht to a place called Berking,[60] and there halted till the 8th, and that day marcht to Gundleslingen; the 9th to Elchingen; the 10th to Sefflingen. Crossing the river Ash the city of Ulm being in our front, a strong and populous citty of Germany in the circle of Swabia and basely surprised by the Elector of Bavaria in the year 1702, and put in the hands of the French in 1703.[61] It stands on the river Danube. All att this place our army got a great deale of linnin cloth that was bleeching in the fields out of towne.

The 15th of August we left Ulm[62] and incampt at Lunzey. The 16th at Seesah, marching this day through Eisling, the strongest pass in all Wittenburgh land. On the 17th we marcht to Hierspack. The 20th crost the river Murtz & incampt at the Stadt Mundelsheime. The 22th marcht over the river Neckar & incampt at Grossing Carty, the 23th at Eppingen, the 24th at Oneheime, the 25th at Long Gabrick, the 26th at Kurlach. The 27th we crossed the river Rhine att Philipsburgh, and campt at Spires and there halted the 28th. The 29th we crossed the river Oveak. This river was in a great wood and a partizan of the enemy fell upon some of our suttlers and plundered them and soe made of[f], and our battalion of Guards marched by themselves that day and the aforesaid suttlers comeing thundering back and desiring our batallion to advance, swearing that all the French army was coming upon us, struck us into such a consternation yt. we ware in a wood alsoe knowing that we ware all alone and a great distance from the army. In short itt putt us into great confusion; and at last it proved nothing but a strong partyzan party and some partyes of French Huzzahs[63]who apeared. Our Grey Draggoons[64] followed them, came up wth. them and cutt them down, and we marcht by them and see them afterwards.

This day as we marcht we left Landau 2 leagues on our right, going over a very strong pass. Our army made this day a verry fine appearance, marching over such ground that the whole army could vew each other. We having there yt. day 120 battalions of Foott and 230 squadrons of Horse and Dragoons.[65] We incampt that night at Swakingham and on the 30th we incampt at Long Candle.

September the 1st we marcht to Crown Wyzenburgh, an old small citty of Germany in Lower Alsatia, once Imperiall but hath been subject to the French ever since 1648.[66] It stands on the river Lutter. Here our army lay incampt as a cover to the King of the Romans[67] and Prince Lewiss of Baden who then layd siege to Landau; a little but strong citty of Germany once Imperiall but subject to the French ever since the treaty of Munster till taken from them in 1702 by the Germans;[68] but the French retook it againe in 1703. Itt stands on the river Quetch. We lay here between our seiging army and the French army, and the strong citty of Strassburgh. Note that by this toun it was that the French fell upon the valliant Prince of Hesse, the last yeare after he parted wth. the Duke of Marlborough at the seige of Limburgh,[69] in his returning home to his winter quarters; and did really slaughter the Princes army bloodily and although Prince Lewiss of Baden lay hard by wth. his army; yett would nott come up to his assistance;[70] which blott will ever remaine in his scutcheon – though *mortuus est.*[71]

The seige of Landlaw now goes on wth vigour; the King of the Romans having built himselfe a little seate to inspect into the works, and could see from his little cabbin how all the works ware carryed on; and the Imperialists did sinck as fine trenches as hath been seen and cutt there approachments as neare as could be expected considering the vast works and strength of the toun as motes and mounts & such like.[72]

While the Imperialists lay before this city, the King of the Romans came to vizitt His Grace the Duke of Marlborough at Wizenbourgh and dyned there, and after consulted wth the Duke concerning the citty of Trier or Treives wch. the French had had in possession ever since 1681. It stands on the river Mozell, and is one of the antientest citties in Europe. And [they] also [consulted about] the castle of Troarback. And it was agreed upon that the Duke should goe and invest Triers; the wch. was accomplished, His Grace, ordering a detachment of English and Dutch [wch.] went leaving the rest of the army at Wizenburgh. But as soon as His Grace appeared with his detachments neare Treir the French quitted it wth. greate precipitation, running as for there lives; and ruining the bores[73] destroying all there corne & forage; butt the castle of Troarbach stood out and was not taken while the Christmans following.[74]

This being done, my Lord Duke returned unto the camp at Wizenburgh, and while we lay here the Citty of Ulm surrendered[75] and likewise brought to the Duke that the cittyes of Ingoldstadt, Munick, and Augsburgh in Byerland and all the touns [scored out] that stood out in that countrey had submitted unto the Emperor.[76]

The citty of Landau holds out still; firing verry thick upon the beseigers day and night; and the Germans went on as vigorously, killing abundance of the besieged, particularly the governour and blinded the deputy governour. Now, Sr., the French had made this toun vast strong since they took itt last yeare, having cast up a high mount of earth wch. mount covered the walls and works and between the walls and the mount they had lately sunk a moat, which moate the besiegers were obleidged to cross wth. ffloates before they come to scale the walls.[77]

We lay at Crown Wizenburgh the 1st of September untill the 2nd of November, and yt. day my Lord Duke ordered all the English that was in the feild to march, the horse by land, to there respective winter garrisons commanded by Lt. Genll. Lumley[78] and Majr. Genll. Wood,[79] and the Foott ware to march down to the Rhine side and there to imbarque in barges and billinders[80] and to fall the Rhine wth. the streeme towards Holland.[81] We being but 4 regiments of Foott besides the battallion of Guards, viz. Coll. Webbs, Coll. Howes, my Ld. Darbyes, and Coll Ffurgasons regiments. The rest of the English being gone the same way about a month before.[82] But the aforesaid regiments being commanded by Lt. Genll. Ingoldsby[83] and Majr. Genll. Withers marcht this day being the 2d of November and cantooned at Long Candle. The 3d marched & cantooned at Garmstone neare the Rhine side. The 4th marched above an English mile and there imbarked, and fell down wth. the stream & had rowing about 10 leagues and then landed and cantooned at Kerch. This day we past by Philipsburgh, a small but extraordinary strong and noble town to the Emperour by the Peace of Reswick 1697. This day we likewise left Spires, a great & famous citty of Germany, taken and burnt down by the French in 1689.[84]

November the 5th we went on board againe and that day left the old citty of Manheime a rich citty [scored out] & strong ffort of Germany burnt by the French twice [in the] last warrs; and about 2 in the afternoone we came to the great, famous and wellbeloved citty of Worms. So much respected by the Emperour yt he wept when he first heard of the destruction of it, being burnt by the French in 1689 likewise – and there cantooned.

November the 6th we went on board againe and fell down to Mentz, or Mayence, an antient large and considerable strong citty of Garmany, lying upon the Rhine, formerly imperial but since subject to its own Prince & Elector, taken from the French in 1689. This day we likewise passed by severall other touns on both sides of the river that had been burnt and destroyed by the French the same yeare that they destroyed Manheime and Hydleburgh; for wch. deed doing the Dauphin[85] gained great displeasure, insomuch that as tis said the French King would never permitt him to bare command in the army since. Wee lay at the little village about a mile from the citty and there cantooned, until other vessells ware provided for to carry us further.

November the 9th in the morning we marcht through the citty of Mayence and through the Electors court & then imbarqued againe in vessels larger than the former, coverd overhead wth. deale boards in order [to make] the best of our way towards Coblentz; but the wind being verry high and tirbulent and withall somewhat contrary, we ware drove aground so yt. that the Lt. Genll. ordered us ashore at a little village called Mumback, about a league from Mayence, and he likewise orderd the masters of the vessels when they ware lightned for to fall down beyond the reach, wch. we found was something difficult, and to waite there till we came to them the next day.

Accordingly the next day being the 10th we marcht about a league and then imbarqued and putt off, butt the weather being bad we could make butt little way. Notwithstanding we ware towed on the shore with horses. We left this day the towne of Pinyer and cantooned at a village called Estricht. On the 11th we fell doun againe and left abundance of fine touns & villages on both sides of the Rhine espetially a place called Sanctuary in the Prince of Hess Darmstadts countrey. This day we sayled above 12 leagues and cantooned that night at Popert in Trierland. The 12th we steered by Coblentz − a strong walled toun, and likewise by Andernach in the Elector of Collogns country and cantooned at Lewidsdorph. The 13th we left Bonne, an antient and verry strong citty of Germany, formerly imperial but now subject to the Elector of Cologne and his usuall seate, taken from the French in 1689; but in the warr wch. commenced in 1702 itt stood by itts Prince[86] for the French interest, but was reduced by the Confederate army under the Duke of Marlborough in 1703.[87] We cantooned this night att a village called Sanma. The 14th we left the famous garrison and citty of Duseldorpe to Kuyzerswaert and cantooned that night at Earden in the Elector of Cologns country. The 15th we left Rhineburgh and the strong citty of Weezell belonging to the King of Prussia in the Circle of Westphalia and Dutchy of Cleeves, and [saw] a curious ferry neare the towne of Zedom, and cantonned that night at Creete belonging to Brandenburghsland. The 16th we left Emmerick and Ginkinsconce and the citty of Cleeves. Just here the river Rhine looses its name and is called the Waell. That night we put into Nimeguen, a large strong and fine citty of the Low Countreys in the Dukedome of Gelderland subject to the States of Holland. Itt stands on the river Waell between the Rhine and the Meuse rivers.

Here we lay untill the 19th and then being putt into Hollands vessells sett sayle and left Bommell and Teelle. The 20th we left Girkham and Workam and the citty of Dort, and on the 22th we came to Swallow & there landed & cantooned.

The 23th of November we marcht by land to the Stadt of Breda, our apoynted garrison, and the other regiments to there respective garrisons.

Since we came to our winter quarters we heare of the capitulation & surrendring of the late besieged city of Landaw, and that the souldiers therein surrendered themselves up [as] prisoners of Warr, and that the burgers ware many of them put to the sword.

I shall now next according to my promiss endeavor to give you an account the best I can of the officers of note that ware taken prisoners and the other officers; and likewise the intire battallions, cannons, standards and Kettledrumms & cullers that ware taken at Blenheim.[88]

Imprimis[89]

The Marshall de Tallard, Ffelt Marshall — (Marshal Tallard)

Mo[nst. de] Hautferrulle, Maitre d'Camp, Genll. d'Draggoons — (M. de Hautefeuille)

Marquiss d'Mervevaux, Lieutenant Generall — (Marquis de Marivaux)

Marshall d'Blansack, Marshall d'Camp, d'Infantry — (Marquis de Blansac)

Mounsr. d'Vausenne, Marshall d'Camp — (M. de Valseme)

Marquiss d'Vallierre, Brigadeire d'Cavalry — (Marquis de la Vallière)

Marquiss d'Scilly, Brigadeire d'Cavalry[90] — (Marquis de Silly)

Monsr. Jolly, Brigadeire d'Draggoones — (M. Jourry or (?) Joigny)

Monsr d'Massalverr, Brigadeire d' la Armory[91] — (M. de Massilière of the *Gendarmerie*)

Marquiss d'Nonvill, Brigadeire d'Infantry[92] — (Marquis d'Enonville)

Monsr. d'Moaney, Brigadeire d'Infantry — (M. d'Amigay)

Le Chevalier de Crossey, Brigadeire d'Infantry — (Chevalier de Croissi)

Monsr. d'St. Second, Brigadeire d'Infantry — (M. de Saint-Second)

Monsr. de Signey, Brigadeire d'Infantry — (M. de Saint-Signey)

Monsr. de Mountford, Brigadeire d'Infantry — (M. de Montfort)

Marquiss d'Septville, Brigadeire d'Gens d'Arms — (Marquis de Seppeville)

Monsr. d'Corman, Lt. des Gens des Arms and Colonell — (M. deCaraman)

Monsr. Oliver, Gussigne de Gens des Arms — (M. d'Ovillars, Engsin)

Monsr. Imssac, Guidon Gens des Arms — (M. Juissac, Standard-bearer)

Marquiss de Sassenage, Aid d'Camp A Gendre d'Marsll Tallard — (Marquis de Sassenage, ADC and son-in-law of Tallard)

Marquiss d'Monan, Coll'll de Dragoons[93] — (Marquis de Nonan)

Marquiss de Loneage, Coll. d'Cavalry	(Marquis de) Saint-Pouange)
La Chevaleire d'Legrady, Coll. d'Cavalry	(Chevalier de Ligondais)
Prince Marley d'Lorraine, Capt. de Cavalry Lorraine)	(Prince Maubec de
Marquiss d'Vassy, Coll. d'Draggoons	(Marquis de Vassé)
Count d'Tobanes, Coll. d'Infantry	(Comte de Tavannes)
Count de Settary, Coll. d'Infantry	(Comte de (?) Schack)
Monsr. Sanbouff, Coll. d'Infantry	(M. Sauboeuf)
Count de Leon, Coll. d'Infantry	(Comte de Lionne or (?) Leone)
La Barron d'Elston, Coll. d'Infantry	(Baron d'Elsen)
Marquiss d'Lasserie, Coll. d'Infantry	(Marquis de Lasse or (?) Lassy)
Marquiss d'Monoanveel, Coll. d'Infantry[94]	(see tenth entry on the list)
Marshall d'Marrivaux, Leiutt. Generall[95]	(see third entry on the list)

(those 35 all made prisoners)[96]

Monsr. Clarenbeave, drowned in the Danube	(Marquis de Clérembault)
Monsr. Blanvill, Lt. Genll, dyed of his wounds	(Marquis de Blainville)

An account of the French troops made prisoners at discretion at Blenheime, August the 2nd 1704:

Ffour Regiments of Dragoons, each regiment consisting of 3 squadrons, as namely:

	Squadrons	
Maitre de Camp	3	(Mâitre de Camp)
La Reyne	3	(La Reine)
Vasseys	3	(Vassé)
Renan	3	(Rohan)
	(in all 12 squa.)	

Officers made prisoners:-
Captains	262
Lieutenants	282
Sub Lieutenants	174
Dragoon Officers	166
	(in all 884)[97]

Officers wounded:-
At Dillingen and Lavingen	60
at Blenheime	30
Artillery Officers	10
	(wounded in all 100)[98]

Infantry taken:-

Rejements[99]	Battallions	
Navarrs	3	(*Navarre* – French)
Sennaterrs	2	(*Santerre* – French)
Groder Almaigne	2	(*Greder Allemagne* – German)
Onyes	2	(*Aunis* – French)
Artois	2	(*Artois* – French)
Proomroys	1	(*Provence* – French)
Longuidoes	2	(*Languedoc* – French)
Plasoise	1	(*Blaisois* – French)
Arjentoise	1	(*Argentois* or *Agenois* – French)
Sarlube	2	(*Zurlauben* – Walloon)
St. Second	1	(*Saint-Second* – Italian)
Lassey	1	(*Lassay* – French)
Boonlanoys	1	(*Boulonnais* – French)
Murreaux	1	(*Montrou* – Italian)
Muntford	3[100]	(*Montfort* – Spanish/Walloon)
Royall	2[101]	(*Royale* – French)
De la Artillery	1	(*Royal-Artillerie* – French)
	(taken in all 28 Regimt)[102]	

Kettledrums taken:-	16[103]

Cannons taken by the English	34[104]
Cannons taken by the Germans	18
(Cannons taken in all 52)[105]	

Standards and Coulors taken:-

From the Gens de Arms by		
Scytenburghs Dragoons	2	(?Schulenburgs)
From ditto by one of		
Vittinghoffs regiment	1	(Vietinghof)
By Mr. Payne of Majr. Petroes		
troope of Carbineers	1	
By Mr. Bellows of the troops		
of Lunenburgh	4	
By the troops of Holland & Hesse	13	
By the English Foote	3	
By the troops of Hess brought		
by Mr. Levingstone [106]	7	
(Standards & Coulers taken in all 31)		

Coulers surrendered:-	Dr. of Coulers
To the English	44

To the troops of Holland & Hesse	16
To the troops of Lunenburgh	30
To the troops of Hess, brought	
By Mr. Levinstone	8
Brought by a souldier of the	
troops of Hesses guards	2
	(Coulers surrendered in all 100)[107]

Here Endeth the Journal of the Yeare
1704.[108]

NOTES

1   *A Royal Dragoon in the Spanish Succession War – a Contemporary Narrative*, by C
    T Atkinson, SAHR Special Publication No. 5, 1938, p. 1.
2   See D G Chandler (ed. & tr.), *The Marlborough Wars* (London, 1968), p. 265.
3   The term 'Private' was only replaced by the designation 'Guardsman' in the
    1920s.
4   Two short passages relating to 1704 and ascribed to a 'Captain Hunter'
    appear in Peter Verney's *Battle of Blenheim* (London, 1976), but, although
    close, are not identical.
5   Letter from Major P H Cordle (PHC/ML/1001), dated 21 April 1976.
6   Letter from Boris Mollo, dated 4 November 1976, enclosing David
    Smurthwaite's note.
7   Letter from David Smurthwaite, ref. 6511, dated 13 January 1977.
8   Roy Porter, 'William Hunter, Surgeon' in *History Today*, September 1983, p.
    52.
9   See A T Hazen, *Catalogue of Horace Walpole's Library*, 3 Vols, London, 1960.
10 J Young and P Henderson Aitkens, *Catalogue of the Manuscripts in the Library
    of the Hunterian Museum*, Glasgow, 1908, Item 315, p. 251.
11 The Editor, the Rev. John Bathurst Deane (1798–1887) was a long-standing
    Fellow of the Society of Antiquaries of London.
12 Rev. Deane tells us that he had only seventy-five copies printed for private
    circulation among his friends.
13 This additional passage is clearly in the same style as the main description of
    later events in 1708, and is of importance in identifying beyond doubt Deane
    as a private soldier.
14 C Dalton, *English Army Lists and Commission Registers*, London, 1904, Vol. VI,
    p. 326. Lt-General Sir F W Hamilton, *Origin & History of the First or Grenadier
    Guards*, London, 1874, Vol. III, Appendix H, p. 441.
15 *Journal of the Campaign in Flanders, AD MDCCVIII*, Preface, p. ii.
16 Dalton, *op. cit.*, Vol. VI, p. 68.
17 As before Malplaquet.
18 Dr Hare's *Journal* does not mention this, but see W S Churchill, *Marlborough,
    His Life and Times*, 1947, Vol. II, p. 361. The authenticity of Hare's *Journal* has
    come in for some close examination. See 'The Authorship of the Manuscript
    Blenheim Journal' by Frances Harris, *Bulletin of the Institute of Historical
    Research*, Vol. LV, No. 132, November 1982. I am indebted to P M Barber of

the Department of Manuscripts, The British Library for bringing this article to my attention. It suggests that a Rev. Josiah Sandby, Secretary to General Charles Churchill (Marlborough's brother) and Chaplain to the Train of Artillery, may be the true author of the Hare *Journal*.

19 Letter from D K Smurthwaite to Arthur Credland, ref 6511, dated 13 January 1977.
20 See D G Chandler (ed.), *A Journal of Marlborough's Campaigns . . . by John Marshall Deane, Private Sentinel*, SAHR Special No. 12 (1984), pp. 1 & 89.
21 *Ibid.*, p. 95.
22 See Alan J Guy, *Regimental Agency in the British Standing Army, 1715–1763* (Manchester University Library, MCMLXXX), and R E Scouller, *The Armies of Queen Anne*, Oxford, 1964.
23 *Ibid.*, and see SAHR Special No. 12, pp. 90–6.
24 *Ibid.*, p. 55.
25 On Oudenarde, see SAHR Special No. 12, pp. 59–63.
26 Hence the general relief when a second battalion of Guards joined in 1708.
27 SAHR Special No. 12, p. xiv.
28 *Ibid.*, p. xiv (bis).
29 *Ibid.*, p. xiv (ter).
30 SAHR Special Publication No. 5, p. 57.
31 Marshall Deane, *op. cit.*, pp. 67–8.
32 See D Francis, *The First Peninsular War*, London, 1975, p. 45.
33 Henry Withers (d. 1729) was first commissioned in 1678, and was Lt Col. in the 1st Guards in 1695 and Brig. Gen. in 1702. A Maj. Gen. in 1704, he was in joint command at the storming of the Schellenberg. Marlborough certainly thought highly of him, and in 1708 he was a Lt Gen. commanding all forces in the Tyne area during the French invasion scare. The following year he was slightly wounded at the siege of Tournai, and at Malplaquet he commanded the 'special force' on the extreme right of the Allied army. In later years he became Governor of Sheerness and lived at Greenwich, where he enjoyed a reputation for hospitality and wit.
34 Sir George Murray (ed.), *Letters and Dispatches of the Duke of Marlborough* (5 vols); and see Chandler, *The Marlborough Wars*, p. 353.
35 See, for example, the full Marshall Deane, SAHR No. 12, p. 25.
36 Deane, *op. cit.*, pp. 66–7.
37 The extra letter, introduction to 1708.
38 Deane, *op. cit.*, SAHR No. 12, p. 80.
39 *Ibid.*, pp. xvii and 125–30.
40 E Fitzgerald, 'The Rubaiyat of Omar Khayyam' (London, 1955), twelfth stanza.
41 Deane, *op. cit.*, p. 79.
42 W S Churchill, *Marlborough: His Life and Times*, Vol. III, p. 308.
43 G M Trevelyan, *England Under Queen Anne*.
44 C T Atkinson, *Marlborough and the Rise of the British Army*, (1921), p. x.
45 Deane exaggerates the number.
46 As Tallard approached Augsburg (reached on 24 July/4 August), Marlborough began to withdraw towards the Danube to link up with Eugene's 18,000 men on the north bank.
47 Baden's force comprised 15,000 men – at Ingolstadt.
48 François-Eugene, Prince of Savoy (1663–1736) was the most distinguished Habsburg commander of his day.
49 Tallard and the Elector had marched from Augsburg, crossed to the north bank of the Danube at Lavingen (30 July/10 August), and then marched

leisurely eastwards, planning to retake Donauwörth, and thus isolate Marlborough south of the river.

50 Marshal Camille d'Hostun, Comte de Tallard (or Tallart) (1652–1728) was a French soldier and diplomat of some distinction. He became a member of the Council of Regency (from 1717) and a Minister of State (from 1726).

51 In fact in Blenheim village.

52 Deane is confused here. Eugene was repulsed twice on the Allied right from Lutzingen by Marsin's and the Elector's troops on the French left, but in fact it was his selfless sending of his last cavalry reserve under Brigadier Fugger to support Marlborough's right-centre when it was caught deploying over the Nebel marshes by Marsin's cavalry that overcame the worst Allied crisis of the day.

53 The village of Blindheim was immediately renamed 'Blenheim' by the English troops. Some accounts, including many French, name the action as the second Battle of Höchstädt.

54 The 1st Guards formed part of Fergusson's Brigade on the left wing during the battle. Deane's account of the fighting around Blenheim village is confused. His positive identification of the presence of Meredith's and Churchill's Regiments is of some importance, as some historians have questioned it. On the other hand, his ideas of timings and sequence are rather odd.

55 Blenheim was certainly on fire. '. . . our poor fellows were grilled amidst the continually collapsing roofs and beams . . .' the Count of Mérode-Westerloo recalled.

56 In this section, Deane has merged the earlier action (mistimed as '3 à clock') with the second major onslaught which began about 6 pm. By this time, the battle had been won in the centre by Marlborough.

57 Deane was clearly an eyewitness of, and probably a participant in, the battle.

58 Ingolstadt's siege was now superfluous and was called off. Baden was furious at having missed the battle.

59 A necessary precaution with all of 14,000 prisoners in the army's midst.

60 All other accounts say Steinheim, near Lavingen and Dillingen.

61 In the sixteenth century, the Holy Roman Empire was divided into 'circles' for administrative purposes. The circle of Swabia comprised Wurtemberg, Baden, the bishopric of Augsburg, and a number of Imperial cities, or 'royall stadts'.

62 The Elector had seized the city and fortress of Ulm by a ruse on 29 August/9 September 1702.

63 The first French hussar regiment had been raised in 1692, but their lax discipline and freebooting ways caused Colonel de la Colonie to describe them as '. . . properly speaking, little more than bandits on horseback'.

64 Hay's Regiment of Dragoons – or the Scots Greys.

65 Another exaggeration – the total Allied strength was ninety-two battalions and 181 squadrons. They faced a French army of eighty-five battalions and 112 squadrons, commanded by Marshal Villeroi.

66 Since the end of the Thirty Years War.

67 This was the title of the heir to the Holy Roman Empire, the future Emperor Joseph I (1678–1711), who succeeded Leopold in 1707.

68 Baden had recaptured Landau from the French on 29 August/8 September 1702.

69 The siege of Limburg lasted from 10 to 27 September 1703 (new style).

70 The Battle of Spirbach (sometimes Spire or Speyerbach) was fought on 4/15 November 1703.

71 'Never speak ill of the dead.' This is a curious insertion, reinforcing the belief that the *Journal* for 1704–8 (as it now stands) is a transcript with additions (see Introduction). Baden died in 1707.

72 Landau was invested on 30 August/9 September 1704, and the siege was conducted by Baden with an army of 30,000. The Governor, M. de Laubanie, and his garrison of 7,000 men held out until 13/28 November.

73 That is boors or peasantry.

74 Treves was surprised and taken on 15/26 October; Trarbach, besieged by the Prince of Hesse-Cassel at the head of 20,000 men, held out from 24 October/4 November to 9/20 December, and cost the besiegers 1,000 casualties.

75 Ulm was besieged by General Thungen and 15,000 men. His siege-guns opened fire on 29 August/8 September and two days later negotiations were opened. On 11 September (new style) the garrison was allowed to march out with the full honours of war. The Allies captured 250 cannon and 1,200 barrels of gunpowder.

76 The French abandoned Augsburg as early as 6/17 August. Ingolstadt surrendered on 10/21 August. On 30 October/10 November a Treaty of Accommodation was signed between the Emperor and the Electress of Bavaria, whereby all remaining towns were surrendered to Leopold I.

77 An interesting example of the conversion of a medieval walled town into a bastion-trace fortress.

78 Henry Lumley (1660–1722), brother of the first Earl of Scarborough, entered the army in 1685. He fought at Namur (1695) and the following year became a Major-General. An MP for Sussex (1701 and 1702–5), he became Governor of Jersey in 1703. He fought in all four of Marlborough's great battles, and was promoted full General in 1711. He left the army in 1717, but from 1715 until his death, he served as MP for Arundel.

79 Cornelius Wood (d. 1712) entered Charles II's army soon after the Restoration, and was a lieutenant in the Life Guards by 1685. He became a Colonel of Horse in 1693, Brigadier-General in 1703, and Major-General in 1704, being wounded at the Schellenberg. In 1707 he was promoted Lt-General.

80 River-boats.

81 During the earlier stages of the march to the Danube, Marlborough had assured the Dutch States-General that he would return with the army by barge down the Rhine in the event of Marshal Villeroi launching a major attack in the Netherlands.

82 In fact Marlborough detached his five weakest battalions to escort the bulk of the French prisoners to Holland – a battalion of the Royal Scots, Churchill's, North and Grey's, Rowe's, and Meredith's, on 1/12 September.

83 Richard Ingoldsby (d. 1712) saw service in Ireland in 1689 and later at Namur (1695). He became Colonel of the 23rd Regiment in 1693, and succeeded to the 18th (Royal Regiment of Foot in Ireland) in succession to Major-General Frederick Hamilton in 1705. He had been promoted Major-General in 1702, and Lt-General in 1704, and saw much service in Germany and Flanders. From 1703 he was MP for Limerick in the Irish Parliament, and from 1707 to 1712 he was Commander-in-Chief of the forces in Ireland and a Lord Justice.

84 These depredations are known as the First French Devastation of the Palatinate.

85 The Grand Dauphin Louis (1661–1711), who predeceased his father, Louis XIV, died of smallpox.

86 Charles Wittelbach, Archbishop and Elector of Cologne (*fl.* 1700) defected

from Habsburg control and switched back to Louis XIV, and thus in support of his brother, Maximilian Emmanuel, Elector of Bavaria (1676–1736).

87 The siege of Bonn lasted from 16/27 April to 4/15 May 1703.

88 Correct names, when known, are placed in brackets after each entry.

89 'Of the First Rank'.

90 De Silly was Tallard's QMG (effectively Chief of Staff), and was sent on parole to Versailles after the battle to report to Louis XIV.

91 The Gendarmerie, one of the crack cavalry regiments of the monarchy.

92 D'Enonville was employed by Marlborough, as a captive, to negotiate the surrender of Blenheim village.

93 In fact de Nonan was commander of the infantry Régiment de Provence.

94 D'Enonville of the Régiment Royal was subsequently made a French scapegoat for the disaster at Blenheim.

95 Deane repeats himself here a second time.

96 Other lists of high-ranking prisoners often include M. de Barrincourt, Colonel of Infantry; the Marquis d'Aurival, Colonel of Dragoons, and the Sieurs de Breuil and La Morcelaire, Commissaries of Artillery. (See Lediard, *op. cit.*, Vol. I, p. 416.)

97 Other sources suggest 987 – 502 falling to Marlborough's share and 485 to Eugene's.

98 This total, repeated in other sources, probably only includes the seriously wounded.

99 The correct spelling of each Regiment, and its native origin, are given in parentheses.

100 In fact two.

101 In fact three.

102 Deane means 'battalions'.

103 Lediard says seventeen pairs.

104 Many accounts say thirty-five.

105 Lediard claims '. . . above 100 great and small' besides twenty-four mortars, but probably exaggerates.

106 Possibly Lt-Colonel Alex Livingstone, later MP for Cheviot, of Ferguson's Regiment of Foot (from 1711) and a Brevet-Colonel from August 1704.

107 Lediard claims 129 pairs of colours and 171 cavalry standards. Marlborough sent them back to England where they were displayed in Westminster Hall, and also at the Thanksgiving Service at St Paul's.

108 The *Journal* for 1704 (incomplete) takes up thirty-two pages in the original. Sergeant John Millner, of the Royal Regiment of Foot of Ireland, in his *Compendious Journal of all the Marches, Famous Battles, Sieges . . .* (London, 1733), says that '. . . the Tedious, but ever glorious, memorable and victorious Campaign of 1704, was in length thirty weeks and one day, commenced the 24th day of April and ended on the 20th of November; of which our corps . . . march'd and sail'd ninety-one days, and therein three hundred ninety-two leagues, or one thousand one hundred and seventy-six miles English' (p. 141).

CHAPTER XV

The Count of Mérode-Westerloo

From the Other Side of the Hill

Private Deane's recollections of the Battle of Blenheim are very interesting from the English infantry point of view, but now we pass on to an even more interesting personal account from the French perspective – this time from a cavalryman, who was a Flemish Major-General under Marshal Tallard's command at the same battle. A future Austrian Field-Marshal, who would leave French service in 1705 but in 1704 was then a General at Blenheim in the French army, this was le Comte de Mérode-Westerloo (1674–1732). Here is another contemporary who throws a considerable amount of light on the day-to-day conduct of Marlborough's most important campaigns.

The *Mémoires* of Eugene-Jean-Philippe, Comte de Mérode-Westerloo were first published in two volumes in Belgium by his great-grandson in 1840. Short passages from the first volume were used by Winston S Churchill in his great study of his distinguished ancestor, *Marlborough: His Life and Times* (London, 1933), but surprisingly Mérode-Westerloo's memories have hardly been employed since.

Here we find a man of a very different type of personality confronting us; a man full of baffling and yet often endearing contradictions. Brave to the point of folly, the Count was also of the most irascible temper, touchy pride and overbearing arrogance – characteristics which continually landed him in trouble of one sort or another throughout his life. A stickler for the last details of the deadening etiquette so dear to his snobbish heart, and firmly convinced of his superb talents as a courtier, landowner and soldier, he bears lasting jealous grudges against the men whom he considered had ruined his military career, namely Marlborough and Eugene, without showing any proof that we can discover. As a commander, the Count has been well described as 'the hero of skirmishes', and it is doubtful, despite his claims, whether he possessed sufficient cool judgement to merit his appointments to posts of the highest responsibility. But this story of the Battle of Blenheim, or rather of 'Blindheim' as it should be called, is the most humorous description of this period that I have ever known.

Biographical note: Mérode-Westerloo was born in 1674 at Brussels. He first saw action fighting for William III in 1692 but later he found himself a subject of the new King of Spain, Louis XIV's grandson. In 1703 he was promoted Major-General. He deserted the French cause in 1706 and joined the Emperor's army – but finally left the forces in 1709 after a quarrel with both Marlborough and Eugene. After a long life spent in the service of the Viennese Court (he was promoted Field Marshal and Vice-President of the Council of War in 1712), he died on his estates from apoplexy on 12 September 1732.

The Count of Mérode-Westerloo was a distinguished Flemish officer who at one stage of his career commanded the Belgian contingent in the service of Spain forming part of Marshal Tallard's army. His spritely and illuminating account of the Blenheim Campaign – as seen through the eyes of an officer serving on the losing side – is a new translation of part of his *Mémoires*, published in French by his great-grandson in 1840. A great deal of the narrative leading up to the battle and the events that followed Marlborough's victory has had to be condensed. In some places the translation is slightly 'free', but it is hoped that something of the spirit of the old Count will thereby be recaptured.

The overall picture we acquire is of a very brave and talented officer – not without a sense of humour for all his lofty rank and station. He has several 'bees in his bonnet'. He was evidently very proud of his Flemish homeland and its soldiers, and in consequence of this – and of the fact that he later deserted the French cause – he is often openly scornful of his French superiors. But in all fairness, he does not conceal the fact that many of the French generals had considerable mental reservations towards him. He is also at considerable pains to inform his contemporaries and posterity that his services were carried out only at grave financial loss. To the ravages of war on his depleted estates was added the lamented extravagance of his wife's household in Brussels, though it must be pointed out that she had the good sense to send 300 pistoles to await the return of our almost penniless hero to Strasbourg.

We can excuse him for falling into the very human temptation of thinking rather highly of his own abilities, and for explaining at length from the security of his old age the ways by which he could have undoubtedly won the battle if only the direction of affairs had been entrusted to his able care. In this respect, he was one of the first – and certainly not the last – in the realm of military autobiography. His ability as a writer is, however, undoubted.

It is hoped that this extract from his *Mémoires* will complement the more readily available Allied accounts. Westerloo is particularly revealing on the state of French morale – both before and after the battle. I have added a few notes to clarify certain points and references, but otherwise the story has been left as far as possible in the Count's own words.

I set out from Brussels at the end of May, sending my suite on in advance; it consisted of more than a hundred horses and mules. At length I joined Marshal Tallard at Lauterbourg. He sent me into quarters with several battalions at Kronweissenburg and also put under my orders Flavacourt's Regiment of Flemish Dragoons. However, the incurable murrain[1] this regiment contracted whilst sharing winter quarters with the French Sommeri Regiment had already put most of the troopers on their own two feet – and shortly afterwards this contagion spread to the whole army under the name of the 'German sickness' for want of a better diagnosis.

Over a month later, M. Tallard ordered me to march to Strasbourg and then on to Kehl,[2] where I arrived slightly behind the rest of the Army. The Marshal had asked me if I wanted to cross into Bavaria and I had answered in the affirmative – although the heavy expenses of the campaign – which alone had already set me back more than 25,000 crowns – and the charges of my young wife's household in Brussels (which was both large and costly due to her over-generosity and general lack of experience) – had sent my financial affairs in the Low Countries from bad to worse; especially as the greater part of my property had been confiscated or ruined in the War.

After making a feint-attack on the lines of Stollhofen, we left[3] the fortress of Kehl and entered into the Black Forest down the Kintezingerthan valley. Before we did so Marshal Tallard formed us into battle-order,[4] giving me the choice of a cavalry or infantry command. I chose the former, and was placed in command of the Right of the second line.[5]

After serving with a detachment sent to capture the mountain-position at Rozburg, we reached Hornberg, and there we camped and rested the space of one day to await the arrival of the head of a huge convoy of no less than 8,000 waggons. Moving on, we next deployed on the Heights above Villingen and duly invested the town[6] as we wished to take the place and use it as our forward depot. However we were eventually forced to abandon the siege after wasting much valuable time and material, and we had no option[7] but to move on and join the Elector of Bavaria.

This Prince was harassed by two armies: the first was the English force of the Duke of Marlborough which had travelled all the way from the Netherlands by long marches[8] to join the second army – that of the Emperor. Earlier the Emperor had attempted to offer the Elector favourable terms – but these he had haughtily rejected on receipt of definite news that we were on our way through the Black Forest. Meanwhile we marched on to Ulm, under observation all the time by Prince Eugene's powerful cavalry force. This forced us to move slowly, thus ensuring the safe arrival of the convoy at Ulm, but at last we arrived late at night within six miles of the city.[9]

Eventually we reached Augsburg and then marched away to the

westward for we were now close to the Danube. We camped at Aislingen, but I enjoyed hardly a wink of sleep – in spite of my most comfortable lodgings – for we were on the march again at one in the morning, reaching the Danube at daybreak. The army crossed at once[10] and marched away to the East towards Dillingen in two long columns.

One thing is certain: we delayed our march from Alsace far too long and quite inexplicably,[11] for it was contrary to the usual diligence, promptness and vivacity of the French.

The army passed a complete day in the camp, but on the 12th marched at break of day. Our next resting-place was sited on the plain – about one and a half miles beyond the little town of Höchstädt. Our right wing was on the left bank of the River Danube with the village of Blenheim some two hundred yards to its front. All the generals of the right wing had quarters there. In front of this village was a small stream running from its swampy source a mile or so away to the left. The camp main guard was posted beyond the village of Blenheim, but in my opinion the left was a trifle over-extended: of course it was due to the usual French desire to appear imposing. The Elector and his men held a position stretching as far as the village of Lutzingen which contained his headquarters – with the woods stretching away towards Nordlingen to his front. Before this position was an area of marshy ground, a few hamlets and one or two mills along the little stream. Blenheim village itself was surrounded by hedges, fences and other obstacles, enclosed gardens and meadows. All in all this position was pretty fair – but had we advanced a mere eight hundred or a thousand paces further to our front we could have held a far more compact position, with our Right still on the Danube and our Left protected by woods, and our Centre more concentrated. There we could have drawn up three if not four lines of infantry, one behind the other, with our 94 guns to the fore, and three or four lines of cavalry to support them in the rear.[12]

Following our arrival, we camped in two long lines in order to cover the vast front selected. We soon saw that our advance guard and outlying picquets were in contact with the enemy's patrols along the edge of the woods a mile away in the direction of Munster. A brisk skirmish took place.[13] All this activity was due to the plots and machinations of the Duke of Marlborough and Prince Eugene who were determined to deprive the Margrave of Baden – in fact the senior commander – of the distinction of giving us battle. They managed this by sending him off to amuse himself by besieging Ingolstadt,[14] which kept him fully occupied, whilst they pretended that their operations were solely designed to cover the siege and keep our army under observation. Indeed, neither were the French Marshals nor the Elector of Bavaria expecting a battle[15] – in spite of the strong indications provided by the enemy's movements: for whilst we were advancing to our position, they too were moving up, and in due course they camped in an area stretching from the Danube on their left, through Munster and into the woods on the right.

So both armies made camp for the night – separated by little more than three miles.[16] The allied army consisted of 182 squadrons, 63 infantry battalions and 60 guns; our force totalled 84 battalions, 140 squadrons supported by 94 cannon.[17] But let me hasten to point out that their battalions were up to one third stronger than ours in respect of soldiers, and as for our squadrons, not one was at its full establishment of one hundred troopers – most containing only 70 or 80. The Bavarian forces and my own troops were in point of fact the most up to strength units; the average French battalion consisted of a mere 350 men.

I arrived in the camp during the skirmish I have mentioned and as a precaution ordered my horse to be left fully saddled in case of an emergency. Filled with curiosity to discover how events were faring, I rode out beyond Blenheim village into the corn-filled plain – taking good care not to get too far away from my escort which I might well have needed. When I saw our troops falling back, I also returned to the camp, and sat down to a good hot plate of soup in Blenheim along with my generals and colonels. These included messieurs de Courtebonne, de Sainte-Hermine, de Saint-Pouange, de Ligondes and de Forsac, together with the old and brave officer commanding the Orléans Regiment whose name escapes me: old Heider was also at the supper party. I was never in better form, and after wining and dining well, we one and all dispersed to our respective quarters. I had placed my Spanish troops under the Duke d'Humières[18] away to the left slightly in rear of my position. I was personally in command of the Right Wing of the second line. I don't believe I ever slept sounder than on that night, and the rest certainly did me good.

Upon my orders, the valet had set up my camp-bed in a barn – and there I spent the night, whilst my servants lodged in the main farm building. I slept deeply until six in the morning when I was abruptly awoken by one of my old retainers – the head groom in fact – who rushed into the barn all out of breath. He had just returned from taking my horses out to grass at four in the morning (as he had been instructed). This fellow, Lefranc, shook me awake and blurted out that the enemy were there. Thinking to mock him, I asked: 'Where? There?' and he at once replied 'Yes – there – there!' flinging wide as he spoke the door of the barn and drawing my bed-curtains. The door opened straight on to the fine, sunlit plain beyond – and the whole area appeared to be covered by enemy squadrons. I rubbed my eyes in disbelief, and then coolly remarked that the foe must at least give me time to take my morning cup of chocolate. Whilst I was hurriedly drinking this and getting dressed, my horses were saddled and harnessed. As my lodging was situated in the very last house in the village and nearest to the enemy, I ordered my servants to pack my kit with all speed, and to watch Marshal Tallard's retainers and do with my belongings exactly what they did with his; but first of all to get everybody and everything clear of the house. Jumping on to my horse I rode off towards the camp accompanied by my two aides-de-camp and taking all my thirteen spare chargers with me.[19]

There was not a single soul stirring as I clattered out of the village: nothing at all might have been happening. The same sight met me when I reached the camp – everyone still snug in their tents – although the enemy was already so close that their standards and colours could easily be counted. They were already pushing back our pickets, but nobody seemed at all worried about it. I could see the enemy advancing ever closer in nine great columns of cavalry and deployed-battalions, filling the whole plain from the Danube to the woods on the horizon. I could even make out that they were organised in alternate pairs of columns, two cavalry and then two infantry. I still hadn't received any instructions, but I ordered my cavalry regiments to mount by way of precaution; I went in person to the standards of each squadron to give them this order, making sure that the trumpeters did not sound 'Boot and saddle' or 'Mount.' Soon everyone was on his horse, and I kept them all drawn up at the head of their tents – and then – and only then – did I notice the first signs of movement at Blenheim village.

A little later Marshal Tallard galloped past the head of the second line of battle, pausing to compliment me on my wise precaution in mounting my men. He asked me to sound 'Boot and Saddle' and 'To Horse' repeatedly, and to send an aide-de-camp to the artillery to order the two signal salvoes fired for the recall of the foragers. He told me he was going over to the left but that he would soon return. My trumpeters were immediately ordered to sound the two calls time and time again, one after the other, and they were repeated all the way down the line. My aide-de-camp with noteworthy rapidity got himself recognised and obeyed by the gunners, and we soon heard the 24 pounders fire the two salvoes. There were in all four pieces of this calibre.

Whilst all this was going on, I saw all the baggage and kit flying precipitately and noisily out of Blenheim village, and everything rushed to the rear through the intervals between my squadrons. A moment later we saw two columns of the enemy filing along the edge of the woods – away on their Right – and this made the French experts declare that the enemy was in full march away towards Nordlingen. This made me smile, for of course it was Prince Eugene marching up to form the Right of their line of battle in order to attack our left whilst their opposite wing made all its preparations to assault us.

At this stage I saw two lines of our infantry forming up behind the village of Blenheim, with their right flank on the Danube's bank. If only they had

278

stayed there – and left the defence of Blenheim's gardens, hedgerows, houses and barricades to smaller detachments – constantly reinforced or replaced as the need arose – things would have gone much better. However, the whole formation was eventually drawn into the defences.

It would be impossible to imagine a more magnificent spectacle. The two armies in full battle array were so close to one another that they exchanged fanfares of trumpet-calls and rolls of kettle-drums. When ours stopped, their music struck up again. This went on until the deployment of their right flank was completed, their left preparing to attack the village. The brightest imaginable sun shone down on the two armies drawn up in the plain. You could even distinguish the uniforms of each successive unit; a number of generals and aides-de-camp galloped here and there: all in all, it was an almost indescribably stirring sight. But a moment later other considerations came to the fore in our minds as the enemy artillery – brought forward and drawn up at the head of their army – loosed a terrible bombardment upon us; our guns at once replied[20] with a similar devastating effect, whilst the French – following their usual deplorable custom – set fire to all the villages, mills and hamlets to our front, and flames and smoke billowed up to the clouds.

This great and magnificent prelude lasted another two hours. We maintained our position at the head of our camping-area, where the tents were not yet struck. Trumpet-call answered trumpet-call; cannon balls inflicted grave disorder on my squadrons. These circumstances made the proceedings even more impressive than any distant view from the safety of a church-tower. I was riding past Forsac's Regiment when a shot carried away the head of my horse and killed two troopers; another of my Spanish mounts was killed behind one of the Orléans squadrons, whilst yet a third received a hit which carried away the butts of my pistols, the pommel of the saddle and a piece of flesh as large as the crown of a hat. He recovered from this wound however without any disfigurement, and years later I gave him to the Duke of Wolfenbuttel.

Following this lengthy prelude, the English infantry – who had waited for the Imperial forces to join battle on the right at last attacked the village of Blenheim, shortly after midday I think it was. The first volleys in this attack had hardly been fired when the two lines of our infantry – some 27 battalions in all, whose orders I believe had been to support the position, entered the village most prematurely and ill-advisedly. What is more, a further 12 regiments of dismounted dragoons[21] were also sent in. Why? – a mere ten battalions would have been capable of defending the place in far better fashion – and all the remainder of this veritable army could have been more usefully employed elsewhere. The men were so crowded in upon one another that they couldn't even fire – let alone receive or carry out any orders. Not a single shot of the enemy missed its mark, whilst only those few of our men at the front could return the fire – and soon many of these were unable to shoot owing to exhaustion or their muskets exploding from over-constant use. Those drawn up in the rear were mowed down without firing a shot at the enemy; if they wanted to reply they could only fire at their own comrades or indiscriminately without aiming. To make things ever worse, the village had been set on fire by the French troops, and our poor fellows were grilled amidst the continually collapsing roofs and beams of the blazing houses, and thus were burnt alive amidst the ashes of this smaller Troy of their own making.

The fire of both attack and defence remained heavy and prolonged. Half an hour after it had started, the Gendarmerie – situated directly in front of me in the first line under the command that day of Lt. General de Zurlauben[22] (a Swiss-born infantry officer) – charged the enemy cavalry stationed on the right of the attacking English infantry.[23] This force was drawn up in five lines – one squadron behind the other. Our charge went well – and the Gendarmerie flung their first line on to their second – but since the troops on the Gendarmerie's left did not ride forward with equal dash – if indeed they charged at all – the Gendarmerie found itself unsupported facing fresh enemy squadrons which charged and in their turn flung them back in rude disorder. [24]

During this period the engagement spread over the whole field of battle, and firing broke out everywhere from one end of the armies to the other. Not only did Prince Eugene attack the Elector, but the Dutch and Hessians attacked the two hamlets Oberglau and Unterglau, which were situated in advance of our centre, and the enemy began to cross the marsh which we had considered impassable, leading their horses by the bridles. So they were allowed to get over and remount right in front of our positions, and then calmly charge and attack us as if we were babes-in-arms.

Our senior generals had been pleased to leave too great an interval between our first and second lines. When the enemy attacked Blenheim in two-column strength, and the Gendarmerie charged over the stream as already related, I wanted to advance with the second line to support them, but this the French high command would not allow.

In spite of this I did march forward when I saw the Gendarmerie break and retire in confusion, hotly pursued by the foe. The broken, disordered cavalry poured through the intervals between my own squadrons; the Gendarmerie was undoubtedly soundly beaten, and the gallant Zurlauben received several grave wounds which caused his death two days later. I came face to face with the enemy after he had passed the stream, and my fresh, well-ordered squadrons charged and flung them back – right over the Nebel; following them up, we then attacked their second line which also crumbled; but then we came up against a third, untired force, and my squadrons – disordered and blown by their exertions – were themselves defeated and pushed back over the stream.

A few of the Gendarmerie, who had rallied and re-formed, and the regiment known as the 'Royal Etranger' – who remained drawn up in a sort of line – caused the enemy to rein in their horses when they saw them. This respite gave me time to rally the greater part of my squadrons; I had it in mind to counter-attack – although I knew there was no longer a second line to support me. Of course there was not a single French general in sight. But I failed to notice that all the forces originally stationed on my left, stretching away towards the centre, had turned about in their tracks and were gone from the field. Their vacated place had been filled by the enemy, who were pouring over the stream, and forming up alongside my position in the very midst of the army; our centre was now under the command of the Duke of Humières,[25] who was wearing a very fine gilt cuirass.

Notwithstanding, I charged with all the men I could rally, and I had the good luck to defeat my adversaries and push them back to the brink of the stream – but I had no wish to recross it for I could see they still had five lines of cavalry. However I failed to notice that they had brought their infantry well forward and they killed and wounded many of our horses at a range of a mere thirty paces. This was promptly followed by an unauthorised but definite movement to the rear by my men – and I too would have been obliged to accompany them had not two musket-balls killed my horse beneath me, so that he subsided gently to the ground and I with him. I really don't understand why there was not a single enemy grenadier with charity enough to come forward and give me a hand to my feet[26] – for I was no more than fifteen paces from the stream and they were drawn up all along the bank, supported by cavalry, five lines deep in all. Luckily, however, one of my aides-de-camp and a groom came up with yet another horse after seeing my fall, and they soon had me hoisted on to horseback again.

I then reformed some sort of a line, and I placed four pieces of artillery in front of my position – I had noticed them trying to sneak off and promptly commandeered them. Whilst these guns were being sited I rode over to Blenheim, wanting to bring out a dozen battalions (which they certainly did not need there) to form a line on the edge of the stream supported by the cannons and the debris of my squadrons. The brigades of Saint-Second and Monfort were setting out to follow me, when M. de Clérembault[27] in person countermanded the order, and shouting and swearing drove them back into the village. However I firmly believe that my proposed move would have been the only way to avert the disaster that ensued. Whilst all this was occurring over on my side, the enemy had cut to ribbons seven newly-raised French battalions after their easy deployment over the marshes. These unfortunate battalions had found themselves completely isolated in the centre,[28] and died to a man where they stood, stationed right out in the open plain – supported by nobody.

Over on the Elector's side, Prince Eugene and the Imperial troops had been repulsed three times – right back to the woods – and had taken a real drubbing.[29] There were some places in the centre too – for instance those areas held by the Vaillac and my Walloon cavalry – where the foe was also defeated three time, and indeed in the case of the men of Flanders the success was gained without the interference of a single general. Thus from a church-tower you would have seen the enemy repulsed on one flank and we on the other, the battle rippling to and fro like waves on the sea, with the entire line engaged in hand-to-hand combat from one end to the other – a rare enough occurrence. All this took place under a deadly hail of fire from the infantry – especially during the various attacks on the villages and hamlets, as well as on Blenheim and the other sectors under attack in the centre. This spectacle, lit by bright sunlight, must have been magnificent for any spectator in a position to view it with 'sang-froid.'

Compelled to abandon my plan, I returned to my cavalry, which now mustered only thirteen troops – I really couldn't call them squadrons. One or two still possessed their standards and kettle-drums. I couldn't help but notice at this moment that the enemy were forming up a complete battle-array at his leisure in the very centre of our army. After Vaillac and five more troops had joined me, I resolved to charge once more.

This we carried through so vigorously that we routed the Prince of Hesse. I was joined by the five remaining troops of the Walloon squadrons who had already performed more than their duty, two more from both Acosta and Heider, and the second Gaetano squadron under their Lt. Colonel, Jobart. By this time the Prince of Hesse had rallied his forces and counter-attacked – but we soundly beat him again. However, in the meantime hordes of the enemy were pushing round our flanks, and we soon found ourselves faced by numerous enemy squadrons[30] on no less than three sides – and we were borne back on top of one another. So tight was the press that my horse was carried along some three hundred paces without putting hoof to ground – right to the edge of a deep ravine: down we plunged a good twenty feet into a swampy meadow; my horse stumbled and fell. A moment later several men and horses fell on top of me, as the remains of my cavalry swept by all-intermingled with the hotly pursuing foe. I spent several minutes trapped beneath my horse.

While all this was going on, the Elector and Marshal Marsin conceded that the day was lost when they saw the enemy in possession of the Centre. They ordered a retreat[31] – which was carried out in good order; but I believe they would not have escaped so easily but for my men keeping the enemy's attention fully occupied. Otherwise the foe could have attacked the head and flank of our left wing as it retreated towards Lavingen. As things turned out, however, our entire left got safely away.

Meantime the enemy sealed all the exits from Blenheim at their leisure, and the general commanding the village rode straight into the Danube and was drowned instead of organising the 27 battalions and 14 dragoon regiments into a square to fight their way out. Good infantry, well disciplined and highly trained, could easily have done this. As it turned out, however, these forces fought on until after seven o'clock, without an experienced commander, and then surrendered as prisoners of war when they saw the enemy bringing up all his artillery.

The French lost this battle for a wide variety of reasons. For one thing, they had too good an opinion of their own ability – and were excessively scornful of their adversaries. Another point was that their field dispositions were badly made, and in addition there was rampant indiscipline and inexperience displayed by Marshal Tallard's army. It took all these faults to lose so celebrated a battle. As regards casualties, I believe these were practically equal on both sides if we discount the prisoners. I calculate that the enemy lost twelve or thirteen thousand killed and wounded on the field of battle and we about the same;[32] but of course the foe also captured the entire Blenheim garrison and other captives during the course of the different actions and the pursuit. M. Tallard was himself taken prisoner. They also took 52 guns, but the other 40 escaped.

Everything happened very quickly, and the crowd soon passed me by; I managed to escape from beneath my horse – which was not dead but utterly exhausted – and extricated myself from the pile of dead horses that had fallen on top of us both. I had barely found my feet when a passing hussar fired his pistol at me. The next moment a huge English Horse-Grenadier – a whole head and shoulders taller than I – came up. He dismounted and came forward to take me prisoner in a leisurely way. I noticed his lackadaisical air, and grasped my long sword which was dangling from my wrist, keeping it pressed well into my side. When he was within two paces I lunged at him, but then discovered my left knee was injured so I stumbled and missed my stroke. The Englishman raised his sword to cut me down, but I parried his blow and ran my sword right through his body up to the hilt. I wrenched my blade free, but as he fell he slashed at me again but only succeeded in cutting the thick edge of my boot which did me no harm. I put my foot on his head and plunged my sword through his throat. My blade penetrated into the soft earth and snapped under the excessive pressure – leaving me with only the hilt.

This left me in a sorry state, but I managed to pick up a pistol from the ground – though I had no idea whether it was loaded or not. Who should then happen to ride past but my valet gazing around in terror. He recognised me stretched out on the ground, and dropped something heavy on my face – a pistol butt I believe it was – making my nose and teeth bleed. 'Is it really you, My Lord?' he asked. I replied in no uncertain terms that it was, and he at once jumped down from his horse and hoisted me on to its back: I was unable to do this unaided because of my bad knee. Once I was firmly in the saddle, I told him to get up behind, but he refused. 'But what on earth will you do then my poor Leblond?' I queried. He never had a chance to answer, for at that moment he fell riddled with shots fired by some passing soldiers. I lost no time in riding off the way I had come, planning to swim across the Danube: the greater part of the cavalry survivors had already attempted this.[33]

As I rode on my way, I removed the white cockade from my hat, and went straight up to a large body of formed cavalry drawn up with their backs to our camp. I reached a large squadron – made up from the debris of two others. As I speak several languages, I was not interfered with as I rode up, and seeing that nobody took any interest in me I resolved to ride straight through the gap in their midst. Finding myself between two of their lines, I rode off to the left to find a path I had followed the day before, coming from Hochstadt. Eventually I found it, and went off passing again between two more enemy squadrons. They never challenged – so I slowly went down my path – speaking to this group in German and answering others in the language they addressed me in. When I reached some wind-mills on a small stream – not far from Hochstadt – some of these soldiers advised me not to go any closer as the enemy were still in possession of the town. I replied that we would soon have them all in the bag, and pretended I was going closer for a reconnaissance. The others stayed behind. As I approached my objective, someone fired several shots at me, but I got past and into the town. Reaching the barrier, I walked my horse for a short distance before being challenged: 'Who goes there?' 'French general officer!' I replied. An officer then let me enter. I went into the square where I found several French generals who had the nerve to tell me I was pretty late. I replied to the effect that they had got there too damned early. We all had a drink at the fountain.

Eventually I passed through the little town and came out onto the ridge behind the marsh – and there I found all the debris of our cavalry in indescribable confusion. It was almost eight o'clock when I reached them, and I at once settled down to reorganise them. As nobody else was doing anything about the disorder, all the officers took their orders direct from me.

Under cover of darkness I marched my men back over the stream and away towards Lavingen, where the Elector and Marshal Marsin were building two bridges over which to evacuate the infantry and baggage. Through an Aide-de-Camp, His Excellency begged me to lose no time in marching on towards Ulm by way of the north bank of the river, bypassing Lavingen without becoming embroiled with the infantry and equipment crossing there. He also placed all his cavalry under my command. I replied I would carry out his orders in spite of my three wounds, but that I couldn't hold myself responsible for what might happen if we came within a mile of Prince Eugene for the troops in their present nervous condition were likely to bolt if a hare got up. I then marched on, and about seven in the evening we marched through Ulm, trumpets and kettle-drums playing. The day's march had been no less than 42 miles.

After being in the saddle for thirty hours with neither sleep nor food – and only one short drink of water – my wounds were in need of attention. On my third day at Ulm, the Elector arrived with the infantry. My baggage was the very last allowed over the bridge at Lavingen, which was very fortunate. I attended his orders-session the next day, and he ended by paying me many fine compliments on my conduct. I received the congratulations of Marshal Marsin and the rest though I could tell they were inwardly seething with indignation.

At this time we heard of the fall of Ingolstadt, and Prince Louis' rage when he learned of the trick Prince Eugene and the Duke of Marlborough had played him. It is quite certain that there would have been no battle had Baden been with them – he was not the sort to risk all to gain all.

When we learnt that the enemy was on the march after the capture of Ingolstadt we left the neighbourhood of Ulm, burning all our baggage. The morale of our army was very low, and had the enemy managed to push a force ahead of us to the lines of Moesskirch, we should have been forced to lay down our arms. Passing Villingen, we re-entered the gorges of the Black Forest, finding Villeroi's men in full control of the passes. His army formed our rearguard. At last the army reached Strasbourg, and a few days later I was sent into a rear area with all that remained of Tallard's cavalry.

Since the battle, I had lost sixty horses through illness, besides those killed in the battle; all my baggage had been burnt; my personal expenditure had been frightful, but my wife had the good sense to forward three hundred pistoles to await my arrival at Strasbourg. At Hochfeld I at long last found enough leisure to write down my account of the battle.

The Battle of Blenheim

I

It was a summer evening,
  Old Kaspar's work was done,
And he before his cottage door
  Was sitting in the sun,
And by him sported on the green
His little grandchild Wilhelmine.

II

She saw her brother Peterkin
  Roll something large and round,
Which he beside the rivulet
  In playing there had found;
He came to ask what he had found,
That was so large, and smooth, and round.

285

III

Old Kaspar took it from the boy,
Who stood expectant by;
And then the old man shook his head,
And, with a natural sigh,
''Tis some poor fellow's skull,' said he,
'Who fell in the great victory.

IV

'I find them in the garden,
For there's many here about;
And often when I go to plough,
The ploughshare turns them out!
For many thousand men,' said he,
'Were slain in that great victory.'

V

'Now tell us what 'twas all about,'
Young Peterkin, he cries;
And little Wilhelmine looks up
With wonder-waiting eyes;
'Now tell us all about the war,
And what they fought each other for.'

VI

'It was the English,' Kaspar cried,
'Who put the French to rout;
But what they fought each other for,
I could not well make out;
But everybody said,' quoth he,
'That 'twas a famous victory.

VII

'My father lived at Blenheim then,
Yon little stream hard by;
They burnt his dwelling to the ground,
And he was forced to fly;
So with his wife and child he fled,
Nor had he where to rest his head.

VIII

'With fire and sword the country round
Was wasted far and wide,
And many a childing mother then,
And new-born baby died;
But things like that, you know, must be
At every famous victory.

IX

'They say it was a shocking sight
After the field was won;
For many thousand bodies here
Lay rotting in the sun;
But things like that, you know, must be
After a famous victory.

X

'Great praise the Duke of Marlbro' won,
And our good Prince Eugene.'
'Why 'twas a very wicked thing!'
Said little Wilhelmine.
'Nay . . . nay . . . my little girl,' quoth he,
'It was a famous victory.

XI

'And everybody praised the Duke
Who this great fight did win.'
'But what good came of it at last?'
Quoth little Peterkin.
'Why that I cannot tell,' said he
'But 'twas a famous victory.'

ROBERT SOUTHEY 1774–1843

NOTES

1   This disease was probably 'glanders'. Eventually it affected a large part of
     Tallard's cavalry. The general condition of Marlborough's cavalry at the end
     of the long march to the Danube contrasted very favourably with the fettle of
     the French.
2   Kehl, on the east bank of the Rhine, close to Strasbourg, was the French
     concentration area for the Danube campaign.
3   1 July 1704.
4   This was a standard and sensible precaution. Earlier in the year (in May),
     Tallard had narrowly avoided being intercepted by Baden's Imperial Army
     during a similar march through the Black Forest to pass 10,000 reinforce-
     ments to Bavaria.
5   Generals commanded sections of the battle-line in accordance with their
     seniority rather than from any consideration of their leading their own
     particular troops – at least, that was the case in the French Army. The post of
     honour was 'Right of the Line', the first line of battle taking precedence over
     the second.
6   The siege lasted from 16 to 22 July.
7   It was Eugene's appearance with 18,000 men near Rothweil that persuaded
     Tallard to abandon the siege.
8   Marlborough's army left Bedburg on 20 May, and joined up with Baden's
     forces at Launsheim on 22 June.
9   5 August.
10   10 August.
11   Tallard waited for Villeroi to take up a position covering the Lines of
     Stollhofen and thus protecting the line of march. Moreover, both generals had
     to refer to Versailles for orders. These they only received on 27 June.
12   Probably a case of 'wisdom after the event'. The actual position occupied was
     very strong if over-extended (four miles).
13   A force of Allied cavalry was escorting Marlborough and Eugene on a
     reconnaissance.
14   Baden left the Allied camp on 9 August. This was a brave flouting of
     'concentration of force', but undoubtedly achieved real 'economy'.
15   Marlborough reputedly planted 'deserters' on the French telling a tale of
     retreat to Nordlingen.
16   In fact six miles.
17   Churchill's figures are: 56,000 Allies (sixty-six battalions, 160 squadrons,
     sixty-six guns) versus 60,000 Franco–Bavarians (eighty-four battalions, 147
     squadrons, ninety guns).
18   Commander of the French second line centre.
19   This may seem a generous number of spare horses for one general, but we
     know from what Westerloo writes that he lost at least three horses killed and
     two wounded during the battle.
20   Mérode-Westerloo implies that the French waited to be fired on first, though
     their guns must almost certainly have been brought into position before the
     British.
21   Probably made up of dragoons whose horses had died of 'German Sickness'.
22   Zurlauben was in fact commander of the whole French right centre first line.
23   The three brigades under Lord Cutts' command.
24   The eight squadrons of the Gendarmerie were in fact defeated by five of
     Lumley's Horse, commanded by Lt. Col. Palmes.

25　D'Humières succeeded to the command of the French right centre after Zurlauben was wounded.

26　The simple reason was that British regimental discipline was too good. No soldier would dare to break ranks without orders even to secure so valuable a captive. Mérode-Westerloo was more fortunate that he wasn't shot on the ground.

27　Clérembault was in command of the defences of Blenheim village. As general commanding the right of the first line, he had seniority over Westerloo and could countermand the latter's orders.

28　Many accounts of the battle say that there were nine recruit battalions.

29　This was not really surprising as the Elector and Marsin outnumbered Eugene two to one.

30　At the critical moment, Marlborough had massed eighty squadrons in the centre facing fifty to sixty French.

31　About 7 pm.

32　In fact the Allies lost about 12,700 men to the French 18,500 casualties and 20,000 prisoners of war.

33　Some contemporary accounts claim that up to thirty squadrons shared the fate of Clérembault and were drowned in the Danube.

CHAPTER XVI

Allies

The Duke and Alliance Warfare

We have suggested that, although Marlborough was successful in his grand strategy for central Europe, he was decidedly unfortunate in Spain. However, we will now examine some other aspects of his international abilities, particularly the group of friends and colleagues he built around him who advised upon and carried out his schemes.

It is important to mention here the Duke's vital aides. He had built up a sound team. Great as he was as a commander, he certainly needed assistance and support. There were three vital men at headquarters in 1704. First there was William Cadogan (1675–1726) who, although later promoted rapidly to general rank, was only a major, but performed the dual roles of Quartermaster-General and inevitably Chief-of-Staff, although no such title existed in the early eighteenth century. He was very important to the Duke, and he kept the post for ten continuous years, being removed from office at the same time as his master in early 1712.

His second vital assistant was Adam Cardonnel (d.1719), the Duke's personal secretary from 1692. The son of a Huguenot refugee, he was particularly responsible for all correspondence. One can only imagine the workload generated by a man who was not only running a war, but keeping in touch with and monitoring all the contacts of the Allied rulers; and also to reporting and 'dealing' with all matters relating to political duties owed to both Tories and Whigs back in Great Britain. Cardonnel's was an enormous responsibility, and his tactfulness was much admired at the time.

The third man was Henry Davenant, who managed the Duke's financial matters, particularly from Frankfurt during the campaign of 1704. Little more is known about him, but he was very instrumental in producing the necessary golden guineas that enabled the army to march to the Danube.

As for the 'secret men' and spies, these are naturally not easy to uncover, but we do know that two Mr James Craggs – father and son – were important and trusted agents of the Duke. Both men appear to have been astute and skilled at both accountancy and diplomacy. Both reaped substantial rewards for their services. The first (1657–1721) was Paymaster General and army clothier, and became Postmaster-General from 1715.

The second (1686–1721) was a great traveller throughout Europe especially in Hanover, and eventually became Secretary-at-War. We know that the Duke set up his own secret organisation. His 'OO' letters are partly known, and it is guessed that his nephew (sister Arabella's bastard from James II), James Fitzjames, Duke of Berwick and Marshal of France, may have been involved!

Winston S Churchill once remarked that during a war there was only one thing worse than having allies – and that was to have none of either, enemies or friends.[1]

John Churchill, the first Duke of Marlborough, has received a 'mixed press', both historically and politically. During the eighteenth and nineteenth centuries the mainly Whig historians and writers, those 'little mercenary scribblers' as the loyal Captain Robert Parker described them[2] were strident in their criticism of the Duke's 'dishonourable integrity'. This was especially true of the famous Lord Macaulay.[3] However, these criticisms were balanced in the twentieth century by both Winston Churchill[4] and G M Trevelyan[5] who produced their famous 'blockbuster' works during the 1920s and 1930s, in four and three volumes respectively, which were both strong in praise and support of Marlborough's fame.

For some years afterwards, British historians remained largely silent regarding the Duke, perhaps feeling somewhat overawed by Churchill and Trevelyan. The writers of the 1960s and later have mostly admired Marlborough and honoured his reputation. However, several authors in the 1990s took the occasional academic 'swipe' against 'the Old Corporal's' reputation, for there is, alas, a modern trend among some historians to display an almost brainwashed antipathy towards 'famous heroes'.

I would like, at this point, to mention three noteworthy historians whose work has embraced the Duke: Professors John Childs[6] of Leeds University, John R Jones[7] of York, and Dr Alan Guy[8] of the National Army Museum; but probably the best modern specialist book has been written by Richard Scouller and I think all those interested in Marlborough should thank him for such a unique work.[9] I have been pleading for writers not to judge the Duke from Whig or extreme Tory points of view, but neither is it correct to judge him by modern morals, for it is a sad mistake to evaluate the past by standards of a later age, which are somewhat irrelevant. Marlborough needs to be seen in his own context, against the background of his own times, peers and social, military and political attitudes. We run great risks if we pronounce upon things seen in the context of a set of values which have little to do with a situation.

This chapter will pass judgement, however, but upon Marlborough's record as a strategist, diplomat and treatymaker, and it will argue that never was his skill as evident as it was in the way he handled his Allies. There may perhaps have been a blemish or two on his record in his later years, but I will contend that his handling of people was always one of his greatest abilities. To prove this I will look at the ways the younger Churchill honed and developed his skills as a negotiator, and then analyse his contribution to the creation of the Second Grand Alliance between 1698 and 1702, together with a resume of his understanding of the wider issues at stake in the ensuing war. As Churchill commented on Duke John, '. . . he was the mainspring of the Grand Alliance and its many signatory states'.[10]

By way of a preliminary we need to focus our minds upon some of the parameters of the subject, and I would draw attention to a quotation from the late Alastair Buchan. Much of what Buchan had to say in 1956 about the NATO Alliance is relevant to the problems of the Second Grand Alliance of some 290 years earlier. Buchan wrote:

> Sovereign states enter into alliances in order to further common political objectives which they are convinced they would not achieve individually. Almost by definition alliances have a limited life-cycle, unless they become transformed into Federations or some organic political relationships. National objectives change, the threat which made it worthwhile to subordinate some national interests to the evolution of a collaborate policy changes also, and the strains of alliance may become too great to bear. For, though alliance has been an essential device of international politics for nearly 3,000 years, it is bound to develop internal strains once the period of clear and present danger is past, since it must involve a relationship between strong and less-strong powers, restricting the freedom of both without giving either a decisive influence upon the policy of the other.[11]

I hope that as my subject unfolds it will become evident that a Second Grand Alliance exhibited almost all of these varied symptoms of internal strain, conflict and decay in full measure.

Alliances at war certainly pose many problems, but to return to W S Churchill, 'It is difficult to wage wars with Allies, but it is still more difficult to fight wars *without* them'. My thesis will revolve around certain enigmatic traits in the personality of the Duke of Marlborough and I make no apology for reviving the 'cult of great men', for his was an age when certain key people exercised immense influence over matters of diplomacy and politics – and 'Milord Duke' was destined to be a very key person indeed; he was, in the modern idiom, a 'major player'.

It is always helpful to try to envisage an historical figure to seek to understand how they were perceived by their contemporaries. How a person was seen by others often influences their behaviour and we begin by examining what Marlborough looked like.

For this we can turn to one of his critics, Sicco van Goslinga, a Dutch

Deputy, politician, soldier and man-of-affairs who was at the Duke's side for many years. He wrote:

> The Duke is a man of birth; about middle height, and the best figure in the world; his features without fault; fine sparkling eyes, good teeth, and his complexion such a mixture of white and red as the fairer sex might envy; in brief, apart from his legs, which are too thin, one of the handsomest men ever seen . . .'[12].

If this is from the pen of one of his greatest critics, what may we expect from those of his admirers? I shall be referring to the views of other contemporaries a little later for further comment and illustrations of the great man in his various roles as a diplomat, statesman and the effective head of the Grand Alliance for ten successive years. Marlborough was a complex character. Napoleon, who never included his name on his St Helena list of Great Commanders, described him as, 'a man whose mind was not narrowly confined to the field of battle; he fought and negotiated; he was, at the same time, a captain and a diplomat'.[13] I feel this was a shrewd assessment but he would certainly be on my list of Great Commanders.

Marlborough's evolution into a diplomat may be said to have had its roots in his childhood at Assche House in Devon. Born in May 1649, the year of King Charles I's execution, young John Churchill spent his early years under the roof of his maternal grandmother, the puritan and staunch Parliamentarian, Lady Eleanor Drake. Her 'protection' was virtually a refuge for the Churchill family, for John's father, the first Sir Winston Churchill who had been in the legal profession, had also been a captain of Royalist horse, while his grandfather had been the Royal Commissioner for Sherbourne. Both had incurred crippling fines from Parliament of £446 and £448 respectively for supporting the royal cause and were totally ruined. Sir Winston, moreover, was banned from practising law, and his family of twelve children, of whom only five survived from infancy, were penniless and dependent upon the generosity of others. Young John presumably learnt early on to guard his tongue, suppress any anger and keep his own counsel, as well as to save every copper piece; certain traits that would persist throughout his life, for good and ill.

The Restoration saw the 16-year-old youth transferred from country to city, to London and the Court of Charles II, where in 1665 his connections secured him a post as page to James, Duke of York, the King's brother.[14] This was achieved through the diplomatic and amorous accomplishments of his elder sister, Arabella, who managed to combine the seemingly incompatible roles of Maid of Honour to the Duchess and mistress to the Duke! These years at the Court of the 'merry monarch' saw developments of future significance to this study. Although his own intriguing amorous adventures and liaisons, alas, do not concern us, during this part of his life he found a lasting friend in a fellow page, Sidney Godolphin, future Lord Treasurer and firm ally of Queen Anne.

The most significant of the developments was the trusted role Churchill established in his patron's household which led him to undertake his first diplomatic mission on behalf of his royal master, the Catholic Duke of York.

The problems of the Protestant Succession Crisis that darkened the later years of Charles II's reign loomed large in these delicate tasks, but Churchill, step by step, became a confidant of the future James II, who appreciated the tact and discretion of his handsome assistant. He shared some of his periods of exile in France, the United Provinces and Scotland. So well did he perform in his duties, that at one point in 1680 his master strongly supported his name for the future Ambassador to France, but nothing came of the effort. However, on four occasions he conducted intricate monetary negotiations for the Duke at Versailles – twice before 1685 and twice more after James succeeded his late brother. He was also entrusted with the task of escorting the future royal consort, George, Prince of Denmark to his marriage with James' younger daughter, the Princess Anne in 1683.

Marlborough became a close friend of the couple and indeed his own wife, Sarah, was later to enjoy their complete confidence, exchanging the famous Morley/Freeman private letters with Anne when she was Queen. Charles II apparently had little time for George, 'I tried him drunk and I tried him sober yet found nothing in him', but Churchill seems to have enjoyed his company as much as Sarah enjoyed that of his wife. This special relationship with the royal family was to have great impact upon international affairs for it enabled Marlborough to wield considerable influence over Allied matters. George died in 1708, but by that time John was firmly established upon the world stage. When the Queen ended the friendship in 1712, the end of the Second Grand Alliance followed within a year.

However, all traits in Marlborough's character were not so admirable. His desertion of James II in 1688 showed there to be a certain ruthlessness and a degree of ingratitude in his make-up, although he had cause to recall what he believed to be the heaping of rewards of his labours upon others after the defeat of Monmouth's Rebellion. His defection led to an important period of distrust for the newly raised Earl of Marlborough in 1689. William III distrusted him for several years and his royal wife, Mary II, disliked both him and his wife, especially resenting Sarah's influence over her sister, Princess Anne. The Earl himself did not like the Dutch who accompanied William into England and into office. He particularly disliked the favourite 'foreign generals' who made up the military hierarchy of the English Army and made his view abundantly clear. The

Queen would not forgive Marlborough for his desertion of her father, although it brought her husband and herself to the throne, and this was further exacerbated when the royal couple discovered he was in secret correspondence with James in exile. Marlborough was sent to the tower. It was only after the death of Queen Mary in 1694 that he was reconciled with William III.

William was increasingly concerned over the maintenance of the balance of power in Europe, especially with the impending death of Charles II of Spain promising to lead to a vast international crisis. Marlborough was most likely involved, directly or indirectly, in the two Partition Treaties of 1698–1700, but was certainly privy to their secret terms. When Parliament, suspicious of the trend in events, accused Lord Portland of leading William III astray, it was the Earl of Marlborough who, not being a minister of state, spoke freely on the implications of policies to the House of Lords.

The great challenge for Marlborough was to be the constructing of the Second Grand Alliance and to become increasingly trusted by William III. When Charles of Spain neared his end, he unexpectedly pronounced an offer to make Philip of Anjou, the grandson of Louis XIV of France, his heir, and the inheritor of all Spanish domains and properties, with the sole provision that Spain and France were not to be united. The crisis exploded for Europe when Louis accepted the promise on behalf of Philip. 'Le Roi Soleil' had thus broken the Partition Treaties and immediately occupied many Italian and Netherlands fortifications with French soldiers in the name of his grandson. William III responded with a requirement that Marlborough immediately set about creating a political alliance to redress the balance of power. He therefore issued instructions at The Hague, dated 26 June 1701, for his 'Ambassador and Plenipotentiary-Extra-ordinary' to rebuild the Grand Alliance for the peace of Europe.

I now turn to Marlborough's abilities as a negotiator of alliances in the difficult waters of international politics. It was evident that there was a real danger of a major European war as France was clearly determined to abandon all previous agreements to secure her new national interests. As well as this pressure, William III fell ill in 1700 and grew impatient for diplomatic success and even more dependent upon Marlborough to achieve it. Coupled with this it would appear the King now accepted the situation that how Marlborough acted would be vital for England. Despite his initial distrust of the man in the 1690s, he had in Marlborough a servant of exceptional abilities and that, because of the closeness between the Churchills and his heir, Anne, England's long-term security lay in his hands. He had William's backing and certain options.

Firstly, should France be willing to return the Spanish fortresses in the Netherlands, and allow the Dutch to recover certain 'cautionary towns as guarantees for good intentions', and important English and Dutch citizens be 'granted equal rights, liberties and privileges in all parts of the Spanish Dominions, as well by sea as by land',[15] he was empowered to make a 'Pacific Treaty' with France on behalf of England and could count upon the United Provinces and the Austrian Empire for support and agreement.

Second, should it become evident that France would make no such dependable and guaranteed professions of pacific intent, he was to commence negotiation of important treaties with the United Provinces, the Austrian Empire and 'other Princes', to include Portugal if possible, so as to enforce, if necessary, satisfactory terms upon France and Spain. In other words he was tasked with creating a Second Grand Alliance with special attention to the security of the United Provinces by 'the entire removal of the forces out of the Spanish Netherlands'.[16] He was also instructed with a second task which would be in noting the interest of the Emperor's 'pretensions to the Succession of Spain', which were to be reported to William III 'for our further directions'. Thirdly, he was to discover 'what it is the King of Portugal do propose . . . and at the same time, to represent to him how necessary it is that he should enter into Common Measures with Us, the Emperor and the United Provinces'.[17] Then lastly, he was to have 'particular record . . . to the security and improvement of the Trades in Our Kingdom'. It was quite an extensive brief!

That Louis XIV would withdraw was dubious from the outset. From early July 1701 hostilities had already commenced in North Italy between Marshal de Catinat and Prince Eugene, so there was no surprise when the 'Sun King' instructed his diplomatic mission in The Hague to withdraw on 5 August. A general war was clearly imminent and every effort was mobilised to create an effective alliance. What did come as a disappointment was that the Wittelsbach family, rulers of Bavaria, Liège and Cologne, all declared for the Franco–Spanish cause.

The twists and turns of diplomatic wrangling need not concern us here. A brief outline must suffice. At first, the work of finding allies was slow, for although the United Provinces and the Elector Palatine fell into line almost at once, it required all of Marlborough's skill, charm and, on occasion, cajoling 'bonhomie' to persuade the rest to comply. Meanwhile the first English battalions were moved to the United Provinces.

Then on 7 September 1701 the major treaty of the Second Grand Alliance was signed between England, the United Provinces and Austria; the 'big three', we might call them. The signatories declared their firm resolve to fight France and Spain until the following concessions should be agreed by Versailles and Madrid:

> First: that the Emperor Leopold 1 would take possession of Milanese, the Two Sicilies, the Spanish Mediterranean islands and, above all, the Spanish Netherlands and Luxembourg, on behalf of Archduke Charles.

Second: that a strong fortress-barrier was to be established to protect the security of the United Provinces.

Third: that the Maritime Powers, the English and the Dutch, were to be given a free hand in the West Indies.

And fourth: the main, 'loyal' German states of the Holy Empire were to receive Anglo–Dutch subsidies if they would join the Alliance – with the Elector of Brandenburg being accorded the dignity of King of Prussia in return for his support.

This 'package' is noteworthy as it contained no suggestion of removing Philip V from the throne, nor any determination to prevent France and Spain from becoming united. However, one contentious area was fudged – that of the proportionate allocations of English and Dutch quotas in terms of fighting men and ships – the notorious *Dénombrement* held over for further careful consideration between the two powers.

Step by step the Second Grand Alliance slowly came together as Prussia, Hesse, Hanover, Celle, Munster and Denmark, and smaller states acceded (Savoy and Portugal joined in 1703). Despite mutual suspicion and doubtful queries, the *Dénombrement* was eventually agreed. Everything depended upon securing ratification from the English House of Commons which was dominated by a Tory majority who demanded the utmost caution. This could have wrecked or possibly badly delayed the treaty, had not the exiled James II died in France on 16 September 1701. Louis XIV responded to this event with rashness and over-emotional sentiment in publicly announcing his recognition of James' son, 'The Old Pretender'[18] as James III, lawful King of England. This French *démarche* caused an immense and immediate furore throughout the country, and William III had worsened things by dissolving Parliament, hoping to dislodge the Tory majority. In the event only the Jacobite Tories were removed but both parties were behind the King; however unwillingly in the case of the Tories. The politicians at home tried to tack 'Eight Articles' onto the international treaty, whereupon the Allied European Powers would formally denounce the claims of the 'Old Pretender'. In fact this was an attempt to delay the treaty's ratification, but the explicit perils of the European situation caused William's view to triumph, and England found itself committed, alongside its European allies, to fight a continental war from 15 May 1702.

What then were the major interests of England and its allies? To understand them we must comprehend the notion of Grand Strategy, or the overall picture, and on this subject I must recommend the work of Dr John B Hattendorf of the USA Naval War College, Newport. I consider his book *England in the War of the Spanish Succession – a study of the English view and conduct of Grand Strategy 1702–1712* (New York, 1987) to be the only important book about Marlborough to have come out of America so far.

Marlborough's affinity for Grand Strategy may have been innate, but we must not forget that he had had an early introduction to the international network of commitments, possessions and interests that influenced policy, and that he also had first-hand experience of the results of policy implications while serving in the Tangier garrison as a young 'volunteer' (or lieutenant) in 1668; taking part in operations against pirates at Algiers in 1670; and fighting at the naval battle of Solebay in June 1672 as a marine, where he earned his Captaincy. Marlborough remained interested in naval matters and the global view of affairs, although almost all of his later military career as Captain-General was in continental campaigning.

England's Grand Strategy had one aim – to defeat Louis XIV, but there was also one basic and important consideration – to secure the Dutch Republic. William III had continued to impress upon Marlborough the necessity to safeguard the Dutch Netherlands ever since the French armies had almost overrun them in 1672. Because of this, lines of fortresses were massed to protect the 'Cockpit of Europe' and all of his campaigns were to be conducted near or in the Netherlands; the only real exception being the Blenheim campaign in 1704.

To achieve the aim of taking pressure off the Netherlands, the Earl needed to persuade the Dutch, German and Austrian allies to divide and defeat the French armies with a triple threat against the frontiers of France, from the English Channel all the way to Savoy and Piedmont. Meanwhile the Anglo–Dutch naval squadrons would exert pressure of their own on other 'targets', which resulted in the seizure of Gibraltar in 1704 and Minorca in 1708, and the protracted blockading and raiding of shipping to isolate the French and Spanish economies. Much depended upon the role of the fast-growing English navy, or rather British from 1707. Not only would it protect our coasts and wealthy merchant ships from enemy attacks, but, because Britain as an island would be safe from the armies of European enemies, it could also indulge in raids, such as attempts to capture the Spanish flotas with its famous annual treasure of South American gold and silver; only once achieved in Vigo in 1702. It could also launch or support attacks against 'Second France' in Canada, or their trading territories in parts of India which competed with the East India Company's Presidencies in Bombay, Calcutta and Madras, while the valuable French West Indies, being virtually undefended, were waiting to be captured.

Thus by starts and stops the Second Grand Alliance came into existence. Much that had been achieved was due to Marlborough's deft diplomacy, even if William III was the main inspiration for the concept.

However, as I have already cited Alastair Buchan as saying, 'to create an

Alliance (such as NATO in modern times) is one thing, to maintain an alliance is quite another matter'. The first grave test of this emerging Alliance came sooner than anyone could have anticipated. On 19 March 1702 King William III, progenitor for thirty years of 'problems with France', died, aged 52, after sustaining the attentions of 'the little gentleman in the moleskin waistcoat' while riding his horse. Most of Europe was shocked and deeply saddened, but France and the Jacobites rejoiced. This cloud may have had a personal silver lining for Marlborough, for Queen Anne's succession meant the Churchills, John and Sarah, became the greatest people in the nation, but could the Alliance survive this blow – or would it disintegrate before being born?

So we now pass on to the third subject of this study – Marlborough's administrative ability. As we know, Marlborough was in fact ready and willing to serve the new Queen, who in recognition of both friendship and great abilities promoted him to a Dukedom. He was probably under no illusion that with the title went the responsibility of ensuring that although the new Alliance was shaken by William's death it was not shattered.

Although England possessed excellent ambassadors abroad, including George Stephney in Vienna, Lord Raby in Berlin and Sir Paul Methuen at Lisbon, the slow passage of instructions between capitals was a challenge and an inevitable handicap for the Alliance. It was, therefore, necessary for the new Duke to add immediately to his already vast load of responsibilities and concerns three vital diplomatic tasks.

The first was to increase his daunting pile of correspondence; an all-year-round job which he managed with the excellent and indispensable aid of Adam Cardonnel, his personal secretary. We can still read today Marlborough's carefully written letters to the Allies, some penned on the very days of the battle, as he did at Blenheim in 1704.

He had to keep in touch with a dozen courts, principalities and powers despite disagreements, charges and sometimes deliberate 'forgetfulness'; he had to keep them all satisfied with everything, and take cognisance of individual peccadilloes. The second task was having to conduct an equally daunting list of personal visits to these courts and seats of government, such as The Hague, Hanover and Berlin. These were important meetings such as those of 1704, but they also included two large-scale conferences every year; one at the start and the other at the end of each campaigning season. Milford Duke's third undertaking was to try to formulate contingency plans for emergency interventions and the occasional 'hiatus' in operations which could plague events after a campaign was over, but sometimes even occurred before it began. As we know, every 'good year' led to a slackening off during the next, as in 1705 and again in 1707.

Marlborough's planning and diplomacy had not only to include this phenomenon but more importantly to ensure that events and considerations pertaining to the Great Northern War (in which Sweden and several smaller Germanic countries lined up against Russia) did not intervene or impinge upon the business of the Second Grand Alliance. In 1707 these potential problems forced Marlborough to travel many long and bad roads to Altranstadt.

In addition to foreseeing, circumnavigating and solving all these events and problems, they all had to be communicated in various forms of explanation or adaptation to every member of the Alliance, not forgetting the English politicians, some of whom were more than keen to see favourites such as Marlborough fall from grace. At times the workload and the atmosphere must have daunted even his spirit: 'I find so little zeal for the common cause that it is enough to break a better heart than mine,' he wrote to Heinsius in May 1705. Yet, amid his tribulations he also made time to write often to his wife, for he and Sarah remained passionately in love despite his Duchess not being the easiest woman to control.

I now wish to describe both Marlborough's famous charm and cunning he used when dealing with his Allies. This is what Lediard calls, 'that eloquence and politeness that was natural to him'.[19] In his endeavours to persuade, cajole or charm his Allies into supporting his view of 'our Great Cause',[20] we must concede that he was not always successful, but on most occasions he was very able, and always did his best on behalf of his Queen, country, wife and, admittedly, himself. I believe him to have been a brilliant man, both as a negotiator and as a soldier. In 1704, with everything to win or lose for the Alliance, it was clearly important for him to gain the confidence and acceptance of the Allies in the growing crisis, otherwise Louis XIV would win the war. In June 1704 the Duke was not so famous as he would become later that year. He was hardly known in Vienna, and even less throughout the Great Holy Roman Empire.[21] Prince Louis-Guillaume, Margrave of Baden (1665–1707), was then aged 49 and was militarily senior to the Duke despite being younger. Marlborough was 54, but his martial abilities were hardly known, except as a young soldier under the great Turenne. Baden had served his apprenticeship under Montecuccoli and the Duke of Lorraine. He had won fame at Vienna in 1633, and won several battles against the Turks: at Nissa in 1689 and Salankamen in 1691. He had, however, been defeated by the French at Friedingen in 1702. As a result, Baden needed to be carefully handled. But whereas in the intricacies of international diplomacy John Churchill was only beginning a successful, ten-year diplomatic career of great achievements, Baden was already 'out of his depth'. The Duke is meant to have had secret orders to arrest Baden if it became necessary – or so it is believed. However, because of Marlborough's tact the necessity never arose and the Alliance avoided such a dramatic event which would have infuriated the Austrian troops. Although he had been handled carefully and skilfully during mid-1704, Baden would never forgive Marlborough for Blenheim, and the famous 'Margrave's foot' became a problem in 1705.

It is now time to study the 'Great Duke's' high command relationship with the Allies, and especially to describe the famous visit to Altranstadt in the spring of 1707. It came at the time of a huge crisis. For several years another great European war had been waged between Sweden and Russia and, although the Allies were not officially involved, there was a terrible danger that these two big international struggles might become linked into one vast all-purpose war similar to, if not worse in scale and devastation than, the notorious struggle of the Thirty Years War. After the shattering defeats of 1706 – Marlborough's triumph at Ramillies, his subsequent capture of half a dozen important fortifications and Eugene's victory at Turin – Louis XIV and his ministers were endeavouring to secure the safety of France and Spain by creating a diversion or second front, through drawing Sweden into the struggle. This would have been a disaster for all the aspirations of William III, Anne and Marlborough and could have brought the Alliance crashing down. The core problem of 1707 was the young, brilliant but uncertain Charles XII of Sweden's proposed invasion of Saxony, which would bring chaos to the Austrian Empire, scatter her 'south-facing' armies and leave the Dutch isolated apart from distant England.

Charles XII was a 'combatant-monarch' whose fame at that time eclipsed that of the 'Twin Captains', Marlborough and Eugene. He had succeeded to the Swedish throne in 1697 and his whole reign had been occupied with bitter wars against the Poles, Danes and, above all, the Russians.[22] A commander of great talent, he had won several amazing victories, including Narva in 1700 and Kissow in 1703, and by 1707 he was at the height of his power and reputation.[23] Some believed that he was obsessed by war, and Louis obviously believed he could easily become a willing pawn in yet another conflict. Marlborough, 'ever watchful, ever right' as Captain Parker styled him,[24] had a different idea and consequently set out to meet with this 'Northern Monarch' making a difficult journey to Altranstadt.

The roads of northern Germany were appalling. Marlborough went by coach and took six days from 20 to 26 April to plough through the deep mud and bounce over the innumerable rocks to prevent the merger of Europe's western and northern wars.

He had despatched messengers ahead to inform the Swedes of his arrival. He had expected a courteous welcome, to be met by Count Carl Piper, the King's most influential minister, and then to be conducted to meet Charles himself. However, when his coach drew up nothing happened. The English out-riders held their steaming and exhausted horses, patting their heads. The Duke stepped down from his coach and stretched while his servant dusted down his red uniform and straightened his wig and hat. But there was no sign of a formed special royal guard nor indeed any senior officers. There were neither generals nor trumpeters, only two Swedish sentinels marching slowly, backwards and forwards, outside the gate. Marlborough's staff were horrified by this snub and even suggested that the French Ambassador had bribed Piper to deliberately insult the Duke. Men held their breath. The Duke returned to his coach.

There are many legends and stories surrounding this inauspicious opening to such a prestigious international meeting upon which hung the future of Europe,[25] but the truth is even more amazing. When Piper at last condescended to come out and greet his important visitor, Marlborough, without saying a word, climbed out of his coach, walked away from Piper to the gate where, as Lediard had it, 'he went aside as if to make water'. When news of this spread, most of Europe applauded. The Duke was clearly ahead of Piper's games of oneupmanship. After this calculated gesture (or was it partially suppressed rage?) '. . . his point made, and feelings generally relieved, he was, at once, courtesy and affability itself'.[26] Upon gaining an audience with Charles XII, he spoke thus:

> Sire, I present to your Majesty a letter, not written from the Chancery, but from the heart of the Queen, my mistress, and written by her own hand. Had not her sex prevented her she would have crossed the seas to see a Prince admired by the whole universe. I am in this respect more happy than the Queen, and I wish I could serve some campaigns under so great a general as your Majesty, that I may learn what I yet want to know in the art of war.[27]

The meeting moved on and was a great success running over several days, 27–29 April. During that time, Piper too was persuaded to be charmed by the Duke who presented him with a gift of a pair of diamond ear-rings for his wife.[28] This was not exactly a bribe, for the gift was bestowed with the full knowledge and consent of Charles; more secret gifts of £1,000 each were given to Olef Harmelin and Josias Caderhielm, two influential Swedish officials.

I do not intend to discuss the details of those important discussions, let it only be said that Marlborough impressed the 25-year-old king and persuaded him to halt his advance into Saxony and to swing his armies eastwards and invade Russia.

Marlborough secured what he intended to gain: the War of Spanish Succession might be contemporary but it would not be merged with the Great Northern War, Louis XIV's Grand Strategy for the defence of France had been thwarted; the security of the Holy Roman Empire was preserved; Europe was spared an all-out struggle; and the Second Grand Alliance remained intact – thanks to the Duke's able negotiations.

Returning west, he paid a visit to Berlin for further discussions to ensure the Swedish–German struggle did not receive a new 'kickstart' from that quarter. The Great Duke was indeed 'Master of the Storm' of all Europe.

However, we must not imagine that Marlborough always got his way. To close, I mention the matter of General Frederick van Baer van Slangenberg. A Dutch senior officer, he had the powers of a Deputy and was attached to Marlborough's headquarters, where he proved a painful thorn in the Duke's flesh. This man was totally impervious to all Marlborough's charms and abilities. He was exceptionally jealous of him, and to such an extent that he appeared to possess an endless determination to ruin certain Allied plans in order to discredit him. Let me quote in full our friend Captain Robert Parker on 30 July 1705:

> Slangenberg was by this time grown so intolerably insolent that there was no bearing him; and because he was not consulted on all occasions he took all opportunity of thwarting the Duke. We were now drawn near the enemy and his Grace had sent orders that the English train of artillery should make all possible haste up to him; but, as they were just upon entering a narrow defile, Slangenberg came up to the head of them and stopped them for some hours, until his baggage had passed on before them, a thing never known before, even for the King's baggage. And it was this delay that prevented the Duke from attacking the enemy. Being disappointed by this means, he turned all thoughts on demolishing their lines, and taking both St. Luc and Xanvelt, tasks which he finished by the middle of October, and then sent the army into quarters.
>
> The Duke made a proper representation of Slangenberg's behaviour to the States-General, who, knowing the pride of the man, really laid hold of this opportunity, and sent him a dismiss.[29]

Before 'making representation', however, we can assume Marlborough often scorned and cursed the man for he also had a reputation for both. Although more than one important figure in European politics felt the lash of his tongue, he was adept at concealing his wrath. The Duke's 'silent rage' was well known by his assistants and I consider that this could have been one of the contributive causes that led to the sad strokes he suffered after 1713. Marlborough was able to master his temper just as he was able to muster his charm. His intellect, which enabled him to understand the implications and nuances of political situations, coupled with his ability to talk with people and lead them gradually to his point of view, made him the supreme controller of the Allies '. . . it was the sense of the whole army. Both officer and soldier, British and foreigner. And indeed we had all reason in the world for it, for he never led us on to any one action [and negotiation] that we did not succeed in'.

There is no denying that our period was a bellicose one; wars of one sort or another filled an approximate total of eighty-two years (taking overlaps into account) between 1688 and 1745. No countries were of course involved in all these struggles, but France was involved in thirty years of conflict, and Austria in all of sixty-three to a greater or lesser extent. The contemporary writer, Casimir Freschot, could justly assert that 'Peace is not always the condition of the world, and is found, if truth be told, only infrequently; and when we have it we do not keep it for long.'[30] But these long spans of near-perpetual war were interspersed with frequent periods of recourse to the conference table. As Professor Ragnhild Hatton has written:

> Negotiations for peace continued throughout the wars – sometimes sincerely meant, sometimes in the hope of breaking the cohesion of the powers ranged on the other side, sometimes for form's sake since it was generally accepted that not to listen to peace offers and a restoration of the *status quo ante bellum* rendered even a just war [i.e. one that the other side had started] unjust.[31]

As we have already seen, another motive for seeking a negotiated settlement was a tactit realisation that a dictated peace based upon an overwhelming military victory was out of the question, as the armies of the day could not achieve the necessary level of decisive success. This did not mean that pacifications were rapidly reached: long months and even years of negotiations all too often proved barren, and disputes over minor points of protocol or procedure could delay or even prevent the reaching of agreement. In the end, however, compromise settlements were arrived at, for 'There comes a time when even Kings have to agree to peace'.[32]

Wars in our period may broadly be said to have been fought out for three principal and overriding reasons: for security, for power, and for *la gloire*. This third reason earned the approval of the French political thinker, Raymond Aron, 'because each of the three terms corresponds to a concretely defined attitude while it also expresses a specific notion'.[33] The search for national or sometimes international security underlay the great Alliances masterminded by William III in his ceaseless attempts to confine the ambitions of France and to maintain a workable basis for the European balance of power. National security was also a matter of great concern for the Habsburgs in their intermittent but bitter struggles with the Ottoman Turks. As for the lust for power, it was one strand of motivation behind Louis XIV's seemingly insatiable territorial ambitions, although it is notable that it was at his suggestion that England and France tried to avert the coming crisis that would be unleashed when Charles II of Spain died by negotiating the Partition Treaties of 1698 and 1699. The hope proved vain – but it was probably genuine enough at the time of its inception.

Frederick II of Prussia entered Silesia in 1740 with deliberate intent to increase the power of Prussia at the expense of its Austrian neighbour – but for part of the War of the Austrian Succession, and for almost all the Seven Years War he fought with increasing desperation in the hope of obtaining a compromise peace when his foes came to appreciate that to beat him would take both vast effort and much time. In the latter struggle he had few illusions about Prussia's ability to conquer the Austro–Russian armies, but he determined to hold out until his opponents fell apart and until war-weariness could blunt both their reserves and morale.

Charles XII of Sweden's motives were largely aggressive. If the maintenance of the security of Sweden's homeland and South Baltic provinces might be invoked as a justifiable *casus belli* at the outset of the Great Northern War, it is not possible to interpret all his successive campaigns in this light. Here was a monarch who was a genuine 'war lord' in our period, whose dedication to the practice of the martial arts and sciences at times bordered on the near-insane.

The pursuit of *la gloire* was indubitably a major factor in the motivation of both the Baltic soldier-king and of le Roi Soleil. Aron concludes:

> Louis XIV probably loved glory as much as power. 'He wanted to be recognised as first amongst monarchs, and he made use of his force in order to seize a city and fortify it, but this half-symbolic exploit was still a way of showing his force. He did not conceive of a disproportionately enlarged France, furnished with resources superior to those of her allied rivals. He dreamed that the names of Louis XIV and of France would be transfigured by the admiration of nations.[34]

War was also regarded as the legitimate expression of the 'last argument of Kings', the ultimate tests for countries and dynasties alike. As Gustavus Adolphus had expressed this, at the time of the Thirty Years War, 'I recognise no one above me, except God and the sword of the conqueror'.

It was not, however, an age devoid of hope. The majority of both the men of action and the men of letters had at least a measure of belief in the possibility of human progress. The pessimism disseminated earlier in the seventeenth century by the horrors of the Thirty Years War –and so clearly reflected in the philosophical writings of Thomas Hobbes – gave place to the more positive ideals of John Locke. Scholars wrote of the rise and fall of successive empires instead of dwelling on the inevitable and rapid decline of hell-bent mankind. Belief in reason led to more optimistic concepts. Some monarchs genuinely attempted to introduce policies of domestic reform out of humanitarian as well as practical concern. Some equally genuinely attempted to avoid recourse to war and bloodshed with the intention of avoiding an increase in human misery and suffering. As

Professor Hatton remarked of the period 1680–1720, 'Wars were in any case more controlled'.[35] Better discipline, better (if still rudimentary) ideas of hygiene had improved the lot of soldier and civilian alike, whilst the general absence if ideological warfare did achieve something to lessen 'some of the terror of war'. A code of conduct was shared between the armies of Europe. The intense indignation when the gentlemanly conventions were transgressed is illustrated by the furore when the Flemish governor of Monzon, the Chevalier de Mous, was ungallant enough to fire cannon at 11 o'clock at night on the house where the Archduke Charles was quartered in 1710.[36] Far more typical was the courtesy of the French gunners who sent a flag of truce to William III's camp to enquire the exact location of his quarters so that they might avoid aiming at them.[37] But such gentlemanly courtesies and niceties must not disguise the fact that the wars of the period still brought misery, famine and pestilence in their train when the mask slipped – as in the case of the Palatinate, twice ravaged by French armies, or of Bavaria (subjected to military execution by Marlborough and Baden in July 1704), or again the burning of Altona by the Swedes in 1712. Such happenings, however, enraged the conscience of the age, as the protests they evoked demonstrated.

Fairly civilised may be the case. Nevertheless, England had its moments of fraud and amusement. As the Duke of Buckingham (having been removed from office by Queen Anne) said:

Good God! How has this poor Nation been governed in my time! During the reign of King Charles II we were governed by a parcel of French whores; in King James II's time by a parcel of Papist priests; in King William's time by a parcel of Dutch footmen; and now we are governed by a dirty chambermaid [Lady Masham], a Welsh attorney [Harley] and a profligate wretch [Bolingbroke] that has neither honour nor honesty.[38]

NOTES

1   See J House, *Winston Churchill – His Wit and Wisdom*, London (n.d.).
2   Captain Parker – see D G Chandler, *The Marlborough Wars*, London, 1968, p. 114.
3   See D G Chandler, *Marlborough as Military Commander*, Staplehurst, 1995, p. 25.
4   W S Churchill, *Marlborough: His Life and Times*, London, 1967 (pb edn).
5   G M Trevelyan, *England Under Queen Anne*, London, 1930.
6   J Childs, *The Nine Years War*, Manchester, 1991.
7   J R Jones, *Marlborough*, London, 1993.
8   A Guy, *Economy and Discipline 1714–1763*, Manchester, 1983.
9   R E Scouller, *The Armies of Queen Anne*, London, 1966.

10   Churchill, *op. cit.*, Vol. II, p. 21.
11   Alastair Buchan, comments on modern affairs, etc., *c.* 1956.
12   Churchill, *op. cit.*, Vol. I, pp. 403–4.
13   Chandler, *Marlborough as Military Commander*, Intro. pp. vi–vii.
14   *Ibid.*, pp. 5, 11, 12 & 258.
15   Churchill, *op. cit.*, Vol. I, pp. 424–5.
16   *Ibid.*, p. 412 & ff.
17   Chandler, *The Marlborough Wars*, pp 254 & 258.
18   Churchill, op. cit., Vol. II, p. 372.
19   T Lediard, *The Life of John, Duke of Marlborough*, London, 1736, Vol. I, pp. xvi–xxvi.
20   Churchill, *op. cit.*, Vol. II, pp. 447, 448 & 453; Vol. III, p. 19.
21   See N Henderson, *Prince Eugen of Savoy*, London, 1968; D McKay, *Prince Eugene of Savoy*, London, 1977.
22   See R M Hatton, *Charles XII of Sweden*, London, 1968.
23   *The New Cambridge Modern History*, Vol. VI, ed. J S Bromley, Cambridge, 1970, pp. 742–62. See Chapter XXI.
24   See Chandler *The Marlborough Wars*, p. 106.
25   Hatton, op. cit., pp. 224–7.
26   *Cf* Hatton, op. cit., p. 11; Churchill, op. cit., pp 157–60; Chandler, *Marlborough as Military Commander*, p. 292.
27   Lediard, *op. cit.*, Vol. II, pp. 151–81.
28   See R M Hatton, *Presents and Pensions, 1688–1709*, London, 1971.
29   See Chandler, *The Marlborough Wars*, pp. 56–7 & 257–8.
30   C Freschot, *Histoire du Congres et la Paix d'Utrecht*, Utrecht, 1716, p. 6.
31   R M Hatton, *War and Peace, 1680–1720* (An Inaugural Lecture), LSE, London, 1969, p. 6.
32   Freschot, *op. cit.*, Preface.
33   R Aron, *Peace and War*, London, 1966, p. 73.
34   *Ibid.*, footnote 19.
35   R M Hatton, *War and Peace*, p. 11.
36   D Francis, *The First Peninsular War* (London, 1974), p. 309.
37   N A Robb, *William of Orange*, London, 1966, Vol. II, pp. 61–2.
38   Churchill, *op. cit.*, Vol. IV, p. 512.

CHAPTER XVII
England's Greatest Soldier
A Final Consideration

The Great Captain-General was extremely professional and practical in all military matters. As we know well, although tired-out but triumphant, on the evening of 13 August 1704 he decided to write immediately to his wife, Sarah, in England in order to inform the Queen of his great victory. As we shall see, his message of triumph was written down on an old tavern bill and entrusted to his senior aide-de-camp, Colonel Parke, with instructions to ride as rapidly as possible across Europe to England. The messenger found Sarah on 21 August at St James's in London. She summoned her carriage at once, taking the exhausted Parke with her to Windsor where the Queen was staying. Thus the Queen had news of the great victory near the Danube before any reports reached the hands of her ministers.

It was clearly impossible for the Duke to return immediately to England, and indeed he only arrived there by ship from Holland to Greenwich on 14 December 1704. With him he brought Marshal Tallard, fifteen other French Generals and twenty more Colonels as prisoners-of-war. With the Duke too came the captured standards and colours – half of the overall tally fell to the Duke's share because the rest were carried by Prince Eugene to Vienna. Of course, Marlborough needed three months before returning to England. He not only had to pursue the enemy back to the Rhine, where the Allies captured the fortresses of Treves, Landau and Trarbach (which did not fall until 20 December), but he had diplomatic missions to complete as well as other army business affairs to settle in Berlin, Hanover and The Hague – especially trying to draw up plans for the next spring campaign. We must never forget that as well as Captain-General of the Anglo–Dutch Field Army he was also the main architect and behind all the international scheming and cementing of the Grand Alliance.

On 3 January 1705 all 128 French and Bavarian standards and colours were brought from the Tower of London and carried in triumph through the City to Westminster Hall, with the Queen watching the parade. Three days later, Marlborough and those of his officers in England were given a banquet by the Lord Mayor and the alderman in Goldsmiths' Hall. Parliament thanked the Duke for his achievements throughout the year and

Admiral Rooke was also saluted for having captured Gibraltar. For all immediate purposes, France was crushed, all England was in triumph, and the rest of Europe was amazed by the events of 1704.

The Duke's admiring soldiers called him 'the old Corporal'. His enemies, the French and Spaniards, were almost equally respectful. Louis Josef, Duke of Vendôme,[1] noted with disquiet after the Battle of Ramillies in 1706 that everyone at French headquarters in Valenciennes 'is only too ready to raise their hats at the mention of Marlborough's name'. This was the type of respect only rarely awarded by fighting soldiers – the adulatory respect evidenced for Napoleon, for Stonewall Jackson by both sides in the American Civil War, and for Rommel by the British Eighth Army in the Second World War are perhaps the nearest equivalents.

All the same, John Churchill, Duke of Marlborough, certainly had his fair share of critics and downright foes; his High Tory opponents dubbed him 'King John II' – a scathing reference to his long-sought but never-attained lifetime appointment to the Captaincy-General.

Ironically, one of the Duke's bitterest critics lined up on his side of the battlefield. It was the Dutch Deputy Sicco Van Goslinga[2] who left this penetrating analysis of Marlborough's character.

> His mind is clear and subtle, his judgment both keen and sound, his insight quick and deep, with an all-embracing knowledge of men which no false show of merit can deceive. He expresses himself well, and even his very bad French is agreeable; he has a harmonious voice, and as a speaker of his own language he is considered amongst the best. His address is most courteous, and while his handsome and well-graced countenance engages everyone in his favour at first glance, his perfect manners and gentleness win over even those who start with a prejudice or grudge against him. He has courage as he has shown on more than one occasion; he is an experienced soldier and plans a campaign to admiration. So far his good qualities. Now for the weak points which I consider I have discovered in him. The Duke is a profound dissembler, all the more dangerous that his manner and his words give the impression of frankness itself. His ambition knows no bounds, and an avarice I can only call sordid guides his entire conduct ... Sometimes on the eve of action he is irresolute or worse; he will not face difficulties, and occasionally lets reverses cast him down ... He is not a strict disciplinarian and allows his men too much rein, who have occasionally indulged in frightful excesses. Moreover he lacks the precise knowledge of military detail which a Commander-in-Chief should possess. But these defects are light when balanced against the rare gifts of this truly great man.

The opinion of Voltaire[3] is also of interest:

> He had, to a degree above all other generals of his time, that calm courage in the midst of tumult, that serenity of soul in danger, which the English call a *cool head*, and it was, perhaps, this quality, the greatest gift of nature for command, which formerly gave the English so many advantages over the French in the plains of Crécy, Poitiers, and Agincourt.

The struggle that will always be mainly associated with Marlborough's name was the War of the Spanish Succession (1701–14), which came about after Charles II of Spain died in 1700. At the time, Spain's holding included the Spanish Netherlands (today Belgium), the Spanish Milanese in northern Italy, and the kingdom of the Two Sicilies (Naples and Sicily) as well as the Philippines and vast areas of South America. If this huge Spanish inheritance fell into the hands of one single European country, it would destroy the fragile balance of power that William III had spent most of his life trying to set up.

Two partition treaties, dividing up the Spanish Empire had been signed while ailing Charles II still lived. On his deathbed, however, he renounced them by dictating a will that left the entire inheritance in both the New and the Old Worlds to Philip, Duke of Anjou[4] (a grandson of Charles's brother-in-law, King Louis XIV of France).

Louis XIV, the ageing 'Sun King', immediately reneged on his agreements, on the one hand to uphold the partition treaties, and on the other to respect the will by keeping Spain separate from France; he promptly sent troops to occupy twenty fortresses in the Spanish Netherlands, in direct contravention of an earlier treaty. Worse, in September 1701 he proceeded formally to recognise the Old Pretender – the son of King James II of England (who had just died in French exile) – as rightful King of England.

These tactless actions set the cat among the pigeons with a vengeance, and the Second Grand Alliance was duly drawn up by England, the United Provinces (Holland), and Austria (Archduke Charles was the rival claimant to the throne of Spain). Most of the Holy Roman Empire followed Austria's lead (except Bavaria and Cologne, which declared for Philip V of Spain), and in 1703 Savoy and Portugal also joined the alliance. Thus were drawn the battle lines for twelve years of war.

Once England declared war (15 May 1702), Marlborough's prime responsibility was to ensure the continued cohesion of the Alliance – of which he was, as his descendant Winston Churchill later wrote, merely 'the informal chairman of a discordant committee'.[5] Associated with these 'grand strategic' roles was the need to influence Queen Anne (who had ascended the throne in March 1702 on William's death) and to walk the tightrope of Stuart Court and Parliamentary politics, balancing Whigs against Tories and striving to avoid becoming too closely associated with any one faction.

Marlborough was also called upon for ten years in succession to lead in person the major Allied army in the field, conceiving strategies acceptable to his confederates, making grand tactical and operational plans for all major campaigns, and supervising the multitude of administrative and logistic problems involved in keeping eighteenth-century armies in the field for six to eight months a year. All of this amounted to a crippling load of responsibilities, and the high degree of overall success that he achieved before the personal political cataclysm of late 1711 ended his career attests to his standing as both statesman and soldier.

Marlborough's rise to prominence came late in life. He was 52 when he first received widespread recognition in 1702. (Napoleon and Wellington, by comparison, were both 46 at Waterloo.) Most soldiers of the early eighteenth century were retired by their mid 50s, but Marlborough was still literally in the saddle at age 62. At the battle of Ramillies on 23 May 1706, the 56-year-old Duke was twenty hours on horseback. Small wonder he suffered from blinding migraines – 'dizziness in my head' – both before and after major crises. Before Oudenarde two years later, he was 'much indisposed and feverish'; by 1710 he was becoming 'sensible of the inconvenience of old age'; and in 1711 he mentions 'frequent and sensible remembrances of my growing old'. Yet he remained to the last the greatest general of his day. He was clearly a tough man beneath his courtly exterior – but, as Goslinga noted, there were certain limitations. John Churchill's earlier career had been varied and fluctuating. Born in 1650, the eldest surviving son of a Royalist Devonshire gentleman in the ruinous aftermath of the Civil War, he grew up in impecunious circumstances. Five years after the restoration of King Charles[6] in 1660, he become a page to the King's brother, James, Duke of York, thanks to his plain elder sister's influence as the Duke's mistress. In 1667 he received a commission in the Foot Guards, and alternated periods of military duty with long sojourns at the very worldly and corrupt Stuart Court. He served against the North African Moors as a member of the garrison of Tangier, was promoted to captain of marines in the Admiralty Regiment after the naval battle of Solebay (where the Duke of York fought the Dutch fleet in May 1672), and then began to learn 'the bless'd trade'[7] on the continent under French tutelage. His valorous conduct at the siege of Maastricht in 1673 attracted the attention of Louis XIV, and he was promoted colonel the next year.

Service under the great Marshal Turenne proved a vital formative period, and the Frenchman prophesied a distinguished military career for his 'handsome Englishman'. During these years the future scourge of the French armies studied the characteristics of other emerging young French officers, including Boufflers, Villeroi and Vendôme, who would one day be his enemies.

Life at Court between campaigns was at times decidedly risky. He shared the favours of Barbara Villiers, Duchess of Cleveland,[8] with the King himself on what was almost a 'shift and shift about' basis and once nearly got caught in flagrante delicto by his monarch. Churchill received substantial sums from this easygoing lady, which helped him purchase military promotions (as remained the custom in the British Army down to 1871). Then in 1677 he fell in love with 17-year-old Sarah Jennings, the favourite of Princess (later Queen) Anne, and after a storybook courtship (which both families opposed), he married her. It was a genuine, lifelong love match, although Sarah's violent temper, shrewish tongue, and Whig politics would prove to be no small embarrassment in later years, and indeed contributed to his downfall. Together they brought up a large family (of which only the girls survived). Churchill was clearly an ardent lover; Sarah told a confidante that on one return from the wars 'my lord pleasured me twice with his boots on'.

For the rest he continued to serve his patron, the Duke of York; and after the Duke came to the throne as James II in 1685, Churchill served the King as second-in-command in the short but decisive Sedgemoor campaign – the last pitched battle on English soil – helping the Earl of Feversham defeat his old friend, the Protestant Duke of Monmouth (an illegitimate son of Charles II) when the latter tried to remove his Catholic uncle from the throne. Three years later, however, Churchill abandoned the King during the Glorious Revolution, transferring his sword to William of Orange at the crucial moment. He claimed that his action was prompted by his Protestant conscience, but this deed of turncoat ingratitude nonetheless left a lasting slur on his reputation.

William III made him Earl of Marlborough, but his fortunes fluctuated wildly. William's wife, Mary II, was the sister of Princess Anne and actively disliked the Marlborough influence over her. The new King welcomed Marlborough's useful military service in Flanders and then in Ireland but distrusted his influence over the English part of the Anglo-Dutch Army. William preferred Dutch favourites[9] and (with justice) suspected the Earl of maintaining links with the former James II in exile.

Marlborough was no better and no worse than many another unscrupulous 'trimmer' at this time, but it earned him a spell as a prisoner in the Tower of London in 1692, and in 1694 he stood accused (probably rightly) of betraying a rival general's plans for what turned out to be a disastrous amphibious raid against Camaret Bay on the French coast – another charge that had pursued him down the centuries. William – who believed the accusation – for a time refused to employ him at home or abroad, and he took no part in the King's major campaigns against France. It even seemed that his military career might effectively be over. If this had been the case, he might well have gone down in history as a soldier-courtier of average ability but endowed with an extraordinary gift for intrigue.

However, after the death of Queen Mary in 1694, and most particularly after the death of William's heir (his sister-in-law's only son, the Duke of Gloucester) in August 1700, Marlborough became steadily reconciled to William, who realised the part the Marlboroughs, man and wife, were likely to play when Princess Anne succeeded to the throne. Marlborough was accordingly made commander of the English troops on the Continent and was employed on vital diplomatic missions. He earned golden opinions for his tactful persuasiveness as the war clouds gathered following the death of Charles II of Spain that same year. The first aggressive French move, against the fortresses in the Spanish Netherlands, had already taken place and Louis XIV and Philip V were already at war with Austria when, on 8 March 1702, William III died.

For the Marlboroughs, their great day had now dawned. Sarah was appointed mistress of the robes to the new Queen, and Marlborough was made a knight of the Garter and master-general of the Board of Ordnance as well as Captain-General over all English troops at home and abroad. At last, on 4 May 1702,[10] England declared war on France and Spain. For Marlborough, ten years of challenge and opportunity, of frustration and achievement, lay ahead. Between 1702 and 1711 he would emerge as the foremost soldier-statesman of his day.

His first two campaigns were fought along the Rhine and the Meuse rivers in broadly conventional fashion, centring upon a siege or two in order to secure the southern flank of the United Provinces. In late 1702 Queen Anne made him Duke for services rendered, but to date these had been unspectacular though worthy enough. In 1704, however, Marlborough revealed his true ability. Afraid that French successes on the Danube would expose Vienna to attack and thus imperil the entire Grand Alliance, he fooled friend and foe alike by marching 250 miles in some five weeks (a record for that era) across Europe to the Danube. He started with 21,000 men but reached the theatre with over 40,000, having picked up Dutch, Hanoverian and Danish allied contingents en route. As a camp follower named Mother Ross recorded, the Duke' seeing some of our Foot drop through the fatigue of the march, took them into his own coach'.

At Gross Heppach he met up with the brilliant (and far younger) Prince Eugene of Savoy and the less inspiring senior Elector of Baden[11] (who was also younger than the Duke). Eugene, an Austrian soldier of Italian–French lineage, had made an immense reputation in wars against the Turks in Hungary. He and Marlborough henceforth developed a remarkable relationship of trust and mutual appreciation, which stood the Alliance in good stead in three of Marlborough's four great battles that were to follow.

With a joint army of some 100,000 men, the Allies now set about defeating the Elector of Bavaria, France's ally, before French reinforcements could arrive to help him. On 2 July they successfully stormed Schellenberg Hill above Donauwörth, thereby gaining a bridgehead over the Danube, from which they set out to drive Bavaria out of the war. In this the Allies failed, and Bavaria's junction with Tallard's army from Strasbourg duly took place at Augsburg in early August, changing the whole complexion of the campaign.

In danger of being isolated south of the Danube, Marlborough sent off the senior but hesitant Baden with 25,000 men to besiege Ingolstadt, and marched hard with the remainder to rejoin Eugene (who had been shadowing Tallard's approach) north of the Danube. There, on 13 August, they forced action on an unsuspecting Tallard at Blenheim. By a display of the greatest tactical mastery, they defeated him completely, inflicting almost 40,000 casualties, against a loss of 12,883 Allies.[12]

This battle reversed the trend of the war, saved Vienna, and by the campaign's close carried the war over the Rhine onto French soil. Europe applauded an outstanding achievement, and Marlborough emerged permanently from obscurity, sharing the praise with his 'twin captain', Prince Eugene, who had willingly taken second place in the battle. A revealing anecdote by the contemporary historian, Thomas Lediard, tells of Marlborough, sorry for Tallard, whose son had been killed, inviting his prisoner to inspect the Allied army. This he glumly did. Then, says Lediard, he turned to say that his courteous captor had 'the honour of having vanquished the best troops in the world', to which the Duke replied, 'What, then, will the world say of those who beat them?'

The next seven campaigns, from 1704 to 1711, were all fought in Flanders and the Spanish Netherlands. Rich cities, strong fortress systems, fertile country, and strategic placement between northern France and the north German plain made the area a favourite site for wars over at least five centuries. Marlborough's plans to transfer the major seat of war to the Moselle in order to turn the French fortress line were foiled in 1705, and a disappointing campaign ensued, Allied support being both tardy and unwillingly given, particularly by Baden, who was furious at his exclusion from the glory of Blenheim the previous year.

The next year Marlborough's intention of transferring his army to Eugene's aid on the important front in northern Italy was foiled, by a French campaign on the central Rhine, which effectively blocked his line of march. Undaunted, Marlborough proceeded to win a battle south-east of Brussels at Ramillies on 23 May.[13] This victory – possibly his greatest – led to the conquest of almost all the Spanish Netherlands before the year was out. Meanwhile Prince Eugene won the equally impressive Battle of Turin in northern Italy, making 1706 indeed the 'annus mirabilis' for the Grand Alliance.

Alas, 1707 proved a frustrating year for both the 'twin generals'. The members of the Grand Alliance again seemed incapable of cooperating effectively for two years in a row. But all was redeemed again in 1708 when Marlborough and Eugene, together once more, won the Battle of Oudenarde on 11 July, after a daring forced march with 80,000 men. They took the 85,000 men under Marshal Vendôme and the Duke of Burgundy by surprise, crossing the Scheldt under the incredulous French gaze. 'If they are there, the Devil must have carried them. Such marching is impossible!' was Vendôme's reaction to the news of the Allied arrival near the river.

The campaign continued with the greatest siege of the period, that of Lille (Marshal Vauban's[14] masterpiece of military engineering) from 12 August to 10 December, when Marshal Boufflers at last surrendered. There followed the recapture of Bruges and Ghent before the Allies at last entered winter quarters after an unprecedentedly long campaign, Marlborough once again sharing the honours with Eugene.

France appeared to be beaten as famine and despair spread. Peace talks opened, but the Allied terms were too harsh, so in 1709 the Allies moved deeper into France, Marlborough and Eugene again campaigning as a team. Tournai was besieged and taken (27 June to 3 September), followed by Mons (beginning on 9 September). Then Marshal Villars[15] – perhaps the best of Louis XIV's later commanders – who had achieved miracles in restoring the morale of the French Army, moved with 85,000 men to attempt to raise the siege. He was met at Malplaquet on 12 September by the Allied army, 110,000 men strong. But Villars had been afforded time to fortify their position, and although the Allies won the battle, it cost them 24,000 casualties; the French (who retired in good order at the end of the day) suffered 12,500 casualties. 'We have had,' Marlborough wrote, 'a very bloody battle . . . it is now in our power to have what peace we please, and I may be pretty well assured of never being in another battle'. Mons eventually fell (on 20 October), and the campaign came to an unmourned end.

In England, meanwhile, the Whig government had given way to a High Tory one, and the Queen was fast transferring her affections and trust from the Duchess Sarah to Mrs Abigail Masham, one of her ladies. The new government, hostile to Marlborough personally and horrified by Malplaquet's casualties, induced the Queen to impose restraints on the Duke. As a result, 1710's campaign saw little action apart from the siege and capture of Douai, Béthune, St-Venant and Aire between April and November.

Meanwhile, the French national recovery proceeded apace, and Allied discord grew. Marlborough's last campaign, however, included a masterly crossing of the lines of 'Ne Plus Ultra' – a defensive position that Villars had constructed – which led to Marlborough's final military virtuoso performance, the siege of Bouchain (9 August–12 September 1711). Despite the proximity of Marshal Villars with a large, strongly encamped army at Cambrai virtually watching the operations, Marlborough and his senior engineer, Colonel John Armstrong,[16] achieved the seemingly impossible – crossing a wide marsh to get close to the fortress, while Villars dared not move to attack.

In all, Marlborough fought and won four major battles, two important engagements, and some thirty sieges – all in the span of ten years of campaigning. But it must be noted that he never managed to win the war outright, and his successors in command were soon privy to the negotiations leading to the Treaty of Utrecht (1713), by which Great Britain reneged on its Allies in return for substantial colonial acquisitions. For this, however, Marlborough was in no way responsible; he was living abroad in exile at the time following his abrupt dismissal from all his offices by Queen Anne, and his political foes' efforts to have him impeached in Parliament for alleged misappropriation of 'bread money' (for ration purchase).

It is also true that on a full dozen favourable occasions between 1701 and 1712, he failed to give battle. But this was due to the powers of veto wielded by the Dutch field deputies (virtual political commissars),[17] who were always at his elbow, and in later years to the restrictions placed on him by his home government. As his great descendent, Winston Churchill, found out to his cost when the electorate turned his government out of office in mid-1945, 'there is no such thing as gratitude in public life'.

Yet he was a master at compelling unwilling enemies to fight and showed an admirable flair for manoeuvring (passing his army unscathed through strong lines of fortified positions in both 1705 and 1711 and displaying a notable ability for all the convolutions of siege warfare). He also found time in his overloaded schedule for complex negotiations, for administration, and for affording political guidance to the lord treasurer, his lifelong friend, Sidney Godolphin.[18] It amounted to an impossible burden for one man to shoulder for a decade without respite. In the end he failed to secure his political base. But it was the failure of a giant surrounded by pygmies.

What were his specific strengths as a 'great commander'? First, we must consider his showing at the level of 'grand strategy' responsibilities, which included national policy formulation and overall Alliance strategy. Working at home through the 'Winter Committee' (a group of influential ministers who met under his unofficial chairmanship between campaigns during the winter), and by means of a ceaseless round of tiring visits to Allied courts throughout Europe, he managed to preserve the basic cohesion of the Grand Alliance. He also kept it moving toward its overall goal of putting an end to French and Spanish pretensions to European – and world – hegemony, and meanwhile ensured that no newcomers should enter the struggle and thus imperil the delicate balance of power.

Not the least of his contributions to the 'common cause' was his diplomatic visit to Altranstadt in April 1707, which dissuaded the maverick soldier-monarch Charles XII of Sweden from intervening.[19]

In one area Marlborough made a grave mistake. By never pressing his doubts about the advisability of prosecuting the costly and ineffective campaigns in Spain – much demanded by the Whigs and Austrians – he doomed the confederacy to cope with a 'Spanish ulcer' as draining as any experienced by Napoleon in the Peninsula a century later.

Following the Allied disaster in 1707 at Almanza,[20] Marlborough should have spoken out and denounced the continuation of the Iberian campaign. Instead he chose to hold his peace, with incalculable long-term effects on the prosecution of the war – which in the end permitted the royal houses of Bourbon (French and Spanish) to survive the storm in better shape than would otherwise have been possible.

For the most part, however, Marlborough maintained a remarkable grasp of the broad issues and problems involved in the struggle. From its inception he could see the war as a whole – a vision shared by few contemporaries. So non-existent was the general appreciation of the simplest rudiments of strategy that it was possible for serious Members of Parliament to declare that he had 'stolen the army' when in the spring of 1704 he transferred the English battalions and squadrons from the Netherlands to the Danube theatre of war.

As a strategist – or planner of campaigns – Marlborough again proved far-sighted and inspired, despite the limitations placed on him by doubting governments and hesitant Allies. Only once – in 1704 – was he able to fool everyone and wage a campaign wholly of his own devising. It can be claimed that he was at his best when campaigning defensively. His first two campaigns, with those of 1704, 1706 and 1708, were fought largely to neutralise earlier enemy gains and retrieve lost ground. Those of 1705, 1707, 1709 and 1710 – fought offensively – tended to produce less dramatic results. However, his handling of the post-Ramillies follow-through was almost as good as Napoleon's after Jena-Auerstädt in 1806 – proving his ability to exploit an unexpected opportunity to the fullest.

A similar opportunity arose after Oudenarde[21] two years later. This time he wished to march well into France along the north coast, bypassing the French fortress barrier, abandoning his land lines of communication, and relying for supply upon the Anglo–Dutch fleet. This 'Great Descent' was too bold a concept for even such a bright spirit as Prince Eugene to grasp and entertain; and Marlborough, aware (again like Napoleon) that at the highest level 'war, like politics, is a matter of tact', had to gracefully accept the lesser course of action – namely the long and costly siege of Lille.

But considering the problems he faced – Allied contingents turning up late (as in the springs of 1704, 1705 and 1707); allied selfishness in prosecuting costly but useless extra campaigns (for example, the Austrian attack on Naples in 1707); and the Dutch concern for their own territorial security as well as their desire to keep both their manpower and their silver guilders to a minimum – it is amazing that he achieved so much.

He was also unique for the time in his appreciation of the significance of seapower used in close support of a Continental war. Early experience aboard the fleet had convinced him of the value of a navy deployed in support of a large army fighting in Europe, employing coastal raiding and larger 'descents' to distract enemy resources from other theatres of war. If this policy had its failures (as at Cádiz in 1702 and Toulon in 1707), it also had its successes (such as the fortuitous capture of Gibraltar by Admiral Sir George Rooke in 1704 and the deliberate capture of Minorca four years later). These gains firmly established Allied naval control over the western Mediterranean.

The imaginative – albeit abortive – concept after Oudenarde of the 'Great Descent', outlined above, also included the seizure of Abbeville by an amphibious attack ahead of the main army, thus providing it with a secure resupply depot before it turned down the Somme toward Paris and Versailles. Marlborough's ability to conceive such bold strategic schemes marrying military and naval concepts illustrates that he was in many ways ahead of his time.

At the grand tactical (or operational) level – the planning of major operations of war to achieve the declared strategic objectives – the Duke also showed the greatest ability. As Hilaire Belloc wrote of generalship, 'the test does not lie so much in the general conception as in the execution of a plan'. Marlborough proved highly adept at deducing his foes' intentions, and then used forced marches under cover of night to confound them. This he did before the Battle of Blenheim, Ramillies and Oudenarde. He also possessed a keen eye for ground, and often used concealed valleys to spring tactical surprises as at Ramillies in 1706, and again in 1708 at Oudenarde.

And was adept at devising unusual lines of battle – as is amply demonstrated by the four-formations-deep array of the allied centre and six-deep deployment of Lord John Cutts' left wing at Blenheim. His adaptability helped him to mass strength at critical points and to fight both fluid, mobile battles, such as Oudenarde, and static, more formalised ones, such as Blenheim and Malplaquet. At all stages he insisted on the proper combination and coordination of horse, foot and guns. He also made a point of keeping large forces of cavalry in reserve, ready to deliver the *coup de grâce*.

Typically, Marlborough developed an action from probing attacks to stronger onslaughts against selected points, sometimes on the flanks (as at

Ramillies) and sometimes in the centre (as against Oberglau village at Blenheim). These were designed to draw in enemy reserves and weaken the enemy battle line at the point already selected for the main attack by superior forces. The enemy line once sundered – as by the second great cavalry charge at both Blenheim and Malplaquet, or by the knocking out of the 'hinge' in the enemy's right-angled line at Ramillies – the battle was almost won. But it still remained to convert the foe's defeat into total rout.

Here Marlborough's penchant for the immediate, all-out, cavalry-led pursuit came into its own when feasible. After both Ramillies and Oudenarde, the exploitation was immediate and remorseless. After Blenheim, the follow-up was initially delayed by the large numbers of prisoners and wounded to be dealt with, but once started it never faltered until the Rhine had been reached and crossed. After sanguinary Malplaquet, there were no fresh troops available.

A major grand-tactical problem shared by all commanders of the day was that of imposing overall control over a battle area several miles in extent and much obscured by black-powder smoke. Marlborough was famous for his knack of turning up at critical times and places as if guided by superhuman knowledge. In fact his secret was use of carefully selected aides-de-camp and 'running footmen' whose task was to report on what was happening at every sector, using their own judgement, as well as to carry messages forward from the Duke. Similar methods were used by Wellington and Montgomery in later centuries – but once again it was Marlborough who first developed the idea of using such 'eyes' to help him keep a sure finger on the pulse of the battle.

If Marlborough had a fault at this level of warfare, it was that he became predictable – as did Napoleon after 1809. His preference for delivering the major blow against a carefully prepared enemy centre became evident after Blenheim and Ramillies. Marshal Villars, a Gascon commander of great ability who in later life was made one of only four marshal-generals of France, was the first to exploit this knowledge, at Malplaquet on 11 September 1709.

Though defeated, the French at least shared the honours of the day, as a weary Marlborough and Prince Eugene were the first to gallantly acknowledge.

In the case of his sieges, of course, Marlborough was bound by the conventions of the science of siegecraft, but the operations he devised to cover the complicated sieges of Lille and Bouchain were outstanding examples of the military art. In the first case (in 1708) he repelled five separate French attempts to raise the siege of 'Vauban's masterpiece' – somehow always ensuring that his supply convoys came through, even when it involved small-scale naval engagements over flooded areas where special carts with larger wheels also had to be provided. At Bouchain (in 1711) he masterminded the storming of the 'cow path' that ran through the marshes by getting his men to advance waist-deep in the mud, the larger men carrying the smaller ones on their shoulders.[22]

As for the passing of lines, he proved a master at fooling the defenders about his proposed point of crossing, through cunning feints, campfires left burning in abandoned camps, and sheer marching speed. 'Milord Duke desires that the Foot shall step out' was an order to which the rank and file responded with a will. Marshal Villeroi was fooled at the Lines of Brabant in July 1705 in this way, and similar treatment was meted out six years later at 'Ne Plus Ultra' to the far abler Villars, who had boasted that 'nothing further was possible' for the Allies against the series of lines he had constructed.

Marlborough placed great reliance on personal reconnaissance of the enemy's pre-battle dispositions – as when he mounted Tapfheim church spire the day before Blenheim. He also made full use of Quartermaster General William Cadogan's[23] intelligence service, and drew much information from a well-placed agent high in the French government, who to this day has eluded identification – a veritable 'Ultra' source. His nephew, the French Marshal James Fitzjames, Duke of Berwick, was also used unwittingly to good purpose, as were tenuous links with the Jacobite (or Stuart) royal family in exile. Marlborough was a formidable opponent.

The Duke's interest and skills also extended to minor tactics. Where the cavalry was concerned, he insisted on their use of cold steel in battle and made sure of it by withdrawing almost all their pistol powder. He also withdrew their armour backplates. Where the 'poor foot' was concerned, he insisted on the adoption of the 'platoon firing system', which conferred considerable advantages of fire control, preparedness, continuity and psychological effect over the French, who still employed battalion, company or line volleys. As Master-General of the Ordnance, he paid special attention to the siting of the guns, encouraged aggressive use of them (as against Taviers village at Ramillies), and ordered that each infantry battalion be equipped with two light pieces by way of what would today be called 'a support company'. For ammunition and supplies he insisted on light, two-wheeled waggons for the army, greatly increasing its speed of movement. His welding of horse, foot, guns and supply services into effective combat teams proved a major factor in achieving success.

He almost always seized the initiative in battle, and he conducted his engagements aggressively, using fire to cover forward movement and even having heavy field guns manhandled over marshy streams. At the crisis around Oberglau at Blenheim, for example, Colonel Holcroft Blood's bringing up of eight guns over the Nebel brook gave the Allies the edge that they needed to rout the hard-fighting Irish Catholic exiles (the 'Wild Geese') who were threatening to drive several Germanic battalions back into the water. All in all, Marlborough's ability to orchestrate the development of a major battle proved to be one of his greatest attainments as a general.

No wonder the French 'raised their hats' at the mention of his name. He brought the reputation of the British arms to a higher level than they had enjoyed since Agincourt in the Middle Ages. How disappointing, then, to be removed from command of the army because of political intrigue by his enemies. But even one of the bitterest of these Tory opponents, Henry St John, Viscount Bolingbroke, who did much to help Robert Harley,[24] Earl of Oxford, bring down the great man in 1711, could not forbear from admitting his greatness. Indeed, after Marlborough's death, Bolingbroke agreed to write the famous panegyric inscribed at the base of the Duke's column that still towers in Blenheim Park.

> These are the acts of the Duke of Marlborough, performed in the compass of few years; sufficient to adorn the annals of ages. The admiration of other nations will be conveyed to latest posterity in the histories even of the enemies of Britain.[25]

But let us leave the final word to that 'hard-marching captain of foot', as Winston Churchill has described him – Robert Parker.

> As to the Duke of Marlborough (for I cannot forbear giving him in precedence), it was allowed by all men, nay even by France itself, that he was more than a match for all the generals of that nation. This he made appear beyond contradiction, in the ten campaigns he made against them; during all of which time it cannot be said that he ever slipped an opportunity of fighting, when there was any probability of coming at his enemy; and upon all occasions he concerted matters with so much judgement and forecast, that he never fought a battle which he did not gain, nor laid siege to a town which he did not take.

Once, shortly before his death in 1722, Marlborough was observed in the still unfinished Blenheim Palace to halt before the portrait of him in the full pride of his youth, painted by Sir Godfrey Kneller. The words he sadly uttered then form a fitting epitaph: 'This', he declared, 'this was once a man'. England has never produced a greater soldier.

NOTES

1   The Duc de Vendôme (1654–1712) was in fact an excellent commander, but was never received as a Marshal.
2   See D G Chandler, *Marlborough as Military Commander*, London, 1973, pp. 27, 69 & 318.
3   François Voltaire (1694–1778) was a brilliant French author.

4   Philip, Duke of Anjou, grandson of Louis XIV, became King of Spain in 1700 following the death of Charles II of Spain. He was crowned Philip V (1700–46).
5   W S Churchill, *Marlborough: His Life and Times*, London, 1967 (pb edn), Vol. III, p. 37. The Duke was very patient with his Allies.
6   King Charles II (Monarch of England, 1660–85).
7   Shakespeare, *Henry V*, Act II, Chorus, v. 1.
8   The Duchess of Cleveland (1640–1709), who had seven bastard children.
9. Including Prince Waldeck and Godart de Ginkel, Earl of Athlone.
10 After the death of James II, Louis XIV recognised the 'Old Pretender' as King of England.
11 Prince Baden (1655–1707) took part in twenty-six European battles.
12 Churchill, *op. cit.*, Vol. II, p. 372.
13 Probably Marlborough's best battle in 1706. Prince Eugene shared his other three major engagements, including Blenheim. Eugene, Prince of Savoy was one of the greatest commanders of the period (and was acknowledged by Napoleon as such).
14 Marshal Vauban (1613–1707). The siege of Lille began on 12 August 1708, with Marshal Boufflers (1644–1711) in command.
15. Marshal-General Villars (1653–1734) was an accomplished French Commander.
16 John Armstrong (1674–1742) was the Duke's chief engineer officer.
17 For example, Goslinga.
18 Sidney Godolphin (1645–1712) was Marlborough's closest friend.
19 King Charles XII of Sweden (1682–1718) fought against Russia.
20 The Battle of Almanza (25 April 1707) was won by the French Marshal Berwick (1670–1734), Marlborough's nephew, against Galway.
21 The Battle of Oudenarde (11 July 1708). Marlborough and Eugene defeated the Duke of Burgundy (1682–1712) and Vendôme.
22 See Captain Parker, *The Marlborough Wars* London, 1968.
23 General William Cadogan (1675–1726) was Marlborough's Quartermaster-General (or Chief-of-Staff, though no such title existed then).
24 Robert Harley, Earl of Oxford (1661–1724) persuaded Queen Anne to dismiss Marlborough.
25 Henry St John, Viscount Bolingbroke (1678–1751). Although he was Marlborough's enemy, he was asked by Sarah to compose the panegyric at Blenheim Palace.

EPILOGUE
The Queen and the Captain-General

Blenheim Palace is a marvellous place. Of course the Great Duke never saw the completed building, but his Duchess, Sarah, certainly saw it and lived in it for many years, as she died in 1744. The book, *Blenheim Palace* (1951) by David Green is both a useful and important work, so too are his other works. His *Sarah, Duchess of Marlborough* (1967), *Blenheim* (1974), *Queen Anne* (1950), *Grindling Gibbons* (1964) and *Gardener to Queen Anne* (1956), present a very valuable scholarly quintet.

Every visitor to Blenheim Palace at Woodstock must carry away vivid memories of the magnificent martial tapestries woven by De Vos in Brussels and displayed in the State Rooms. They have been reproduced many times in countless books but to see these ten fine 'Marlborough Tapestries' in the correct setting is a fabulous experience. A fine volume about these works was written by the late Alan Wace (Phaidon, 1968) and focuses upon the representation of Donauwörth (the storm of the Schellenberg), Hoochstat (Blenheim), the Forcing of the Lines of Brabant, Audenarde (Oudenarde), Wynendel, Insula (the siege of Lille), Montes Hannoniae (Malaplaquet) and lastly three versions of the siege of Bouchain, which the duke was particularly pleased to style his final campaign.

Perhaps the most fascinating relic is the famous Column of Victory, which was erected in 1730 and stands on a hill loftily overlooking the Palace, and was intended to remain forever to recall the deeds of the Great Duke. The author of the Column's celebrated panegyric was Henry St John, Viscount Bolingbroke, whose relationship with the First Duke was not exactly cordial, particularly in later years. However, during her widowhood, Duchess Sarah could find no statesman, soldier or scholar with a more apt or a more polished style than her husband's erstwhile adversary. Lord Bolingbroke was consequently entrusted with the composition, which is acknowledged to be a masterpiece in its conciseness, completeness and expression. It is a fine column – but it is surprising that Prince Eugene, one of the 'Two Captains', is only mentioned once.

Today at Blenheim Palace we may gaze upon the portraits of John Churchill as he once did himself. For we know that one day, as the old Duke looked at a portrait of himself as a young man, he said quietly, 'this was once a man'. But what sort of a man was he? The final summary is best left to her who knew him best. Years after his death, when invited by another Duke to remarry, Sarah spoke his most memorable epitaph:

> Where I as young and handsome as I was, instead of old and faded as I am, and you could lay the empire of the world at my feet, you should never share the heart and hand that belonged to John, Duke of Marlborough.

Emperor Joseph of Austria, as well as creating for the Duke a small princedom of Mindelheim near the Neckar river, south of Laffen town, set up a generous plaque near Blindheim in Latin. Unfortunately, but possibly understandably, Maximillian-Emmanuel, Elector of Bavaria, having been allowed to return to his lands in 1714 by the generosity of Emperor Leopold, destroyed the monument. However, it was recorded and translated into an English version:

On the 13th Day of August 1704
In, and Near this Place
Were routed, after an incidental Slaughter
The French and Bavarians Armies,
Under the command
Of Emmanuel, the elector
And the Marshals of France, Tallard and Marsin:
The first of whom was taken
Prisoner in the Battle,
With 40 other generals of the First Rank
900 officers of Lesser Note
and 12,000 Common soldiers,
besides 14,000 put to the Sword in the Field of Battle,
and 4,000 pushed into the Danube.
With an Immortal Glory
By
John, Duke of Marlborough, an Englishman
Who
Under the happy influence of his Mistress, Great Anne
And the States-General of the United Netherlands:
Led a Valiant Army from the Thames and the Meuse to the Danube,
To succour Germany that was reduced to the last Extremity,
Which Expedition he began to accomplish with the greatest Courage,
In Conjunction with the Forces under Lewis, Prince of Baden

By taking the strong Pass and Mount of Donawert,
That seemed Impregnable through its deep Entrenchments;
And afterwards, having rejoined the Forces Commanded by
Prince Eugene of Savoy, brought to Perfection,
With the same Constancy of Kind and Success
In the decisive Battle that was fought here
Between Blindheim and Hochstedt
The Enemy Army
Had the Advantage of Numbers, and Ground on their Side;
Nor was there any other Passage to Victory,
For the Confederates than through Rivers and Morasses,
From which the Generals of the Confederate Armies may
know,
That valour overcomes all Obstacles,
Princes may learn,
Conspiracies with the Enemies of their native country
Go seldom unpunished;
And Lewis XIV
Must at least confess
That no Prince whatsoever ought to be called
Great
And happy
Before his death.

To conclude this final chapter, I have decided to re-employ Lord Bolingbroke's celebrated panegyric written on the Column above Blenheim Palace, and the Eleventh Duke of Marlborough has kindly allowed it to be published here. The description is completed here (as written in the period) by Thomas Lediard, *Duke of Marlborough* (London, 1736), Vol. 111, pp.438–45.

The castle of *Blenheim* was founded by Q.ANN(E), [sic]
In the fourth Year of her Reign;
In the Year of the Christian *AEra* 1705;
A Monument defign'd to perpetual the Memory of the
fignal Victory
Obtained over the *French* and *Bavarians*
Near the village of *Blenheim*
On the Banks of the *Danube*
By *John Duke of Marlborough;*
The Hero not only of his Nation, but of his Age;
Whofe Glory was equal in the Council and in the Field;
Who by Wifdom, Juftice, Candour and Addrefs,
Reconciled various, and even opposite Interests;

Acquired an Influence, which no Rank, no Authority can
give.
Nor any Force but that of superior Virtue;
Because the fixed important Centre,
Which united in one common Cause
The principle States of *Europe*;
Who by military Knowledge, and irrefutable Valour,
In a long Series of uninterrupted Triumphs,
Broke the power of France,
Broke the Power of *France*;
When raised the highest, when exerted the most;
Rescued the *Empire* from Desolation;
Asserted confirmed the Liberties of *Europe*
PHILIP, a Grandson of the House of *France*,
United to the Interests, directed by the Policy,
Supported by the Arms of the Crown, was placed on the
Throne of *Spain*. King *William* the Third beheld this
formidable Union of two great, and once rival Monarchies.
At the End of a Life spent in defending the Liberties of
Europe, He saw them be their greatest Danger.
He provided for their Security, in the most effectual
Manner. He took the Duke of *Marlborough* into his Service.
Ambassador extraordinary and Plenipotentiary
To the *States General* of the United Provinces.
The Duke contracted several Alliances before the Death of
King *William*. He confirmed and improved these. He
contracted others, after the Ascension of Queen ANNE; and
reunited the Confederacy, which had been dissolved at the
End of a former War, in a ftrier and firmer League.
Captain General and Commander in Chief
Of the Forces of *Great Britain*.

The Duke led to the field the Army of the Allies.
He took with surprising Rapidity *Venlo, Ruremode
Stevenswaert, Liege*. He extended and secured the Frontiers
of the *Dutch*. The Enemies, whom he found insulting at the
Gates of *Nimweghen*, were driven to seek for Shelter behind
their Lines. He forced *Bonne, Huy, Limbourg* in another
Campaign. He opened the Communications of the *Rhine*, as
well as the *Maes*. He added all the Country between these
Rivers to his former Conquests. The Army of *France*,
favoured by the Defection of the Elector of *Bavaria*, had
penetrated into the Heart of the *Empire*. This mighty Body
lay exposed to immediate Ruin. In that memorable Crisis,

the Duke of *Marlborough* led his Troops with unexampled
Celerity, Secrecy, Orders, from the *Ocean* to the *Danube*. He
saw; he attacked; not stopped, but to conquer the Enemy.
He forced the *Bavarians*, sustained by the *French*, in their
strong Intrenchments at *Schellenberg*.
He passed the *Danube*. A second royal Army, composed of
the best Troops of *France*, was sent to reinforce the first.
That of the Confederates was divided. With one part of it
the Siege of *Ingolftadt* was carried on. With the other the
Duke gave Battle to he United Strength of *France* and
Bavaria. On the second Day of *August*, 1704, he gained a
more or glorious Victory than the Histories of any Age can
boast.
The Heapes of Slain were dreadful Proofs of his valour. A
marshal of *France*, whole Legions of *France*, his prisoners,
proclaimed his Mercy *Bavaria* was subdued. *Ratisbon,
Augsburg, Ulm, Meminghem*, all the Usurpation of the
Enemy, were recovered. The Liberty of the *Diet*, the Peace of
the *Empire*, were restored.
From the *Danube* the Duke turned his victorious Arms
toward the *Rhine*, and the *Moselle, Dandu, Treves, Traerbach*
were taken. In the Course of one Campaign the very Nature
of the War was changed. The Invaders of other States, were
reduced to defend their own. The Frontier of *France* was
exposed in its weakest Part the Efforts of the Allies.

That he might improve his advantage, that he might push
the Sum of Things to a speedy Decision, the Duke of
MARLBOROUGH led his Troops early in the following Year
once more to the Moselle. They, whom he had saved a few
months before, neglected to second him now. They, who
might have been his Companion in Conquest, refused to
join him. When he saw the generous Design he had formed
frustrated by private Interest, by Pique, by Jealousy, he
returned with Speed to the Mars. He returned; and Fortune
and Victory returned with him. *Liege* was relieved; *Huy* re-
taken; the *French*, who had pressed the Army of the States-
General with superior Numbers, retired behind
Intrenchments, which they deemed impregnable.
The Duke forced these Intrenchments, with inconsiderable
loss, on the seventh day of July, 1705. He defeated a great
Part of the escaped by a precipitate Retreat. It Advantages
proportionable to this Success were not immediately
obtained, let the Failure be ascribed to that Misfortune,

which attends most Confederacies, a Division of Opinions, where one alone should judge; a Division of Powers, where one alone should command. The Disappointment itself did Honour to the Duke. It became the Wonder of Mankind how he could do so much under those Restraints, which had hindered him from doing more.

Powers more absolute were given him afterwards. The increase of his Powers multiplied his Victories. At the opening of the next Campaign, when all his Army was not yet assembled, when it was hardly known that he had taken the Field, the Notice of his Triumphs was heard over *Europe*. On the 12th of *May* 1706, he attacked the *French* at *Eamillies*. In the Space of two hours, the whole Army was put to flight. The Vigour and Conduct, with which he improved this success, were equal to those, with which he gained it. *Louvaine, Brussels, Malines, Liere, Ghent, Oudenard, Antwerp, Damme, Bruges, Courtray* surrendered. *Ostend, Menin, Dendermond, Ath* were taken. *Brabant* and *Flanders* were recovered Places, which had resisted the greatest Generals for Months, for Years; Provinces, disputed for Ages, where the Conquests of a Summer. Nor was the Duke content to triumph alone. Solicitous for the general Interest, his Care extended to the remotest Scenes of the Year. He chose to lessen his own Army, that he might enable the leaders of other Armies to conquor. To this it must be ascribed that *Turin* was relieved, the Duke of *Savoy* re-instated, the *French* driven with Confusion out of *italy*.

These Victories gave the Confederates an Opportunity of carrying the War, on either Side, into the Dominions of *France*. But the continrued to enjoy a King of peaceful Neutrality in *Germany*. From *Italy* was once alarmed, and had no more to tear. The entire Reduction of this Power. whose Ambition had caused, whose Strength supported the war, seemed reserved for him alone, who had so triumphantly begun the glorious Work,

The barrier of *France*, on the Side of the *Low-Countries*, had been forming for more than half a Century. What Art, Power, Expence could do, had been done to render it impenetrable. Yet here she was most exposed; for here the Duke of *MARLBOROUGH* threatened to attack her. To cover what they had gained by Surprise, or had been

yielded to them by Treachery, the *French* marched to the
Banks of the *Scheldt*. At their Head were the Princes of the
Blood, and their most fortunate General, the Duke of
Vendome. Thus commanded, thus posted, they hoped to
check the Victor in his Course. Vain were their Hopes. The
Duke of *MARLBOROUGH* passed the River in their sight.
He defeated their whole Army. The Approach of Night
concealed, the Proximity of *Ghent* favoured their Flight.
They neglected nothing to repair their loss; to defend their
Frontier. New Generals, new Armies, appeared to enhance
the Glory, none were able to retard the Progress of the
Confederate Arms.

Lille, the Bulwark of this Barrier, was besieged. A numerous
Garrison and a Marshal of *France* defended the Place. Prince
Eugene of *Savoy* commanded, the Duke of *MARLBOROUGH*
covered and sustained the Siege. The Rivers were seized,
and the Communication with *Holland* interrupted. The
Duke opened new communications with great Labour and
much greater Art. Through Countries, overrun by the
Enemy, the necessary Convoys arrived in Safety. One alone
was attacked. The Troops, were attacked it, were beat.
The defence of *Lille* was animated by Assurances of Relief.
The *French* assembled all their Force. They marched
towards the Town. The Duke of *MARLBOROUGH* offered
them Battle, without suspending the Siege. They abandoned
the Enterprize. They came to save the Town.
They were Spectators of its Fall. From this Conquest the
Duke hastened to others. The Post takes by the Enemy on
the Scheldt were surprised. That River was pasted a second
time; not withstanding the great Preparations made to
prevent it, without Opposition.
Brussels, besieged by the Elector of *Bavaria*, was refeved.
Ghent surrendered to the Duke in the Middle of a Winter
remarkably severe. An Army, little inferior to his own,
marched out of the place.
As soon as the Season of the Year permitted him to open
another Campaign, the Duke besieged and took *Tournay*.
He invested *Mons*.
Near this City the *French* Army, covered Intrenchments,
waited to molest, nor presumed to offer battle.
Even this was not attained by them with impunity.
On the last Day of *August* 1709, the Duke attacked them in
their Camp. All was employed, nothing availed against the

Resolution of such a General; against the Fury of such
Troops. The Battle was bloody. The Event decisive. The
Woods were pierced.
The Fortifications trampled down. The Enemy fled. The
Town was taken. *Douay, Bethune, Aire, St. Venant, Bouchain*
underwent the same Fate in two succeeding Years. Their
vigorous Resistance could not face them. The Army of
France durft not attempt to relieve them. It feared prefered
to defend the Capitol of the Monarchy.
The Prospect of this extreme Distress was neither distant,
nor dubious. The *French* acknowledged their Conqueror,
and sued for Peace.

These are the Actions of the D. of *MARLBRO'* [sic]
Performed in the Compass of few Years,
Sufficient to adorn the Annals of Ages.
The Admiration of other Nations
Will be conveyed to latest Prosterity,
In Histories even of the Enemies of *BRITAIN.*
The sense, which the *BRITISH* Nation had Of his
transcendent Merit, Was expressed in the most solemn,
most effectual, most durable Manner.
The ACTS of PARLIAMENT, inscribed on this Pillar,
Should stand
As long as the *BRITISH* Name and language Last,
Ilustrious monuments
Of *MARLBOROUGH's* Glory
AND
Of *BRITAIN'S* Gratitude.

*   *   *

In peaceful thought the field of death surveyed
To fainting squadrons sent the Timely aid,
Inspired, repulsed battalions to engage,
And taught the doubtful battle where to rage
Joseph Addison
The Campaign 1704

Select Bibliography

A. Contemporary Memoirs of Military Significance

1.British Sources
Ailesbury, Thomas Bruce, Earl of, *Memoirs* (Edinburgh, 1890)
Bishop, Matthew, *The Life and Adventures of Matthew Bishop ... from 1701–11* (London, 1744)
Blackadder, Lt-Col. John, *Diary* (1/00–1/28), ed. A Crichton (London, 1824)
Cadogan, William, *Correspondence*, Add. Mss 28918, 42176, Add Mss 2196 (British Library)
Cranstoun, Col., *Letters*, included in the Bath Papers, Vol. I, 1904 (R. Hist. Mss C.)
Deane, Pte John Marshall, *A Journal of the Campaign in Flanders AD MDCCVIII...* (privately printed, Edinburgh, 1846)
Hare, Chaplain-General Francis, *Journal*, Report XIV (appx) (R. Hist. Mss C.)
Kane, Brig.-Gen. Richard, *Campaigns of King William and Queen Anne...* (London, 1745)
Millner, Sjt John, *A Compendious Journal...begun in AD 1701 and ended in 1712* (London, 1733)
Noyes, Dr Samuel, *Diary of 1/05 and 1/06* (privately owned)
Orkney, George Hamilton, Earl of, *Letters...during Marlborough's Campaigns* (English Historical Review, April 1904)
Parker, Capt. Robert, *Memoirs of the Most Remarkable Military Transactions from the Year 1638 to 1718* (London, 1747; new edn, London, 1968)
Pope, Capt. Richard, *Letters*, Cowper Papers, Vol. III (R. Hist. Mss C.)
Richards, Maj.-Gen. John, *Journal* and *Letters*, Add. Mss Stowe 4/4 and 5 (British Library)
Sterne, Brig.-Gen. Robert in Cannon, R, *Historical Records of the British Army* (London, 1835)
Swift, Jonathan, *The Conduct of the Allies* (London, 1712)
Wilson, Sjt John, privately owned by the Duke of Northumberland

2. Continental Sources

Eugene, Prince of Savoy, *Feldzuge, Series One and Two* (Vienna, 1876–81)

Goslinga, Sicco van, *Mémoires* (The Hague, 1857)

Klopp, O, *Der Fall des Hauses Stuart*, 14 vols (Vienna 1875–88)

La Colonie, Jean-Martin de, *The Chronicles of an Old Campaigner*, trans. & ed. by W Horsley (London, 1904)

Mérode-Westerloo, le Comte de, *Mémoires*, 2 vols (Brussels, 1840; trans. & ed. by D G Chandler, London, 1968)

Puysegur, le Maréchal de, *L'Art de la Guerre*, 2 vols (Paris, 1748)

Saint-Simon, le Duc de, *Mémoires*, eds Cheruel and Regnier, 40 vols (Paris, 1881–1907)

Schulenburg, J M, *Leben and Denkwurdigkeiten*, 2 vols (Paris, 1887)

Villars, le Maréchal Claude-Louis-Hector, Duc de, *Mémoires* (Paris, 1887)

B. General Histories, Documentation and Lives of Marlborough and the Period

Burnet, Bishop G, *History of his own Time* (London, 1832)

Belfield, E, *Oudenarde* (London, 1972)

Butler, I, *Rule of Three* (London, 1967)

Chandler, D G, *The Art of Warfare in the Age of Marlborough* (Staplehurst, 1990)

_____ *The Marlborough Wars* (London, 1968 reprinted 1998)

Childs, J, *The Army of Charles II* (London, 1976)

_____ *The Army, James II and the Glorious Revolution* (Manchester, 1980)

_____ *Warfare of the 17th Century* (London, 2001)

_____ *The Nine Years War and the British Army* (London, 1991)

Dalton, C, *English Army Lists and Commission Registers*, 6 vols (London, 1904)

Falkner, J, *Great and Glorious Days* (Staplehurst, 2002)

Francis, D, *The First Peninsular War* (London, 1974)

Guy, A J, *Oeconomy and Discipline* (London, 1985)

_____ *The Glorious Revolution* (NAM, 1988)

Haddington, J B, *England in the War of the Spanish Succession ... Grand Strategy* (London, 1987)

Hatton, R M, *Charles XII of Sweden* (London, 1968)

Henderson, N, *Prince Eugen of Savoy* (London, 1964)

Houlding, J A, *Fit for Service. The Training of the British Army 1715–1795* (Oxford, 1981)

Jones, D W, *World Economy in the Age of William III and Marlborough* (Oxford, 1988)

Jones, R J, *Marlborough* (Cambridge, 1993)

Leslie, N B, *The Succession of Colonels of the British Army from 1660 to the Present Day* (Special publication No. 11, SAHR, 1974)
McKay, D, *Prince Eugene of Savoy* (London, 1977)
Marlborough, John, Duke of, *The Letters and Dispatches of The Duke of Marlborough*, ed. Gen. Sir George Murray, 5 vols (London, 1845)
Parker, G, *The Military Revolution* (Cambridge, 1988)
Pelet, J J G and Vault, F E de, *Mémoires militaries relatifs à la succession d'Espagne sous Louis XIV*, 11 vols and Atlas (Paris, 1846–52)
Rogers, Col. H C B, *The British Army in the 18th Century* (London, 1977)
Sautai, M, *La Bataille de Malplaquet* (Paris, 1904)
Scouller, R E, *The Armies of Queen Anne* (Oxford, 1966)
T'Hoff, B van (ed.), *The Correspondence 1701–11 of John Churchill and Anthonie Heinsius* (The Hague, 1951)
_____ *The Correspondence of Marlborough and Godolphin*, 3 vols (Oxford, 1971)
Tomlinson, H C, *Guns and Government* (London, 1979)
Trevelyan, G M, *England under Queen Anne*, 3 vols (London, 1930–4)
Verney, P, *The Battle of Blenheim* (London, 1976)
Walton, C, *History of the British Standing Army, 1660–1700* (London, 1894)
Watson, J N P, *Marlborough's Shadow: The Life of the First Earl Cadogan* (Barnsley, 2003)
Wright, Q, *A Study of War* (Chicago, 1952)

C. Lives and Historical Studies of Marlborough and the Period

Anon., *Memoirs of the Lives and Conduct of…Prince Eugene of Savoy and John, Duke of Marlborough* (London, 1742)
Alison, A, *Life of John, Duke of Marlborough* (London, 1852)
Ashley, M, *Marlborough* (London, 1939)
Atkinson, C T, *Marlborough and the Rise of the British Army* (London, 1924)
Barnett, Correlli, *Marlborough* (London, 1974)
Baxter, S B, *William III* (London, 1966)
Belloc, H, *The Tactics and Strategy of the Great Duke of Marlborough* (London, 1933)
Burton, I, *The Captain-General* (London, 1968)
Carre, H, *De Villars* (Paris, 1936)
Chandler, D G, *Marlborough as Military Commander* (London, 1973)
Childs, J, *The British Army of William III, 1682–1702* (Manchester, 1987)
Churchill, W S, *Marlborough, his Life and Times*, 4 vols (London, 1933–8), 2-book edition (London, 1947) and pb edn (London, 1967)
Clarke, G N, *English Society* (London, 1985)
_____ *The Character of the Nine Years War* (Cambridge, 1953)

Corvisier, A, *La Bataille de Malplaquet 1709* (Paris, 1997)

_____ *Louvois* (Paris, 1983)

Cowles, V, *The Great Marlborough and his Duchess* (London, 1973)

Coxe, W C, *Memoirs of John, Duke of Marlborough*, 6 vols and Atlas (London, 1820)

Dutems, J F, *l'Histoire de Jean, Duc de Marlborough*, revised by Duclos (Paris, 1806)

Green, D, *Sarah, Duchess of Marlborough* (London, 1967)

Grey, E and M S, *The Court of William III* (London, 1910)

Hattendorf, J, *England in the War of the Spanish Succession* (New York, 1988)

Hebbert, F J and Rothrock, *Soldier of France: Vauban* (New York, 1989)

Hibbert, C, *The Marlboroughs* (London, 2001)

Hugill, J A, *No Peace Without Spain* (Oxford, 1991)

Lediard, T, *Life of the Duke of Marlborough* (London, 1736)

Mitford, Nancy, *The Sun King* (London, 1966)

Parnell, A R, *The War of the Succession in Spain* (Oxford, 1905)

Phelan, I P, *Marlborough, as Logistician* (London, 1985, *JSAHR*, Nos 272–4)

Rowse, A L, *The Early Churchills* (London, 1956)

Taylor, F, *The Wars of Marlborough, 1702–1709* (Oxford, 1921)

Thomson, G M, *The First Churchill* (London, 1959)

Watson, J N P, *Captain-General and Rebel Chief* (London, 1979)

Wigfield, W M, *The Monmouth Rebellion* (Bradford-on-Avon, 1980)

_____ *The Monmouth Rebels* (Sutton, 1985)

Wolseley, Lord G, *Life of Marlborough*, 2 vols (London, 1894)

Index